This Quiet Place

A DAILY DEVOTIONAL
FOR WOMEN BY WOMEN

Dorothy Eaton Watts, Editor

Ardis Dick Stenbakken, Associate Editor

REVIEW AND HERALD® PUBLISHING ASSOCIATION
HAGERSTOWN, MD 21740

The authors assume full responsibility for the accuracy of all facts and
quotations as cited in this book.

This book was
Edited by Jeannette R. Johnson
Copyedited by Jocelyn Fay/James Cavil
Designed by Patricia S. Wegh
Cover illustration by Kim Jacobs
Typeset: 11/13 Stempel Schneidler

PRINTED IN U.S.A.

02 01 00 99 98   10 9 8 7 6 5 4 3 2 1

R&H Cataloging Service
Watts, Dorothy Eaton, 1937-   ed
    This quiet place, edited by Dorothy Eaton
Watts and Ardis Dick Stenbakken.

    1. Devotional calendars—SDA.   2. Devotional
calendars—women.   3. Women—religious life.   4. Devotional
litarature—SDA.   I. Stenbakken, Ardis Dick, ed.
II. Title.

                    242.643

ISBN 0-8280-1346-2

I Want to Hold You, Lord!

Hold me, and I will be safe. Ps. 119:117, TEV.

Bethany, my 2-year-old granddaughter, lifted chubby arms and lisped, "I want to hold you, Grandma!"

Stooping, I swooped her to my heart. Her small arms circled my neck, and I felt her soft cheek against mine. She sighed contentedly. I could feel her whole body relax.

"I like to hold you, Grandma," she whispered. "I love you."

"And I love you, too," I replied, rubbing my cheek against her silky hair.

Bethany knows that when she holds me, I am also holding her. Oh, the warmth, the joy, of such an embrace of love! Could this be what God wants from us in prayer?

Bethany's oft-repeated request came to my mind as I read Brian Manning's words in *The Signature of Jesus:* "Grabbing ahold of God in faith means simultaneously being seized by the power of a great affection of being grabbed ahold of."

In prayer we reach out our arms, crying, "I want to hold You, God!" He responds by enfolding us with His love, lifting us close to His heart, holding us tight. Oh, the delight of those moments of an embrace with God in prayer!

I feel very much the need of God's embrace as I begin this new year. From the warm safety of His arms, I have no fear for what this year may bring of good or ill.

As I look at my to-do list for this week, I realize there aren't enough hours! I don't have the wisdom or the strength to meet the challenges that face me. I cry out, "I want to hold You, Lord! It feels so good to hold You!" From my position in the arms of God I know that anything is possible!

My wish for each of you is that you will often take time out to go to God with outstretched arms of need, crying, "I want to hold You, Lord!" We all need to take our busy hands out of the mixing bowl of activity for God long enough to be swept up into His embrace of love.

DOROTHY EATON WATTS

Hurry, Before They Sand the Hill!

And at midnight Paul and Silas prayed, and sang praises unto God: and the prisoners heard them. Acts 16:25.

Our church has closed only twice in more than two decades, both times because of winter storms. The 1996 weather closed stores, schools, roads—nothing escaped. The whole weekend was ruined—no food, no travel, no electricity, lights, heat, or hot water.

We live on the top of a mountain. The roads up to the house are curvy, icy, and treacherous. Griping dominated all conversations. My husband's air flight was canceled, the college's concert was canceled, and life itself was canceled—or so it seemed to those of us used to twentieth-century conveniences.

The novelty of the storm had long before ceased to intrigue. The house was freezing, and we were sick of sandwiches. Then our son, Stacey, came in with a most welcome invitation: "The neighbors have invited us over for chili and cheese toast; their Buck stove is working." We didn't need to be asked twice.

What I remember most about the evening was a conversation I overheard between Stacey and the neighbor's son.

"Hurry up, Jimmy; let's get going before they sand the hill! Get on your snow skis. We can get in a couple long runs down that curvy road if we get going before those sand trucks come up and spoil everything!"

And they did ski—in Collegedale, Tennessee, on an icy mountain road unfit for cars, but exactly right for teenagers who took a weather disaster and turned it into a one-of-a-kind experience.

"If life gives you a lemon, make lemonade." I'd heard the expression before many times. But never had that philosophy meant more to me than on that bitter cold winter evening. We were snowbound on a mountaintop with hospitable neighbors, chili, and cheese toast, and two exuberant youth who gave me an object lesson in perspective—how to turn a paralyzing storm into a winter vacation. Like Paul and Silas, fettered in prison, but who could still sing, I hope to find some way to enjoy life "before they sand the hill," thus transforming a misery into a moment to remember.

WILMA MCCLARTY

Lamplighters

Let your good deeds glow for all to see, so that they will praise your heavenly Father. Matt. 5:16, TLB.

In the days before electric lights there was an occupation known as lamplighting. A friend of mine told me about her childhood memories of Chicago, when she saw the lamplighter making rounds just about dusk every evening. I never knew that kind of lamplighter, yet I do know many people who light my life.

My friend Lois glows with radiant character. She's the kind of friend who doesn't just say "Have courage" or "Keep the faith"—she suggests how to do it. She's totally practical in the art of being a friend.

As a fellow writer, she's helped me to dip my pen in the sweet Spirit's power. She's a real sister-of-kind, a true bright light in my life—the kind of friend Ralph Waldo Emerson wrote about: "A true friend is someone who can make us do what we can."

Lois wrote a poem that expresses her kind of lamplighting:

> To walk, to run, perhaps to fly
> To always set my goals on high—
> Though if my wings could never spread,
> Make no complaint but joy instead,
> If I have helped some life to soar,
> Where mine has never been before.
>
> —LOIS PECCE

Marianne is another lamplighter. She supported me through one of the most difficult times in my life; a candle glow during those shadow times, assuring me that God was at work in my life.

Early in our friendship we both became aware that God's needlework was weaving our hearts into a sturdy fabric that clothed us in gracious, bright garments of caring. She was, and remains, a bright candle of encouragement.

My friend Kandi reflects the shine of her friend Jesus, the light of the world. Because of distance Kandi and I depend on letters; however, her letters are filled with the same joy as her presence. She doesn't write letters, she lights them—treasures to store away and read another day.

Do others feel warmed by the light you and I share? Let's light someone's life today.

BETTY KOSSICK

The Best Christmas Pageant Ever!

*And she gave birth to her firstborn, a son. She wrapped him in cloths
and placed him in a manger, because there was no room
for them in the inn. Luke 2:7, NIV.*

Our Christmas pageant was delayed while the snow melted and
the roads cleared. On January 4 I awoke two and a half hours
earlier than necessary but could not go back to sleep. This was the
day of the pageant, and it was not snowing! I thanked God for the
beautiful clear weather and asked Him to protect each one who
would be coming to church that day.

A few minutes after arriving at church, I knew it was very ques-
tionable whether everything would be going smoothly. Where was
the angel of the Lord, the one who had all the lines? For several minutes the Wise Men's gifts were misplaced. One of the shepherds had
not come. Another shepherd was quickly coached to learn an additional line. Two of the smaller angels did not show up. Mary forgot
to bring a doll to represent Baby Jesus. Several people scurried around
to find a doll and swaddling clothes to wrap it in. This caused a slight
delay, as the "baby" could not be placed behind the manger before-
hand. I asked the audience to excuse us while a music stand was
moved and some props were put in place. Melissa became a minute-
person and read the lines of the angel. Someone did not realize that
the red cape was to be used to complement a Wise Man's costume,
so Tommy did his part not completely attired. They sang only one
verse of "Away in a Manger," rather than the two verses we had
planned. However, most of the lines went quite smoothly, and soon
it was over.

We received many compliments, and no one thought January was
a bad time to have a Nativity scene. We were all pleased that the
audience had been blessed by our simple portrayal of the story of
God's ultimate gift. In spite of all our human failings, it really turned
out to be "the best Christmas pageant ever"!

*Lord, help me to remember that this is what Christmas is all about—the
gift of Your Son, Jesus, and His power to turn our failures into success.*

LILLIAN MUSGRAVE

Seek and You Will Find

"Ask, and it will be given to you; seek, and you will find; knock, and it will be opened to you." Matt. 7:7, NKJV.

With great anticipation we stepped into the rubber raft to experience our first white-water trip down the Ocoee River.

Chuck had experience, but for the rest of us, this was a first! It was an exhilarating ride being thrown up and over terrifying rapids. Suddenly our raft got hung up on rocks. Water pounded on both sides of us. We tried bouncing; we tried prying ourselves off with the paddles, but nothing worked.

Chuck stepped out to lighten the load. When he did, the force of the water broke his hold on the raft. In horror we watched our guide being swept away downstream, leaving us high—but not necessarily dry! However, with the raft now lighter, we were able to move, and moments later we picked up Chuck where he clung to branches.

As we neared the end of the run, Chuck felt his pocket. "Oh, no, my wallet's gone!" There was no way we would ever find a wallet in that raging river, even in a plastic bag! It was a significant loss.

It took us a while to dismantle the raft, and by the time we headed back up the road, the river water had been diverted for electrical purposes. Now there were mere pools where just an hour before there had been fierce rapids. When Chuck pointed out the rock on which we had gotten stuck, my husband said, "Well, since there's no water there now, let's go look for the wallet."

"No way! Impossible!" The skeptics shook their heads.

We prayed, and as Chuck headed across the riverbed, he prayed again. "Lord, I should have been more careful with my wallet; if You want to teach me a lesson, that's OK. But if You want me to find it, You'll have to impress upon me where to look."

Chuck noticed the branches that he had grabbed earlier and moved toward them. Looking down, he saw a plastic bag floating among the branches. Could it be? Yes, there was his wallet!

KAY KUZMA

God or the Baker?

*Bring ye all the tithes into the storehouse . . . and prove me now . . .
saith the Lord of hosts. Mal. 3:10.*

It was difficult for my mother, a single parent, to provide for herself
and her five children on her small salary as a schoolteacher in India.
We gathered daily for family worship and attended church faithfully.
Somehow she managed to give each of us children an offering to put
in the plate each week. I observed, though, that other people put
money in the tithe envelopes.

"Why don't you pay tithe?" I asked her once.

"God knows everything, and He knows my struggle. Surely He
doesn't expect me to pay tithe when I have so little," she replied.

That made sense to me.

Then one day the pastor preached on Malachi 3:8-10. He made it
very clear, even to us children, that one tenth of our earnings is to be
returned to God.

When we got home, Mother told us, "Starting with next month's
salary, I am going to return a faithful tithe to the Lord."

True to her word, at the beginning of the month my mother
made the budget and put the tithe first on the list. She found she'd be
able to pay all the listed items except for two—the tithe and the
baker. Both were 14 rupees. She had only 14 rupees left. Which one
should she pay? We prayed about it at family worship that evening,
then Mother made her decision. "I'm going to pay my tithe."

The next morning at church she seemed happier than usual, even
though there was no money left.

That evening a woman came to the house and asked my mother
to give her daughter tutoring. Mother agreed. Then the woman gave
Mother 25 rupees in advance.

"See, children," she said, after the woman left. "God's promises
are true. He has just opened the windows of heaven for us and
poured us out a blessing that's more than we need to pay the baker."

We were all so happy; we praised God and thanked Him for His
faithfulness. Mother gave 14 rupees to the baker, and the extra 11 rupees saw us through the month.   WINNIE KURIAN

Cookies and Confession

He that covereth his sins shall not prosper: but whoso confesseth and forsaketh them shall have mercy. Prov. 28:13.

Just before I left for work one morning, I wrapped up a few freshly baked cookies and put them in my purse. I could hardly wait for the chance to call my friend Roseline. "I brought something delicious for you! Come to my office!"

"OK," she promised. "I'll be there as soon as I can."

The morning passed; she did not appear. The more I thought about it, the more upset I got. *She doesn't care that I brought something for her. She's done this before. She promises to come by, but forgets to do it. Why do I bother?*

The cookies stayed in my purse all day. In the middle of the afternoon I needed Roseline's help with a computer program, so I called her again. She came immediately. After helping me with the program, she said, "Oh! Cookies! I meant to come this morning, but I had so much to do!"

I was upset, so I replied, "Well, since you didn't come in the morning, I took them home. Anyway, they got all crumbled."

"What a pity!" she said. "I'm so sorry I forgot. I feel really bad about it."

After she left, I couldn't concentrate on my work. My mind was in a turmoil. I knew I had lied twice. The cookies were in my purse. They were not crumbled at all. The thought of telling two lies burned my soul. I tried to do my work, but I couldn't because of the war inside me. I knew I should confess, but I didn't want to!

Finally I picked up the phone. "Roseline, please come to my office!"

She came at once. I met her at the door. "Roseline," I began before I lost my nerve, "I want to confess my sin. I lied to you. I was upset because you didn't answer my call this morning. I thought you didn't care. Here are the cookies—whole. I'm sorry. Will you forgive me?"

"Of course," Roseline replied.

We hugged each other, and I felt so good! I went back to work with a prayer in my heart. "Lord, how good it is to confess! Thank You for the joy of forgiveness!" NILMA PIMENTEL MONTEIRO

The Vanilla Cream Pie

When pride comes, then comes disgrace,
but with humility comes wisdom. Prov. 11:2, NIV.

While my husband and I were at Andrews University doing graduate studies, Raymond Moore and his wife invited our family to dinner. Knowing that they both worked hard, I offered to contribute something for the dinner. I prepared potato salad, a small vegetarian dish, and a vanilla cream pie, pleased that I could contribute to the function.

We looked forward to a good visit with the Moores, who had been at Philippine Union College when my husband and I were students there. We anticipated reminiscing about good old college days.

On the day of the dinner I asked my daughter and my husband to carry the potato salad and vegetarian dish. I would carry the pie. It was topped with a very high meringue, and I wanted to be sure that it received extra care. Also, I wanted to present the pie myself. I was proud of my ability to cook an American dessert.

Turning to Lynda and my husband, I said, "Please be very careful as you carry the dishes."

"Everything will be OK," my husband assured me as we walked up the front steps of the house. "I'll open the door."

Holding my precious pie, I stepped on the snow-covered driveway. Suddenly my feet slipped. As I struggled to keep my balance, I let go of the pie. It landed upside down on the driveway. *Oh, no!* I thought. *There goes my beautiful dessert creation! It's ruined!*

Raymond Moore came to help. "Don't worry about the pie," he said. "We'll just scoop it up from the snow. It will taste just as good, no matter how it looks."

I felt embarrassed. I had so wanted them to see my beautiful creation in perfect condition. "Mom, I'm glad it was you carrying the pie and not me!" my daughter said.

I was so proud of myself and that pie! Was the Lord trying to teach me something? I certainly did learn from that experience that excessive pride can lead to embarrassment and humiliation, just as the wise man said long ago. OFELIA A. PANGAN

Surprise, Surprise!

The earth was formless and empty, darkness was over the surface of the deep. . . . And God said, "Let there be light," and there was light. God saw that the light was good. Gen. 1:2-4, NIV.

All was dark, silent, expectant. How long the planning for this birthing event had gone on, we don't know, but now all was in readiness. Then suddenly, surprise! All the lights came on.

Women love surprises. Baby showers. Bridal showers. Birthdays. Hiding in the dark, waiting to spring the trap. Once I dragged my husband to the airport to meet, he thought, some unknown soul, only to watch our daughter, Rikki, walk off the jetway. Another time my husband went to see "someone with a problem" and returned with Rikki to surprise me. Nothing could have pleased us more. And the planning was half the fun!

God also loves surprises. In fact, the Bible record is full of surprises. Think of Sarah when she discovered that she really was pregnant. Or Abraham when he saw the ram caught in the bushes. Or Joseph's brothers when they discovered who the ruler of Egypt really was. Of course, there was the surprise of the Samaritan woman when Jesus spoke to her and revealed what He knew about her. Or the woman caught in adultery—Jesus did not condemn her, but rather forgave her. The list can go on: Esther when she was chosen queen "for such a time as this," or the woman with an issue of blood when Jesus felt her touch. Just think of young Mary when the angel appeared and announced she was to be the mother of the Messiah! Mary Magdalene's surprise when Jesus spoke to her the morning of the Resurrection must have been mind-boggling.

Our lives seem so ordinary, yet often full of surprises when we let God lead. He always takes us beyond the ordinary. Each of the Bible men and women had one characteristic in common: they were willing to let God lead. There was a commitment. Sometimes there was discouragement, because they could not see the future. Things did not always seem to be going well, but behind the scenes God was waiting to spring His ideal surprise at the perfect moment.

Lord, give me the patience and trust today to let You lead and again surprise me with Your goodness. ARDIS DICK STENBAKKEN

The Bunch of Parsley

*As cold waters to a thirsty soul, so is good news
from a far country. Prov. 25:25.*

The parsley was wilted, dried up, almost dead, almost useless. It
looked unattractive, undesirable, and unwanted. It had been picked
at the peak of perfection, tied into bundles, and taken to the market to
be sold. Some vendor then bought it to sell in his roadside stall.

The hot tropical sun smiled on the bunch of parsley. It tried to
hide, but there was no shade. The sun moved across the sky and
evening came. The stall would soon close for the night. People
stopped to look at the bunch of wilted parsley and shook their heads.
Some picked it up, then put it down, choosing a better bunch. Others
walked farther to buy from another stall.

Finally a man stopped at the stall. He needed parsley. He had
been to the other stalls, but there was no parsley to be had. This was
the last stall, the last bunch of parsley. He looked at the wilted leaves.
"I'll let you have it cheap," the vendor said, wanting to get rid of the
useless parsley.

"I'll buy it," the man said. "After all, it is cheap."

He hurried home and apologized to his wife. "I'm sorry, but this
is all I could find. Can you use it at all?"

She didn't reply, but grabbed a jug and filled it with cold water.
She stood the bunch of parsley in the jug and went about her other
chores. You should have seen the parsley come alive! It was soon refreshed, standing up straight and tall. It didn't resemble that bunch of
old wilted parsley at all.

At times our lives are like that bunch of parsley. Our spirits have
long since lost their sparkle, and life, its meaning. We need Christ to
come to us. He is not turned aside by our appearance or our unfavorable surroundings. We might be wilted and scorched by the criticism
of others, but Christ sees some hope in us. He knows that all we
need is a drink of the water of life, the good news of salvation.

When Christ comes into our lives, He will renew our hearts and
refresh our thoughts and actions. We will no longer be unattractive,
undesirable, and unwanted.

PRISCILLA ADONIS

Look for the Signs

Teach me your way, O Lord; and lead me in a straight path. Ps. 27:11, NIV.

My husband, Ed, and I had an appointment; however, he was unable to get the day off. So we decided that I would pick him up during his break, and we would drive to the appointment together.

Since I was unfamiliar with the area where he worked, he gave me precise directions how to get there. That morning I got on the highway, just as he had directed, but for some unknown reason I found myself headed in the wrong direction. I had missed the signs that would have kept me on the right track. I quickly took the nearest exit and headed back to the route I was supposed to have taken.

As I got back on the highway, I saw the signs my husband had mentioned. Better yet, I spotted one of his company's trucks heading toward the same place I was. Then, deciding that the truck was too slow, I overtook it—and guess what happened? Yes, I ended up going the wrong direction again! Fortunately for me, my husband's job site was close by, and I was able to find it without further trouble.

My experience that day reminded me of the numerous times I fail to observe the signs my heavenly Father has so clearly outlined in His Word. The minute I focus on my own instincts or my own strength, I immediately start heading in the wrong direction. And though He often sends someone to guide me back to the right path, my spiritual stubbornness prohibits me from accepting His guidance.

My husband's directions were very precise, and had I followed the signs he had given, I would have reached him without losing my way. Likewise, the signs that the Lord has given in His Word are very precise. If I follow them I will never go wrong.

My prayer each day is "Teach me your way, O Lord; and lead me in a straight path." He helps me to follow the directions given me in His Word. JUDITH A. SULLIVAN

Airport Prayer

*As a father has compassion on his children, so the Lord has compassion
on those who fear him; for he knows how we are formed,
he remembers that we are dust. Ps. 103:13, 14, NIV.*

I sat in the airport, waiting for my plane to arrive. After an intense weekend of speaking, I looked forward to greeting my husband and son, driving home, taking a shower, and crawling into my own bed.

Time passed too slowly. *We should be boarding now,* I thought. I checked the board above the receiving desk. "Delayed 40 minutes," it read. "Oh, no," I gasped, "surely not!" I had only a half hour to make my connecting flight in Houston. With the delay it was highly unlikely I would arrive in time to catch my connecting flight home to Ontario, California.

When boarding time finally came, I found my seat. *I surely don't want to spend the night in the Houston airport,* I thought. *I want to be home in my own bed.* I looked down at my swollen feet and began praying.

"Lord, I'm just so tired. I'm willing to do whatever is in Your will, but I'd surely love it if You'd just get me home tonight."

I checked my ticket. I was arriving in Houston at gate C-35; my connecting flight left at gate C-36. That looked hopeful. At least I wouldn't have to run the length of the airport to find my flight. But there was still the matter of 10 minutes' overlap in time. Dared I hope that my second flight would be delayed also?

I gathered my things about me and was ready to deplane quickly. As I passed the counter, empty of the usual boarding crowd, I glanced toward the attendant.

"Are you the passenger for Ontario?" she called.

"Yes," I eagerly responded.

"Hurry," she said, "they're holding the plane for you."

I rushed down the hallway she designated and into the plane, praising the Lord for taking notice of my tiredness and answering my prayer. God remembered that I was dust—a human being who was wearied and needed help.

CARROL JOHNSON SHEWMAKE

Water for the Harvest

"The water I give him will become in him a spring of water welling up to eternal life." John 4:14, NIV.

It's the season for consulting seed catalogues and checking on special offers. But one offer, never made but quite crucial to the success of seed sowing, is for someone to keep up with the watering.

As far as gardens go (in our country, anyway), watering can be a very dodgy business. Either there is too much rain, and your seeds get washed away, or you don't get sufficient and your tomatoes crack. Certainly, plants do need water.

I became aware of this during a particularly dry summer. Friends whom we visited in France had no rain from March to August. The wheat and maize crops were poor, and the well was dry. A neighbor of ours here in England carried 80 two-gallon bucketfuls of water to her flower border to save her shrubs from wilting away.

In early summer we had the promise of a good crop of peas from our vegetable patch. When there was no rain, we realized we would need to water them. It was a long way to carry buckets from the tap, and the hose would reach only so far. At harvesttime the peas told their own story: fat peas at the watered end of the row, very thin peas at the other!

One day late in the season I decided to go blackberry picking. I took along large containers, but I found one and a half blackberries. The rest were all shriveled. No moisture, no harvest.

As far as our lives are concerned, the Master Gardener has promised to take care of the watering. He has promised, "The water I give . . . will become . . . a spring of water leading up to eternal life."

"He who drinks of the living water becomes a fountain of life. The receiver becomes a giver. The grace of Christ in the soul is like a spring in the desert, welling up to refresh all" *(The Desire of Ages,* p. 195). The indwelling of His Spirit will make you blossom. And as you sow seeds of love in someone else's life, showing them something of Jesus, you will have a harvest.   PEGGY MASON

The Tapestry

"He will call upon me, and I will answer him." Ps. 91:15, NIV.

I sat at the piano and began to play as I looked at the photos of my loved ones I had placed there. Tears flowed down my cheeks. We had moved to a remote region of Brazil where we had no friends or relatives. There was no telephone, either. My husband went on long trips, leaving me alone in the strange city.

One morning I opened my heart up to God. "Lord, You know how lonely I am. What can I do about it?" As I prayed, the idea came to me that I could begin making tapestry. I got dressed immediately and went shopping for materials.

I was excited when I found what I needed in the small shopping area. Hurrying home, I sat down on the sofa and opened my package. I threaded the needle with yarn and held the canvas on my lap. *What do I do now?* I wondered. (I hadn't asked anyone for instructions.)

When I couldn't figure out what to do, I threw the canvas to the floor and began to cry, complaining all the while to God.

Still weeping, I got up and went to the piano. The hymn I chose was based on Jeremiah 29:12: "You will seek me and find me when you seek for me with all your heart" (NIV). My heart longed to feel God's presence, to know He heard me and understood my loneliness and frustration.

The doorbell rang. I opened the door to see a smiling woman. "I'm your neighbor," she said. "I've been wanting to introduce myself for several days, but I was afraid of interrupting your piano practice."

As we visited, I learned she was an arts teacher, specializing in painting and tapestry. Quickly I picked the canvas up off the floor and told her my story.

"I'll teach you to do tapestry in exchange for some of your music scores," she offered. "I'm learning to play the piano, and I really liked the song I heard you playing a few minutes ago."

She and I became great friends. From that day I have known that God is concerned with our happiness. He is eager for our call; He sent a good friend in my time of need.

DJANE MEIRI PEREIRA DANTAS

Unscheduled Stops

Who knoweth whether thou art come to the kingdom
for such a time as this? Esther 4:14.

I had planned my day's visits before I left the Beaumont City health department, organizing them according to where they were located. My first stop was in a section of town I had visited many times.

I pulled my car to the curb, got out, and locked the doors. As I walked toward the houses, I realized I was nowhere close to where I intended to be. How had I made a mistake like this? Why had I stopped in an area I had never even been in before?

I turned back to my car. But instead of getting into the car, I turned full circle and headed back to the houses. I stood looking at the houses. Once again I turned to go back to my car. And again I made a complete circle and was facing the houses. I started to question my sanity, thinking I had better just start walking before someone saw me standing there, turning around in circles.

Just then a girl came out of one of the houses. "Are you the nurse from the health department?"

"Yes, I am!"

"Please, come in and check my friend," she begged. "She needs help!"

In the tiny living room was a 19-year-old girl in agonizing pain. She'd had a cesarian section a few days before. She was holding her abdomen and said that her belly hurt terribly.

"May I take a look at it?" I asked. She nodded. When I looked at the incision, I saw a gaping hole; the incision had popped open. As the girl was also a diabetic, I tried to convince her to go to the hospital right away. Because she had no health insurance, she did not want to go.

After a long discussion her friend was able to convince her to go. I then headed back to my car. This time I had no trouble. I realized then that the Lord had wanted me to go see that girl. He was watching out for her and compelled me to help her. What an honor to be singled out by Him to bless others! SUSAN L. BERRIDGE

Excused, or Forgiven?

You, O Lord, are good and forgiving, abounding in steadfast love to all who call on you. Ps. 86:5, NRSV.

I pushed a shopping cart along the aisles of the grocery store, looking for items on my list. Stopping in front of the canned beans, I didn't notice that my cart obstructed the aisle.

"Ahem!" Someone cleared her throat to get my attention.

Two shoppers were obviously wanting to proceed. I was embarrassed, and hurried to move the cart so there was room to pass. "Excuse me," I said.

Pleasant smiles and nods from the delayed shoppers let me know they accepted my apology.

Later a friend at church related a tantalizing bit of information about a shortcoming of a mutual acquaintance. I told this tale to another friend, who then passed it on to someone else. It wasn't long until the whole congregation buzzed with the news. Off to one side stood the one accused, hurt in her eyes. I tried to put those pain-filled eyes out of my mind, but I could not.

Kneeling at bedtime to pray, I thanked God for His blessings and asked for His protection. Then I remembered the episode of the morning. I saw again the pain-filled eyes. "Excuse me," I said. "It's too bad she was hurt, but You know that information was accurate. I only told the truth." With a hasty amen I got into bed.

Sleep wouldn't come. I tossed and turned and adjusted my pillow. "Please, God, help me to sleep," I prayed.

Instead He showed me a picture of myself. I saw a miserable gossip, an ugly, self-righteous sinner in need of forgiveness. And all I could do was cry, "Be merciful to me, a sinner."

He set me free. He gave me peace. He made my heart sing a song of joy and gratitude. I sought His smile of approval, and He assured me that I was forgiven.

That night a powerful truth burned itself into my soul: God is not in the business of excusing. He is in the business of forgiving.

BARBARA ROBERTS

No Trespassing

Resist the devil, and he will flee from you. James 4:7.

I passed Sylvia's home twice daily on my way to and from school. It wasn't unusual to see this large Saint Bernard romping with the neighborhood children. She seemed as gentle as she was beautiful. On days when her youthful companions were not with her, I would often call her name softly, and she would walk a few feet with me, all the while wagging her tail.

Then one day as I neared home a strong gust of wind snatched my notebook, scattering its precious contents about Sylvia's lawn. Those papers represented hours of diligent study, hours of "midnight oil." I couldn't afford to lose them. I hurried across the street to rescue whatever I could.

When Sylvia first spotted me, she came bounding out to give her usual greeting. Giving her a pat on the head, I headed for her lawn to retrieve my homework. As soon as I set foot on that well-manicured lawn, Sylvia growled a low, threatening rumble, like distant thunder.

I was stunned! In the months I had known her I could not remember Sylvia's making such a sound even once. My first reaction was that I must have imagined the growl. And because the wind was still merrily tossing my papers indiscriminately about the yard, I decided it was time for immediate action and once again stepped onto the lawn. Sylvia gave a second growl, more menacing than the first, and this time lowered her massive head while her body language shouted to me, "No! Stay off my property!"

I was no match for this huge growling canine, but I was reluctant to leave the scene without recovering even one hard-earned paper. I made one more try. Sylvia had not changed her mind. I was not going to receive permission to trespass on her property.

As I reluctantly left, I thought of my own battle with Satan, the enemy of souls. How often, when faced with this formidable foe, do I give in and allow him to gain ground on the lawn of my heart? Am I as persistent and immovable in my resistance to the trespassers of my soul as Sylvia was to me?   JAYNE DOSWELL DARBY

Home Is Where the Heart Is

"I go to prepare a place for you. . . . Where I am,
there ye may be also." John 14:2, 3.

It has been more than 30 years since I left Belfast, and although I have been extremely happy in England, having married, raised a family, and made many friends there, Ireland is still "home." I was born there. My character and my values were formed there. My roots are there, and the older I get, the more I long to return to the land of my birth.

On return trips, as the plane descends, I never cease to thrill to the vivid green of the patchwork fields, nestling in the valley formed between the hills, and the sparkling waters of Belfast Lough. The poet Louis MacNeice tells how he was born "between the mountains and the gantries," and I identify with his sentiments, for my father worked in the shipbuilding yards. When I see Goliath, the giant crane, outlined against the sky, I know I am home.

The Irish are a sentimental people. In one of our folk songs we say that Ireland is "a little bit of heaven" that "fell from out the sky one day." Talking with the warm, friendly people, soaking up the culture, or driving along an empty country road with the sun shining and the birds singing, one can almost believe it. And yet Ireland is not heaven. As in every country in this world, however beautiful, sin and wickedness and corruption lurk in the shadows.

Nor is Ireland my true home. When I accepted the sacrifice of Jesus for my sins, I became a child of God and a citizen of the heavenly kingdom. Jesus is re-forming my character and my values. My roots are growing deep in His love, and He has gone to prepare a home for me where He lives. I should long for heaven even more than I long for Ireland. My thoughts should be continually on the day when He will return to take me home.

Will you, with me, pray for, work for, and long for the land of our rebirth?   AUDREY BALDERSTONE

Trapped!

Hereby perceive we the love of God, because he laid down his life for us: and we ought to lay down our lives for the brethren. 1 John 3:16.

A gentle, steady drizzle was falling. The traffic flowed smoothly despite the raindrops, and I was glad that in 10 minutes I'd be at work. Suddenly I noticed there was no oncoming traffic. My lane had come to an abrupt standstill and was now inching along at a snail's pace. Within seconds I saw a car flipped upside down in the opposite lane of traffic. The wheels on the car were still spinning. Tiny puffs of smoke circled about the car.

Fear gripped me. Several drivers jumped from their cars and ran to the disabled car. I could see the car's driver frantically crawling back and forth, window to window, like a caged animal, desperately trying to escape. He appeared dazed and confused, but was fighting to escape with what strength he could muster.

That poor man, I thought. *Should I stop and help? I know CPR. Maybe he'll need my help. But so many other drivers have left their cars and are running to his aid, maybe I'm not needed. Suppose the car explodes? He'll be killed, and those who are now running to help may be killed or injured. What should I do?*

I decided to keep on driving; however, I sent up a petition to heaven. "Lord, please, don't let this man suffer. Please, let one of the drivers be able to rescue him soon."

Once at work I could hardly think of anything but the accident. *Was the man alive? Did he have broken bones? Did he go into shock? How long before an ambulance arrived? Was one of the drivers able to extract him from the car? Did the car explode?*

As I relived the entire scene I began to understand even more what it means to lay down my life for my sister or brother. It means loving someone else more than myself. It is recognizing that someone's life is in jeopardy, and acting quickly to save her no matter what the cost. It means being willing to sacrifice for the man trapped in his car, as those drivers were willing to do. It means making the ultimate sacrifice as God's only Son did for you and for me when He gave His life on Calvary.   IRIS L. STOVALL

The Budget Dilemma

The Lord shall open unto thee his good treasure. Deut. 28:12.

T he room was quiet except for the ticking of the clock on the mantel and the steady, rythmic breathing of my dog, who was peacefully sleeping by my feet. It was two minutes until midnight, and the rest of the family was in bed.

Spread out on the table in front of me were the checkbook, pen, calculator, a stack of bills to be paid, and a bank statement waiting to be balanced. Would we ever have enough money to cover all the bills? For years we lived from month to month, returning tithe and giving offerings, stretching each dollar, hoping to have a tax refund for a vacation, keeping five children in church school, and keeping everyone clothed and the car running.

I breathed a silent prayer for a miracle and for wisdom as I began the painful task of paying the bills once again. Because of confused priorities and uncontrolled spending, I was caught in the trap of more bills than money.

In my search for a solution to our financial dilemma, I found that the Bible is full of texts dealing with finances. I discovered that what we are doing in our management of money is a clear indicator of what is happening in our spiritual life. I found that stewardship is more than returning our tithes and offerings—it encompasses our whole life and lifestyle. I learned that we needed to set a goal, control our spending, and set up a yearly budget.

So my husband and I figured out a budget based on biblical principles and prayed over it. I calculated it would take us one year to get out of debt. The thought was overwhelming, but we decided we had nothing to lose.

We made some sacrifices, but as we paid off each small loan, it freed up money that we applied toward another debt. Instead of taking 12 months to pay off all our debts, we were able to do it in eight months! We were thrilled!

If you are experiencing financial problems, why not decide today to seek help in turning your finances around and becoming a faithful steward of all God entrusts you with? Then you can claim the promise of Deuteronomy 28:12 and 13 and live a happier life.   CELIA MEJIA CRUZ

Night Prayer

I will lie down and sleep in peace, for you alone, O Lord,
make me dwell in safety. Ps. 4:8, NIV.

I loved bedtime at Grandma's house. No matter how scary things were at home, no matter what troubles came, a snugly time with Grandma made it all right.

Each night I nestled in Grandma's lap in front of the coal stove. She rocked me, sang songs, talked of the day's events, and told stories of the family's past. The family had had hard times aplenty, and the faith-filled grandparents, aunts, and uncles who nurtured us through them were the stuff of our bedtime stories. I felt better knowing we had always come through.

The best moment each evening was always saved for last: "The Night Prayer." Grandma had found the prayer in a newspaper during World War I and clipped it out. While her loved ones were away at war, she said "The Night Prayer" and it made her feel better. Then after the war she lost it.

But then came World War II, and her sons were called to battle. Once again "The Night Prayer" turned up in the paper. Once again she clipped it out and read it every night her boys were gone. I still remember the first four lines, how my grandma recited them so softly to me, warming me and rocking me to sleep:

"Night is falling, dear Father; the long day is o'er.
And in Thy loved presence I'm kneeling once more
To thank Thee for keeping me safe through the day,
To ask Thee this night to keep evil away."

When I was little, it was always enough to know that my Father knew all about my sorrows and had them firmly in hand, infinitely more able than I to deal with them. It was enough to carry me into sleep and through the next day to the precious time when "The Night Prayer" would again commit the day's events to Him.

As a mom with children of my own, it is still enough to know that as we gather for bedtime worship, the worries, hopes, sorrows, joys, failures, and successes of my family are committed to my dear Father.

JULIA C. S. VERNON

The Power Outage

"You also must be ready, because the Son of Man will come at an hour when you do not expect him." Matt. 24:44, NIV.

Sometime around 1:00 a.m. during a January storm, the power went off, and I had no heat. The night-light in the bathroom was off, and the red figures on the digital wall clock no longer blinked. As the electric blanket cooled, I shivered, finally getting up to add a quilt to the bed.

Between fitful naps, I wondered how I would cope if the power outage should last. I had a dozen short, fat candles. If I clustered them in a cake pan and lit all of them, would the flames be enough to take the chill off the air in some corner of the house?

Maybe I could get out a large, round metal tray on which to burn a few logs of rolled up newspaper. But where would the smoke go? Up the vent over the range? Not without power to turn on the blower fan. Would I have to walk through the snow to the friendly neighbors who had fireplaces or woodburning stoves?

My husband and I had talked about having a fireplace or a wood-burning stove put in. We finally decided on gas, but did nothing more than look at gas heaters in a couple places. Then in November my husband was called to Korea. We decided to take a chance on getting through the winter without a power crisis.

And now here I was. I dressed warmly, but our mobile home is not well insulated, and it still felt cold. I stepped outside to sweep a path to the bird feeder. The beauty was breathtaking! Even with a gentle wind, the swaying branches held their load of snow. I hurried to find my camera. Under the gray sky, even with all the white snow, my automatic flash went off as I took shots in all directions.

Then with a *swish* the furnace came on. I flipped a switch and light blazed. I was safe—until next time. When my husband gets home, we're going to have a serious talk about being prepared.

And we will renew our resolve to be prepared for a time of trouble far worse than a home without heat in winter.

Irene Wakeham Lee

Priorities

"Martha, Martha," the Lord answered, "you are worried and upset about many things, but only one thing is needed. Mary has chosen what is better, and it will not be taken away from her." Luke 10:41, 42, NIV.

There was so much to do that morning as I bustled about the house. Our daughter and two of her friends were coming to visit, and I wanted everything to be just right. My husband had left for the hour's drive to the airport, where he would pick up the girls, so I thought I had plenty of time to complete the necessary preparations.

When the food was ready to pop in the oven, I turned my attention to cleaning the house. Soon the bathroom was sparkling, and I started sweeping the floors. Just as I got to the family room and kitchen area, I heard a car in the driveway. Since it wasn't time for my husband to return, I went out to see who was there.

To my great surprise, the plane had not been late, my husband had made record time, and here was my daughter's smiling face greeting me. My first reaction was despair as I thought of the unfinished cleaning and the pile of dirt I had just swept into the family room.

But in spite of my initial reaction, I was able to welcome my guests into my home. Even though the kitchen didn't get swept or mopped, we had a great time together. And no one even seemed to notice that there was dust in the living room and the rug wasn't vacuumed. Lack of some preparations I had deemed as absolutely necessary didn't spoil our visit together at all.

Then I think of the times that seemingly necessary cooking, cleaning, or other chores take first priority in my life. My best friend Jesus is waiting to visit with me, but I'm too busy. On the days when I "choose what is better," putting personal worship and prayer time first on my agenda, everything goes much smoother. The really important things are completed in less time, and I feel blessed.

Lord, help me get my priorities in order and make that better choice today so that Your blessing will not be taken away from me. BETTY J. ADAMS

Rearranging the Furniture

Be renewed in the spirit of your mind. Eph. 4:23.

T he children were little and their language was not yet perfect, but their father quickly understood when he saw the rearranged furniture. The couch was where the table had been. The bookcase was now on the opposite side of the room, the piano beside the fireplace. His favorite chair stood in front of the window. Even pictures and lamps were relocated.

I liked change, so this happened every several months. Because I was a stay-at-home mommy who could not afford new furnishings, rearranging the furniture satisfied my desire for "newness."

I have also followed this same pattern in my spiritual life. Periodically I revamp it. Sometimes it's quite intentional; I want to be refreshed, so I change my approach. I may arise earlier or pray as I exercise. As I gain additional insights from reading inspiring authors, I may try worshiping differently. For a while my prayer time was separate from my Bible study. Often when I'm invited to share the corporate worship experience of others, as at women's retreats, I adapt lessons and formats shared there into my devotional time. From one such spiritual retreat I began "practicing the presence" of God. I designated a physical place for Him to reside. At other times, in carelessness, I neglect any form of worship—yet another change.

Perhaps my spiritual life is reflected in my human need for difference. My comfort is that as I express my devotion to God, each of the approaches I may choose as an avenue of seeking to be in His presence helps me to see Him from another dimension.

I have found that just as there are many ways to arrange furniture, there are different forms of worship. Each serves the purpose of supplying freshness, giving pleasure, providing contentment, and glorifying God. Whatever form we choose, the end result of time with God will be a renewing of our minds and of our spiritual lives.

ELIZABETH DARBY WATSON

The Sudden Fall

If you think you are standing,
watch out that you do not fall. 1 Cor. 10:12, NRSV.

Recent thaws and freezing weather in northern Idaho had made both walking and cross-country skiing difficult. "What shall we do for our daily exercise?" I asked my husband.

"Let's hike our trail down the hill to the railroad track. It should be safe and simple with our ski poles," he suggested.

The snow was covered by a thin crust of ice, so most of the time we could walk on top of the snow, leaving only slight footprints. Every once in a while, however, we'd hit a softer place, and with a sudden jolt we'd sink up to our knees.

Although the trail was steep, we successfully made it to the railroad track and started back. Drifting snow had filled the trail, making it hard to follow. Jay was ahead when I hit a soft spot and my uphill leg disappeared to my thighs. Sitting on the slick snow, I struggled to get it out, but my big boot stuck. As I jerked on it I called, "I can't stand up, and I'm slipping!"

Jay cautiously inched in my direction.

Now with both legs free and facing downhill, I teetered on the brink of the slope. As I tried to stand, I began to slip and started downhill, gaining speed with every second. With astonishment Jay stared at his wife speeding down the hill. Slick ski pants and my anatomy filled the role of sled quite well under the circumstances.

Knowing that piles of snow and ice chunks at the bottom would stop me, and thankful there were no trees or bushes sticking out of the snow, I laid back and went with the slide. My skid terminated with my feet not quite reaching the bank of ice chunks. The ski pole, like a javelin, followed me to the bottom, stopping just short of my head. Far above me on the hill I heard uproarious laughter.

How often I have tried to negotiate the slippery paths of life on my own, only to have my spiritual balance slip right out from under me. *Hold my hand today, Lord, lest I slip and fall.*   EILEEN E. LANTRY

Bronwen's "Revenge"

*"Don't be afraid; you are worth more than
many sparrows." Luke 12:7, NIV.*

P ssst! Pssst!"
    The sharp sound pierces my sleep. "Go away," I murmur.
    "Psssst!" It's our third daughter, Bronwen. I know there's no
chance she'll go away. Her voice is urgent. "Get up."
    "Why?"
    "There's a woodpecker at the bird feeder!"
    A weekend morning. A chance to snuggle deep under the covers a
little longer. I sigh. My eyes feel glued shut with sleep. "OK," I moan.
    I remember the hours Bronwen, then 4 years old, had spent tip-
toeing after sparrows, a saltshaker in her hand. I'd thoughtlessly told
her one could catch a bird by putting salt on its tail. But now she had
her "revenge." She'd put four feeders on our front porch, in a tree,
and in the front yard.
    I shrug into my chenille robe, pulling it tight against the chill, then
feel my way down the stairs. I'm not a morning person.
    At first I don't see the woodpecker, only the usual flock of purple
finches darting around the pole feeder on the lawn. Small and quick,
they look like they've been dipped in raspberry juice.
    "There it is," she says. "On the tree trunk. It's called a red-bellied,
even though its belly is white and the red is on its head."
    I see it too, busily pecking for insects in the trunk of the ornamen-
tal plum tree; suddenly this begins to be fun. I'm watching a flock of
chickadees elbowing the mourning doves for seed on the ground
when Bronwen says, "Look! There's a downy woodpecker." Awe fills
her voice. Its black-and-white checkered coat looks soft and fluffy. I
wish I could touch it .
    A red-winged blackbird catches our eye next. It spreads its wings,
showing its colors, before swooping to the bar of the pole feeder.
Finches and sparrows flutter out of its way.
    Ribbons of late-winter sunlight fall across the greening lawn. The
air holds a pink glow. I scoot my rocking chair toward the window
for a better view. I can't imagine why the bed seemed so inviting. It's
a perfect way to begin a morning.   PENNY ESTES WHEELER

Blizzard Conditions

*Cleanse me with hyssop, and I will be clean; wash me,
and I will be whiter than snow. Ps. 51:7, NIV.*

The seventh blizzard of the season is sweeping through North Dakota. The wind is howling, and the snow is swirling in every direction. Weather reports are warning of "blizzard conditions" and "life-threatening windchill." We are instructed to stay indoors unless it is absolutely necessary to venture out into the storm.

When our family moved here from Mexico last summer, every North Dakotan we met wanted to tell us about the force of winter and the shock we soon were going to get. There have indeed been adjustments for our family concerning the weather. We spent a small fortune for appropriate coats, boots, hats, and gloves. We learned how to insulate water pipes as we prepared our house for the cold weather. We had a block heater installed in our car. We are learning firsthand what "cabin fever" means. However, the climate changes have been less difficult for us than we'd imagined. We are enjoying the winter and marveling in the wonder of all the snow.

The empty field across the street is a blanket of white—a blanket about five feet deep! It looks so beautiful, so pure, so perfectly white. There's something peaceful and calming about a winter scene. Between snowstorms the snowmobilers flock to the open field, leaving their mark on the still-white blanket. In a couple days the snow in that field will be dirty and covered with crisscrossing trails. The view from my kitchen window won't be so serene—until the next snowfall, when all the marks will be covered over in new soft snow.

Lord, when the blizzard hits my life, when the wind of trouble howls and swirls, help me to trust in You. Remind me that this is my chance to let You smooth out the ruts and the tracks of sin that crisscross my life. Show me how to be pure and gentle in the face of difficulty. Today, Lord, I pray the prayer of David: "Wash me, and I will be whiter than snow." SANDRA SIMANTON

Thank You, Lord!

It is a good thing to give thanks unto the Lord, and to sing praises unto thy name, O most High. Ps. 92:1.

A few days ago I felt overwhelmed by a lot of problems that had been piling up for months and years; there seemed to be no way out. As usual, I took my problems to the Lord in prayer, and within a few days the problem that topped the list was miraculously solved by Him. My immediate response was to shout "Hallelujah!" and to sing praises to the Lord.

This set me thinking, and I took my pen and began to write a letter to the Lord, telling Him how good He has been to me.

I reminded Him about when I was very young and my mother gave me two pence. When I lost the money, I prayed. As I opened my eyes, I found the two pence. *Thank You, Lord.*

I wrote of the time I went to hawk fish with another neighbor in the savannah bush of the middle belt of Nigeria. Both of us became lost and wandered around without finding the bush path to take us back home. We cried and shouted and prayed for deliverance. How God led us back to the path after wandering around for more than two hours is one of His miracles in my life. *Thank You, Lord.*

In 1955 I wanted to travel back to my parents, a journey I had never taken before. I traveled in a truck that had to visit various villages. A trip that today takes only about 30 minutes took us almost four hours, and we arrived late in the night. I could not find my way home and could not sleep in the truck, but God sent me a sister who kept me for the night and took me home the following morning. *Thank You, Lord.*

I remember when I was very young, our house was built at the foot of a hill of igneous rock, where reptiles abound. One morning I started to sweep a storeroom, not knowing that during the night an eight-foot-long python had climbed to the rafters on top of the building. God kept me safe. It was a few minutes later that the python crawled down and attacked our goat. The snake was eventually killed. *Thank You, Lord!*

Lord, how can I say thank You for what You have done, things so undeserved but which You do to prove Your love to me?   BECKY DADA

A Way of Escape

*God is faithful, who will not suffer you to be tempted above that
ye are able; but will with the temptation also make
a way to escape, that ye may be able to bear it. 1 Cor. 10:13.*

I was wallowing in self-pity, totally depressed, desperately lonely,
irretrievably rejected. My husband, the father of my four children,
ages 2 to 7, had left us for another woman. He was no doubt out having a good time, while I, who always tried to do "the right thing" and
serve God, was alone this Saturday night, lonely, miserable, forgotten
by everyone. *Who cares? Not a soul. Least of all God. It just isn't worth
"doing the right thing." It doesn't pay!*

I decided to go to a party I knew would end up with partner
swapping. I knew it was wrong, but I didn't care. So I set about finding a baby-sitter for the night. Baby-sitters were always easy to
find—two or three phone calls, and I'd be on my way.

Eleven phone calls and no more options later, I was more dejected
than ever. With angry tears and rebellious thoughts, I eventually went
to bed and fell into a troubled sleep.

Seemingly only moments later, the sun streamed in my window
and my four children bounced all over me. They hugged and kissed
me and cuddled close. "I love you!" they said.

The depression and rebellion of the night before seemed far
away. *God does care,* I thought. *Always.* I remembered when He'd sent
a friend with a birthday cake at 9:30 at night. That was the night I
felt suicide was the only option. I thought of the time He'd sent a casual acquaintance with a huge food parcel when there was literally
nothing left to eat. Then too, He had led me to people who could understand my problems and be there for me.

Now He'd intervened and not let me go to a party that He knew
would totally wreck me. It was not really the way I wanted to go in
life. He loved me enough to say no when it really mattered. He intervened gently when things were beyond my endurance.

Gratefully I hugged my children and we laughed and played.
*Thank You, God, for once again providing a way of escape, even when I was
turning my back on You. Thank You.*   HELEN CHRISTIAN

Mental Pictures

Whatever is admirable — if anything is excellent or
praiseworthy — think about such things. Phil. 4:8, NIV.

Sometimes when I want to switch off from the problems of the day, I sit or lie down quietly. Usually I begin "letting go" physically, starting with my toes and gradually relaxing each part of my body in turn, breathing slowly and feeling the tension drain away.

Relaxing mentally isn't as easy, so I decide to travel in my imagination to one of my favorite places—perhaps a beautiful garden or a mountain stream.

Today I thought of Granada, a beautiful island in the West Indies. I visited there many years ago, but I can still picture the scene easily. I see the vivid tropical sea in glorious greens and blues. I seem to actually feel the warmth of the sun and the ice-cold freshness of a lemon squash. I remember that when the sun is too hot, I can run into the sea and feel the cool salty water splashing over me. I can almost taste the salt.

I picture the coconut palms in the distance. On the beach nearby I see "seaside grapes," adding more green to the picture. The picture changes. It is night, and the moon is out. I hear the soothing sound of waves gently lapping against the shore.

I always feel a sense of gratitude after I have "painted" one of my mental pictures. I have the blessing of memory, sight, and hearing, God-given gifts I tend to take for granted. Even if I were poor, uneducated, isolated, or disabled, I could still paint my pictures.

In my little period of letting go, I experience physical, mental, and spiritual rest from this busy world, escaping from the sadness and violence that easily confront me, and enjoy a few minutes of relaxing in the beauty God has created.

What mental picture could you paint? What feelings would it bring to you? Thank God for the ability to remember and enjoy. God invites us to take time today to think on things that are lovely, and especially to spend time with Him.

PHILIPPA MARSHALL

The Prayer Meeting

*Before they call I will answer, while they are yet speaking
I will hear. Isa. 65:24, NRSV.*

When I applied to a community college to enroll in the registered nursing program, I was encouraged by my counselor to take preparatory biology. The classes were scheduled to meet on Monday and Wednesday evenings, from February to June.

I was grateful to be able to get into the course but was very concerned about missing prayer meeting on Wednesday evenings. But I knew God wanted me in the nursing program, because I had prayed about it and followed His directions. The day I got into the preparatory biology class was the final day of registration.

Many thoughts tumbled through my head. Not even one holiday fell on Wednesday that year. I would miss prayer meeting for five months. I hated to miss it, but didn't see how I could help it. I decided to do as I always did, and talked to God about my problem.

As soon as I got home a friend from church telephoned me. She said, "Sister Rose, I don't know what has gotten into the pastor. He came here and saw prayer meeting on Wednesdays, and he has gone right ahead and changed it to Tuesdays without asking anyone about it. You know, Sister Rose, that my girlfriend and I have gone out every Tuesday for lunch for the past 35 years. Now what am I going to do?"

All the while she was speaking, I was thinking, *Thank You, Jesus! Praise the Lord!*

"Why don't you still go to lunch, and then invite your friend to attend prayer meeting with you?" I suggested.

I didn't miss one prayer meeting. I passed the course and got into the nursing program. A few weeks later the pastor changed prayer meeting back to Wednesdays. I just continue to praise Him.

No problem is too big—or small—for God to handle. He is so good! He even cared about my desire to attend prayer meeting! I believe He especially loves to help us when we want to spend time with Him.

JANICE ROSE

Shut the Lions' Mouths!

My God hath sent his angel, and hath shut the lions' mouths. Dan. 6:22.

I was scheduled to speak at a writer's conference for professionals, most of them men. With no presentations the first day, I had time to observe. The more I saw, the more apprehensive I became. They often interrupted the male presenters, asking questions, challenging statements, or offering comments. The presenters handled these interruptions with graceful skill, but I knew I could not do it! I have a fear of being tongue-tied in public, so I write out and time every presentation, word for word. I don't read my script, but I know it is there in case I should forget. My system leaves no room for interruptions from the audience! I often ask my audience to hold their questions until the end, or to see me privately. This time I was reluctant even to do that.

Lord, what am I going to do? I prayed the morning of my first presentation. *I feel intimidated by these men. I'm scared. Please give me some courage for today.*

Immediately to my mind came the story of Daniel in the lions' den. I smiled. *Yes, Lord, I agree that if You could be with Daniel in the lions' den, You can be with me. I honestly do feel as though I'm standing up before a group of professional lions. It's comforting to know that You will be with me in my presentations.*

I wasn't completely satisfied, so I continued. *Lord, I have one more request. Please shut the lions' mouths!* I was relaxed during my presentation. My students sat meek as lambs. Not one opened his mouth! They did the exercises I requested without protest! It was marvelous!

Near the end of the week I decided to share with the class my fears of the first day and my prayer about shutting the lions' mouths. They burst into laughter! Whenever they saw me after that they teased me by pretending to roar. We had great fun!

"I wanted so badly to speak up during your first presentation," one distinguished brother admitted. "But somehow I just couldn't get my mouth open!"

Thank You, Lord, for shutting the lions' mouths. What an amazing God You are to make it possible for me to do each task You call me to do. With You by my side, I need never fear!   DOROTHY EATON WATTS

Canning Compliments

*A word aptly spoken is like
apples of gold in settings of silver. Prov. 25:11, NIV.*

I watched her, standing alone on the front steps. The church service had just concluded, and it was obvious to my 13-year-old eyes that she was a visitor. One after another, people walked right past her as though they didn't see her. How they could have missed her was beyond me. Her bright-orange dress was at least two sizes too small, contrasting with her shoes that were an off shade of red.

Out of the corner of my eye I saw my mother move toward the visitor. As the minister's wife, she sought out individuals who didn't quite fit in. She had a knack for saying something appropriate, a gracious way of making them feel welcome. This time I was sure that even she would be stumped. I was wrong.

"I'm so glad you could worship with us today," Mother said. "Oh!" she added. "In this light your hair is absolutely alive with sunbeams!"

The woman sighed with relief. "I didn't expect to be in town this long," she explained. "So I didn't bring any dress clothes. When my visit lasted over the weekend, I borrowed some clothes so I could come to church." They began to chat.

She wanted to come to church badly enough to borrow clothes! I was thoroughly ashamed of my earlier not-well-put-together assessment. Later I asked my mother, "How do you always think of something appropriate to say?" That's when she told me about canning compliments. Now, I knew about canning. (You know, the predecessor of freezing.) If I had a dollar for every vegetable and fruit I've stuffed into a mason jar, I'd be rich! But canning *compliments?*

We talked about her belief that there's always something about which one can compliment another individual. A genuine compliment was the fastest way she knew of to help someone feel comfortable. It turned out that Mother had made a habit of looking for those somethings and canning them.

"That way," she explained, "no matter whom I meet, there's always a jar I can open and tailor the contents to the specific situation."

How about your pantry? Any jars of canned compliments on the shelf? ARLENE TAYLOR

Miracle Tracks in the Snow

God also bearing them witness, both with signs and wonders, and with divers miracles, and gifts of the Holy Ghost, according to his own will. Heb. 2:4.

I t was dusk. Clouds were gathering in the sky, casting a primitive darkness. I picked up my daughter, Gail, from her friend's home, where she had stayed while I shopped in town. And then we were heading home in a blinding snowstorm.

It was bad. The snowflakes fell with a marked determination that filled us with apprehension. It was so hard to see the road. The mailboxes on each side stood up like sentinels, marking the path home. But we knew those faithful markers would soon come to an end when the road made a jog by one last house.

We had traveled the road so many times—to church, to the city, to the school. How well we knew it! But now the snow was a solid wall of white that faded into darkness around the edges of the headlights. It did no good to know the road so well. It would be easy to slip off the pavement into a ditch or to sideswipe a tree.

Gail began to cry, sensing our danger. In our great need, she remembered the One who is ever ready to hear a plea for help. "Oh, Jesus, come and help us. Please take us safely home."

In the snow ahead, two car tracks appeared, as though a car had gone ahead of our station wagon in that blinding snow. There was no side road or driveway from which those tracks could have come. They simply began—so clear, so pronounced. The car that made them would have had to be immediately ahead of our bumper or the snow would have covered the tracks in a second. But there was no glow of taillights.

Using the tracks as a guide, I maneuvered the car, making good progress. Soon the snow let up enough so we could see familiar landmarks again, and the tracks disappeared as mysteriously as they had appeared.

A miracle? Why not! Did not God manifest His power in the cloud by day and the pillar of fire by night to the children of Israel? Will He not use that same power today to help His people when we call upon Him in faith?   LAURIE DIXON-McCLANAHAN

Forgiveness

Confess your faults one to another, and pray one for another, that ye may be healed. James 5:16.

I suppose one of the most difficult things a person ever has to do is to admit when she is wrong and then try to make amends.

I don't know what it is that makes this so unpleasant; surely everyone already knows we are only human and are subject to making some mistakes. To admit to a mistake, and thus prove we are less than perfect, is very difficult for most of us. I am no exception. I've gone through many sleepless nights and miserable days before I gave in to that still small voice urging me to confess.

When I was a small child, I picked up a penny sucker from under the counter of our neighborhood grocery store. That bothered me for more than 20 years. Even though the store had changed hands once or twice, I wrote a letter of apology and sent sufficient pennies to cover my sin.

When I was 15 years old, I bought a two-piece suit from a friend of a friend. But I never had the $5 to pay for it. My conscience bothered me for many years until I drove to that woman's home and paid my debt.

Most recently, while out to lunch with a friend and her husband on Valentine's Day, the restaurant was offering its women patrons free strawberry shortcake with their meal. Since I have a problem with sugar, I was about to turn down the offer, when my friend's husband whispered to me to accept it and give it to him, which I did.

Long before I arrived home that day the still small voice was speaking to my heart. I felt that what I had done was wrong, so I wrote a letter of apology to the manager of the lunchroom and enclosed a check for the dessert.

I like to be able to go to bed at night and go to sleep. I can't do that if I have unconfessed sins keeping me awake. I always feel so good when I confess my wrongs. Why do I sometimes wait so long to do it?

We should right our wrongs as soon as we know iniquity is happening. Don't give it time to fester; that way the wound isn't as deep and takes less time to heal. That sounds good to me.

CLAREEN COLCLESSER

From House to Home

May the Lord continually bless you with heaven's blessings as well as with human joys. Ps. 128:5, TLB.

After a year of house hunting and house selling, we were finally able to move into a larger house. Our family of four had outgrown the small two-bedroom house my husband and I had bought shortly after we were married. We were so excited to be moving into a place with three bedrooms, a large kitchen, a formal dining room (high on my priority list!), a big master bedroom with a cozy dormer window and a walk-in closet, and a garage. There was even a porch with a swing. Oh, it seemed too good to be true!

About a week after moving in, though, Michelle, age 7, summed it up: "I like our new house, but I miss the old one."

I began to think about just what makes a house a home. Our old house had been cramped, the windows were drafty, and the basement smelled funny. But the memories of laughter and love were there. We'd been through good times and bad, but that's what makes a house a home—not the structure, but what happens inside.

Our new house was purchased from a couple who were in the process of divorcing. As our furniture and friends filled the house, we began making memories right away. My two sisters, Mom, Dad, and Grandmother visited soon after we moved, creating some precious memories.

One evening the previous owner stopped by to pick up some mail. The girls had friends over, and I was busy feeding them amid the usual evening chaos of supper and Daddy arriving home. The house was far from neat and tidy. When we had first looked at the house, the owner's wife had already moved, and he was living alone with only a few pieces of furniture. Everything was clean and neat, but didn't look lived-in. Now the man looked around and commented, "This looks really good. It's nice to see furniture here."

I think what he really meant was "It's nice to see 'living' here—the noise of children, the smell of good food, the love of a husband and wife."

It takes a lot of work and emotional investment, but memory by memory our house is becoming a home. ANN MALONEY-HALIM

A Mother's Prayer

But ye have not so learned Christ. Eph. 4:20.

I was giving a piano lesson when my mother brought my little daughter, Rebeca, an 8-month-old baby, to me. I looked at the baby and was worried to see that she had dark spots all over her body and was having difficulty breathing.

Though her color and respiration gradually returned to normal, her fever remained constant. I prayed, asking God to restore my child's health, but it seemed my prayers were not answered. Many nights I stayed awake all night, bathing her burning body.

In my despair, I began studying the symptoms that my daughter presented. My husband and I took our baby to the doctor frequently. Then I consulted another physician, who told me that Rebeca was preleukemic.

My heart could no longer stand the pain of seeing my baby so ill. Rebeca could no longer swallow the medication. Her tongue was full of wounds and irregular spots. I thought to myself, *I am going to lose my baby.*

And then one night, unable to continue to see her suffering, I knelt by the bed and in a cry of anguish I placed my child in God's hands. "I no longer ask for healing," I prayed, "only that Your will be done in her."

After that I had peace in my heart. The next morning a friend gave me the name of a pediatrician whose specialty was cases similar to Rebeca's, and, as incredible as it seems, day by day my baby recovered.

Today Rebeca is 10 years old. She is a beautiful and healthy child. Her skin can be compared to a fruit: rosy and soft. Rebeca loves Jesus very much. Her healing has helped me understand that we are nothing, but that God can still perform miracles today.

God heard my prayer when I forgot my personal pain a little and was able to put my daughter in His hands.   MARILISA FOFFA STINA

Rumorosa

"The gate is wide and the way is easy, that leads to destruction, and those who enter by it are many." Matt. 7:13, RSV.

There is a road in Mexico that parallels the United States border from Tijuana to Mexicali. The road has always been hazardous as it climbs up and up over the barren mountains. It is called Rumorosa. This narrow highway with many curves was noted for many accidents. I rode a bus over this road at night and was told that if I had known the road I would never have taken a bus over those mountains. Ignorance—or Providence—got me to Mexicali.

Not long ago the government built a new two-lane highway over these mountains. The old road is used for traffic going one way, and the two new lanes are used for traffic in the opposite direction. The road looks beautiful and wide, but the engineers neglected to bank the many curves. But with two lanes each way, drivers naturally think that one can go faster than before.

A friend and I, riding over this road, pulled out and stopped to take a look at the view. As we peered over the steep cliff, cars sped by us, screeching their tires at every turn. From our vantage point I counted seven cars in just one area that had misjudged the turns and ended up far below in the gulleys. Much of this chaos was caused by drinking drivers. As we continued on, we looked back at the turns. We could see cars, trucks, and even a double tanker that had misjudged the turns and ended up in disaster.

As we travel along life's roads, we may feel exhilaration in the fast lane. We may doze at the wheel. Satan does not bank the turns or curves, but delights when we crash, physically as well as spiritually.

Praise the Lord, we can stay on the narrow and difficult way that leads to life. We have no fear for the future as we see how God has led us in the past. Let us keep on keeping on our upward way with our eyes ever fixed on Jesus.

DOTTIE O. BOWEN

World's Largest Flower

"Whoever remains in me, and I in him, will bear much fruit;
for you can do nothing without me." John 15:5, TEV.

We rounded a curve on the highway in Sabah's Crocker Range mountains, when we saw the sign, "Rafflesia Jungle Reserve." "Let's stop!" I exclaimed. "Maybe we can see one."

The rafflesia, with its monstrous maroon-and-orange blossom, grows only in Southeast Asia. Its five thick, fleshy, petal-like lobes can measure three feet across and weigh up to four pounds. But it's only a flower, nothing more. Rafflesia has no roots, no leaves, nor stems—nothing green. It is beautifully decorated with light warty spots and spikes in its center tube.

Rafflesia is a mystery flower. No one knows how its seeds germinate or grow, or how this parasite plant begins life inside a trailing forest grapevine on which it is totally dependent for food. Fine microscopic threads develop from its tiny seeds, growing into the host vine for about 18 months. Then in just a few exciting hours the brown bracts split and the full flower blooms.

We followed our guide down the steep trail. At a fenced-in site we saw many brown buds the size of large cabbage heads showing among the forest rubble. The bracts had split, showing the orange lobes of the flower.

Many never mature because of drought, predators, and native witch doctors, who boil the buds for medicine. Exposed to great risks from damage or destruction, rafflesia's 15 species are on the rare and endangered list.

What a wonderful fragrance this huge flower could produce! But instead it is repulsive. Not all species smell terrible; some have no odor at all. Bluebottle flies, lured by the smell, come loaded with pollen from the male flowers to deposit on the female flowers. A few days after blooming, rafflesia shrivels up, turns black, and waits for rain to wash its many tiny seeds to other vines.

Like the rafflesia, which must remain in the vine, we must remain in the true Vine, Jesus. Neither can do anything worthwhile apart from the vine. It's our choice: live apart from Him and die, or remain and have life. Thank God, when we choose to remain in Him, He takes the responsibility to enable us to be fruitful.   EILEEN E. LANTRY

Missionary Life

Trust in the Lord with all your heart and lean not on your own understanding; in all your ways acknowledge him, and he will make your paths straight. Prov. 3:5, NIV.

I had always dreamed of becoming a missionary, but it seemed the doors were closed. Then my husband and I heard of the need for young pastors who would go for a year to France to learn the language, and then go on to Africa. We didn't hesitate. We applied and were accepted.

I had longed to be totally dependent on God. In Europe I had the feeling that my everyday duties pushed God to the background. When I came to the Central African Republic, I learned to depend on God for every little thing.

We went to Bambari, the second largest town of the country. The trip by car over the 235 miles took us 10 hours. The first 95 miles (150 kilometers) were paved. For the rest of the way we mostly bumped from one hole to the next no faster than you could walk. Our little daughter called one rocky spot, more like a stony staircase than a road, "Mount Ararat."

The house that had been rented for us had once been the best house of the town, but now it was dilapidated and dirty. Cockroaches and mice droppings dotted the floors and cupboards. We had no appliances, no electricity, and no water. If we had had enough gasoline, we would have returned to Bangui the next day.

I was exhausted, hot, dusty, and pregnant. I sat down on the once-beautiful steps and thought, *It's quite good things are as they are. At least it can't get any worse!*

Our petroleum lamp would not burn, so we spent our first night sitting with two candles, listening to all the little creatures in our house, not even daring to use the bed because there was no time to do any cleaning before the tropical night engulfed us. The next morning we bought new lamps that worked, a petroleum cooker, and a few pails with which we could carry water from the well 165 yards (150 meters) away.

Step by step, we learned to live in Africa. I am so thankful for those difficult but at the same time wonderful years. *Thank You, Lord, that You taught me to trust in You in all things and that You have led me on Your paths.*

HANNELE OTTSCHOFSKI

To Make Your Mark for God

The eyes of the Lord are on the righteous and his ears are attentive to their prayer. 1 Peter 3:12, NIV.

I was in my late 30s when I asked God to give me a special work to do for Him. I waited three years before He showed me I was to write.

Most writers are people who yearned to be such. Not I. Art was my love. Awards over the years proved my mettle, with commercial art being my particular best.

Without any training, my writing until that time had been mediocre. Then I was asked to write press releases for my church. This volunteer work led to my becoming a journalist.

I see writing as an extension of a Christian lifestyle. Editors know me as a dependable writer, one who meets deadlines, who generates ideas, who is people oriented. However, the larger part of my work is the special task God gave me when He answered my prayer to serve Him in a special way. As a writer I have God-given opportunities to meet people and pray for them.

With interviewing being a major part of my writing life, I meet hundreds of people. Most interviews are face-to-face, but many are via the telephone. During interviews people's needs often come to the fore. Often God impresses me to pray with them, sometimes at kitchen tables, sometimes in a major corporate office, sometimes by telephone.

I simply cannot let these opportunities to minister escape. Prayer is not always generated because of some dilemma, but often it is a prayer of thanks, a time to let my contact know that I'm rejoicing for him or her.

Prayer is a wonderful thing; like writing, it can reach out and touch so many.

If you yearn for God to use you in a special way, to make your mark for Him, ask Him what He wants you to do. Then with a patient heart go about your Christian living. He will answer in His time. You will be excited when you discover what He has planned for you!

BETTY KOSSICK

Daydreaming

*In my Father's house are many mansions: . . . I go to prepare
a place for you. John 14:2.*

I remember going through catalogs and magazines as a child. First I would choose my family: a husband and four perfectly beautiful children. Then I would outfit each one with lovely clothes, fancy toys, and a beautiful car. The daydream also included a perfect mansion.

When I was a young wife, the daydreams diminished to how I would furnish our first little two-bedroom house. As the children came, my daydreams became dreams for them, of seeing each one of them growing to be happy, mature young Christians. My dream included seeing each of the four become college graduates so that they might embark on their own dreams.

On a vacation trip to Rhode Island I saw not just one but several streets of mansions, miles of them. However, most of the mansions were uninhabited! They were not the culmination of someone's dream, but rather they were simply possessions of their owners. It was as if each one had tried to outdo the others by having the largest house, the best-manicured grounds, and the most spectacular view. There were walls of polished marble, rich tapestries, furnishings and fixtures imported from all over the world. The beauty was beyond my wildest imagination.

I have been able to live a large portion of my dream. The four beautiful children, now educated, live happy lives of their own. Nice cars sit in my driveway, and I have a comfortable home. Though attractive, it is not a mansion. I still daydream, but in a much larger perspective! Now I am planning a mansion that will put the ones in Rhode Island to shame. Love and everlasting peace will be there, and all will be perfect beyond my imagination.

I don't believe we dream enough about what it will be like in heaven. If we did, we would be more excited.

We can live the dream of a mansion in a city with streets of pure gold. If you become discouraged about how little you have here on earth and how few of your daydreams have come true, try a little heavenly daydreaming! Don't let your mansion sit uninhabited; reach out to Jesus and receive your keys.   BARBARA SMITH MORRIS

Reflection

Love does no wrong to a neighbor; therefore, love is the fulfilling of the law.
Rom. 13:10, NRSV.

If ebony and ivory
live together on the keyboard
side by side on the piano
in perfect harmony
producing melodies
of such beauty, so many,
why can't we?

If cat and dog
(natural enemies) can live
under the same roof as equals
each one in its own space
giving happiness
to the hand that caresses them,
why can't we?

If rose and thorn,
opposites in their manner of being
(one shares beauty and perfume;
one intimidates and wounds),
live together on the same plant
forming a total, one complete in the other,
why can't we?

If rain and sun,
each one with its own value
(one refreshes, the other parches;
one dampens, the other dries),
unite, and the result
is the beautiful rainbow of colors,
why can't we?

HULDA CYRELLI DE SOUZA

A Special Gift

The greatest of these is love. 1 Cor. 13:13, NIV.

Sidney was my high school chum. We were juniors together in academy. We spent days together at the beach, all night waiting for the Pasadena Rose Parade, and many hours talking.

After graduation I went to college; Sidney took nurse's training, married, and moved away. At first we wrote, then settled for the usual Christmas letter. Eventually we lost track of each other.

Years later Sidney returned alone. She was in a wheel chair in a nursing home. I visited her as often as I could—especially when I needed cheering up. Sidney had a great sense of humor and a lot of courage. She "adopted" two overseas children and sent them gifts and money for an education. She kept their pictures on her wall and called them her "kids."

But there were times of deep discouragement, too, when she'd call at night and ask me to read from the Bible and pray with her. We walked together through the darker part of her life.

Although Sidney didn't have a lot of money to buy gifts for her friends, she gave me one of my most treasured gifts, a little block of wood wrapped in "teddy bear" paper and tied with a bright little bow. Pasted on the front wrapper was this message:

> This is a very special gift
> That you can never see.
> The reason it's so special?
> It's just for you from me.
>
> Whenever you are lonely
> Or ever feeling blue,
> You have only to hold this gift;
> It's filled with love for you.
>
> You can never unwrap it,
> Please leave the ribbon tied.
> Just hold the box close to the heart—
> It's filled with love inside.

Who needs a gift of love from you this Valentine's Day?

EDNA MAYE GALLINGTON

Love

If I had the gift of speaking any language, including the language that angels use, but didn't have love, I would be nothing but a noisy gong or clangling cymbals. 1 Cor. 13:1, Clear Word.

Though I speak with eloquence at a women's retreat, but show not love in my speech, I am nothing but a piece of noisy machinery.

And though I have exceptional intuition, understanding all the mysteries of each and every church member, and though I believe I am capable of all things, but show no love, I am nothing.

And though I give generously to the food bank and myriads of other charities, and though I wear out my body volunteering at the local shelter, but show not love, no one really benefits.

True love can take a lot of battering and still be kind. It can stand being told its dress is inappropriate, its husband is not as good as the last man, its children are very noisy; and still it can be gracious. True love doesn't envy its friend's new suit or church positions. It doesn't even strive to outdo the other cooks or singers or mothers. True love never brags about its achievements but gives all the glory to God, the Giver.

True love refrains from being rude to the tactless, doesn't store up treasures on earth (even shoes or clothes), doesn't spout off in anger at those who are blowing out their ignorance or those who just differ in view, and gives the benefit of the doubt to everyone (even the chronic liar).

True love sorrows with the sinner and shares the joy of others' happiness. True love handles life with womanly grace and dignity (sometimes with lots of swallowing), has a positive attitude in good times and bad, doesn't give up easily, but endures in the strength of the Lord. True love never fails.

Know-it-alls will pass away, as will gossips and nosy people. We all are frail humans in the eyes of God. But when God puts His perfect love in our hearts, all frailty will dim in His glory.

When I was little, I acted and played like a child. But I became a woman and put away my childish attitudes toward God. I still see Him only dimly, but soon I'll see Him face-to-face. Then I will know Him perfectly as He knows me.

There are three beautiful things in life: faith, hope, and love. The greatest of these is love!

DAWNA BEAUSOLEIL

Good News!

As cold waters to a thirsty soul, so is good news
from a far country. Prov. 25:25.

I was excited. There was a new free E-mail service. The company actually encouraged people to log on to their computers and use it at absolutely no charge. They also wanted users to tell family and friends the good news of how they could use this free service, copy the program onto computer disks, and mail it to them. Or we could provide the names to the company and they would mail out the disks. There were absolutely no strings attached, except a brief and simple user's agreement.

The deal sounded fantastic. I quickly logged on and filled out my information, eager to get in touch with those I had neglected to call or write to. I could see it now. Soon I'd be "talking" to people I hadn't talked to in years—brothers, nieces and nephews, and college chums.

In the days that followed I tried to remember all the people I knew who had computers with modems. The list gradually grew, but it was not large enough for me. I began to think about those who had computers, but no modems. Maybe they'd consider getting a modem if they saw how useful it would be. Then I started thinking about those who didn't have a computer. Perhaps they'd be motivated to get one. After all, free E-mail. Wow! They would be able to correspond with me as often as they liked, no matter where they were. There was so much I wanted to share with them, and I was sure there was lots they wanted to tell me as well. I made disk copies and wasted no time getting them in the mail.

Good news, sprinklings of my life down through the years, refreshing information for the receiver, like cold water to a thirsty soul. As I thought of all the news that I could share, I thought of the good news, freely given by our loving Saviour, to be shared generously by those who know it and have accepted it. Good news, available to everyone. Good news, indeed, like water for a thirsty soul. Would I give up my time, duplicate anything necessary, or use my personal postage stamps to provide good news to others? Would I be as eager to share His good news as I was to share all the insignificant little tidbits of my life? Would you?

IRIS L. STOVALL

Ten Minutes, Please

Unless you speak intelligible words with your tongue,
how will anyone know what you are saying? 1 Cor. 14:9, NIV.

I had given two major presentations already that day and was grateful to be able to sit back, let my mind go blank, and enjoy the
singing and watch the young people participate in the vespers.

Suddenly I heard my name. I looked around to see what was happening; the vespers leader was looking at me and repeated, "And
now, Mrs. Stenbakken." I had no idea what I was supposed to do, but
stood up and walked toward the front of the room. As I passed the
women's ministries leader, she whispered, "About 10 minutes."

I could not think. It all came as such a total surprise. As far as I
knew there was no theme to the vespers—so far it had been only
singing. I was only about five steps from the front of the room, so I
didn't even have time to come up with anything en route. "Lord,
help!" I whispered.

I began talking. I couldn't tell you what about. I wanted to say
something about women, so I think I talked about Sarah in the Old
Testament, drawing on something I had written for a devotional a year
before. But a devotional is not even close to being 10 minutes in length.

Finally I decided that surely 10 minutes must have passed and sat
down. I was miserable. What an opportunity I'd had, and I felt as
though I had blown it because I was unprepared. I determined then
and there that I would always have something intelligent for my
tongue to say if I should ever be caught by surprise again. Fortunately
the experience hasn't repeated itself, but I do have something tucked
in the back of my mind, just in case.

My situation was unique (I hope!), but how often we have an occasion to say something for Christ and we blow it because we aren't
prepared; we haven't filled our minds with ideas and thoughts of Him
and what He has done for us. I want to be ready to share with a
neighbor, a friend, a chance encounter, should I have that opportunity
today. And that preparation must begin right now.

ARDIS DICK STENBAKKEN

The View From My Kitchen Window

For his compassions never fail. They are new every morning;
great is your faithfulness. Lam. 3:22, 23, NIV.

My husband was traveling again. This time it would take him three weeks to finish his itinerary. A few days after he left, I began to feel sick. At first I experienced constant sneezing, then a sore throat. Muscle pain, headache, and high fever followed.

"Influenza," the doctor said. "Stay home and drink lots of fluids."

"Why now?" I asked God. "I can't get sick now. I have to teach the junior class in church. And I can't leave my support group by themselves. Besides, Lord," I added, "the day after tomorrow is my birthday. I can't be sick on my birthday." My complaints were endless.

But sick I was. I stayed in bed until my birthday. That morning I decided to fix some soup. I was getting a little hungry and wasn't as sick as I'd been two days before. Though weak and still feeling sorry for myself, I stood up and went to the kitchen. I opened the window to let in some fresh air. That's when the most beautiful sight came into view. The cherry tree that had been bare and brown only a few days before was now in full bloom. Shades of pink and lavender mingled with the softest white, making a beautiful picture. It was only mid-February, but early spring had come to the little Mediterranean island where I lived.

I felt ashamed of my self-pitying. I told my Father I was truly sorry. Instantly I knew He forgave, because I felt His presence. I felt the warmth of His love enveloping me that very moment. In spite of all my complaining and whining He had prepared this splendid view for me to enjoy. A birthday gift indeed! I stood a while longer, soaking in the beauty of the view before me. I no longer felt alone or miserable.

When times are difficult, I return to the memory of that day when I received from my Father a tree full of blossoms as a birthday gift. The flowers lasted only a week, but the inspiration and courage they gave me will last a lifetime. MERCY M. FERRER

Stress Relief

He gives power to the tired and worn out,
and strength to the weak. Isa. 40:29, TLB.

I awakened with a strange feeling in my stomach. Definitely not butterflies. No, more like that uptight feeling I recognized as my old enemy, anxiety. My mind raced with thoughts of what I needed to accomplish. It was the last day to complete my 40 hours of work before flying out for a much-needed vacation with friends and family. Only 10 more hours of work, and I would have completed my work week in three days! I had already cared for the household duties, packed, and checked off a long list of "to-do's."

Whoa! I thought. *Let's stop this "stinking thinking." I have a source of strength that will get me through this day, and I can choose anxiety or I can choose peace.*

I absorbed the glorious spring morning as I looked out my window. I lifted my eyes up to the beautiful Chugach Mountains. I really needed the text about lifting your eyes to the hills and getting strength from the Lord. I couldn't remember where it was found, so I leafed through the Old Testament. My eyes fell on just the words I needed for comfort:

"Lift up your eyes on high, and see who has created these things" (Isa. 40:26, NKJV). *Yes, Lord, what power!*

"He gives power to the tired and worn out, and strength to the weak" (Isa. 40:29, TLB). *That's me today, Lord.*

"But they that wait upon the Lord shall renew their strength. They shall mount up with wings like eagles; they shall run and not be weary; they shall walk and not faint" (verse 31). *I know, Lord, I need to stop being so stressed and wait on You.*

Just two weeks before I had attended a Christian women's retreat on stress and grief recovery and the brain/body connection. I needed to bring my stresses to God. I prayed, *Lord, let me restart this day, allowing You to take control. I lay all my plans at Your feet. Use me today in Your service. Take away what I recognize as "stinking thinking," and I know I can do what You would have me accomplish today.*

I looked at my watch. Forty-five minutes had passed as I talked with God about stress. Not only had it been a wonderful prayer time, but the anxious feelings had disappeared. RITA KAY STEVENS

The New Manager

*All things work together for good to them that love God,
to them who are called according to his purpose. Rom. 8:28.*

I had just received another letter of inquiry from my supervising manager. It had become a weekly pattern. Nothing I did seemed to satisfy him. I was sure the letter of termination would be coming soon. Only my family's support prevented me from resigning out of utter frustration.

Then the manager got a letter of transfer. I still felt bitter toward him, even though I received a promotion from the new manager. However, the Lord had a plan that would free me from the burden of bitterness.

I was transferred to the main bank branch office and, to my chagrin, the old manager was my new supervisor! The thought that I was going to work directly under him as a clerk was a nightmare for me. Then the question came into my mind: *Why can't you commit the problem to the Lord in prayer?* Then and there I asked the Lord to help me forgive the man. I also prayed He would protect me from his harsh treatment.

When I reported to my new department, he greeted me coldly. Then he completely ignored me. After one month I received a letter instructing me to proceed with my annual leave. At 4:00 on the day I was preparing to go on leave, I received another letter of transfer, this time to the head office.

Indeed, God always has the best for His children who trust in Him. After two months at the head office I was promoted from clerk to credit management officer, which placed me in a supervisory position over my previous tormentor.

If we learn to ask God to solve our problems—and don't dictate to Him—He will be able to work for us. The experience in the bank was a difficult one, but it taught me to allow God to lead in my life.

MARGARET KAMARA

Who Is Listening?

Whether you turn to the right or to the left, your ears will hear a voice behind you, saying, "This is the way; walk in it." Isa. 30:21, NIV.

T he prayer ended, but before I got off my knees the folks around me started singing an after-prayer song. I was visiting in a new church and was unfamiliar with their order of service, but as the congregation moved along in the song, I was able to join them.

"Hear our prayer, O Lord; incline my ear to Thee—"

As soon as I sang those words I realized that my words were different from everyone else's, as they followed the songwriter's request for God to turn *His* ear to *us*.

As my mind weighed those contrasting phrases, I decided it *was* my ears that needed to be made alert—not God's! I've often wished I could recognize God's voice—especially when I'm facing a dilemma and need an answer to a problem.

The story of young Samuel is a classic example of a human hearing God's voice and following His instruction. Even Samuel didn't recognize God's voice the first time. It took someone older and more experienced to turn Samuel's hearing the right direction. The older I get the more responsibility I feel to mentor my young friends, to help them learn the sound of God's voice.

The Lord "revealed himself to Samuel through his word" (1 Sam. 3:21, NIV). Samuel audibly heard God's instruction—he didn't have access to His written Word. I've never had an audible divine message, but I have a great opportunity to know God's will through His written Word. However, when I'm reading His Word it takes effort to keep my mind from wandering and concentration to keep my thoughts focused. This is where I need God's special help to incline my ear toward Him. The Lord's promise to reveal Himself to Samuel through His word is equally relevant for me.

I certainly want God's ear to recognize my voice—to hear my praise, to listen to my pleas, and to respond to my cries for help. But I do also need to incline my ear to Him. At the beginning of every day wouldn't you like to know that "your ears will hear a voice behind you, saying, 'This is the way; walk in it'"?   ROXY HOEHN

Even the Smallest Things

*My God shall supply all your need according to
His riches in glory by Christ Jesus. Phil. 4:19, NKJV.*

I thought it was too small a thing to pray about. Especially after all that God had done for us that week. Just the week before, my husband, Tim, while working on electrical lines at work, had fallen two stories off a ladder to the sidewalk. Miraculously, he only shattered both wrists. He could have landed on his back and been paralyzed for the rest of his life. Or he could have hit his head and suffered severe head injuries, if he had survived. They X-rayed him from head to toe and found no other damage. The surgeon on call was able to do emergency surgery so that there was no permanent nerve damage.

Then Tim came home. That week in church he shared his testimony of how God spoke to him in his hospital room. As he lay on his bed looking up at the ceiling, he realized that he hadn't been "reaching up" much lately. He renewed his commitment to God.

After all this, could I ask this small request? My request seemed too insignificant in the scheme of that week. Our home was full of friends from my mom's group, so I had plenty of salad and odds and ends for a meal. But I had nothing to drink except water. Such a tiny thing. As I stood there thinking about what to do, there was a knock at the door.

My friend Judy had brought dinner for that evening: Mexican pizza—and a gallon of homemade grape juice! Such a small thing, yet God cared. He knew I wanted to be able to offer a good meal to our company, that I had never gotten used to offering only water to drink. And He supplied my need. Regardless if it is a big need or a small one, He is faithful.

God wants us to bring all our needs and concerns to Him. He wants us to give Him permission to supply all our needs. He wants us to know that He cares about every aspect of our lives, big or small.

TAMYRA HORST

Mirror, Mirror on the Wall

Look unto me, and be ye saved, all the ends of the earth: for I am God, and there is none else. Isa. 45:22.

The words of an old fairy tale came to me as I stood in front of the mirror getting ready for church. The line was familiar to me; I'd read it so many times to the children in my class.

"Mirror, mirror on the wall, who's the fairest of them all?" I asked. The mirror was silent as I checked my appearance. *Is my hair in place? How does this dress look? Should I put on my suit instead?* Finally satisfied that I was ready to face the world, I turned to walk away. But something drew me back to the mirror.

This time I asked a different question as I gazed at my image in the mirror. "Mirror, mirror on the wall, how am I *really* looking? I'm looking good on the outside, but what about the inside? God sees in there. What does He see? Does He see the unpleasant thoughts I've had lately? How does my heart look to Him? Am I pleasing in His sight?" Again the mirror was silent as I thought about my soul's appearance before God.

Mirror, mirror on the wall, who's the fairest of them all? Although the mirror did not speak, I knew the answer was not "Annie Best is fairest of them all." My life is marred by sins and mistakes. I am not as good as I may look on the outside. The mirror may not reflect the things of the heart, but I know what is there. I am not the fairest of them all.

There is only One who is the fairest of them all. He is the only one who has never sinned. He is the only one who has no blemishes to mar His appearance or His character. He is all lovely, within and without.

The beautiful thing is that Jesus died to forgive all the ugliness He finds inside of *me*. Because I have accepted His gift of salvation, God does not see the ugliness that is there; instead He sees the lovely image of His Son, Jesus, who died for me.

In the words of an old chorus, "He's the Lily of the Valley, He's the Bright and Morning Star; He's the fairest of ten thousand—everybody ought to know."

ANNIE B. BEST

The Book of Memories

A book of remembrance was written before him for them that feared the Lord, and that thought upon his name. Mal. 3:16.

It was a moving experience for me to visit Limone, the tiny mountain town of my ancestors. My great-grandfather had once lived here. As I walked those narrow stone streets, I asked myself, *Did he once run on these streets where I now walk? Which house was his? Was he baptized and married in the ancient majestic church that dominates the village?*

We visited the small church cemetery. Many of the last names—and even some complete names common to our family—I found on the gravestones. I felt more certain this must be my great-grandfather's village. Yet I still felt some doubts. I would be really sure about it only if I could see my grandfather's birth certificate with my own eyes. Someone told us we could ask to see the registry at the city hall.

Very early the next morning I awoke, excited and eager to know the truth. In the registry office a young woman introduced herself. Her last name was the same as my great-grandfather's. She led us into what I call "the hall of memories." The shelves were lined with large old books, beautifully bound, with dates on their spines.

I gave her the name and birth date of my great-grandfather. She took the book for 1844 off the shelf, and there, on November 22, 1844, was my great-grandfather's name: Giovanni Antonio Bellone. It was his birth certificate, with his parents' names and the names of witnesses to his birth and baptism.

Yes, the memories, the stories of my grandmother Magdalena were true! This was the town of my maternal ancestors. I got a photocopy of the document and felt suddenly rich.

There is another book of memories, one that we each have in heaven. Not only is the date and place of birth recorded, but shown there is when we experienced our new spiritual birth. It also records the actions that show our love for the Lord.

Have you accepted Jesus as your personal Saviour? If so, your name is recorded in God's "book of memories." What remembrances of your life are recorded there? What thoughts, words, and deeds are written beside your name?   EUNICE PEVERINI

The Fun of Giving

"It is more blessed to give than to receive." Acts 20:35, NIV.

I was driving my children home from school through the crowded streets of Managua, Nicaragua, when one small girl caught our attention. "Look at that little girl," I said. "That big skirt is tucked up under her arms. It must belong to an older sister. She probably doesn't have anything else to wear, so that's better than nothing."

"We could give her our red dress," Loysi suggested.

"Neither one of us wears it anymore," Gabi agreed.

As soon as we got home, they ran inside and found the red dress, then jumped back into the car. "Hurry, Mama! Let's see if we can find that girl with no dress of her own."

We hurried back the way we had come. There she was, almost in the same spot where we had seen her earlier. Gabi and Loysi jumped out and handed her the red dress.

I watched the little girl's eyes open wide with wonder as she saw the beautiful red dress. She grinned as she took it. I noticed that the joy in her eyes was reflected in my daughters' eyes.

"That was fun!" they agreed. This wasn't the first time they had shared their outgrown clothes with a child who had less, and I was pleased to see how happy it made them.

Not long ago my son came into the house laughing and said, "The kids at the gate are so funny." At the gate I found 10 children, from toddlers to teenagers, giggling as they waited for a handout they knew they could expect. We always tried to help whoever came, although we usually asked them to help with chores for which we always rewarded them.

What can I do for them? I wondered. *There are too many to give them all chores to do.* I looked up just then to see Henry coming our way, pushing a wheelbarrow full of coconuts from our trees. As he distributed them, I found some Bible verse cards that friends had sent. One of my daughters handed a card to each child.

The children's faces were bright with joy, both the ones who received and those who gave. The sight warmed my heart.

"Lord," I prayed, "please speak through these gifts to the children's hearts. And help each member of our family to always participate in the joy of giving." PAM BAUMGARTNER

Creative Hospitality

Practice hospitality ungrudgingly to one another. 1 Peter 4:9, RSV.

After my husband died, an older widow telephoned me every Friday night for more than a year. "I know you live alone, and I'm just checking to see if you're OK," she'd often say. I wasn't the only one she offered hospitality to over the phone.

Another friend always plants a garden that is much larger than what she and her husband can use. "I like to give the extra vegetables to the married students at the university," she told me. "They're always glad for the boost it gives their food budget."

I know a woman who often asks her two small daughters to take a box of homemade cookies to an older couple. "It's always such a pleasant surprise when they come," the old folks told me. "It's nice to know that someone cares, that we are not forgotten."

Another friend knits baby blankets. When a new baby arrives, she uses that as an excuse to go for a visit, taking with her the lovely gift she has created.

My own way to show hospitality is to share the flowers that grow around my house. I find it a great joy to share them with someone in the hospital or with a shut-in friend.

I used to think that hospitality meant inviting people to one's house for food or to stay overnight. That can be one way to show hospitality, but it isn't the only way. There are many creative ways to show true Christian hospitality. All we need to do is to love each other in a tangible way. This can be different for each of us.

Hospitality can be flowers, as well as food. It can be a blanket for a new baby, as well as a bed offered to a stranger. Hospitality is shown over the telephone, as well as over a basket of vegetables. A box of cookies delivered to someone's home may give the same message of love as an invitation to enjoy a bowl of soup.

Dear Lord, give me eyes to see the many opportunities I have for sharing love in a tangible way. Give me perception to use what I have at hand, however meager, and the creativity to use it to make someone feel loved. And then, Lord, help me to have the grace to do it joyfully!　　　　FONDA CORDIS CHAFFEE

Message in a Plastic Bag

Evening, morning and noon I cry out in distress,
and he hears my voice. Ps. 55:17, NIV.

There was a sharp breeze blowing sea spray across the sand. As I walked along the seaweed-littered shoreline, I knew a few tears would not be noticed in the stinging spray. I wanted an answer from God. "Forty-two years is a long time to pray for someone," I began. "Your will is that none should perish, so I know You too are interested in his salvation. Now he is old and sick; doctors offer little hope. Please save him so he can serve You before it's too late!"

"Father," I continued, "I need encouragement and assurance that You hear me. I am going to ask You a trivial prayer. It is not a matter of life and death like the prayer that hangs heavy on my heart, but I need to know You are listening and that You love me and hear my prayers. So please give me a plastic bag so that I can carry some of this seaweed home for my garden!"

A white plastic bag suddenly floated up to me on the tide. I thanked the Lord for His swift answer as I pushed the sticky seaweed into the bag.

The next day I was up at sunrise, walking along the beach. There was another plastic bag lying on the high-tide mark, ready for me to gather the seaweed. Then I thought perhaps there must always be a plastic bag lying discarded on the sand. Not so. The next day there was no seaweed and no plastic bag. The day after that there were masses of seaweed, but I couldn't find a plastic bag until I dug deeper. There, under the seaweed, I found a brown plastic bag.

"You are answering me a different way every day, Lord!" Then I realized that He always answers when we call. Not always in the way we would expect. He is not limited; He has a thousand ways to answer our prayers when we may know only one. He hadn't said no to my larger prayer, only "Wait."

Although I didn't yet have the desires of my heart, I knew He wasn't ignoring me. I will cling to His promises until it is time for Him to say "Yes!"

NOELENE CURTIS

Multiplied Blessings

The Lord will bless everything you do. Deut. 28:6, TEV.

W hen I retired from nursing, I began to seek God's will for my life. I was eager to find out what He planned for me to do.

The day after my retirement party I had an appointment with my accountant to file my income tax papers. For many years my refund had amounted to about $100. So I was astonished to learn that I would receive a refund of $1,258.

This is exciting! I thought. *Does this have something to do with God's will for my life? Why so large a refund now?*

Four days later I was asked to join a group of volunteers going to hold evangelistic meetings in the Ukraine. "How much will the trip cost me?" I asked.

"The plane ticket will cost $1,228," he told me.

Almost exactly the amount of my refund! I thought. "Yes, I'll go! This is God's will for me."

I was to help with the children's meetings, so I collected craft supplies for the 100 children they expected. Besides 150 crowns from a local business owner, we gathered bookmarks, erasers, small books, and pictures to give away as gifts each night.

When we arrived in Kiev, we discovered that the place of the meetings had been changed from a small town to a large city. "You can now expect 500 children every night," they told us.

"Five hundred!" we groaned. "But we brought enough for only 100 children. What are we going to do?"

There was only one thing to do: pray and go forward. We began to make more crowns out of extra poster paper we had brought along. Even though we knew we hadn't brought enough paper to make sufficient crowns, as we used up the paper, more paper seemed to replace it in our suitcases! We made a total of 496 crowns! While we were adding, God was multiplying!

Our other supplies multiplied each day as well. Every child went home with a gift every night. We knew there weren't enough gifts, but each day we went to our suitcases for fresh supplies and were never disappointed.   PHYLLIS ALEXANDER

My Shepherd

The Lord is my shepherd; my soul will lack nothing. Ps. 23:1, Clear Word.

On my way to work every day I used to pass a small field surrounded by a hedgerow. It lay just outside the pretty village of Crawley in Hampshire, with its thatch-roofed houses and a duck pond. The field is part of that rural Old World, for often it has a small flock of sheep in it as in days of long ago.

As autumn progressed, I watched the ewes grow round with fleece and pregnancy. After Christmas snowy white flakes of lambs appeared upon the ground. Soon they wobbled after their dams on woolly legs that soon became like springs as they bounced over the field. By late summer the new lambs had grown dignified and stout, almost mature, getting down to serious grazing and growing.

There were two scenes I will always remember. Each occurred in a matter of seconds, but they made a deep impression in my mind.

On a dull winter's day the retired farmer, tweed-clad, stood at the gate. The sheep looked up from where they were and of one accord, from every corner of the field, all came bouncing to greet him. What love! What joy!

On a bright spring dawn I passed by the same spot. The farmer was in the field, walking. The sheep and lambs, in silhouette, their coats silver-edged with sun, pressed close to him, looking up. A few gamboled behind him in a line, following wherever he went. Such love! Such devotion!

In the few seconds it took me to drive past, I received such a deep impression. I wonder, as people pass me in a few seconds on our everyday commute, do they catch a glimpse of Christ's radiance? Do they see a moment of His magnet's aura of love? *Shepherd God, lend me this gift to share. Help others to see my love, my joy, my devotion to You!*

These short scenes, which tell me something about the human shepherd, also tell me about mine. Only love can call forth such joyous greetings. Only love can cause such trust, such following. *Teach me that love day by day, my Shepherd! Help me to follow You always with love and joy!*

APRIL DUNNETT

The Glass Cat

"Don't take on troubles ahead of time because tomorrow will have its own problems. . . . Live one day at a time." Matt. 6:34, Clear Word.

M att, my golden retriever, was overjoyed to see me after spending a weekend in the kennel. After he had calmed somewhat, I took his leash in hand and headed outdoors.

"Can you handle him by yourself?" the attendant asked.

"No problem," I responded.

But I hadn't figured on the cats. A gray tabby sat just outside the door. The moment she saw Matt she streaked across the lawn. Matt, breaking free of my control, dashed after her, dragging his leash along the ground.

"Matt! Come back here! Now!" I ordered. He just kept chasing that cat until she reached a tree and climbed to safety.

The attendant retrieved Matt. "I'd better control him for you," he offered.

I was grateful. There was no way I could restrain Matt's 100 pounds when he made up his mind to go somewhere.

Suddenly Matt strained again at the leash. The attendant hung on and was hustled toward another tree where a large white Persian lay asleep at its base. As Matt rapidly advanced, the cat lay perfectly still. Then Matt was upon her, and still she never moved, even when the dog sniffed her from head to tail. She didn't lift a hair or spit at him. He looked back at me, clearly baffled by this cat!

"You silly dog," the attendant laughed. "Can't you tell the difference between a real cat and a glass one?"

Matt walked toward our car with what dignity he could muster while the attendant and I chuckled all the way.

Often I'm like Matt, chasing after something that isn't even real. I get all excited over future problems that are no more likely to threaten me than that glass cat. I fret and stew over dangers of the future that will never come to life.

Lord, just for today, help me to stop chasing the glass cats of imagined problems. Help me to take to heart Your advice to stop pursuing tomorrow's worries. Today's real problems are enough, and even those will not harm me if I stay under Your control!   DOROTHY EATON WATTS

The Brother I Look the Most Like

We, who with unveiled faces all reflect the Lord's glory,
are being transformed into his likeness with ever-increasing glory,
which comes from the Lord, who is the Spirit. 2 Cor. 3:18, NIV.

I had been invited to give a weekend prayer seminar in a beautiful new church near San Francisco. The church congregation was a cosmopolitan mix with a warm, friendly spirit.

My husband was with me this time, and our hosts for the weekend were a pleasant couple with three teenage children. On Friday night we met several members of our host's family—his father and mother, a sister, and her family. The next morning we met the younger brother, a tall, well-built young man. We commented that no one in this family looked alike. Our host, a rather short, stout man, laughed at the difference between himself and his athletic younger brother.

As my husband and I sat at the dinner table in the fellowship hall, our host appeared at the end of the table to introduce yet another family member.

"I want you to meet the brother I look most like," he announced.

We looked up and smiled immediately, for it was true that these two men *did* look alike. Same height, both slightly chubby, receding hairlines. Same twinkling eyes. Identical smiles curving both their mouths. But we laughed along with our host when it dawned on us that one man was Black and one was White.

"He loves to do that," our hostess remarked. "Those two men are such good friends they've even begun to look alike! So they claim to be brothers."

Shouldn't it be that way with all our brothers and sisters in Christ? No color lines to separate us. We should just love each other, work together, and share our faith as family members.

The closer our friendship with Jesus grows, the more we begin to look like *Him*—as well as each other. That is God's promise. We can look like Jesus—the same smile, the same warm, loving eyes, the same love for others.

Then we can introduce others to Jesus by saying, "I want you to meet the Brother I look the most like."　　　CARROL JOHNSON SHEWMAKE

Feeding Thirdo

"Yes, Lord; You know that I love You." He said to him, "Feed My lambs." John 21:15, NKJV.

Wading through a corral filled with leaping lambs, my ruddy-cheeked husband announced with a chuckle, "I think I'll call these three Primo, Secondo, and Thirdo."

I surveyed the triplets, my eyes resting on Thirdo, the smallest. He wasn't particularly handsome, and his siblings certainly got to mother's milk ahead of him.

A few days later I noted the lassitude of Thirdo as he lay under the light in the pen with his mother and siblings. Something was seriously wrong. Thirdo could no longer get up to feed from his mother. I made an emergency call to an experienced sheep farmer's wife.

"He's starving," she said simply. "You can bring him over."

So I took Thirdo to the neighboring sheep farm, where the woman and her husband examined him.

"What are his chances?" I murmured, scanning the man's face for any sign of hope.

"Oh, about 60/40," he said softly. "Should have got to him sooner."

With a good lesson in tube feeding and some frozen colostrum, I sadly traveled the gravel road home, promising the best of care to the languishing lamb.

My tear-stained face hovered over Thirdo for the next several hours. But three hours after my first successful tube feeding, he softly breathed his last. Heartbroken, I felt like a great failure. If only I had done something sooner.

Sometimes while walking near Thirdo's grave I think, *It shouldn't have happened. Why didn't I get help sooner?* No, Thirdo didn't have the robust constitution of his siblings or his mother's undivided attention. Because of my inexperience, I hadn't asked for help soon enough. He had fallen through the cracks, as we sometimes say about the less fortunate in our society.

I sensed God's voice speaking to me as He did to Peter long ago: "Feed My lambs. Don't let them slip through the cracks."

Dear Father, please point out Your starving lambs to me. And help me to nourish them before it's too late.   BONNIE WILDE

The Light of the World

The Lord shall be unto thee an everlasting light,
and thy God thy glory. Isa. 60:19.

One morning I faced a problem for which I had no answer. I desperately needed peace. In my prayer time I asked God to reveal Himself to me. I continued to pray about this as I began my walk in the misty morning air. Beams of light streamed from the sun, piercing through the trees and falling at my feet.

I hastened to the middle of the road, where the shafts of sun pooled into a sea of warmth. Proceeding up the street, moving in and out of shafts of light, I soaked in the beautiful warm rays as I experienced God's love enveloping me.

As I reached a curve in the road, the sun was directly above the cul-de-sac, shafting its rays downward, casting the end of the street in deep shadow. As I praised God and walked toward the delightful display of light, I felt as though I could just keep walking right on into that glorious world above. *O, God, can't I just keep going and go on home? I want to go home!*

Suddenly something else caught my attention—a slightly bluish glow approximately halfway between the ground and the sun. I felt slightly alarmed. The glow looked like pictures I'd seen of UFOs. I took a few more slow steps, my mind trying to take in the ethereal vision before me. I stopped and waited. Gradually my mind and eyes joined in focus, and with a sigh of relief I finally determined this glowing object to be a fluorescent light at the end of our street. Because the sun in my eyes had obliterated all other objects, the bluish glow of the streetlight was all that pierced through the shadows.

I realized my attention had been diverted from the beautiful healing scene God had prepared for me that morning. As I once again continued toward the sunlight streaming down through the trees, I thought of how Satan tries to counterfeit God's heavenly light in an effort to distract us from the Sun of righteousness.

O, God, don't let me allow Satan to interpose his fraudulent imitations on my pathway and divert my mind from Christ, the true Light of the world.

JODI EULENE DODSON

Why Me?

"I have told you these things, so that in me you may have peace.
In this world you will have trouble. But take heart!
I have overcome the world." John 16:33, NIV.

Why me? I can't count the times I've said those words or felt them in my heart. The car won't start, and I fear being late for an appointment. *Why me?* My back is injured, and physical limitations slow me down and limit my activities. *Why me?* An employer in whom I have placed my trust betrays me. *Why me?* Events in my childhood caused devastating hurt and pain. *Why me?*

This question implies that life is usually not as difficult for others as it is for me. Perhaps I'm not a good enough Christian or I would never even ask the question. Then I read the words of Jesus, "In this world you will have trouble."

What might happen if we accepted loss, pain, disease, or trouble as something we have been given, rather than a retribution for something we have done? What might happen if we considered trouble as normal in this world of sin, rather than abnormal?

What might happen if I always expected that the car might not start? Would I be more thankful when it worked? What if I recognized that humans have increased vulnerability to the spine because we stand upright, and therefore I expected to have problems with my back? Would I be more thankful for the things I still can do?

What if I were to expect that employers, like employees, sometimes feel powerless and inadvertently betray our trust? Would I have more compassion? What if I acknowledged that I live in an imperfect world where no one is perfect? Would I be more tolerant of those who have hurt me?

What if I were to see trouble as an opportunity to go deeper into my relationship with God and to go deeper into my understanding of my own heart? What if I could learn to at least welcome the possibilities posed by trouble—the chances to solve problems in new ways, the opportunities to understand myself and others better, the new ability to feel compassion for those who have shared my kind of trouble?

KATHLEEN TONN-OLIVER

The Detour

My God shall supply all your need according to his riches in glory by Christ Jesus. Phil. 4:19.

Three commitments faced me. The tremendous heat took much out of me, physically and emotionally. My whole being desired rest, but I had no time to stop for that. I was teaching two-teacher improvement courses in Espírito Santo and Rio de Janeiro, Brazil, and I still had two more courses to teach before regular classes began.

My mother-in-law was not well and needed my attention. My husband pitched in and did what he could to help care for her while I continued teaching.

The third commitment was an appointment in Curitiba, 523 miles (847 kilometers) away. My husband would make the trip with me. We were finally ready to go by Friday afternoon. I dreaded the heat, but God provided clouds that helped make our trip more pleasant.

We were looking for a quiet place to spend Friday night and Saturday before we resumed our journey on Sunday. We both needed rest and time away from people. As my husband drove, I prayed that God would help us find the ideal quiet retreat so that we could re-plenish our spiritual, physical, and emotional resources.

As evening approached, we were disappointed to find ourselves no farther than the city of São Paulo. Where could we find a quiet oasis in such a noisy, pollution-ridden city? And traffic was backed up. It took us more than an hour to cross the city. I was feeling agitated. *Lord, why are You allowing this to happen?* I complained. *Here we are, longing for a secluded location so that we can have a quiet day with You, and now just this!*

Looking up, I noticed a neon sign advertising a hotel in a place we had never expected to find one. But there it was, nestled in the middle of a wide expanse of tree-covered lawn. The wind whispered through the pines, and birds sang in their branches. It was the perfect retreat spot!

We learned that because of heavy rains a bridge had collapsed. If we had continued farther on Friday we would have been stuck in traffic. By Sunday the traffic was still congested, and it took us five hours to reach our destination, but we were rested and able to cope. It was fantastic how the Lord had cared for our needs!

HULDA CYRELLI DE SOUZA

The Power of Music

Sing psalms, hymns and spiritual songs
with gratitude in your hearts to God. Col. 3:16, NIV.

The music on the radio played softly as I sat by my favorite window listening. The distant hills and fields formed a complete panorama, unobstructed by the now-bare branches of the trees. I sat quite still, drinking in the view and enjoying the sounds.

A big white cloud drifted slowly across the sky. Gradually the blue sky changed to a soft blue-gray, with the slightest tinge of pale mauve just above a hill. The winter sun lit up the clouds, but not for long. The soft plaintive music of the violins seemed to capture the mood of the winter.

What was the music? It didn't really matter. Just listening to it was relaxing, making me feel rested and at peace. The music seemed part of the scenery.

I closed my eyes and wondered what the composer had been thinking as he or she wrote and how the musicians felt as they interpreted it for me.

"Another blessing," I whispered to myself. "Thank You, Lord, for the gift of music that helps me cope with modern life."

Sometimes we are poor spiritually because we attach too much importance to material values. Sometimes we work too hard mentally and become uptight. Music helps us unwind, putting our body, mind, and spirit in balance.

It is no wonder that the apostle Paul suggests that music can dwell in us richly, teaching and admonishing us with all wisdom. He adds, "Giving thanks to God the Father through him" (Col. 3:17, NIV).

Music has the wonderful power to reach the heart, bringing us nearer to our Father as we praise Him with song. Music brings harmony, joy, and peace to our lives.   PHILIPPA MARSHALL

Spilled Paint

*Blot out my transgressions. Wash me thoroughly
from mine iniquity, and cleanse me from my sin. Ps. 51:1, 2.*

One day I decided to paint my daughter's dresser, a project that had been on my list for a long time. The weather was cloudy, so I decided to paint the dresser right there in her bedroom.

I couldn't wait to open the brand-new can of bright white paint. I set the can of paint on top of the dresser beside the brush and rags. Then I noticed I had forgotten to put newspaper under the dresser to protect the carpet. So I lifted the end of the dresser ever so slightly to shove the newspaper underneath, not thinking about the paint on top of the dresser. The can of paint tipped over and hit the floor in such a way that the lid popped off, and paint spread rapidly into the brown carpeting.

I have to do something quick, I thought. *But what? Maybe I could sacrifice the vacuum cleaner to suck up the unwanted paint. . . . No, that would just ruin it, and there isn't any guarantee it would even work.*

It was inexpensive carpet, but I knew we didn't have the money then to replace it. I was frantic. I had to do something quickly. There was only one thing I could think of to do to save the carpet. I quickly found the utility knife and cut around the damaged area. Then, flinging the carpet piece into a laundry basket, I ran outside and soaked it with the hose. I worked at it for what seemed like an eternity, but gradually the carpet returned to its original color. After it dried, I placed it back into position, and one could hardly see where I had done the surgery.

I thought about the little sins in my life that would eventually spread like spilled paint. Left unattended, they would set in and become impossible to remove. I knew what I had to do. I had to give every fiber of my heart to Jesus, and He would cleanse me, making me clean again.

Lord, take my life today and wash it in the fountain of Your blood. Take the stains of my life, returning me to the original color of Your plan for my life.

JO ANN HILTON

Take Out the Garbage

Listen to me; pay attention to what I say. Prov. 7:24, NIV.

My friend Gladys and her 12-year-old grandson, Sven, were enjoying a trip by Greyhound to Alberta. They made my home one of their stopping places for a weekend.

On the last day of their stay we toured Michener House, the renovated birthplace of Canada's twentieth governor-general, Roland Michener. We hiked around Cranna Lake, sighting waterfowl and muskrats. Sven skipped rocks across the water. Then, since Sven's mother had attended Canadian Union College and taught on the staff for two years, we meandered around the college as he tried to visualize her life as she had lived it on the campus. By the time we got back home, we were tired and hungry. As I drove into the garage, my mind was busy with what to prepare for supper.

The next day promised to be an exciting one for Sven. He and his grandmother would continue their trip to Calgary. More important, they had tickets to watch a game by their favorite football team. But the greatest feature would be to watch Gladys's nephew, one of the professional players on the team, in action.

After Sven and his grandmother went to bed, I tidied up the kitchen. An inner voice urged me to take out the garbage. I tried to ignore the promptings, because I didn't like going to the dumpster in the back alley at night. Since I had to take my friends to catch the early morning bus, I told myself, "I can do it first thing in the morning while the car warms up."

When the urging continued after I brushed my teeth, I gave in. "Oh, all right!" I muttered. As I made my way to the back door that exited through the garage, I twirled a twister around the plastic bag. Bright lights startled me when I opened the door. In my preoccupation with supper, I had forgotten to turn off the car headlights after our day's drive.

"Thank You, Lord!" I breathed. "I'm glad I listened to Your sweet promptings!" What a scurry the next morning would have been with a dead battery and two passengers needing to catch the bus. I had been spared a dilemma, and Sven didn't miss seeing the British Columbia Lions game.

EDITH FITCH

Beware of the Yeast!

"Beware of the yeast of the Pharisees." Matt. 16:6, NRSV.

Making bread is an art, and a good loaf is a delight. While serving with the military overseas I fed Christian military personnel on weekends. I always included fresh, home-baked bread on the menu, usually baking six loaves at a time.

One breadmaking day I set out my ingredients. I had my doubts about the freshness of the yeast. Should I use it, or not? I hated to waste it, so I mixed it with the other ingredients. What if it proved to be inactive? I didn't want to take the chance of being without bread. I decided I'd better get some fresh yeast, just in case.

At the commissary I picked up the yeast and a couple other items I needed. Then I remembered a baby shower coming up soon, so I ran upstairs to the baby department. There I met a neighbor and stopped to chat a moment. Suddenly I thought of my bread. My heart did a flip. Suppose that yeast had been good; what then?

I hurried home and ran up the back steps and into my kitchen—and stopped. What a mess! The soft mixture had overflowed the mixing bowl, run onto the table beneath the shelf where I had placed it, gone across the table, and spilled onto the floor. Obviously the yeast had been good!

After the mess was cleaned up and the bread was rising again, I thought about the power of yeast. The grains of yeast had been small, but what a big mess they had created in my kitchen!

Perhaps this is what Jesus had in mind when He spoke of the "leaven of the Pharisees." The evil they hid in their hearts grew and created a problem in their lives.

Do we sometimes think that little sins don't matter? Do we trifle with little white lies or small acts of deceit, not realizing the multiplied results they produce in our lives? Are we enticed to speak words of gossip that grow, causing great harm?

Making bread is an art; so is forming Christian character.

DOTTIE O. BOWEN

My Father's Hand

*Even there shall thy hand lead me,
and thy right hand shall hold me. Ps. 139:10.*

As Mother stood talking to the grocery store owner, I wandered up and down the aisles. Large open barrels of dried food lined the counter and the walls of the store. One barrelful of peanuts sat out of my mother's sight. I was 7 years old and should have known better, but the temptation was too great. I reached in and took several peanuts, stuffing them into my overalls pocket.

On the way home Mother realized that something was strange. "What's wrong, Phyllis?" she asked.

"Nothing," I replied.

She was not convinced.

"No. Nothing is wrong," I insisted.

That evening I went into the living room and placed the peanuts on the table in front of Father and Mother. "I'm sorry I took the peanuts," I cried.

They knelt in prayer and helped me to ask God for forgiveness. When we finished, Mother reached for my coat and said, "Now you must take these peanuts back and tell Elsie what you did. Jesus forgave you, and now you must ask Elsie to forgive you."

No amount of persuasion to wait until the next day deterred my parents. Getting to the store involved walking on a path through a tall cornfield that was ready to harvest. Slowly I proceeded, but the gentle breezes encouraged the stalks of corn to wave back and forth. The bright moon enlarged every imaginary object a 7-year-old girl could think lurked along the path. Terrified and crying, I continued to the edge of the field and into the store.

"I took these peanuts," I sobbed. "I'm sorry. Please forgive me."

"Of course I forgive you, Phyllis," Elsie said, hugging and kissing me.

What sweet release and relief! Now there was one thing left—the walk home. No ghost or goblins hovered nearby, but as I reached the edge of the field near home, Father stepped out to take my hand. Without my knowledge, Father had been there all the time, only a few feet away.

PHYLLIS ALEXANDER

Even Shoes Can Instruct!

If you think you are standing firm,
be careful that you don't fall! 1 Cor. 10:12, NIV.

I had a pair of shoes I liked very much. There were reasons. First, they were of good quality and suppleness. And their heels were neither too flat nor too high, but just what made me comfortable. In addition, they were plain, simple but elegant. And finally, they were black and could go with any dress.

I wore them often, and they quickly wore out. I couldn't repair them because the inside of the heels was plastic. I realized they were slippery and could be dangerous, but I liked them so much! I believed I had only to be cautious and it would be OK. I continued to wear them.

One day at the market I slipped and fell. People helped me up, but my left side hurt, especially my left hand. When I arrived home, however, my pain decreased, and I didn't need to send for the doctor. I put the worn-out shoes in a corner and let them rest. I should have thrown them away, but I liked them too much.

Several weeks later when I feared I might be late to work, I put the shoes on and hurried off to the office. At 4:00 I tidied my desk, locked my drawers and my office door, and left. I went down the stairs and passed along the cemented outside wall.

Suddenly it happened. I slipped and fell. My left side hurt again and my left wrist swelled. I went to the doctor's office, and he sent me to the hospital for an X-ray.

As I waited for my turn, I thought, *My shoes are like a cherished thing that leads to a spiritual fall, or a beloved person who may cause me to slip spiritually. Even though I liked my shoes, as soon as they became slippery I should have left them at once, because they threatened my physical life. Likewise, even if I enjoy a practice or a person, as soon as these become spiritually slippery for me, I have to leave them immediately lest I lose my eternal life.*

Lord, help me to be willing to give up those practices or persons that may cause me to slip and fall. I want to stand firm in my daily walk with You.

JEANNE D'HARIMALA RASOANINDRAINY

The Little Cottage

Trust in the Lord with all thine heart; . . .
and he shall direct thy paths. Prov. 3:5, 6.

We fell in love with the little seventeenth-century cottage as soon as we saw it. Its front door opened onto an Old World garden, over which a huge tree kept a watchful eye. Ancient beams supported the low-ceiling front room, whose open fireplace spoke of cozy evenings to come. Narrow, crooked stairs led to a timbered bedroom. From its window we looked out on wide meadows and the village.

Not only was this house within our budget; it was near Bentwaters Air Force Base, Suffolk. There we could obtain military retiree medical, postal, and grocery shopping privileges. Miss Wood, the house's owner, wanted to move to town. We took her to the so-licitor's office, where we exchanged contracts. When we returned to the cottage, we excitedly measured for carpets and curtains while she stayed downstairs.

On one trip to the car I noticed tears streaming down her cheeks and knew instantly she had changed her mind about selling. Although we had the signed papers, we decided not to oppose her. We had prayed about it, and it was not meant to be.

Although disappointed, we searched for something else in the area but could find nothing. Finally we found a house near Lakenheath Air Force Base about 50 miles away. We could move immediately. The day we moved, Miss Wood's solicitor called to say she was now willing to sell to us. It was too late, of course. We wished we had waited longer before buying the new house.

Two years later, to everyone's surprise, Bentwaters Air Force Base closed, and property prices plummeted. Those who worked for the American military lost their jobs, shops and businesses went bankrupt, and military retirees in the area were left without any support.

It hit home then that had we had our way, we would have been left with a house greatly decreased in value, as well as loss of our retiree privileges. How grateful we are that our heavenly Father cares so much about us that He closed the door on what could have been a disastrous mistake. Now, that's a God we can trust!   EDNA MAY OLSEN

Adoption Papers

But when the fullness of time had come, God sent his Son, born of a woman, born under the law, in order to redeem those who were under the law, so that we might receive adoption as children. Gal. 4:4, 5, NRSV.

He has a different name now, but when I met him at an orphanage, he was called Nelson. He was a little boy with dark, despondent eyes and a medical condition that made his face look sallow and puffy. The doctor said if Nelson didn't receive the proper medical treatment, his life would be in serious jeopardy. The treatment he needed was not available in Central America.

During a phone call to the director of children's services for the orphanage, we talked about Nelson's situation. "I'll write about little Nelson's needs in our next newsletter," she said. "Maybe there's a family who would be willing to adopt him."

I thought, *Who would adopt a sick, possibly dying, child?*

A few weeks later news came. Not one but two families were willing to consider adopting Nelson. Paperwork for international adoptions takes a long time, but once the decision about Nelson's future had been made in prayer and faith, we tried to hurry the paperwork along. Finally the day came for our director to board the plane and take Nelson to his new home.

Recently I received a photo of Nelson from his mother. He is no longer the child with sad eyes. His eyes look mischievous and full of life. His smile reflects the joy and love he shares with his brothers and his parents. His medical treatments continue, and there is every reason to hope for his future. I'm sure that without the adoption Nelson would not have survived past his fifth or sixth birthday.

It was my privilege to see several other children undergo a beautiful, miraculous change because of a loving family, but none will remain in my mind as clearly as the transformation of Nelson.

God, through Jesus, has arranged for the adoption of each one of us. We have the chance to be His daughters. The adoption papers are filed. The forms have been stamped. Jesus has already paid the costs. It is my prayer that your life and mine will reflect the joy that is ours through the life-changing adoption that has redeemed us from certain death.

SANDRA SIMANTON

It Doesn't Add Up

*It doesn't matter how much you have. What matters is
how much you are willing to give from what you have. 2 Cor. 8:12, CEV.*

A*nother opportunity to tackle life head-on,* I told myself, standing in the
schoolhouse supply store. I'd never pass my qualifying exams with
my poor math skills, so I was looking for some practice workbooks.

I asked the woman lingering in front of the remedial math section
if she'd spotted books about fractions. Yes, she knew exactly where
they were. "Is this for your children, or students?" she inquired.

"Neither," I began bravely. "They're for me."

She straightened up, jerking her head sideways to see me better.

"I have a math learning problem and have to take a test to get
into school," I explained. "So I need to brush up on basics."

"Basics?" she asked. "What grade are you entering?"

I laughed. "I'm starting my doctoral studies."

"What?" she exploded. "And you can't do simple math?"

"You wouldn't want to see it!" I replied.

She pressed on. "What do you do?"

"I'm a teacher." I was beginning to enjoy this.

She visibly jumped. "Who do you teach?"

I smiled broadly. "Graduate students."

She reached for the rack to steady herself. "Where?" she asked in
an almost inaudible voice.

I winked at her. "I don't teach math." Gathering up my workbooks, I sang out, "Thanks for your help!" Heading for the sales desk,
I could sense her staring. I could imagine her thoughts: *University professor? Can't do math? It doesn't add up!*

Her response to me that day set me to thinking. We don't all possess the ability to perform well in every area of life. Some of us may
be very good at one thing and not talented in another. God knows
this and understands our limitations. He views us according to what
we can do, not for our lack of ability.

I smile when I remember the consternation of the woman at the
store. But then, humor may not be *her* talent. BARBARA COUDEN

A Testing Time

But the Comforter, . . . whom the Father will send in my name,
he shall teach you all things, and bring all things to your remembrance,
whatsoever I have said unto you. John 14:26.

This past year has been dominated by finals—the culmination of three years of intense study. It is not easy being a wife, mother, friend, church worker, and student, especially at an age when memory is not so sharp as it used to be!

Many times I wondered why I chose a university that tested on examinations alone instead of on course work. How was I to remember everything I had read over three years when I could hardly remember what I did yesterday?

As I traveled to the first examination I reflected on my first days as a university student. The lectures outlining our course of study seemed way over my head, and I spent the first few days in a panic. *I can't do this. I don't know what they are talking about.*

Then came the lecture entitled "The Bible as an Intellectual and Cultural Source." It was inspiring, and what's more, I knew what the lecturer was talking about. He emphasized that a knowledge of the Bible is fundamental to our understanding of English literature and urged us to study its great truths. Although I was expected to explore the writings of philosophers and classicists, my tutors accepted my arguments backed up by biblical texts.

Now I faced my biggest challenge. Each day was a nightmare, but God is good. On every paper there was at least one question that required an answer based on biblical sources. I found scriptures learned as a child readily coming to my rescue.

Hard work, reliance upon God, prayer, and the Bible got me through. I was very conscious, however, that God cannot call to our remembrance that which we have never learned. As children we are expected to commit Bible passages to memory, but as adults we often become lax, knowing that we can look it up. There may be times, however, when we have no access to the Scriptures.

My experience has made me resolve to be more diligent in my study of Scripture, with a prayer that the Spirit will help me to retain those passages I may need in the future. AUDREY BALDERSTONE

First Airplane Ride

Peace I leave with you, my peace I give unto you. . . .
Let not your heart be troubled, neither let it be afraid. John 14:27.

I'll never forget my first ride in an airplane when I was only 6 years old. I stood in the prop wash of a small airplane as my father and big brother got ready for a ride over Fargo, North Dakota. Suddenly I burst into tears.

"You can't go, Faith," Dad explained. "It costs too much." I continued to cry.

The pilot looked down at my tear-stained face and smiled. Then he spoke to my father. "She's small. She can go for free."

My tears stopped immediately. Someone lifted me into Dad's lap, and he buckled me in. They couldn't find a helmet small enough for me, so I went without.

The sides were open to the wind, and the noise was terrible. But the view was wonderful! I looked over the side as far as my father would allow me, watching as the trees and houses seemed to shrink to the size of toys. I felt I could reach out, pick them up, and play with them. My eyes were wide with wonder and delight.

Then I made a discovery. Since the plane was piloted from behind, I couldn't see the pilot. It was clear to me that we needed help, and I knew how to get it. I scrunched my eyes tight and prayed silently, *Dear Jesus, please take care of us and help us to get down safely.*

I opened my eyes then and enjoyed the rest of the ride. The adventure continued as exciting as before, for I knew Jesus would take care of everything. My heart was at peace.

Sure enough, in a little while the plane banked and turned back toward the airport, where it landed safely. I was delighted. The fact that I then saw the pilot climb out of the plane didn't lessen my feeling of genuine answered prayer.

On those occasions since when I've seen an airplane slice a path across the blue prairie skies, I remember the wonder of that day and the peace I had knowing Jesus was in control of our airplane. It brings a new sense of peace to my heart for the present. Peace can always be mine as I trust Him to take care of things.   FAITH KEENEY

The Lost Sale

"Judge not, that you be not judged." Matt. 7:1, NKJV.

One Sunday afternoon my daughter Lynda and her husband, Pierre, went shopping for a bigger car to meet the needs of their growing family. They stopped at a dealership recommended to them by a friend. The selection in the lot was great! They asked the sales representative many questions about the different models. He seemed impatient when they asked about yet another model.

Finally they settled on the car they wanted, but the sales representative wasn't eager to talk terms. He seemed to be trying to get rid of them. He mumbled something about "We can't talk about a deal until we've done a computer search on your credit."

"Let's go," Pierre said. "This salesman isn't interested in selling us a car. Let's go somewhere else where somebody is."

They were upset when they told me about the rude treatment. "He wasn't interested in answering any of our questions," Lynda said. "He judged us as being unable to buy a car, so I guess he figured Why bother?"

"What kind of clothes were you wearing?" I asked.

"Very casual," she replied.

So could it be that they were judged by the clothes they were wearing? Did the sales representative judge them to be curious people who were only passing the time? Lynda and Pierre found another car dealer who showed them respect, and they bought the car they wanted.

The first sales representative lost a good customer because his perception of Lynda and Pierre was wrong. I wonder if the story would have been different had they gone in smart business attire.

Before we condemn the man, perhaps we need to look at ourselves. Do we ever judge people by the clothes they wear, the car they drive, or the way their hair is fixed? Do we let external appearances keep us from discovering the beauty of the person on the inside? Do we exclude people from our friendship based on first impressions? Do we pay more attention to some people than we do to others based on our perception of their wealth or status?

Lord, please help me today to have an open heart to others, regardless of how they look. Help me to show warmth and acceptance to all. Free my heart from any desire to discriminate. OFELIA A. PANGAN

The Immunization Records

"I have written your name on the palms of my hands." Isa. 49:16, TEV.

Today I browsed through last year's prayer journal. What a reassuring experience it was to see a record of many answered prayers! I found there big "important" prayers, as well as "insignificant" prayers.

I imagined God sitting in His majestic throne room, with Jesus in the holy place in the heavenly sanctuary, surrounded with the incense-like essence of the prayers of people from around the world. There are prayers of the mothers whose children are starving, prayers of the families who have lost loved ones, prayers of those living in war zones. These are the "important" prayers.

Then I think of my prayer, written one day last year. "Lord, I can't find the girls' immunization records. Please help me to find them." In comparison to others, this seems to be one of those little "insignificant" prayers.

Yet in the midst of all of those urgent petitions, my prayers reached the ears of Jesus. He did not rebuke my petty prayer or become impatient with me. Instead He dispatched an angel to answer my prayer. I was able to record, "I found the immunization papers." It may have been small, but to me it was important.

My God is an intimate God, a personal God. He is interested in my personal needs, for He has engraved me in the palms of His hands. He knows my urgent needs and my petty wants. He cares for them all.

This entry in my prayer journal reminds me that Jesus loves me. He is not just the God of the big emergencies; He is the God of the day-to-day life of His children. He is a God who tends to the small, seemingly insignificant details of our lives.

The Lord is attentive to all the needs of His daughters. He tends to us as individuals, by name. He even knows the number of hairs on our heads. What a mighty, gracious God we serve!

"Take to Him everything that perplexes the mind. Nothing is too great for Him to bear, for He holds up worlds, He rules over all the affairs of the universe. Nothing that in any way concerns our peace is too small for Him to notice" *(Steps to Christ, p. 100).*

EILEEN TEJADA KNIGHT

The Real Thing

Love must be completely sincere. Hate what is evil,
hold on to what is good. Rom. 12:9, TEV.

Our neighbor didn't wait to be invited in. Breathlessly she summoned, "Come quickly. See what's in our yard."

Living in tropical Singapore, we'd seen lots of surprises. Dropping everything, we rushed to see. Tenaciously clinging to a tree branch, we found a thick green insect, 11 inches long.

"It has six legs, but insects aren't that big!" I exclaimed. "Don't let it get away before I go get our book."

I brought the book outside and pointed to a picture. "It's an unusual species of walking stick, one of the largest of insects, and lives only on guava leaves."

"Mommy, let's make it a pet. I'll give it fresh guava branches every day. We've got a big gallon bottle we could put it in and keep it on the kitchen counter," our 7-year-old Kevin begged.

So we captured the insect, and wonder of wonders, it thrived on the fresh guava leaves. As she dropped her eggs, we saved them. Later almost transparent masses of crawling babies covered the sides of the jar. Though never successful in raising them to adulthood, we deposited scores on the guava tree.

The insect's wings were too small to support her heavy body in flight. She seemed content in our kitchen for almost a year.

Our pet was a phony. Looking at the walking stick, you'd think you saw a twig or branch, not something alive. They can't fly or jump—just crawl. Though some birds and insects feed on them, most think they are a dead stick. If disturbed, they remain motionless and stiff, pretending to be dead, an instinct God gave them to preserve the species.

Unfortunately, some people are phonies too. They pretend to be Christians when they really haven't learned to love and trust Jesus. Oh, they go through the motions—church, Bible reading, prayer. But there's no deep love, no personal relationship with their Lord. Pretending may fool others, but not God.

If you feel like a phony, why not ask God to turn you into the real thing? He can give you a love that is sincere. You can have a personal relationship with God that is the real thing.   EILEEN E. LANTRY

A Personal Mission Statement

God did not give us a spirit of timidity, but a spirit of power, of love and of self-discipline. So do not be ashamed to testify about our Lord. 2 Tim. 1:7, 8, NIV.

At a recent convention Laurie Beth Jones, a marketing consultant and best-selling author, shared her conviction that everyone should have her personal mission statement.

In the late 1980s, when the term *perestroika* was little more than a political buzzword, I met a young Russian woman in the city of Alma-Ata, Kazakhstan, who was in her final year of university studies. Although Anna Volkaslavsky did not know the concept of a mission statement as we know it, she had hers in mind. Though quiet and demure, Anna was a woman with a purpose.

Anna had approached me with a translator and shared, "I want to write books about Jesus for children." She didn't seem to sense that she had left me momentarily speechless, because in 1987 Anna's mission statement seemed unattainable. Communism still had a grip in the U.S.S.R., and children were the prime target of Communism. Communist leaders had decided that religion would be tolerated among the "older citizens," but on every front the children would be discouraged from believing in Jesus.

Anna asked if I could get her a book on how to write from a Christian perspective. I did. You can imagine my joy when four years later I received a copy of Anna's first children's book and a handwritten thank-you note. I couldn't keep the tears from flowing. The book was beautiful! The artwork compelled me to read the words that spoke of Jesus' love in language that speaks to children's hearts. Anna's books are like water in a desert as she continues to be guided by her personal mission statement by publishing other materials for the children.

Why not write your own mission statement? Pray about it. Ask the Holy Spirit to guide you. Keep it short—one sentence. Write it in language a 12-year-old can understand, and then memorize it. Make it bold, full of love for others, and infused with self-discipline. Then embrace your mission statement; it will assist you in setting priorities and guide you in the way you respond to everything that comes your way in life—from this day forward!   ROSE OTIS

Safe Behind the Door

Because he hath set his love upon me, therefore will I deliver him. Ps. 91:14.

Madam, I have a knife in my pocket and I am going to kill you."
The words rang in my ears as I faced the young man standing by my bathroom door.

My husband and a visitor had just left our upstairs apartment to return to the office after our lunch. I was also about to leave when the confrontation took place.

"Why do you want to kill me?" I asked.

"Because I am hungry, and I need some money."

"Please, go outside and I will get you something to eat," I pleaded.

The young intruder looked at me, but never offered to move. Anxious to relieve the tension, I headed for the kitchen, praying in my heart that the Lord would direct me to do the correct thing. I saw the front door open, and the thought came to me to call the garden boy. I stepped out on the veranda and called to James.

Immediately my intruder responded, "He's not down there. He's gone to lunch."

I faced my assailant, my mind racing in circles. *What shall I do? Shall I run down the stairs and scream for help, or shall I make a dash through the door, back into my apartment?* The thought had hardly entered my mind before I found myself locking the door from the inside and running to the phone to call my husband. I was safe behind the door. Now I knew he could not harm me.

In that moment, safe behind the door, I experienced a peace I had never known before. I knew that God loved me, that He had heard my prayer, and that He had just saved my life. The young man disappeared, and I never saw him again.

God has given me another door of safety. I have only to go through the door of salvation and I am safe, not only now, but for eternity. Jesus Christ, my Saviour, is the Door. Hiding behind Him I am safe from the evil one who would destroy my soul eternally. Safe inside the door, I know a peace that is beyond understanding.

ELEANOR L. HEWES

Counting My Blessings

Bless the Lord, O my soul: and all that is within me,
bless his holy name. Ps. 103:1.

Sometimes it seems that my problems are too many. At those times I try to think deeply and to count my blessings. I can see that blessings far outnumber my problems. I can see that the times when my problems seemed more than I could bear were the times the Lord was closest to me.

One of those times occurred while I was a student in Nigeria. We were fond of taking excursions to new areas. It's a large country, and there are many interesting sights to visit. Once we were scheduled to travel with a group of students to the midwestern part of the country. I wrote my parents that I'd stay behind at the school and wouldn't go on the trip. Later I changed my mind and went, but I didn't write to tell my parents of the change of plans.

On the way we had an accident, but the Lord protected me and all the other students. When the accident was announced, my sister rejoiced that I wasn't on the trip. Later, when she learned that I was there, she rejoiced again, this time because we were all safe and well. *Thank You, Lord!*

Another blessing happened during my first pregnancy. I had a transverse pregnancy, which was difficult for me. I carried the baby for 10 months and four days. It may not have come then, but my water broke, and it was necessary to induce labor. When the nurse discovered the problem, she turned the baby's head downward and my baby was born safely. I believe He led that nurse to do the right thing to save my baby. *Thank You, Lord!*

A third blessing in the midst of difficulty came when I had a serious infection. The doctors gave me an injection to which I had a violent reaction. I could easily have died, but the Lord miraculously saved my life. *Thank You, Lord!*

Take a moment now to think deeply about your life. Think of those difficult times when it seemed your problems were many. Can you see God at work during those times? Can you find His blessings that are greater than your problems?

Write down your blessings. Then praise God for His them.

BECKY DADA

Remembering My Sins

Remember not the sins of my youth, nor my transgressions: according to thy mercy remember thou me for thy goodness' sake, O Lord. Ps. 25:7.

I have lost more than 60 pounds during the past year. That's right; after many years of overeating, snacking, or eating the wrong foods, I was finally able to conquer the urge to indulge. But what helped to jump-start my weight loss was using God's herbs to satisfy my hunger and take away my desire for unhealthy things. My mind is clearer, I have a new, improved look, and of course I feel great.

My friends, especially those who haven't seen me in a long time, are shocked at the change. Whenever they see me, they remind me of what I used to look like, as if I could ever forget! Comments about my clothes being too big or about my needing a new wardrobe, or worst of all, showing me pictures of the way I was, are a part of most of their conversations lately. Even people I don't know at work or in the grocery store have stopped me to ask how I did it. So forgetting about my past isn't an easy thing to do.

For me, those things are past. Being overweight is definitely in my past. Transgressing the laws of health is in my past. Eating junk food is in my past. Not drinking enough water is in my past. Too much fattening food, sugar, and salt are in my past.

I think about it sometimes, how I used to be. I was often tired, sick, brain-cluttered, and with aches and pains. Indeed, I was in pitiful shape. But thank God, as I matured and realized what I was doing to my body, I desired to live a healthier life. He doesn't remind me of my sins or even remember my sins or transgressions. He sees me as I am today, a new creature in Christ.

What a wonderful life we would all live if each day we saw our spouses, children, bosses, pastors, coworkers, and friends as new-borns. How great it would be if we had no knowledge of their old ways, and they had no knowledge of ours. What a joy life would be for each of us if no one remembered (or even knew) the sins of our youth, but fully accepted us as we are each moment of the day. May we ever trust God to help us to love each other unconditionally, where we are, instead of where we were or where we could be.

IRIS L. STOVALL

Trust

*"Unless you change and become like little children,
you will never enter the kingdom of heaven." Matt. 18:3, NIV.*

The morning was dull and gray. Heavy clouds lurked over the Tennessee hills surrounding our valley. My mood matched the atmosphere. Concerns of family, health, and retirement played tug-of-war with my thoughts.

Two days of early spring rains had swollen the streams and caused flooding in the valleys. The air was crisp and invigorating. Donning winter garb and borrowed knee-high boots, I started out walking, thinking to banish my gloom with the freshness of the morning. The crisp cool air slapped at my face and mood. I looked at the winter landscape, the beauty of the leafless trees, and the crunchy pad of leaves still covering the ground. *There is still a beauty to the winter landscape,* I thought.

Making my way down the hill, I walked beside the swift-flowing stream of clear mountain spring water. It was now overflowing its banks and flooding my path. For a moment my adult mind dictated, *Turn back. It's too wet.* Then from somewhere deep within a small child's voice said, *Have fun. Splash in the puddles. Enjoy the moment.*

For the next few minutes I was a child again, splashing water to the top of the knee-high boots, and laughing at the spectacle. My mood changed, banishing worry in the joy of the moment. I was a child again, trusting. For that moment I was calm; worry was gone. My mind flashed back to my carefree childhood, when under similar circumstances I had splashed in the puddles after the rains. I had no worries. My parents cared for my needs. Now my heavenly Father has promised to supply all my need. My heavenly Parent cares for me. He is concerned about my happiness. Nothing that affects my peace is too small for Him to notice. Nothing that confronts me is too big for Him to handle. His arms of love reach out to me. His ear is always alert to my cries for help. He is always there for me. Why not trust Him?

O, God, make me a joyous child again, trusting You always for what You have promised. Amen. JOAN MINCHIN NEALL

Cracked China

"Do not store up for yourselves treasures on earth, where moth and rust consume and where thieves break in and steal; but store up for yourselves treasures in heaven." Matt. 6:19, 20, NRSV.

One day, walking through the streets of downtown Toronto, I saw an elegant set of china service for eight in an unusual contemporary styling. "A luncheon set," the proprietor informed me.

I was enchanted. The price was right. I planned how I would use them at Sabbath lunches. An elegant setting would mask the truth: given my cooking history, the food served on them would be mediocre at best.

On that first weekend, exclamations of aesthetic approval prefaced the collegiate chatter. But later, when a helpful young man almost dropped a plate, I began to reconsider my decision. *Maybe I should use these only for special guests*, I mused. So I packed the dishes back in their boxes. Five years later I made a disheartening discovery. Two of the plates had cracked.

"The dishes were made to be used, madam," the proprietor reminded me when I called to complain. "If you can't use them regularly, at least soak them constantly."

That evening as I slid the fragile crockery into the soapy water, I paused, aghast at my past actions. I had been storing up earthly treasures, thinking them too precious for use by the unsophisticated. The china had become more important than those brilliant young scholars who were willing to risk indigestion to share their afternoons with me.

I began to understand what Jesus meant when He lamented about how hard it was for the rich to enter the kingdom (Mark 10:25). I wasn't even rich. I simply owned 38 pieces of fine china, yet I was allowing them to block my path to the kingdom.

Distressed, I began to wonder. Had I been hoarding more than the china? Did I have other talents packed away? Immediately unused talents came rushing to my mind. Duly chastened, I determined to adjust my lifestyle. As the china came out of hiding, so did my talents, including some I had not even realized I possessed. I'm loving every moment of the spontaneous acts of sharing. Now, that is heaven-stored treasure!   GLENDA-MAE GREENE

Rejoicing in One Found Sheep

*"Does he not leave the ninety-nine and go to the mountains to seek
the one that is straying? And if he should find it, assuredly,
I say to you, he rejoices more over that sheep than
over the ninety-nine that did not go astray." Matt. 18:12-14, NKJV.*

One evening my friend Lona and I discussed how we had once again fallen out of our spiritual walks. Her face was distressed as she asked me, "Do you think God gets angry or maybe even fed up with us? When my own children repeatedly do things they have been told not to, I get furious! Do you think God's like that?"

"He probably is," I responded.

That next week as I was leaving a church dinner, I stopped to talk with a friend. My daughter, Rebekah, 2 years old, ran back toward the fellowship hall. I assumed it was safe, as her older brothers were still there. As I conversed, my sons came out without their sister; they hadn't seen her.

I went to get her myself; she was not there. I tried to looked in all the rooms, but they were locked. I looked in both restrooms. I was becoming anxious. Could she have slipped out without being seen? I frantically ran around the outside of the church, calling her name.

Other church members joined the search. We called and again searched places I had already looked. I checked the car. Others began driving up and down the streets, searching for Rebekah, but she was not to be found.

By now I was dreadfully frightened. I told myself not to panic; I had to remain calm to find her. I cried out to God, "You know where she is, Lord. Keep her safe and help us to find her."

Finally the pastor arrived with the keys and began unlocking doors. At last! There she was, sitting quietly, playing in her classroom. "Why didn't you answer when I called?" I asked.

"I was just right here, Mommy," she replied.

A few days later I recalled the conversation that Lona and I had had. I realized how foolish my response had been. Sometimes we wander off, thinking we are safe, but God knows the real dangers that lie waiting. He doesn't give up on us. He worries when we stray. He diligently works to bring us back into His fold and rejoices when we return.

BETHANY SORENSON

Are You Watching?

Watch therefore: for ye know not what hour your
Lord doth come. Matt. 24:42.

My 4-year-old granddaughter was coming to visit. Her instructions to me on the telephone the night before had been very specific.

"Grandma, I want you to sit on the couch by the window and watch for me."

"Surely I will be there watching for you," I promised.

On the day of her expected visit I had many things to do. I got so involved preparing for her arrival that I forgot to watch. Suddenly I heard a car in the driveway and hurried to open the door to welcome my family.

I greeted my granddaughter with a smile and open arms, expecting that she would run up the steps to give me a hug. But she just stood on the sidewalk with a very disappointed look on her face. Finally she said, "Grandma, you weren't watching for me!"

"I'm sorry," I apologized. "I really meant to watch for you, but I just got so busy I forgot." I could tell that didn't make her feel much better.

Needless to say, on her next visit I sat on the couch and watched for her out of the window. I saw the car drive down the street to our house. I saw it turn into our driveway. I watched the door open and my little granddaughter step out. Her eyes were focused on the window. Her face lit up with the most beautiful smile, and she ran into the house. Throwing her arms around me she exclaimed, "I'm so happy, Grandma. You were watching!"

Jesus has given us specific instructions too. He has told us, "I want you to be watching for My return." But how often we become caught up in the busyness of life. In the hustle and bustle of everyday activities we may forget to watch for Him.

I want to live so that He will welcome me with open arms and a smile of joy. I don't want Him to be disappointed because I wasn't waiting and watching for His return.

NORMA GREENIDGE

The Belt Buckle

Be ye kind one to another. Eph. 4:32.

As a registered nurse I frequently have the opportunity to be a special blessing to someone who is frightened and vulnerable. One morning my assignment included a young woman who had recently had a miscarriage.

I tiptoed into the darkened room to see my new patient. Her face was drawn and sad, her hair uncombed. She didn't seem to notice me. *I can see this one needs some personal attention and love,* I thought. I helped her with a shower and made her bed. After a little while together, she opened up to me.

"I really wanted this baby," she whispered. "I love the father so much." Then she unburdened her heart. She told how her family had disowned her and would not permit her to see her two children from a previous marriage.

As she talked I didn't say much; mostly I just listened. I tried to be gentle as I went about my duties. "I'm sorry you've had it so hard," I said.

Later when I visited her room, I met her boyfriend. "I'm very sorry about the loss of your baby," I said. I offered to bring him something to drink, and he seemed to appreciate that.

When I went to check on her later, the boyfriend reached into his jacket pocket and took out a small unwrapped box. "Here's a gift for you," he said, "for being so kind."

I opened the box. Inside was a slightly tarnished belt buckle with the words "Grown in the U.S.A." engraved on it. "Now, don't you go and give this away!" he said. "It's for you to keep for yourself."

I wonder what he thinks I'm going to do with such a large belt buckle, I thought. "Thank you," I said aloud. "I'll keep it to remember you both."

That afternoon the woman was released. I helped her to the car in a wheelchair. It was an old car stacked full of possessions. When I realized they probably lived in the car, the old belt buckle seemed a precious gift of love. I still have that belt buckle. When I open the cabinet where I keep it, I remember that couple and the gift warms my heart again. *Help me to give my best to each of my patients today,* I pray as I return the treasured gift to its shelf. ROSE NEFF SIKORA

Change

I the Lord do not change. Mal. 3:6, NIV.

The other day I heard someone comment, "The only human being who likes change is a baby with a wet diaper."

Researchers say that fewer than 20 percent of people like change—and most of those have a preference for processing information with the upper right brain quadrant. These people sometimes even initiate change just for variety because they tend to become bored with routine and sameness.

The remainder of the population, with different brain quadrant preferences, value routines, tradition, and predictability. They are creatures of habit and quickly become comfortable with the status quo and build their routines around it. They often resist change. This can be stressful both for them and for those who are trying to implement the change.

The loss of the status quo can cause intellectual problems of readjustment, as well as emotional feelings of grief. Some people go through the same stages that people who are facing death go through. They experience denial, anger, resistance, and bargaining before they finally move into exploration and acceptance.

Much of the pain and stress perceived during the process of change can be minimized by living the serenity prayer:

God grant me the serenity
To accept the things I cannot change,
The courage to change the things I can,
And the wisdom to know the difference.

The Bible is the greatest book ever written about change. Paul talks about putting on a new self (Col. 3:10). That's change! In Ezekiel 36:26 God promises that "I will give you a new heart and put a new spirit in you" (NIV). That's change!

While promising us the security that God never changes, the Bible challenges us to embrace change; to become more like the person that God wants us to become; to strive to emulate Christ. When we look at change as a healthy growth process with lessons in every situation, it will lose its power to threaten and stress. The constant amid the change is God—"I the Lord do not change."   ARLENE TAYLOR

The "Bum" Lamb

"Whoever comes to me I will never drive away." John 6:37, NIV.

Last night we visited the ranch of people who had offered to give our daughter a "bum" lamb. We went out to the barn and saw the big woolly mama. She had a baby of her own that she readily accepted, but the other little fellow, the bum lamb, was having a hard time.

Oh, how that orphan lamb wanted to nurse! He would move right in like he was supposed to, and every time Mom would lower her head and send him scrambling. He didn't smell right, and she knew it. He would stand in the corner, blinking his eyes, trying to get up enough courage to try it again.

The rancher then tied mama sheep up and let the little fellow nurse awhile.

"How long will you have to tie the mama up?" we asked.

"In about a week this mother's milk will have saturated him enough so that he will smell like the mother, and she will probably accept him as her own," the rancher explained.

How interesting! I thought.

Have you ever felt like a bum lamb, longing to be accepted and loved by God, but feeling that surely you smell so sinful He would never want to adopt you? The wonderful truth is we don't have to feel rejected or miss out on the blessings. If Christ is in us, we "have received the Spirit of adoption, whereby we cry, Abba, Father. The Spirit itself beareth witness with our spirit, that we are the children of God" (Rom. 8:15, 16).

And Peter adds, "As newborn babes, desire the sincere milk of the word, that ye may grow thereby" (1 Peter 2:2).

The heavenly Father will never drive you away, no matter what you have done. He's a Father who will never reject you. He accepts you just as you are.

Wonderful heavenly Father! He adopts us and provides nourishment for us that we may grow, not because He is forced to, as was the mama sheep, but because He very much delights to!

GERITA LIEBELT

Supermarket Comedy

The grace of the Lord Jesus Christ be with your spirit. Phil. 4:23, NRSV.

I need You today, Lord," I wrote one morning. "I need Your love, strength, patience, and peace." Then with confidence I looked forward to a great day.

Instead it turned out to be a disappointing day. My computer wouldn't cooperate, and errands took twice as long as expected. My husband showed up for lunch after I'd put it away. He'd just spent a frustrating two hours in a line to get new license plates for our car. Nothing was on schedule. There were interruptions all day.

It was almost bedtime before I remembered I hadn't done the grocery shopping. Wearily I put on my coat and drove to the nearest supermarket. My shopping done, I parked cart number 912, with its seven bags of groceries, and went to get the car to load up. By the time I got to the car, no more than 50 steps away, I'd forgotten why I was there. I drove home, pulled into the garage, and opened the trunk to get the groceries. The trunk was empty, of course.

Dorothy, how can you be so stupid? I berated myself as I jumped back into the car and drove the 10 blocks to the supermarket. There sat lonely shopping cart number 912 beside the curb where I had left it 15 minutes before.

A cheerful teenager loaded my trunk. "I can't believe what I just did," I told him.

"I saw you hit the speed bump!" he grinned.

"But that's not the worst thing I did," I continued. "I went all the way home and left my groceries sitting here!"

He laughed. "You're allowed to make a few mistakes."

"You're right!" I agreed, but inside I wished I would stop making such stupid ones. It was as if my mind had gone out of gear and I was coasting along in neutral.

I told the Lord all about it. "Thank You for watching over my groceries while I played out this little comedy. Do You sometimes laugh at the crazy things Your creatures do?"

Surprised at my own sense of humor after such a trying day, I realized God had indeed given me much grace for that day.

DOROTHY EATON WATTS

A Few More Steps

A little child shall lead them. Isa. 11:6.

It was in the early spring of 1988 when our family, together with some friends, decided to drive to the Sinai Peninsula and scale Mount Sinai. We started the seven-hour drive in good spirits. Everyone anticipated walking on the very place where the Israelites had walked. We all were excited to see the mountain where God had handed Moses the Ten Commandments. We thought that although it may not be the right mountain, it must have been the same area.

At 3:00 in the morning we awoke and dressed warmly. Each took water, food, and a flashlight. As we trekked around the mountainside, we talked about how God had provided the Israelites with water, manna, and protection.

After an hour of walking our son began to get tired. He asked, "Why do we have to climb to the very top?"

Again my husband related the story of how Moses received the Ten Commandments. So our son walked on and was one of the first to reach the top.

The last few meters were steep, stairlike steps. By now I was exhausted, so I called it quits. I found a flat rock and decided to lie down and wait for the group to come down. Soon our son was back.

"Mom, you have to come. It's not far," he said.

"I'm really tired," I replied. "Please let me rest here."

"Mom, come on. Only a few more steps," he coaxed.

I couldn't bear to disappoint him. He had come down all the way from the top for me. So with all the strength I could muster, I stood up, took five or six steps at a time, and before I knew it, we reached the top. What a wonderful view! What a beautiful sunrise! The mountain air was invigorating. The feeling of being able to conquer what was seemingly an impossible task was great! And I could have missed it all, but I didn't because our son came back for me. He coached me as though I was a child. With him, I made it to the top.

My God is like that. When I fall back, He's there for me. When I call it quits, He gives me courage. He is ever patient and loving. With Him, I'll still make it to Zion, the heavenly mountain.   MERCY M. FERRER

Visit to Skull Caves

The trumpet will sound, and the dead will be raised incorruptible,
and we shall be changed. 1 Cor. 15:52, NKJV.

My friend and I went as student missionaries to an isolated part of Fiji to teach English. We lived in a small bamboo bure, ate Western food when we could afford it, local food when we couldn't, and busied ourselves in every aspect of campus life.

Life was humid, hurried, and hectic, but weekends offered a peaceful change to scheduled life. Sometimes we simply took an afternoon nap or wrote letters home, but more often than not we would have a relaxing outing with some of the students, learning more about their culture. On one of those friendly afternoons a small band of multicultural students offered to take us to the Skull Caves. Curious to learn more, we eagerly accepted.

After miles in the blazing tropical heat, we made our way up the rugged hillside to the hidden tombs. The dense tropical jungle produced deep shade, and in the semidarkness our voices softened as we began our ascent. The going was challenging, and teacher-student barriers disappeared as we each relied on the other to clamber through the thick jungle undergrowth.

Finally we saw the caves ahead of us. In silence we moved slowly forward to view skeletons of those loved ones of long ago. Pieces of pandanus mat, once the shroud of the deceased, were still visible.

I wondered, *Who were these people who had been so faithfully laid to rest here? Were they young or old? tribal chiefs or teenage sons? Were they wives, mothers, young women? Who were they? What sort of people were they? Who placed them here? Who loved them enough to complete the arduous task of carrying their bodies so far up this difficult hill? Had they ever heard the gospel story, or had they died Christ-unknown?*

I didn't know the answers, but God does. I remained silent all the way through the jungle to the village. I thought, *Life is a brief blink in the eternity of time. From dust we were made and to dust we shall return. Yes,* I pondered, *if Christ doesn't come first, I too shall become but dust.*

And I wonder if there may be life again on that hillside, when He who died on a hill far away comes back to claim His own. For this reason He died and rose again. This is the message of Easter. RUTH RAWSON

A Lot Can Happen

The women hurried away from the tomb, afraid yet filled with joy, and ran to tell his disciples. Matt. 28:8, NIV.

On the way home from church one fine Easter weekend my husband and I drove down a country lane to see which trees were in bloom. We found that we had to close the car's sunroof, as the sun was too warm and bright.

Within 20 minutes of our arrival home, however, the sky had clouded over and the wind had begun to blow. The weather station warned of hail. Lightning cracked the sky, and thunder rolled back over it instantly. Rain hit the windows with a loud splashing. Instead of eating on the deck, as we had hoped to do, we wondered if we should take our lunch to the basement!

Two hours later the sky was clear and the sun was shining. A lot can happen in a short time.

I think of Mary that Friday afternoon long ago as she stood at the foot of the cross. How could her world have come to this? It was less than a week since this same mob had been shouting "Hosanna!" and proclaiming Christ king. Even death came quickly. Her heart was breaking. It was too much to fathom. A lot can happen in a short time.

Sunday morning the women headed for the garden tomb. They had followed Jesus, supporting His ministry. They had stood close to the foot of the cross and watched as His body was laid in the tomb. As they now approached, carrying their spices, they no doubt were discussing the past three days. Everything had happened so quickly it all seemed unreal. But now they were headed for the tomb and reality. They had thought He was their hope and future. Now He represented despair.

But a lot can happen in a very short time. The tomb was empty, the cloths were neatly folded, the Roman guard scattered.

"Where have you laid my Lord?"

"Mary."

A lot can happen in a short time.

Please go with me through this day and this night, Lord. Keep me close. I need the steadiness of Your hand and Your hope when I cannot see the future. A lot can happen in a short time. ARDIS DICK STENBAKKEN

A Contented Violet

Be content, look upon me. Job 6:28.

I was busy being a wife, the mother of three active children, and a foster parent. I helped with gardening, then canning and freezing hundreds of quarts of produce each year. I helped to build and decorate a do-it-yourself-on-a-shoestring-style country home. I led out in the children's programs each week at church, plus a host of other duties. Busy I was, but contented I was not! That elusive dream of fulfillment, of making a name for myself and being noticed, was always beyond my fingertips.

One warm Sabbath afternoon I slipped away from my busyness. Crossing our large garden-orchard-vineyard, I went down the hill into a rocky wilderness adjoining our property. As I walked among the trees along a tiny bubbling creek, I prayed, "Lord, please quiet my soul. Give me a purpose in life and the assurance of Your love."

The rippling water soothed my jangled nerves. The weed smells delighted, and the gentle whisper of leaves helped refresh my troubled mind. Suddenly I stopped. There by the creek bank, barely noticeable, was a tiny wood violet. One lone blossom, but what a gorgeously perfect blossom it was! As I drank in its simple, pure beauty, it was as though God spoke to me.

Do you see that brave little violet? It is where I put it, far from human observation. You, no doubt, are the only person who will ever see it. It may be trodden upon by one of My wild creatures. Yet it grows contentedly where I put it, blooming bravely, though it is not noticed or praised. It is happy to fulfill My design and do My pleasure, seeking no reward, but simply doing as I ask. Will you do the same, being willing to "bloom" where I put you, to go unnoticed, or to be "stepped on"?

I will never forget that contented violet, nor the lesson it taught. I pray only that I may be like it, doing my Father's will, for the sheer joy of pleasing Him.

Lord, make me like the wood violet, content to bloom where You have planted me today. MYRNA FORBES

Two Suppers

*Behold, I stand at the door, and knock: if any man hear my voice,
and open the door, I will come in to him,
and will sup with him, and he with me. Rev. 3:20.*

Supper number 1: After church today a friend invited me to eat lunch with her and her roommate. The townhouse had a cheery decor; the brightness of the afternoon sun shining through the windows created a warm, cozy atmosphere. The table was nicely set. The food was scrumptious! We had a great time.

Then the conversation turned to spiritual themes. They spoke of what it would be like in heaven, and how wonderful it would be to talk to Jesus face-to-face. Spiritually I was filled. Physically I was stuffed. But even as I write this, I'm hungry again!

Supper number 2: Today I went to a wonderful meal. Many people were present. The table was exquisitely set with starched white linen and shiny silver tableware. The meal was simple, but "out of this world." The Host was never physically visible; nonetheless His presence was obvious.

As I sat there in church, eating the bread and drinking the juice of the Lord's Supper, I really didn't feel worthy to be there. In fact, "someone" had almost convinced me not to attend the supper for that very reason. But then Satan is always trying to do that. Even though of myself I am unworthy, through these very symbols of His body and blood I was reminded that Jesus had paid the ultimate price.

Before the end of the service the minister asked two very interesting questions: "Did you notice that when you ate the small piece of bread, which was a symbol of the body of Christ, it made you hungry for more bread? And when you drank the swallow of juice, which was a symbol of Christ's spilled blood, it made you thirsty for more juice?" He continued, "That's the way it's supposed to be. When you take Christ and His Word into your life, it makes you hunger and thirst for more. When you truly seek to know Him, you will find that you will want more and more."

I left the Lord's Supper table hungering to know Jesus more. *Lord, help me always to have that hungering and thirsting after You—but then continually fill me.*
NANCY CACHERO VASQUEZ

The Blackbird's Song

I offer in his tabernacle sacrifices of joy;
I will sing, yea, I will sing praises unto the Lord. Ps. 27:6.

A red-winged blackbird came to my feeder at 6:30 this morning. I paused during my quiet time to watch it hopping on a branch of forsythia just above the feeder, its black suit shimmering like silk. Its bright chevron of red and gold gleamed in the rays of the morning sun.

"How handsome you are!" I whispered.

And then it opened its mouth and began to sing—melodious clear notes filled with the joy of spring. It danced back and forth along the branch, singing a trill with each hop. It flew to another branch and repeated the performance.

"How can you be so happy so early in the day?" I asked. (I'm a night person myself, and getting up at 6:00 for an hour with the Lord takes a great deal of effort on my part.)

A sense of awe came over me, as though I had walked uninvited into the blackbird's private time with God. No one was there in that sun-dappled sanctuary but the blackbird and me, and I sat, quietly listening to its song of joy, its sacrifice of praise to its Creator.

I imagined its song went something like this: "Thank You, Lord, for such a lovely morning! Thank You for the sunshine and the budding trees! Thank You for sunflower seeds in the feeder! I will eat well today. Thank You for supplying all my needs."

It stopped a moment, cocked its head to one side, then jumped down to the feeder and helped itself to a seed. In a moment it was back on its branch, singing its heart out among the forsythia blossoms, its black suit fairly bursting with joy.

My own heart responded in written words of joy and praise in my prayer journal. I felt drawn into the very gates of the tabernacle, the very presence of God, by the blackbird's song. I began to count my blessings of the moment and the many answered prayers of recent weeks. I felt overcome by God's faithfulness to supply my every need.

Dear Lord, I prayed, *I would be a bird singing in Your tree, coming to Your feeder, rejoicing in Your goodness for all the world to hear. You have put a song of joy in my heart, and I feel it bursting forth, filling my world with gladness and praise.* DOROTHY EATON WATTS

Count Your Blessings

A merry heart doeth good like a medicine. Prov. 17:22.

A series of moves created problems in trying to sell our home during a time of recession. We had a major engine repair on our not-so-old car. Now, during my routine physical, the doctor found a tumor. *How many of life's pressures and tensions can one family stand?* I wondered. *Why us?*

Then I remembered a song from years before: "Count your blessings, name them one by one; count your many blessings, see what God has done." In those days as we sang the song, however, we would count our blessings by twos or threes instead of just "one by one." I decided to make a list of my blessings and my problems and see what the score would be.

I was truly amazed at the results. We did have a heavy financial burden with an unsold house in another state, yet the Lord had provided us with a comfortable home we could afford. It was convenient to school and work. Our car problem was major, but could be repaired. One of the major blessings in my life has been a husband who is careful to see that we have a nest egg for such emergencies.

That covered two of the three negatives on my list, but how could I find a blessing in having major surgery? I had tried to follow a healthy lifestyle. But I learned that some things just happen and can't be accounted for. My tumor was one of them. It was fast-growing and needed immediate removal.

I hardly had time to think about it because there were so many things needing to be cared for before entering the hospital. My husband was able to change his work schedule so that he would be home to give moral support and care for the children. The tumor was benign. I was back to full-time work within three weeks.

My list of problems seemed to have been covered with blessings, and yet I had barely begun my list: a loving, supportive family, an interesting and rewarding job, wonderful and caring friends who made life fun and special. The list went on and on.

Take time to write down your own "cursings" and then your "blessings." Perhaps a new perspective can make the problems seem less important.

ANITA L. JACOBS

The Christmas Wreath

"I know the plans I have for you," declares the Lord, "plans to prosper you and not to harm you, plans to give you hope and a future." Jer. 29:11, NIV.

The Christmas wreath still hung on the front door. The artistic combination of pinecones, velvet ribbon bows, and pine branches added a special touch to the entry porch and looked right in place while the cool winds and snow flurries of late winter prevailed. I liked seeing it there—a little reminder of the warmth of the holiday season.

I must take it down, I thought, as the cold of winter blended into the coolness of early spring. To my surprise, I found that a bird was building its nest right in the heart of the wreath. Soon it would be home to a little feathered family. I could not remove it.

We watched as the nest was finished and two small eggs were laid within. Daily the mother bird covered the eggs with her outstretched wings. We used a different entrance to the house to avoid disturbing her.

Before her babies had time to hatch, a bird of prey raided the nest, killed the mother bird, and pushed the eggs out of the nest to be smashed on the porch below. The mother's body lay in the branches beside the nest, wings still outstretched in her struggle to save her babies.

In nature and in human life alike a stalker is at work. The prince of this world, the devil, is our saboteur who tries to snatch away every good thing that our God has planned for us. Have your plans been thwarted? Remember, these are not the plans of your heavenly Father, for He has promised, "I know the plans I have for you, plans to prosper you and not to harm you, plans to give you hope and a future."

Lord, help me to remember today that the message You have for us is Jesus. Thank You for the reminder of Your plan of salvation, Your plan to bring me a future and a hope. Today I ask for Your presence in my life, a presence and a power that will keep the devil far away from all the good You have planted in me.   JOAN MINCHIN NEALL

Lord, Remove the Stuff

Draw nigh to God, and he will draw nigh to you. James 4:8.

Instead of saying to my 6-year-old daughter "Let's say our prayers," I use the phrase "Let's talk to Jesus." This approach to prayer seems to remove the formality, routine, and stiffness from what can turn into a ritual. I wanted Rachel to experience a free-flowing conversation with her Friend.

One night Rachel had a difficult time getting focused as we knelt to pray.

"Try closing your eyes and pretending you see Jesus," I suggested. "Then just talk to Him as you would to me." I smiled to myself, confident that this was really all she had to do.

"I can't; I have too much stuff in there," Rachel responded.

"Ask Jesus to help you remove that stuff so you can talk to Him," I countered.

Rachel closed her eyes tightly and began, "Lord, remove this stuff so I can talk to You."

It seemed that no sooner did she make this request than the Lord answered. Immediately she began a free-flowing conversation with her Friend.

I thought about the times I have entered into a season of prayer only to discover my mind wandering off in other directions, focusing on the activities planned for tomorrow or what someone had earlier said or done. My mind has been cluttered with "stuff," as Rachel put it. Many times I've not had a real conversation with my Best Friend.

Wait a minute! If He really is my Best Friend, what kind of friend am I that I cannot give Him my undivided attention and focus? My earthly friends would think that anything less would be rude! The next time I experienced a cluttered mind when I tried talking to the Lord, I prayed Rachel's prayer, "Lord, remove the stuff so I can talk to You." And He did. After that I had a good time sharing with Jesus, my Friend.

Lord, remove all the stuff from my mind just now. I want to talk to You, to hear You share with me. VICKI GALLON-CLARK

Paper or Plastic?

Be not conformed to this world: but be ye transformed
by the renewing of your mind. Rom. 12:2.

Paper or plastic? One more decision to make!
I have a vinyl wire rack frame that fits on the inside of a door beneath my kitchen sink. It holds a paper or plastic bag for trash. I like it. But it's not squared off—it has rounded edges. So if I use paper sacks, I have to make some adjustments. By folding and bending and smoothing and ignoring the surprising amount of noise a paper bag makes, I can eventually make the sack fit the rack and become a useful container. When I use a plastic sack from the market, the material is pliable and easily molds itself to conform to the wire rack.

Grocery sacks aren't the only things that need some adjusting on our part before they fit comfortably into our lives. For instance, when moving from one house to another, adjustments need to be made for differences in wall space and furniture. We often fold towels according to the way they fit in the cupboards or drawers.

I don't like changes. With my daily schedule I find it difficult to shape my plans to fit into a 24-hour day. Maybe God is telling me to bend a little and be more flexible.

Sometimes I'm like a paper sack; it's hard for me to readjust, bend, or mold to fit into the plan that God has for me. When He tries, I make a lot of noise. On rare occasions I'm like the pliable plastic sack. I let God readjust, bend, and shape me so I can better fit His plan for my life.

No matter what kind of sack I use, the frame in my cupboard never changes. It's always there—a steady, sturdy, dependable support. In a similar way, no matter how I twist and fuss or question, I know I can rely on the Lord's steady, sturdy, dependable support. He's the frame that holds me, and it's His love that molds me.

God is the framework; we are His containers. He wants us to be willing to bend to His will so He can fill us with His Spirit and use us for His glory. In reality, isn't that what we desire too?

MARCIA MOLLENKOPF

Is My Name Written There?

"Whosoever was not found written in the book of life was cast into the lake of fire." Rev. 20:15.

A s we had been doing for almost five years, we confidently approached the prison control room window. However, instead of pushing the book through the slot for my husband and me to sign, a voice echoed from behind the tinted glass. "Mr. Norman can enter, but Mrs. Norman's name isn't on the list."

While my husband asked questions and waited for answers, I took out my copy of prison rules and read them to determine what rule I'd broken. Satisfied that my record was clear, I listened while the officer made calls to the prison chaplain and the warden.

For validation, we showed the officer our seminar material that we received from Prison Fellowship, listing the names of all participants. But somehow my name was not on the prison list.

Finally the officer, as an afterthought, said that she recognized us as regular volunteers, but my name needed to appear on their computer list. The other eight volunteers were already in the waiting room, unaware of why my husband and I were delayed. They couldn't go to the chapel until we were cleared.

Eventually my name was cleared for entry, and the book placed on the window ledge for us to sign. Once inside, we were surprised to find the new Prison Fellowship area director there. His presence was providential, for he had helped clear my name for entry.

A long-forgotten hymn came to mind—"Tell me, Jesus, my Saviour, is my name written there?"

I reflected: *When the books are opened on that great judgment day, will my name be recorded in the book of life? Will I be found wanting, or will my sins all be washed away?*

We were told that omission of my name was a computer error. On that day of all days, computers won't be responsible, for the angels who keep the records don't make mistakes. Our Intercessor will have ceased intercession, and probation will have ended. There will be no second chance. Is my name written there? Is yours?

MABEL ROLLINS NORMAN

Not as Man Sees

The Lord does not look at the things man looks at. Man looks at the outward appearance, but the Lord looks at the heart. 1 Sam. 16:7, NIV.

I had been riding all day, and now I sat, trying to center down and relax before my next bus arrived.

A woman sat next to me on the row of connected chairs in the bus depot. A small person. Almost a nonperson, skeletal, in chino pants and jacket, with a narrow scarf tied around her fuzz-covered head, the ties trailing down her back. At first I thought she was a man, perhaps some far-out sect member hanging around the bus depot.

Putting her out of my mind, I read until I heard someone say "Hi, Mom!" Glancing up, I saw a young woman with a bonny small girl and a tall sturdy man coming toward us. The small person next to me stood up.

The young woman gathered her into her arms, hugging her close. Turning to the little girl she said, "This is your grandma."

The frail, almost bald little woman stooped and hugged the small girl. Then she stood up and hugged her son-in-law. A smile warmed her face. The young man picked up the woman's luggage, and they walked away together, talking and laughing.

As they walked away I wondered, *Does she have cancer? Has she been through a course of chemotherapy treatments? Is she coming to her daughter's to recuperate? Shame on me! To think I so misjudged her, going entirely by sight.*

My companion was not a small, skinny man from some far-out sect. No! She was a waiting grandmother, waiting for the loving reception she would receive from her family.

I'm so glad God's way is not our way. He always knows what is in our hearts.

I thought of Jesus' words in Matthew 7:1, 2: "Judge not, that ye be not judged. For with what judgment ye judge, ye shall be judged."

Dear Lord, teach me to have a generous mind and not be so quick to judge. Give me a thoughtful, caring heart where others are concerned. Amen.

EVA ALICE COVEY

The Quilt

How very good and pleasant it is
when kindred live together in unity! Ps. 133:1, NRSV.

Not long ago I pieced my first full-sized quilt. I thought that since there were only 30 blocks, I could average one a day and be finished in a month. How wrong I was! There were, in fact, 1,230 tiny pieces comprising those 30 blocks, plus all the strips to connect them.

Try as I might, I could never seem to make a perfectly square block. Always there was some little point that didn't match perfectly with the others. And being "geometrically challenged," I had to check every single block against the pattern. Occasionally a piece would need to be rotated or reversed. How thankful I was for a good clear pattern!

After many days—yes, even months—of sewing, the quilt is finally finished. And when you stand back and look at the whole thing, it really is beautiful. Not perfect—but still beautiful. I'm glad now as I look at the quilt on our bed that I didn't say "This project is too big for me!" and give up on it.

Each woman in the body of Christ is unique. And not one of us is perfect. But as we daily learn to let God choose the pattern for our lives, we can come together in unity. Our points may not always match up exactly, but we can still be in harmony together, each in her own place in God's great design.

I'm glad that Jesus never gives up on us, no matter how messed up our lives may seem. He truly is the Master Craftsman, "the author and finisher of our faith" (Heb. 12:2). God, who has begun a good work in each of us, promises to be faithful to complete it (Phil. 1:6). Then as the world stands back to take a look, they will indeed behold a unified work of great beauty!

As a favorite author of mine puts it, "the secret of true unity in the church and in the family is not diplomacy, not management, not a superhuman effort to overcome difficulties—though there will be much of this to do—but union with Christ" (Ellen G. White, *The Adventist Home,* p. 179).

Christ has that ability to take the imperfect "quilt squares" of our individual lives and stitch them into a thing of great beauty.

BRENDA FORBES DICKERSON

The Pattern

Ask, and it shall be given you; seek, and ye shall find. Matt. 7:7.

It was 6:00 in the morning. In one week I would be serving at a wedding reception, and I had only this day to make my dress. I assembled my material, scissors, pins, thread, trim, and—Where was my pattern? It was missing!

I looked through everything again. No pattern. I reviewed my store receipt. Yes, I had purchased it. I searched my pattern drawer, my fabric cupboard, and throughout the house. It wasn't there. Seven o'clock. Eight o'clock. My morning was wasting. Every minute was precious. Stores were closed; I had no options.

Then, and only then, I remembered something I had failed to do—talk with my Father. I analyzed all the clutter I had gathered around me, and since He is a God of order, I felt compelled to go upstairs to the study my husband and I shared. I knelt at the little couch right by my office file and began to pour out my problem. I asked my heavenly Friend to forgive me for my negligence. I told Him I had done my best to have everything ready, and that I needed to have my dress finished that day. I reminded Him that I believed He knew where the pattern was and pleaded with Him to show me where to look.

Somehow comforted and calmed, I rose from my knees. To keep my balance, I reached out and grasped the handle of the bottom file drawer. The drawer slid open. Then I did something I had no reason for doing. I cannot explain why, but I reached about halfway back into the drawer of correspondence, and felt something familiar—my pattern! Astonished beyond description, I felt tears stream down my cheeks. I thanked Him again and again.

To this day I am baffled as to how the pattern got in that drawer. I am equally amazed at the personal and direct way God heard and answered my plea. He not only knows my name; He knows about everything I possess. He does not intrude when He is neglected, but stands ready and waiting to help when He is bidden. I've learned to place Him first in my life, and more and more He has become my friend.

Yes, the dress was finished that day—all because my heavenly Father cares.

LORRAINE HUDGINS

Truckers or Angels?

It shall come to pass, that before they call, I will answer;
and while they are yet speaking, I will hear. Isa. 65:24.

I traveled alone to a school reunion. After enjoying the day with old friends, I decided to visit my niece and spend the night with her. At 4:00 the next morning I left to go home. I was anxious to get there in time for a meeting I'd promised to attend.

It was still very dark; the highway was completely deserted except for my vehicle. I had not even seen another car on the road since leaving my niece's house. I had the road all to myself.

I was doing about 60 miles per hour when suddenly a red pickup truck passed me. Then a second vehicle pulled in behind me. The red pickup slowed down to 40 miles per hour. The one behind me slowed to the same speed. Because I was in a hurry, I pulled around the red pickup. The driver sped around me and again forced me to slow down. The car behind me stayed right on my rear bumper.

"Oh, Lord, help me!" I prayed. "I'm frightened!" All sorts of thoughts raced through my mind about what could happen to me on that lonely stretch of road should the men in these vehicles force me to stop. "Please send Your angels to protect me!"

I glanced at my rearview mirror. An 18-wheeler bore down upon us. Immediately I saw a way out of my predicament. *I'll pull out as soon as it's past me, and stick close to its bumper,* I thought. *Maybe that will discourage the red pickup and the other vehicle from following me.*

As soon as the tractor-trailer passed, I pulled in behind. Suddenly—from nowhere, it seemed—a second 18-wheeler appeared in my lane. *Amazing how a deserted highway suddenly has five vehicles!* I thought. *I wonder if God sent two guardian angels to protect me from the men in the other two vehicles. They surely seem like angels to me.*

For the next hour I drove sandwiched between those two 18-wheelers, singing praises to God for His protection, certain that they had come in answer to my cry for help. I arrived safely home, thankful for God's loving care.

SUZANNE ELLIOTT

Call 911!

You shall call, and the Lord will answer; you shall cry,
and He will say, "Here I am." Isa. 58:9, NKJV.

O h, Mary," my pastor husband, Ben, phoned one afternoon when
our children were toddlers. "Joe and Lori are here, and I thought
we could have them over to supper. Would that be OK?" Joe and Lori
were special friends from a former pastorate.

Well, at least this time he remembered to call ahead! I thought. "Sure,"
I agreed. "That's great."

What on earth am I going to do with this house! I felt near panic. Looking
around, I saw only a dirty diaper in the toilet, a sink half-filled with water
from Laura's playtime, the kitchen cabinets piled high with dirty pots and
pans, and a living room floor scattered with toys. I knew other rooms
were just as cluttered. *How can I clean this place up before Joe and Lori arrive?*

I felt frustrated, exasperated, lonely, and desperate. So I just
stopped and prayed my 911 prayer: "Oh, Lord!" Just then I remembered something I had read about how to clean a house in a hurry. I
decided to give it a try.

I put all the dirty pots and pans into the oven to be done later.
Now just remember not to turn the oven on while they are inside, I warned
myself. Taking a laundry basket, I enlisted the children to help me
pick up the toys and put them into a closet until there was more time
to put them away where they belonged.

Benjie loved playing with toys that made noise, so I asked him to help
me push the vacuum. We did only the living room. I then closed the doors
to rooms in the house I didn't want our guests to see. Using window
cleaner I polished the sinks, mirrors, and cabinets. It gave everything a
quick shine, and the house began to smell clean. I sprayed the whole house
with air freshener and lit some candles. *Voilà!* I was ready for company.

Wow! God is good! He had impressed me with tips from a book I
had read; He helped me remember them in my time of emergency. I
know God is very interested in my day-to-day chores.

That incident happened many years ago. My toddlers are now
young adults. I have more time now to call on God, but I think He
still loves my 911 calls. "Help, Lord, I'm checking in again. 911!"

MARY MAXSON

I Just Can't Wait That Long

Even so, come, Lord Jesus. Rev. 22:20.

Some years ago, when her sons were quite young, my daughter, Loni, was taking her boys, Eric and Chris, on a trip to see their great-grandmother. As the trip progressed, Loni wasn't surprised to hear Chris say, "I can't wait that long." She assumed he needed a rest stop. Every little while Chris piped up, "I can't wait that long!" After many hours and many passing miles (and many rest stops), they were close to their destination. Still Chris kept saying, "I can't wait that long."

Loni was baffled, and she didn't want to stop again so close to Grandma's house. "What do you mean, Chris? We just stopped at a restroom!"

"No, Mommy," he explained. "I don't need a rest stop; I just can't wait to get to Grandma's house!"

That's exactly the way I feel about Jesus coming back to take us home. I just can't wait to get there. The journey has been long enough. I'm so eager to see my Father. I can't wait to see my dear Saviour, and I long to meet my guardian angel. *Oh, Jesus, please come soon and take us home. Like Chris, I just can't wait that long!*

How intense are we about Jesus coming back to get us? Years ago, when I sang "Do You Really Want Jesus to Come?" in all honesty I really didn't—not yet, at least. I didn't have a clear assurance of salvation in my heart. I didn't believe I was doing the work I was supposed to do perfectly enough. I felt I wasn't ready, so I wasn't sure I wanted Him to come.

Now I have the abundant assurance of salvation through the unclouded significance of the gospel. Now I have caught a vision of the unfathomable love of Jesus on the cross as He hung alone in the darkness, separated from His Father. Now I have caught a glimpse of the boundless love of God.

Now I *really* want Jesus to come! I just can't wait to get to my Father's house!

JODI EULENE DODSON

Promise Under the Dead Leaves

I am the resurrection, and the life. John 11:25.

I miss my mother.

She died in the early spring just as alumni weekend was beginning at Atlantic Union College, our alma mater, where I worked. Good friends joined Dad and me as we laid Mom to rest that Saturday afternoon.

Sunday morning we had to decide where to begin picking up the pieces. "Let's get rid of the wheelchair first," I suggested to Dad. "I'd just as soon remember my mother as she was when she was healthy and not have to keep seeing reminders that she wasn't." So we started the sorting and giving-away process.

By Monday we'd finished that task, and I looked around for some other project to keep my mind occupied. No point in going back to my job—it was Patriots Day, a legal holiday in Massachusetts celebrated by the running of the Boston Marathon.

The sun was shining. It was warm for mid-April. Why not rake the dead leaves from Mom's garden beside the house? I got a rake and started in, gingerly lifting the oak leaves layer by layer so as not to damage whatever might lie underneath.

There, just beginning their season of growth and flowering, were tender green shoots full of promise. Spring bulbs. Perennials. Even weeds.

I couldn't have picked a better task for this weekend, I thought. *What better way to be reminded of God's power, the very same creative energy that will restore Mom to life someday?*

That spring and summer I became a regular customer at several of the area's greenhouses as I added more and more plants to the garden. My inexperience made the project a great learning experience. Dad and I dug out grassy areas that threatened the garden's borders and expanded it. We even unearthed stepping-stones that through the years had become buried. Gardening proved to be good therapy as well as a constant reminder of the God of growth and renewal.

I still miss my mother. Friends tell me I probably always will. But the garden's cycle of death and rebirth for me illustrates the power of the resurrection. It assures me I'll see her again.   JOCELYN FAY

Do You Work Here?

*By this shall all men know
that ye are my disciples, if ye have love one to another. John 13:35.*

Do you work here?" a woman asked.

"Yes," I nodded and smiled. "May I help you?"

At the library where I work as a page, patrons generally ask "Do you work here?" before asking how to find a particular book. Of course it's reasonable to assume that I work there if I am pushing a book cart, but many times I am just walking through the library when I am asked. I wondered how they could guess that I was an employee and not another patron.

After careful observation of my fellow workers, I realized that we act differently when we walk through the library. We push in chairs and pick up stray books. We don't wander aimlessly through the stacks. We know our way around. The library is a second home to us, and we feel at ease surrounded by books.

A doctor dressed in jeans and a flannel shirt would be just as efficient as any other physician, but he or she would not be acceptable to many patients. We are used to seeing doctors wear white lab coats, and we might worry about their credentials if they didn't dress like doctors. Without the customary lab coat, a hospital worker could easily be mistaken for a patient or a visitor. We would have to ask them to find out if they were doctors. An airline pilot in a sweat suit could fly a Boeing 747 jet as well as one in a uniform, but the passengers might not feel as confident.

There is no universal Christian uniform to identify us. We can be identified only by our actions. Do people know we're Christians, or do they have to ask? Can they tell by the way we walk, by the optimistic attitude of faith we maintain through life's ups and downs? Do people know we're Christians because of our integrity in business, our patience in dealing with workday problems? Does our welcoming smile in church show visitors that we are members, that we belong there? Do our neighbors see our smiles, our love, our patience, and know that we are Christians? We need to let our Christianity show so that people know that we work—and walk—with God.

"Excuse me, but are you a Christian?"

"Yes; may I help you?"

GINA LEE

Rescued

*God sent not his Son into the world to condemn the world;
but that the world through him might be saved. John 3:17.*

Her tiny body trembled from her first encounter with the rough-
ness of the world. Dragging her broken tail, she fled from the
pain and rain through the first open door—into a dormitory. Sandra
rescued the kitten and gave her safety and security. For many months
Sandra gently nursed the little one through surgeries, serious falls, and
heart disease. The cat welcomed Sandra home and became a precious
companion for lonely and sad hours. The two bonded with real and
lasting affection.

The trees and plants in the valley below Sandra's home could not
flee, as the kitten had, before total annihilation from the bulldozers.
One rainy night Sandra, the rescurer, dug up one of the small willows
and gave it the security of a clay pot. The little tree lost all its leaves
from shock, but it survived and became a graceful work of art.

One night Sandra discovered that her beloved cat's hind legs
were paralyzed. The cat tried to drag her now helpless body over the
floor, but could not. The vet could not restore her body, and 28
hours later the cat died. The grief of the household was like that of
losing a family member.

Sandra dug a grave for her precious pet near the end of the porch
where the cat loved to sit, enjoying the potted willow below her. As
the sun rose, Sandra gently laid the still body on a pillow of soft grass
and her favorite blue towel and blanketed her with Queen Anne's
lace and lilies.

Then Sandra gave the dear little rescued cat the most precious
memorial she could—the rescued willow tree. Always the tree will
grow as a graceful memory of the love and affection so freely given
by a cat to her adoptive family.

As I think of Sandra's tender heart, how she loves to rescue doomed
animals and plants, I remember Someone else with a tender heart,
Someone who loved a doomed world enough to rescue the helpless
lives on our planet. How tenderly He has cared for us, giving the ultimate sacrifice. What a rescue! What a Rescuer!   RUTH WATSON

The Banana Theory

"Neither do I condemn you," Jesus declared.
"Go now and leave your life of sin." John 8:11, NIV.

When I finally passed my driving test, I experienced both excitement and depression. You see, I hated driving. I learned only at the insistence of my husband. I suspect he didn't want to be the only man in Britain with a wife who didn't know what to do with a steering wheel.

As a new driver I struggled with reversing. I could never remember which way to turn the wheel. So Jonathan reversed for me. If he was not around, I just kept driving until I came to a roundabout. (You will be surprised at just how few roundabouts we have in Britain!)

All went well until the day I needed to back out of the garage. Jonathan was busy. I had to do it myself. I remembered being told that if I followed the shape of a banana when reversing, all would go well. I focused on the shape of a banana and slowly eased back. Suddenly I recalled I was to use this technique only when reversing around a corner, not in a straight line. Instead of driving out of the garage, I had simply driven into the side of it.

I scrambled out of the car and stood by the garage with my hand over my mouth in horror. At that moment the garage door, which was a flick-up type, decided to flick down—on top of the car roof. I had driven the car into the hinges of the garage door. The hand that covered my mouth now covered my eyes. I had managed to damage the side of the car and the roof of the car without even getting our vehicle on the road!

Jonathan came bounding out of our house. He looked at the car encased in the garage like filling oozing out of a sandwich. I was sure he was going to be angry. I was planning my defense about the "banana" theory when Jonathan came over and burst out laughing! I thought the poor man was in shock. He didn't get angry with me or lecture me or book me in for another set of driving lessons. Rather, he consoled me. He didn't respond in the way that I imagined he should.

Neither does Jesus respond to us in the way He should. For our sin, our rebellion, our ugliness within, He should cast us aside. Instead He offers us love, acceptance, and a fresh start each day.

MARY BARRETT

Prayer for Pain

*The Lord is nigh unto them that are of a broken heart;
and saveth such as be of a contrite spirit. Ps. 34:18.*

Lois, my youngest sister and the mother of two small children, was very sick. In the beginning it was just a simple headache which, as time went by, became more and more intense. The diagnosis of these intense headaches was not encouraging: "cerebral angioma followed by a stroke." Immediate surgery was necessary.

This was the first major crisis our family had to face. It was a stressful time for us, but we had many friends who gave us encouragement. People all over the country prayed. We knew that God was there with us, leading, guiding, and supporting us.

The doctors prepared for the surgery, but they cautioned us not to get our hopes up. The problem was very severe. Twelve hours we spent waiting in front of the operating room. She survived, but the neurosurgeon had little hope for her recovery.

For many days she lay in a coma in intensive care. As we watched her, our faith seemed to be slipping away. Using what little faith we had left, we cried out to God: "Please do something, Lord, for our precious Lois; give us a miracle." His response was her complete recovery. All pain was gone. Praise the Lord!

At the hospital doctors, nurses, and employees came to visit her, because they knew that in her case God had manifested His power. They were amazed at her rapid recovery.

When she returned home, Lois told us of her experience in the intensive-care unit. Although she gave no outward sign of consciousness, she was aware of her critical condition. As she lay there she silently sang hymns, repeated Bible verses, and pleaded with God. Many times she sent a silent plea to God, "Please spare my life so I can see my children grow up to serve You."

We are promised that if we come to God and in humble, trusting faith make known our wants to Him, He can and will hear our cry.

Lois did not feel God's visible contact, but His hand covered us with love and compassionate caring. He was there with our family. He touched Lois and made her whole again. He took away the darkness and let light shine in our hearts again.   LEILA RIBEIRO NADALINE

Walking on the Water

With God all things are possible. Matt. 19:26.

I recently attended Atlanta's passion play. More than 30,000 attendees each year experience a new rendition of this dramatic reenactment of the final scenes of Christ's life. The cast begins practice for the next year immediately after the current year's season is over. The actors spend much time in prayer and Bible study, recreating in themselves the spiritual impact of the characters.

The scene that most touched me was the one of Christ walking on the rolling sea. The whole stage was transformed into a storm at sea. Plastic waves rose high. Hefty fishermen strained at the sails, rigging, and anchor. In the midst of the panic, Peter stepped out of the boat through faith and walked on the water to meet Christ. For a moment the disciple's faith overcame fear. He believed in the power of the Ruler of the laws of nature long enough to experience God's power over the laws.

I imagine how happy Christ must have felt to see Peter taking those first few steps of faith. It must have been something like a mother's joy in seeing a child take its first few steps. How proud the mother feels. How gratified Christ must have felt.

Then Peter took his eyes off Jesus, focusing instead on his experience, and began to sink. How disappointed Christ must have felt.

I wonder what Christ thinks as He watches me today. As He sees me have victory for a moment, then resume my treadmill life of materialism and self-defeat, what is in His mind? Does He feel as a mother does when a child refuses help, then falls and gets hurt? "Why will you die? How long and how patiently have I knocked at the entrance to the door of your heart and urged you to let Me in? But you wouldn't let Me! You have been the object of My care. You have the potential to be a princess, but you refuse the King's finest offer!"

Our greatest need is to believe we can gain strength from focusing on Jesus, visualizing our potential in Him, and truly incorporating that belief into our hearts. Then our victories will be sure. Like Peter, we can walk on water by faith in our mighty God.　　SHARI CHAMBERLAIN

Under His Wings

The Lord watch between me and thee,
when we are absent one from another. Gen. 31:49.

My niece was getting married, and I was planning to attend the wedding in Sydney, Australia. I saw to the necessary documents; I was in and out of the travel agent offices. She asked me to insure myself against any accident or sickness, but I felt it wasn't necessary. We were working in East London, South Africa, at the time.

It seemed that every news program reported another air crash. Each time my husband would come running to me, wherever I was in the house, and say, "No, Cilla, I cannot let you go! Look! There is another plane crash."

I didn't argue or say much, but quietly prayed that the Lord would grant me this opportunity to see my brother and his family.

The time came to leave. My two daughters were busy with exams, so they couldn't go to the airport. This left only my husband to see me off. Although this was my first experience to venture so far all by myself, I felt calm. I had it all figured out. I would wait at the Jan Smuts airport in Gauteng, and after a few hours would board another plane to Zimbabwe, where my sister would be waiting to visit with me until my flight for Australia.

My poor husband was thinking, *What if I don't see her again? What if her plane crashes? What if she gets ill and I can't get to her?*

I told him to cling to the Bible promise: "The Lord watch between me and thee, when we are absent one from another." "You must claim it too," I told him. I reminded him of God's protecting hand over me.

The hymn I adopted as my own was "Under His Wings I Am Safely Abiding." This hymn gave me inner peace and wonderful calmness. I sang it over and over in my mind all during the journey.

Everything went well. I never became ill, got lost, or anything. I was God's special child, and He promised to protect me. The wedding was beautiful, and the family was happy to have me with them for a while. The Lord kept His promise. He kept me safe while we were absent one from another. Priscilla Adonis

Angel in a Pickup Truck

He shall give his angels charge over thee,
to keep thee in all thy ways. Ps. 91:11.

I drove along country roads lined with blossoming dogwood one spring morning on my way to work. Stopping to yield to the oncoming traffic, I noticed a pickup truck inching up behind me. I thought it was nothing out of the ordinary until I began to track how closely the driver followed me for the next seven miles. I braked; he slowed down. I sped up; he accelerated. I turned right; he turned right. Puzzled, I checked my rearview mirror again. I did not recognize him. The tousled blond curls were as unfamiliar as his truck. Clearly I was being followed.

Turning onto the university campus, I noted that he was still right behind me. When I drove into the safety of my parking space he pulled up behind me. I got out of my car. So did he. Curious, I waited for him to join me on the crowd-filled sidewalk.

"Ma'am" (his Midwestern drawl was obvious), "your brake lights aren't working. I almost slammed into you a few miles down the road. I had to follow you all the way here to make sure you arrived safely."

Without waiting for my stammered words of gratitude, he climbed into his truck and drove off. I never saw him again.

I may never know who that man was, but one thing I do know: he was a God-sent reminder of the Father's unflagging love and care. He was indeed an angel in working clothes.

God taught me a lesson that day. There is no such thing as the right model. That my good Samaritan did not look like my picture of an angel was irrelevant. He simply answered a call to service. My angel did not need to be well-dressed or articulate. Wrapping his words in layered tissues of immaculate or long-winded politeness was unnecessary. What I had needed, unknown to me, was safety. My Father had sent the young man in the pickup truck to provide that.

Solomon says, "The human mind plans the way, but the Lord directs the steps" (Prov. 16:9, NRSV). How many times has my God protected me while I remained blissfully unaware of imminent danger?

Thank You, loving Lord, for sending angels I may never recognize or realize I need.   GLENDA-MAE GREENE

Good Morning!

This is the day which the Lord hath made;
we will rejoice and be glad in it. Ps. 118:24.

G ood morning!" I greeted two carpenters who were installing cabinets in the school office.

"What's good about it?" Stewart grumped.

I was taken aback. I had to think quickly. Did I sincerely mean
"Good morning"? Or was I simply going through a polite formality
like many who say, "Have a nice day"?

"Give me three good reasons," Stewart mumbled through his
drooping moustache. It was obvious he had gotten out of bed on the
wrong side.

"The sun is shining, I was able to get out of bed, and I have a
job," I enumerated for him.

"Humph," he grunted.

The other man raised his eyebrows and gave me a smile.

Throughout the morning I had time to think. *Yes, it is a good morning.*
Even if the sun doesn't shine every day my attitude can brighten the day. No
aches or pains prevented me from getting out of bed. I have a job that I love.

I decided the last reason embodied a wealth of blessings that can
erase the cloudiest day. I compiled the following 10 beatitudes about
the blessings of work. Blessed am I, because work:

provides an honorable reason to get up in the morning.

whets my appetite so I enjoy my meals.

keeps me too busy to get into trouble.

allows me to enjoy my vacation more fully.

brings me many compliments or rewards.

supplies my basic needs of food, clothing, shelter, security, and
recreation—a reason for living.

instills self-respect so I can face any crisis with dignity.

gives me an appreciation for rest at the end of the day.

cures many mental afflictions.

glorifies God, in whose image I am created.

"This is the day which the Lord hath made; [I] will rejoice and be
glad in it." Good morning, everyone!   EDITH FITCH

Give Me All Your Keys

I will give unto thee the keys of the kingdom of heaven:
and whatsoever thou shalt bind on earth shall be bound in heaven: and
whatsoever thou shalt loose on earth shall be loosed in heaven. Matt. 16:19.

I had been at Andrews University for only a month when my Volkswagen started giving me trouble. There were no funds for extensive repair and certainly none for another car. However, I took the car to a mechanic who had been recommended to me. My heart broke when he bluntly reported, "Lady, you should find an enemy and sell him this car."

It couldn't even be repaired. Sitting in my little VW, I wept and rehearsed my griefs to my heavenly Father. *Lord, why am I here, anyhow? I've been recently divorced, rejected. I have no job, no money, no home, no one. All my things are in storage; my sister is footing that bill. Lord, all I have is this one bent key—and now the car won't run.*

The car was rusted through so that it flooded when it rained. The windshield wipers didn't work in snow, and the only way to defrost was to roll down windows to let in cold air. But until now the car had always taken me where I needed to go. Now even my mobility was threatened. *Lord, where are You?*

Then I heard a still small voice. *Wanda, give Me your keys, and I will give you the keys to the kingdom.* It was not the answer I expected, but all the answer I needed. I gladly gave Him my last possession. Like the widow with her mites, why bother to hold on to a couple mites when we serve a God rich in love and grace?

Holding the rusty bent key in my hand, I surrendered it to God and asked Him to keep the VW running until I got a job. And He did! Through three severe winters, potholed streets, and miles and miles of roads from Michigan to Virginia to Ohio, the VW and I plodded along. Sometimes I had to jump-start it, but it always ran. The week I got a new job as chaplain at a regional medical center, I traded in that old VW and got $50 more than I paid for it.

In my hand I held a new key to a Toyota Tercel, and more: I received the keys to the kingdom—the assurance that my heavenly Father is my sure help and defense, my salvation and my joy. Hallelujah!

WANDA GRIMES DAVIS

My Friend

There is a friend who sticks closer than a brother. Prov. 18:24, NIV.

My friend Pat is a very special person. While others are asking "What can I do?" she gets it done. She instinctively knows what is needed and when, and nothing is ever too much trouble.

Her gift of friendship extends to all; she is the first to notice when someone needs help. As she relates to young and old alike, her warm personality, enthusiasm, and energy make her popular with all age groups. She is a motivator who is able to inspire others to go on the Soup Run, help with charity sales, pack relief boxes for refugees, or play hockey.

Effortlessly, it seems, she holds down a demanding job, runs her home, entertains extensively, and caters for functions within the church. She knows all the young people by name, is interested in their hopes and aspirations, and runs an open home for them. Pat is everyone's friend and helper.

Those who have been bereaved have found comfort in her warm understanding and practical help. Those who rejoice are gladdened by her delight in their achievements. Always there, always dependable, she is a treasure. Pat is my friend, one who means a lot to me.

I have another friend like her. He too knows what I need before I ask. He too is a motivator. He enables me to achieve; helps me to gain satisfaction. He comforts me when I grieve and brings joy out of the darkest hours. Before I ask, He too is always there, always de-pendable, bearing me up when I am down, and giving me strength to climb life's hills again. What a privilege it is to have a friend like that!

Although He cares for the whole world, He knows my name. He is interested in my goals and aspirations, my trials and struggles. He offers me warm understanding and practical help. He is my helper, my inspiration, and my treasure. Other friends may fail me, but He will never fail me nor forsake me.

Jesus is my dearest friend. Is He your friend too?

AUDREY BALDERSTONE

He Understands

*When the Lord saw her, he had compassion on her,
and said unto her, Weep not. Luke 7:13.*

Widow of Nain

Jesus felt compassion
As He watched the funeral train
Bearing through the city gates
The widow's son, of Nain.

Her mother's heart was broken,
It was more than she could bear,
To see her only son
Lying lifeless there.

Jesus walked beside her;
He asked her not to weep.
And then He touched her lifeless son
And wakened him from sleep.

He changed her grief to happiness
And gave her back her boy.
And they embraced each other
With gladness and with joy.

He who stood beside that mother
Still says, "I am He
That was dead but now liveth;
Come and follow Me.

"I will give you life eternal,
Just believe in Me.
I broke the confines of the tomb;
My power can set you free!"

He stands beside us in our sorrow; He is touched by our grief. So ask and believe! If we receive His promise, we have the answer!

ELVA E. SPRINGER

Bethany's Gospel

As the Father has loved me, so have I loved you. John 15:9.

My 2-year-old granddaughter, Bethany, has difficulty pronouncing the letter G. I am "Bamma," and Ron is "Bampa." On a recent visit, after a series of hugs and kisses for "Bamma," I said, "Bethany, you are just so sweet!"

"You wouldn't think she was sweet if you saw how she has been acting recently," our daughter Esther replied.

Esther explained that Bethany had for several days been the epitome of stubbornness. Daily she put on a classic performance of "the terrible twos." No discipline Esther used seemed to do any good. After yet another display of independence, her mother finally sighed and said, "Oh, Bethany, you are so bad!"

Immediately Bethany began singing her version of a children's song, "I am so *bad* that Jesus loves me, Jesus loves me, Jesus love me, I am so *bad* that Jesus loves me, Jesus loves even me." Because of her difficulty with the letter G she had substituted "bad" for "glad"!

"Pretty good theology," I commented with a chuckle.

I've thought a lot about that incident. We've come to call it "Bethany's gospel." God does indeed love us, even when we're bad, in spite of all the mistakes we've made and the stubbornness we have shown. God loves us just as we are. Nothing we can ever do will cause Him to stop loving us. No matter how many times He has to discipline us, He loves us still.

"Jesus loves us as we are and not as we should be, since none of us is as he should be," says Brian Manning in his book *The Signature of Jesus* (p. 177). I am so glad that Jesus loves me like that!

What a joy it is, Lord, to know that You love me just as I am, in spite of my faults, mistakes, sins, and blunders. Thank You, Lord, for loving me, even when I am so bad!

I want to be so filled with this knowledge of Your unconditional love and acceptance that I will be able to love others in the same way. Help me to look at people in my life and think, You may be so bad, but I love you anyhow, just as Jesus does. Nothing you can do will make me stop loving you, just as nothing I do will cause God to stop loving me.

DOROTHY EATON WATTS

Dirty Windshields

Wash me thoroughly from my iniquity, and cleanse me from my sin. Ps. 51:2, NKJV.

The windshield wipers flip-flopped back and forth numerous times across the glass. I pushed the button one last time. The cleaning solution squirted up, swishing away the last traces of dirt. Instantly I could see clearly. I continued my drive, turning like clockwork at all the right places. I'd driven this road to work hundreds of times before and didn't need to think about where I was going. My mind wandered to the grocery list, church duties, my daughter's basketball game, and buying new clothes.

Oops! The windshield had accumulated some salt residue from the recent snow. I gave a quick squirt and let the windshield wipers do their thing. Soon the glass was spotless again.

My mind wandered to a request from my son, the next time my husband would be traveling out of town, and the bills. Suddenly I came back to reality, noticing that the windshield was dirty, top to bottom and side to side. It was caked up with salt, dirt, and grime, and I could barely see where I was going. How in the world could I have driven this far and not seen, right before my eyes, how filthy the windshield was?

A couple more squirts of the magic button and all was well, and none too soon, for up ahead were several crater-like potholes. Surely I'd have been jolted back to reality if I had hit one—and probably damaged my car too.

Isn't life like that? We go about our business day by day, mechanically giving little thought to what we're doing. We are like robots, with no brains sometimes, wrapped up in life. Meanwhile, right before our eyes, we've picked up all the crud life throws at us: gossip, revenge, jealousy, worry, sadness, and bitterness. Bit by bit it accumulates, clinging to our souls and turning our clean hearts into filthiness—in thought and in action. And many times we don't even know it. All is well, we think as we travel along life's road. Then *bumpety-bump, bang!* We're stuck in a pothole of sin, wondering what happened.

Lord, help me to see every bit of life's dirt as it is flung in my direction. May I ever be ready to push the button that will release Your cleansing solution into my life before it's too late.

IRIS L. STOVALL

Prayer Opportunity

*The Lord is my strength and my shield; my heart trusted in him,
and I am helped: therefore my heart greatly rejoiceth;
and with my song will I praise him. Ps. 28:7.*

My husband and I had just completed a 3,000-mile trip from British Columbia to Maryland, bouncing along the rough highways in our one-ton pickup. As we began conducting an evangelistic series, I began experiencing severe pain that radiated from my low back all the way down my right leg. A visit to the doctor confirmed I had partially ruptured the last lumbar disk. He prescribed bed rest for six weeks.

"I can't go to bed now; I've got to give health lectures and sing for the meetings!" I protested. Although I tried to continue with the series, the pain was so severe that I finally accepted his wise prescription.

As I climbed into bed, I began to weep. "Dear Lord," I cried, "I don't know why You have permitted this injury, but, there's one thing I know: You and I are going to have lots of time together."

Each evening around 6:00 I began interceding in prayer. I prayed that heaven's angels would be sent to impress sincere people to attend the meeting. As I knew the nightly schedule, I would pray specifically for those taking part. Especially did I pray when I knew my husband was giving an altar call.

At the close of the meetings 42 people were baptized! Heaven must have realized that special grace was needed to enable those souls to break the bonds of sin and to have victory over their sinful habits, enabling them to understand and appreciate the Bible. The special time I shared with the Lord drew me into a more precious relationship with Him and gave me a deeper insight into the value of intercessory prayer.

God is able to take the unfortunate circumstances of our lives and turn them into beautiful experiences. As I lay in bed for the entire month, I turned my heart toward heaven. In my earnest intercession for others Jesus drew so close that I look back upon that trial as a great blessing.

KAY COLLINS

Smother With Kindness

Always try to be kind to each other. 1 Thess. 5:15, NIV.

My first nursing job was in a small, struggling 30-bed hospital that mainly served government-assisted families. I came to work one Friday morning to begin a three-day weekend of 12-hour shifts. The night nurses reported about the difficult mother in room 17. I expected that I would be assigned there, for I was often given the pediatric patients because I liked children. I assumed that I was going to have a terrible weekend.

As soon as I walked into my patient's room, the mother gave me a suspicious look. She began to complain how terrible the hospital was compared to a large state university hospital where her other child had been hospitalized in the past. "I wish we still had insurance so we could go to a real hospital," she said.

Her comments offended me. I felt like telling her that she should be thankful there were people willing to serve her, even though she was dependent on the government. But God held my tongue. He impressed me to smother her with kindness.

I worked really hard the rest of the day to be pleasant to this mother. I explained everything that I was doing for her child and updated her on her son's tests. I included her in his care and allowed her to talk about the problems she was experiencing in her personal life. She never left her son's bedside.

Saturday I gave her some soap, towels, and scrubs so she could take a shower and change her clothes. I shared my lunch with her. As the weekend progressed, the other nurses noticed that the difficult mother was becoming much less difficult.

When I told the mother I would be off the next couple days and that her son would soon be discharged, she had tears in her eyes. She hugged me and said, "Thank you for being so kind. You were the only one who seemed to care about me."

I'm so glad I listened to God's counsel. It made a big difference for a mother going through a difficult time.

Lord, help me always to be willing to suspend judgment on another's actions. Help me to hold my tongue. Teach me to treat difficult people with kindness.

K. ELAINE PASCUAL

Where Are You, Lord?

The King shall answer . . . Inasmuch as ye have done it unto one of the least of these my brethren, ye have done it unto me. Matt. 25:40.

I saw a homeless child of God with shopping cart.
    'Twas filled with all the things that he possessed:
A dirty quilt, some trinkets, rags, a duffle bag.
    The air was sharp, and he was poorly dressed.

I hurried by. My nostrils caught the reeking stench
    That issued from this mute, discarded soul.
He asked for nothing, but his need for love screamed out.
    I closed my ears, and tarried not to console.

I sat before the fire in warmth and gratitude,
    Forgetting this poor wretch of low degree;
But words of Jesus echoed in my callous heart,
    As you have done to him, you've done to Me.

But Lord, I do not know him, silently I pled.
    It's risky to take chances, You can see.
As you have done to him . . .
    Lord, I did not know! I would not treat You thus!
. . . you've done to Me.

I threw my jacket on and hastened from my house
    Back to the spot. It had begun to rain.
I shivered as I ventured down forsaken streets.
    But he was gone. My searching was in vain.

Despondent, I returned and fell upon my knees.
    "Where are You, Lord?" in sad reproach I cried;
"I cannot bear to see You homeless, hungry, cold,
    Rejected by the ones for whom You died!"

I rose. New purpose kindled in my heart. I know
    I'll find Him—recognize Him at a glance!
I'll offer Him a meal; a coat; I'll speak a word
    Of comfort, if He'll give me one more chance!

LORRAINE HUDGINS

By Ravens or by Truckers

The ravens brought him bread and meat in the morning and bread and meat in the evening, and he drank from the brook. 1 Kings 17:6, NIV.

The cliffs and caves of Pangna, Thailand, had always intrigued me. However, whenever we traveled through that picturesque area, we never had time to stop to explore them. My husband had preceded me back to the United States, and soon I would follow. It was visit the caves now or never.

My 14-year-old son and two of his friends agreed to go with me on my excursion over the mountains. In Pangna we dug sea animal fossils from the seashore beds; we explored the mysterious caves and tried unsuccessfully to find a way to scale the cliffs. The villagers were not even curious about how to climb the intriguing pink stone walls that crowned their village in majesty.

When we left for home, we fell in behind a logging truck loaded with giant teakwood logs struggling up the steep grade. Because of the winding road, we could not pass the truck. I was concerned lest the motor overheat, so stopped to rest the engine for a while.

We got out to stretch our legs. The first thing I noticed was a dark liquid running down the asphalt from our motor. It was water, not oil or gas. We opened the hood and saw that the water pump belt had broken. What could we do now? Here we were in a mountain jungle where no one lived, and at least 10 miles from a village.

It was past noon, and my growing boys were very hungry. Traffic was sparse, and we could not leave the car unattended. We decided that Payop, the oldest boy, would hitchhike to the next town to try to find a water hose that would fit our car. I flagged the first vehicle that appeared.

"What's the trouble?" asked the driver. When we showed him, he opened a box in his truck and pulled out a water hose—exactly what we needed. He put it on; it fit perfectly! We went on our way, rejoicing for the miracle hose the Lord had sent. God can send bread by ravens, or a water hose by a trucker. He specializes in the impossible.

RUTH WATSON

Thank God for Failure

Since the Lord is directing our steps, why try to understand everything that happens along the way? Prov. 20:24, TLB.

I was 18 and could attend the university if I gained certain grades in the qualifying examination. When the results came, my grades were not good enough. I admit feeling let down.

Yes, there had been extenuating circumstances, but I still couldn't understand why this bad thing had happened to me. I had committed my life to God. I had worked hard for all my exams, and from the first time I had thought of becoming a teacher I had planned to teach in a Christian school. Now here I was—a failure. It just didn't add up. How sick I felt! How final defeat seemed! I had to go back to school and on the treadmill again for another year—a lost year, a year that seemed to last forever.

When I finally started teaching in a Christian school, though, I began to understand why God had allowed that apparent blow to fall. I discovered that students tend to think that their teachers sail effortlessly through all their studies, pass all their exams in a blaze of glory, and therefore cannot really be expected to understand a struggler. Having faced failure myself, I was much better equipped to enter into other people's discouragements and help them to keep on trying. I learned not to take success for granted and to trust that God knows what He is doing. So I'm thankful for the time I didn't make it to the university the first time around.

Incidentally, a few days after receiving those dismal qualifying results I heard that I had failed to gain my music degree by five marks, a second blow that pointed my musical inclination in quite another and very satisfying direction.

Maybe there are apparently negative experiences in your autobiography. If you cannot understand now, hang on, and in time you will. I have discovered that Proverbs 3:6 is absolutely true: "In all your ways acknowledge Him, and He shall direct your paths" (NKJV). God trains some of us by bringing us disappointment and apparent failure. It is His purpose that we learn to master difficulties. Success will come as we struggle against insurmountable difficulties.   PEGGY MASON

Getting in the Way

*You have turned aside from the way; you have caused many
to stumble by your instruction. Mal. 2:8, RSV.*

I put on the brakes the minute I heard the ambulance. With lights
flashing and siren blaring, it rushed to the intersection. Once there,
however, it had to wait as four drivers turned left in front of it. They
paid no heed to the lights and siren.

Didn't they stop to think about the consequences of their actions?
Was their desire to get where they were going more important than
saving someone's life? What if it were their loved ones waiting for
the ambulance? I kept thinking of the person the ambulance was trying to reach—waiting and suffering. I thought of the anxiety their
loved ones must be experiencing.

Like the drivers who made the ambulance wait, Christians can
hinder the work of the Holy Spirit in people's lives. When we criti-
cize ministers and find fault with others, we are getting in the way.
The people who are doing God's work in helping to spread the gospel
are in special need of our prayers and support. Monopolizing their
time with petty grievances means that they may not be available to
counsel those who are in real need. Our selfishness can prevent someone from receiving the blessing they need.

Likewise, we can be guilty of selfishness when we get in the way
of people who are trying to do right. When new Christians struggle
to adopt better lifestyles, we need to offer encouragement and moral
support. Rather than being their judges, we should be their examples
and encouragers. Instead of nagging and pointing out what we believe
to be faults, we need to let go and let God work on their hearts. Only
He knows what needs they have.

We need to examine our own lives and make sure we are helping,
not hurting, God's cause. Setting ourselves up as being "superior
Christians" only gets in the way and hinders their journey to God.

*Lord, please help me to be sensitive to Your presence in the lives of others. Help
me to stop interfering so that You can work! Help me to cause no one to stumble
because of my selfishness. Help me not to block the work of the Holy Spirit.*

GINA LEE

Joys, Hugs, and Rainbows

The joy of the Lord is your strength. Neh. 8:10.

One morning I felt spiritually low as I went outside to water my flower garden. Then I noticed that as the spray from the hose shot through the air, the sun and the water were creating a gorgeous rainbow. I immediately became excited. I love rainbows and prisms. In fact, I've asked God to make my home in heaven out of prisms.

As I moved the spray to my left, I saw a rainbow circling toward the ground. Playing with the position of the spray, I found I could bring the rainbow almost to my feet. Then I reversed directions and sprayed to the right. Again I could see a rainbow circling around and down. The colors were so vivid and awesome! The more I played with the water, the more excited I became.

Slowly I sprayed back and forth, right to left, left to right. Not only was my garden watered, but the rocks and the stone wall were soaked. In creating my rainbows I sprayed the storage shed, the grass on the hill, and the sidewalk in the middle. I sprayed the trees, the driveway, the flowers, and the weeds. But I was experiencing the most beautiful rainbow, my own personal rainbow.

"O God," I ecstatically announced, "I don't want to quit!"

By then the tears were running down my cheeks. I was laughing, crying, and praising God all at the same time. Then I discovered I could carefully angle the hose as it came toward me and actually create a connected rainbow! I didn't know a rainbow was connected: I've always seen half circles. But there it was—a giant, gorgeous, color circle just for my pleasure!

But God had yet another lesson for me in this rapturous encounter. If I stood directly between the sun and the rainbow, the brilliant circuit was broken right at the spot where my shadow was cast. God knows how to teach us effective lessons through nature.

Then I glanced up where my spray had accidentally gone still higher, creating yet another rainbow—a double promise of God's love to a hungry, needy soul.

"God, this is too much for me! I don't think I can handle it," I cried. But there they were. Double rainbows. It was like a hug from God. I felt strengthened by this joyful encounter with God.   JODI EULENE DODSON

House for Sale

For you yourselves know very well that the Day of the Lord will come
as a thief comes at night. When people say, "Everything is quiet
and safe," then suddenly destruction will hit them! . . .
People will not escape. 1 Thess. 5:2, 3, TEV.

I well remember those beautiful spring days when we outgrew our little house. With three children in grade school, a dog, a turtle, and a variety of other pets, we needed a larger home where we could stretch our arms without knocking something over. So we decided to sell.

Our real estate agent had advised us of the best way to prepare the house for a quick sale. We carefully followed his advice. We painted and fixed to make a good impression on the first buyer. We never left home unless everything was neat and clean, the curtains were open for light, and each room smelled good. Our buyer could come at any moment.

But when the buyer didn't come, we started to leave the house without doing the necessary things.

Then one day, when we thought for sure the buyer wasn't coming, we decided it was OK to leave shoes all over the floor, clothing out of the hamper, and dirty dishes in the sink. It was then that the first buyer showed up at our door.

We were not ready to show the house. He had come without calling. He took a quick look but was not interested. We learned from that experience always to be prepared, and we sold a couple months later.

What about our spiritual lives? Could the same be true? Can we change our deeds after the Son of man appears in the sky? What will it be for those who, like Judas, are determined to reject God's word and scorn His name? What will happen to those who neglect their preparation for that great day?

The return of our Lord Jesus to this earth is closer than we know. The great conflict is about to end. Have you been waiting so long for your heavenly home that in your busy life you have neglected your spiritual home? Have you allowed filthiness, mildew, and the darkness in to corrupt walls that were once clean? Is there trash scattered around your spiritual home? Have you neglected to keep things in order in your heart? Are you ready for Jesus to come?   OLGA VALDIVIA

A Gardener's Commission

You crown the year with your bounty, and your carts overflow with abundance. Ps. 65:11, NIV.

She hears the whisper
of "garden" in her ear
And stirs within herself,
Responding to the call.
It's time to plan, to design
Her plot of earth
To hold summer's cache;
An artist's vision
Grand, bursting forth
Through tended soil
From minikin seeds sown
By her gentle hands.
Then, fruits emerging
Like fine artwork,
As offerings of love,
Bouquets and loaves and
Canning jars fat-full
With tasty pantry fare.
Ah, yes! Her very soul
reaches up like eager crocus
When she hears the garden whisper.
For surely the bounty
Equals her commission.

Gardening is not something I do well. I never was very good with a spade. My admiration goes especially deep for my friend Emma, walking toward age 90, who so loves her garden. But she never tends it just for herself; to her it's a commission from God. When Emma hears "garden," she knows her work is for others, and she goes at it with gusto.

By her example as a good gardener I understand that I am a gardener too, albeit a spiritual one. I can till a heart, be a blessing, share the love of Jesus. I can help people grow. I too can have a harvest, rich and fragrant. Yes, I have a gardener's commission too, and it isn't just for me.

BETTY KOSSICK

Food for the Journey

*Joseph gave orders to fill their bags with grain . . .
and to give them provisions for their journey. Gen. 42:25, NIV.*

I have to admit that I didn't enjoy studying at Sparsholt. Yet I had to drive there every morning and back again in the evenings, five days a week, for two full years. With classmates and most teachers unfavorable to Christianity, my spirit often felt starved. Sparsholt was a land of famine for me.

How grateful, then, I was for the daily journey! While others fought their way through traffic jams, most of my journey was along little English lanes. Already keyed up, tense for the fearsome day ahead, I would find a sense of sudden relaxation as I dropped off the third exit into the depths of the countryside.

In autumn I discovered the bridge of gold, where sycamores joined their yellow-leaved branches overhead, lighting up the dullest rainy day. In winter God traced fine lines of beech twigs in black ink against the sky for my delight. For spring He opened a picnic box of delicious sights! He embroidered pink petal rosettes all over a small cherry tree opposite the Littleton village church. He drifted a sequence of wildflowers along two banks: modest bells of snowdrops, shiny stars of yellow celandine, paler primroses, purple sweet violets, and wild trumpets of daffodils.

Throughout the year He charmed away my anxieties with the gamesome frolic of a wild rabbit on the verge; the thrill of a roe deer leaping the lane; the metallic shine of green on a pheasant's neck above his russet body and long-decked tail; or just a bright-eyed English robin; a lonely horse, head over gate, waiting for company; and the artistry, the moods of many clouds.

Coming home tired and worn, I'd swing out of the city boundary line into a lane so small that it seemed a lane to peace. There I'd find a moon bathing in a foam of clouds; the winter velvet dark; the song of a thrush to cheer me; solitude to revel in; the curving contours of the hills to lap me round.

If Joseph, being human, could give good gifts to his brothers and food for the journey, how much more my best Brother opens gifts to me, hides more in sacks of time, and gives me heart food for my daily journeys.

APRIL DUNNETT

Scrubbing Toilets and Wiping Bottoms

Whatever you do, whether in word or deed, do it all in the name of the Lord Jesus, giving thanks to God the Father through him. Col. 3:17, NIV.

When I quit nursing to stay home to be a full-time mother, I imagined my life taking a dramatic turn for the better. Somehow I saw myself becoming a woman of leisure, with nothing to do but dote on adorable children in cute bonnets and booties.

At work I could singlehandedly manage nine infants in the new-born nursery. Certainly one little baby at home could hardly demand any time at all! After all, don't babies sleep most of the time? (I can hear mothers of great wisdom snickering at such inexperience. With two children now, I laugh just recalling my foolish expectations.)

So today, after nine years of motherhood, I still wipe bottoms, use a little bit of elbow grease to erase scuff marks off the kitchen floor, and yes, every Wednesday scrub the toilets. Sometimes I wonder, *What's a nice girl like me doing in a place like this? It's so routine, dull, mundane.*

But that's the point. God began to show me that I could be thankful that I have two healthy children who need to be wiped. I can be glad that we have shoes to scuff up the floor and that I have strong hands to scrub. There is a godly dignity in scrubbing the toilets. I can scrub those toilets to the glory of God. I can count it a privilege to bring Him honor as I cheerfully fulfill my seemingly dull routine.

Isn't it interesting that the King of kings, and the Lord of lords, Creator of all, spent most of His life in a carpenter's shop? Certainly Christ's work was often routine, dull, and mundane. He could have said, "What's the Messiah doing in a place like this?" Yet our Saviour did not consider any task too unimportant for His attention. His life was quiet and simple as He walked in humility upon this earth. Our Lord was doing God's service at the carpenter's bench just as surely as when He was thronged by the multitudes.

Yes, I too can follow Christ's example of faithfulness in my humble duties. When I find myself performing what may be considered a lowly task, I just remember my humble Saviour. I experience great joy in glorifying my Father in heaven in all that I do for Him.

JULIE REYNOLDS

Touched by an Angel

*"Behold, I send an Angel before you to keep you in the way,
and to bring you into the place which I have prepared." Ex. 23:20, NKJV.*

Here are my 11 cents," I called to the clerk at the back of the store as I set my money on the counter for the one cigarette that would relieve my terrible cravings.

As I turned, a tap came on my shoulder, and there stood a very handsome man, about six feet tall. He said, "You're trying to quit, aren't you?"

"Yes," I said. "I just need one, and then I can continue to quit. I can't take it anymore."

He reached out and took the cigarette from my hand and replaced it in the jar on the counter, handed back my 11 cents, and said, "Go home; everything will be fine." His was the most gentle voice that I have ever heard.

I immediately left the convenience store as if someone were leading me. The tall handsome man . . . Where was he? I didn't see anyone in the store, no one on the sidewalk, and nobody driving away in a car. Where had my benefactor gone?

There was no hesitation on my part as I hastened home. Safely inside, I realized that an angel had come to my rescue and saved me from a near crisis. After smoking for more than 35 years (and at times three packs a day), I had now accepted Christ. With Christ in my life there was no room for a lifestyle riddled with unhealthy practices. It was not by my might or power but by God's Spirit that I was able to live according to His will. I believe God intervened that day to give me the victory over nicotine.

But fleshly cravings do not give up without a battle. This experience did not mean that all cravings and needs were gone. In my moments of weakness I could hear a gentle voice saying, "Go home; it will be fine."

I think of 1 Corinthians 10:13: "God is faithful, who will not allow you to be tempted beyond what you are able, but with the temptation will also make the way of escape, that you may be able to bear it" (NKJV). God knew I would be unable to resist without my angel's help, and He made a way of escape for me. I long for the day when my Lord says, "Come home; it will be fine."   PHYLLIS ALEXANDER

Yes, Jesus Loves Me!

If we confess our sins, he is faithful and just and will forgive us our sins and purify us from all unrighteousness. 1 John 1:9, NIV.

C an God really love me?" is the lament often voiced by women who have been sexually abused in childhood. Where was God when I was hurt? Did He abandon me? Is this just a sinful world where bad things happen to innocent children? Sometimes the woman still feels unloved, especially by God. She feels tarnished, used, secondhand. These are powerful emotions and must be validated.

One day I was meditating on 1 John 1:9. I humbly and in solemn awe believed that through the life and death of Jesus I could be given a fair and just forgiveness of all my sins, remembered or forgotten.

I had always thought this text was to encourage me that God will wash me from the dirt of daily sins. But the nagging fear that never left me was *Am I really good enough for God to love?* It was an intrinsic fear that no matter what I did, it would never be good enough for a holy God.

As I studied and prayed for wisdom, this text became clear in a way that I had never understood before. It was as if God encircled the last portion of the text in bright letters and was saying, "My beautiful daughter, please see that I am making a promise to you."

Suddenly it was as though my eyes were opened and my mind able to understand a new concept. God was saying to me that He is loving enough, powerful enough, and able enough to purify me from all the unrighteousness done to me. He would cleanse me of the sins perpetrated on me as a young, innocent child and for which I had carried shame. God would completely make me "white as snow" in His eyes. I felt a peace and acceptance of His cleansing love wash over me. My heart lifted with praise.

It's not always easy to remember that God loves me and sees me as His perfect and purified child. So when I am confronted with my human failings and start to berate myself for not being perfect, I go to my room, where I have a picture of me as a 4-year-old hanging on the wall. I look at that precious little child and sing out loud, "Yes, Jesus loves me."

JANIS CLARK VANCE

Tire Blowout

*He will give His angels charge concerning you, to guard you in all your
ways. Ps. 91:11, NASB.*

My mother and I were driving home from visiting relatives
about 10:00 at night. We were laughing, singing, and talking
over old family memories when suddenly there was a loud bang, and
the car wobbled wildly.

"What was that?" I asked, fighting to control the car.

"I think we've had a blowout," Mother said. "Just get safely off
the road."

As I tried to steer the car off the highway, my mother began to
pray aloud. "Heavenly Father, please help Eleanor to control the car
and get us off the highway safely."

I was able to pull off the highway, but help would have to come
from a passing motorist. Neither Mom nor I had any idea how to
change a tire. Automobiles whizzed past. Some blinked their lights.
Some honked. None stopped. A half hour passed.

"You know," Mother said, "I think I'll just ask the Lord to send us
someone to change this tire." With that she closed her eyes and
prayed aloud, "Lord, You see where we are. You see what's wrong.
Now send us someone to change this tire."

Car lights beamed into the back of our window. A young man got
out of his truck with a jack in his hand. My mother leaped out of the
car and said, "Praise the Lord for sending you. I was just asking the
Lord to send us someone to change our tire. Are you an angel?"

The man smiled and set about efficiently changing our tire. He
seemed to know exactly what he was doing. I handed him the trunk
key. In a matter of minutes the spare was on the car and the trunk
closed. He smiled again and wordlessly handed me the car keys.

"Can I pay you?" I called after him as he turned toward his truck.

Again he just smiled and waved, hopped into his truck, and drove
away. Strange that he had not spoken a word, and that he had
changed the tire in less than five minutes. We both stood motionless
in the darkness as he pulled onto the highway and drove away.

"Do you think God sent an angel?" I asked Mother in hushed tones.

ELLIE GREEN

Rest in the Lord

Come unto me, all ye that labour and are heavy laden,
and I will give you rest. Matt. 11:28.

Getting a good night's sleep comes easier for some people than it does for others. My husband, for example, can crawl into bed, get himself in a comfortable position, and be snoring away in a matter of minutes. My two daughters have also been blessed with this ability.

I, on the other hand, have the most trouble getting to sleep. As tired as my body may be, my mind seems to be overcharged with energy. It has always been that way with me. Sometimes hours go by, and no matter how much tossing and turning I do trying to get in a comfortable position, sleep seems to elude me.

One night I had a most unforgettable experience. I lay in bed long after my husband fell asleep, having the usual trouble getting my own rest. I kept thinking of my day's experiences, those of the past week, and before I knew it, it seemed that my whole life was passing before me, with all my mistakes and failures. I simply could not rest, much less sleep.

In pure desperation I cried out to God, remembering some of the promises He has given us in His Word. It was time to claim them for myself.

Lord, You said that we should come to You if we are heavy laden and You would give us rest. Then there's the song, "Roll, Roll Your Burdens Away." You said to cast our burdens upon You and You would sustain us. You have promised to give us peace and rest. I need that, Lord.

Then I said, *Open Your arms wide, Lord, here come all my burdens!* I could picture those burdens rolling away from me into the arms of God.

After naming everything that was bothering me, from the most recent back to the incidents that had happened years before, I said, *All right, Lord, they're Yours now; I don't want them anymore. I need my rest now. Good night, Lord.*

Then I turned over on my side and immediately fell asleep. I don't think I have ever had such a good night's sleep.

Thank You, God, for Your promises, especially those that provide rest.

ROSE MARIE BROWN

Fire in the Manse

*"When you walk through the fire, you will not be burned;
the flames will not set you ablaze." Isa. 43:2, NIV.*

One morning my phone rang. Our young pastor's wife, calling
from a neighbor's phone, was sobbing. "My house is on fire!"
she cried. "Can you come?"

We went immediately. The scene was devastating. Fire trucks were
everywhere. It was several hours before we could enter what was left
of the house. Everything they owned was either gone or badly damaged by the fire. What was not in ashes was covered with black soot.
The smoke smell was almost unbearable. We were all in shock.

But God began providing for every need. One neighbor offered a
two-bedroom apartment in their basement. Another neighbor
brought in groceries. The Red Cross provided funds for clothing. The
dry cleaners offered to clean, without charge, everything that could
not be washed. The school did a large load of linens in their laundry.
Folks took bags of items home to be cleaned. Money came from their
family, church members, fellow pastors, and the community.

Someone brought a new Bosch and mill grinder. This special ap-
pliance for baking and cooking, although a small item compared to
the family's larger needs, brought such joy to our pastor's wife. It
demonstrated that God provides even the small things in life.

Just when they would be overwhelmed and discouraged, God
sent someone or something to remind them, "I am God; I love you
and will care for you." Taking one step at a time and one day at a
time they pieced their lives back together. It was evident that God
walked with them through their trial by fire.

And our faith was strengthened as we saw how God provided.
Our love for fellow church members and neighbors who helped deepened. Our respect for community people who used their means and
influence increased. In a very secular and often selfish society we
were reminded of not only God's love, but the love and caring spirit
of friends, church members, and even total strangers. We were inspired as we saw the family meet each hurdle with trust in the Lord. I
am more certain that God will always walk with us as we pass
through the fires of life.

JUNE E. LOOR

Simple Pleasures

I have learned to be content with whatever I have. Phil. 4:11, NRSV.

I enjoy the sound of the mourning dove. I often hear its almost haunting call through my open window, reminding me of the whistle of a freight train off in the distance. If someone were to ask me to make a list of my life's pleasures, I would be hard-pressed to number them in order of their importance because I have so many.

My faith in God and my fellowship with my church are high on my list. My family is very important to me—my two children and their spouses, my six grandchildren, and my two great-grandbabies hold that special place in my heart.

I really look forward to that quiet time by myself, curled up with a good book or video, or maybe just relaxing contemplation. I find pleasure in writing letters and short stories, even though some of them may wind up in the cylindrical file. I enjoy listening to good music, ranging from symphonies to gospel or whatever suits my fancy at the moment.

I have nourishing food to sustain me, and I find enormous pleasure in crawling between clean crisp sheets when I'm tired and my body is crying for sleep.

I'm not a big spender, so closets full of clothes and hoards of "stuff" and "things" do not impress me. But I'm thankful for my 1989 Ford Tempo that may be in need of repairs soon. For the time being, though, it gets me where I want to go, and I appreciate that.

I'm basking in the warm sunshine as I watch a blanket of white clouds nesting in a bright blue sky. I love the fragrance of the old-fashioned pink roses growing in profusion along my driveway hedge. It seems as though they've been there forever.

I look forward to the rain. I love the sound of it on the roof and its musical spattering on my window sill.

What is it about life that can be so pleasurable for some people and so miserable for others? I don't have the answer, but I do know that sometimes we have to make our own happy times.

Life can be filled with joy if we learn to appreciate the simple pleasures God gives.

CLAREEN COLCLESSER

Highway Breakdown

Call unto me, and I will answer thee, and shew thee great and mighty things, which thou knowest not. Jer. 33:3.

My children and I were traveling on Interstate 95 from Huntsville, Alabama, to Sicklerville, New Jersey. We had attended a college alumni weekend and were on the last portion of our trip homeward. The van seemed to be performing well when all of a sudden it stopped, and we steered it to the side of the road.

I got out and lifted the hood. "Everything looks fine to me," I told the children. I tried again to start the engine. No response. I had no idea what to do next.

"We could pray," one child suggested.

"Jesus will help us," another agreed.

So we had a season of prayer right there with trucks and cars whizzing past. We each asked the Lord to intervene. We had just stopped praying when a man drove up in a red Camaro.

"You need some help?" he asked. "What can I do for you?"

After we explained our trouble, he offered to take someone to the nearest exit to call a tow truck. I decided my two oldest children would accompany him. As the car drove away, I prayed for their safe return.

The children returned with the man and informed me a repair shop was at the next exit and a tow truck was en route. We thanked the man for being so helpful. The tow truck came and towed the van, but the repair shop was closing as we arrived. "We'll fix it first thing in the morning," a mechanic informed me.

Our funds were very low, and we had just enough money for supper. "Lord, help us!" I sent another petition to the throne. "Now what do we do? How can I pay for repairs or a motel?"

Then I thought of friends who lived not far away. They helped us get a place to stay for the night. The shop repaired the van the next day, and my husband wired the money for the repairs.

The Lord had answered all our prayers and blessed us with safe travel the remainder of the trip home. My heart was filled with joy just to realize that God had been with us every mile of our trip. He had seen us through each trial as we trusted in Him.

SHARON MARSHALL-RANDALL

Weeds or Flowers?

Take heed that ye despise not one of these little ones. Matt. 18:10.

Your girls are growing like weeds," a church member observed. The girls *had* been growing, I knew. I had just packed away too-small clothes and brought out boxes of the next size up. "Oh, they're not growing like weeds," I shot back. "They're growing like beautiful flowers." I didn't want my precious girls ever to think of themselves as weeds.

"Flowers don't grow that fast—only weeds do!" came the somewhat cynical reply.

Later the same person passed me on the way out the door. "My kids sure aren't flowers. They're more like weeds."

The hurt, pain, and disappointment in his voice made my heart ache. I wondered if this man's children grew up thinking of themselves as weeds or flowers.

"Growing" children cannot be rushed. Like fine flowers, they must be nurtured and tended constantly. Weeds grow with no outside intervention, but tender, desirable flower shoots must be protected, fed, and watered if they are to be hardy and productive.

My grandmother loved flowers, especially wildflowers that she would gather from the woods and transplant into her garden. The common little purple violets flourished in her yard, threatening to become a nuisance. I dug a large clump and gave them a place of honor in my flower beds, where they grew large and lush. To some they are just a wildflower, but I love their joyful little faces, and the heart-shaped leaves add a nice undergrowth.

Grandma, however, did not like the tall, stately, old-fashioned hollyhocks that I use to add height to my flower beds. I think they are beautiful, easy to grow, and indispensable in a country garden. But then, beauty is in the eye of the beholder.

Am I conveying to my children that they are beautiful flowers to me? They may be only common violets to others, but they will have a place of honor in my garden. If we parents aren't our children's chief cheering section, who will help them to feel they are lovely flowers in the garden of God?   ANN MALONEY-HALIM

God Works in Our Lives

I am convinced that neither death nor life, neither angels nor demons,
neither the present nor the future, nor any powers, neither height nor depth,
nor anything else in all creation, will be able to separate us from
the love of God that is in Christ Jesus our Lord. Rom. 8:38, 39, NIV.

That afternoon was like all others. There was nothing interesting happening. Things were running so monotonously normal that I no longer looked for anything new. Suddenly my son placed a letter in my hands from my sister, Celia. Before I opened it, a lifetime of memories flowed through my mind.

I saw a frail little girl who was so skinny that her bones showed. Her freckle-covered face wasn't all that pretty; she was plain and unattractive. A later picture showed Celia holding her son, Caio, in her arms. No longer plain or skinny, she looked healthy and strong. A shining smile made her face beautiful.

Eagerly I opened her letter. We lived so far apart that letters were our only contact. This letter told news of her family, her son, his mischief, and how God was blessing her life.

Few in my family are religious. Most do not care for God. We never had the opportunity to study the Bible. Father never allowed us to attend church. He thought it a waste of time and felt that the church never saved anybody.

After I grew up, I decided to study the Holy Scriptures. But no one else in the family seemed interested. I was even asked not to comment on God's Word. Whenever the opportunity came, I invited someone from my family to go to church with me, but chores, laziness, or indifference always prevented them from going.

Celia wrote, "You may be surprised to know this, but I always have admired you for your faith. I wanted to have the happiness, peace, and joy that you have, so I began reading the Bible as you do. I find it a great help. Jesus is changing my life." Then she quoted Romans 8:38, 39.

Tears of joy rolled down my cheeks. I felt so happy to know God had used me to touch my sister's life. Sometimes speaking of Jesus to people seems in vain, but it is good to remember that the seed remains. One day it will germinate and bear fruit, eternal fruit for our Saviour Jesus Christ. RUTI RODRIGUES DE CARVALHO GARCIA DOS SANTOS

Honeybun's Choice

*You are a people holy to the Lord your God. Out of all the peoples
on the face of the earth, the Lord has chosen
you to be his treasured possession. Deut. 14:2, NIV.*

My cousin, Sue, is married to a very happy, friendly trucker named David. At one house where David frequently made deliveries lived a dog named Honeybun, who just loved David. Every time David brought a package to this house, Honeybun came out and greeted him, tail wagging, a happy dog smile on her face.

David began to notice that Honeybun was getting rounder, and eventually it was certain that she was expecting puppies. Most mother dogs become a bit crabby when they have new puppies. Not Honeybun. In fact, the first time David made a delivery after the puppies were born, Honeybun actually ran out to meet him. Then she made it very clear that she wanted David to follow her to see her babies. Now, that was unusual in itself, but you'd never guess what Honeybun did next. She picked up one of her puppies and laid it at David's feet.

Several weeks later Sue and David decided they would like to have a puppy and thought they might adopt one of Honeybun's babies. So David called the family and learned that there was one puppy left. When Sue and David arrived, they discovered that the remaining puppy was the one that Honeybun had already picked out and presented to David. There was no question—they were supposed to have that very dog! She had already been chosen for them!

They named her Mindy. And Mindy has grown up to be a hairy, bearlike dog who is just as sweet as her mother was. Mindy is getting to be an old dog now, but she still brings lots of joy to my cousin and her husband.

You and I are chosen too, but we're chosen by God. Each morning when you wake up, say to Him, "Here I am, God. If there is anything You want me to do for You today, just send Your Holy Spirit to tell me. I'm already Yours, because You have chosen me."

BARBARA HUFF

Trusting God With My Friends

This also cometh forth from the Lord of hosts, which is wonderful in counsel, and excellent in working. Isa. 28:29.

I knew I had read the passage before, but never had its words spoken so clearly. In my devotions that morning I had been praying for friends on my prayer list. They were friends who were immersed in pressing problems, more so now than ever before, it seemed, and all I could give them was encouragement and prayer.

One had had a leg surgically removed and was grieving. Another was in constant pain because of a back injury, but couldn't rest or stop working because of financial and family responsibilities. Others were mourning the loss of loved ones. Some had financial difficulties. It seemed there was no way out.

As I prayed, I longed to make a difference. I lingered over each name, asking God for solutions, for His presence, for blessings for them, for comfort. This time as I prayed I felt sad. "Are my prayers really making a difference?" I asked God. "Why am I so sad? Why doesn't anything seem to happen? Why can't I see Your power at work?"

I opened my Bible and read Isaiah 28. When I got to verses 24 to 29, I took note. It told how the farmer plowed the ground. He didn't plow all day, only long enough to break up the ground. He scattered the seed precisely as needed and where needed.

Suddenly my heart thrilled as I caught the significance of what I was reading. God knows what is happening. He doesn't allow "plowing" more than necessary. The passage went on to say that the fragile herbs are harvested gently. Even though our trials don't feel gentle to us, God is working with us carefully and gently, as the farmer works with the crops. Then the passage is summed up with this: "The Lord . . . is wonderful in counsel, and excellent in working."

That text seemed to say, "Trust your friends with Me. I will take care of those you are praying for so earnestly. I will do what is best for each one. I will work carefully in their lives so that there is a rich harvest. I know what I'm doing."

Help me, Lord, just for today, to trust my friends in Your loving care. Plow, plant, cultivate, and harvest Your will in their lives. Help me to be patient as I wait for You to do Your work. EDNA MAYE GALLINGTON

A Taste of Kindness

She extends her hand to the poor, . . . and on her tongue
is the law of kindness. Prov. 31:20-26, NKJV.

We were traveling from our mission field in West Africa to Britain on furlough, stopping over in Amsterdam. We had written ahead to the church, asking for some inexpensive accommodation.

When we arrived, we were alarmed to find no one to meet us and no message. We had a phone number, but the office was closed. Our financial resources were limited, and our three small boys were noisy and irritable from a day of being cooped up in a plane. Explaining our situation to the man at the hotel reservation desk, we asked if he could find us some inexpensive accommodations. A few phone calls later he called a cab and gave directions.

We seemed to travel for miles. Finally we were ushered up the steps and into a warm, inviting guesthouse. Our room was large with space for the cots brought in for the boys.

As we unpacked, our host said, "Why don't you give the boys their supper and settle them in bed? Then you and your husband go out and have a nice meal together. We'll listen out for them."

What a treat! It seemed like years since we had been alone together.

The next morning I remarked that I very much liked one of the cheeses our host had served for breakfast. She smiled and told me how famous Holland is for its cheeses. When we came to settle our bill, we had a surprise. The cost of the room was less than anticipated. Then she reached under the counter and pulled out a package wrapped in aluminum foil.

"This is for you," she assured me. "We have been so happy to have you staying with us." She was treating us like invited guests, not paying customers. "I cannot go and be a missionary, but you have brought the mission field to us. God bless you."

The package turned out to be two kilos of the cheese I had liked. I have never forgotten her, though that was 25 years ago. I never knew her name, but I shall never forget her, and I continue to thank God for her ministry.

I have tried to follow her example by being generous, thoughtful, kindhearted. VALERIA FIDELIA

As a Child

Except ye be converted, and become as little children,
ye shall not enter into the kingdom of heaven. Matt. 18:3.

R ecently we were faced with an international move. There were
hundreds of details to attend to, both with the home we would
be leaving and the one we would be moving to. Although this was to
be a temporary assignment for my husband's job, it created myriad
deadlines and mounds of paperwork. So many loose ends needed to be
tied up before we could leave. The task seemed unending, yet we
looked forward to the move with a certain excitement and expectation.

Interspersed with the excitement, anticipation, and planning was
our concern for our three girls, all under the age of 5. Of concern was
not only their physical needs, but the emotional impact of such a
move. From my reading on the subject I discovered that the baby
would be least affected. She would take her cues from us, her parents. Her needs would center around the love and nurture that we
would offer. We would provide the stability she needed for contentment and security. As long as her physical needs continued to be met,
and we continued to give her the usual level of love and nurture, she
would be little affected by the upheaval.

What a lesson that holds! If I am as a child, then it doesn't matter
where I am. As long as I live in the presence of my heavenly Father
with daily interaction through my devotional life, I will be little affected by the major changes. God has promised that He will never
leave me. He has promised to meet my every need. With Him by my
side I can be content no matter where life takes me, and in whatever
situations come my way I can remain secure. Should I miss this daily
interaction with Him through Bible study and prayer, I miss the stability He can provide. Without Him I will easily be overwhelmed by
the changes in my life. I am complete in Him. Like a small child, I
need nothing more.

Resting in the arms of my heavenly Father I have nothing to fear
from the upheaval around me. He provides the stability I need. It
doesn't matter where I am or what conditions I face, I am content
knowing He loves me and cares for my every need.

SHERYL A. CALHOUN

The Wedgwood Egg

Whom have I in heaven but you?
And earth has nothing I desire besides you. Ps. 73:25, NIV.

I will never forget my twenty-first birthday, the most important birthday I ever had. On it I received my first gift from Jonathan.

Jonathan and I lived about 90 miles apart. We hardly ever saw each other, as both of us were planning to go to college and needed to save as much money as we could. We nurtured our friendship through the mail service.

The mail carriers received plenty of exercise with the numerous 10-to 12-page letters we exchanged. One time Jonathan ran after the mail carrier and made him rummage through his sack, as he was sure there was a letter from me. That was the one day I hadn't written!

One day the mail carrier delivered a little box that contained a blue and white Wedgwood egg. I still treasure it—it sits in a very special place in our bedroom. The gift was important, as it showed me that Jonathan cared.

Since then I have received many gifts from Jonathan and have valued each one. The gifts have not only been practical, but something that I really wanted or needed.

As much as I appreciate the gifts that my husband has given me, I value his friendship more. Memories of walking hand in hand, talking late into the night, sharing a joke, are treasures I cherish. I'm glad Jonathan is my friend, and not just a giver of gifts.

Sometimes we can view God as the giver of gifts instead of a friend. We too easily forget that the primary purpose of a relationship with God is enjoying each other's company. Talking late at night, chuckling over a joke, walking and sharing together are not only for those in our earthly home, but can happen with God, too.

It is those times when we make no requests of God that a real depth of friendship is forged. When we permit God to be a part of our lives for the sheer pleasure of being in His presence, something very special occurs in our fellowship.

In your relationship with God, aim to value Him for what He is. It will make an incredible difference in your friendship.

MARY BARRETT

Caught in the Act

All have sinned, and come short of the glory of God. Rom. 3:23.

I was spending my holidays with my sister's family. My 3-year-old niece liked to eat a cereal that was kept on the top of a cupboard. We didn't know she had a habit of eating it dry when no one was around. One day she thought nobody was watching, so she pulled out the shelves, climbed up, opened the tin, and started eating cereal. She was so absorbed she did not see the housemaid come in. The surprised housemaid was about to speak when my niece noticed her and began to shout, *"Cerelac mi ni, Cerelac mi ni."* ("It is my Cerelac. It is my Cerelac.")

It was the cry of ownership that brought me to the scene. There my niece was, perched lightly like a bird on the high shelf, tin cover in hand, boldly defending her actions. She was unaware of the fact that she could fall down and injure herself.

I burst out laughing when I saw her. I brought her down and pacified her, but I couldn't stop laughing.

How like my niece we all are! When caught in sin we defend ourselves instead of acknowledging our guilt. My niece couldn't help herself out of her situation. She was in danger but didn't understand that. She needed somebody greater than herself to help her down. She needed someone wiser than herself to help her understand. She needed to learn, to grow.

Often we do not realize our danger either. We need someone to help us. Of course that Somebody is Jesus. We cannot get out of our dangerous situations without His power, without His taking us in His strong, secure arms. We cannot break away from sin without His assistance. We may not realize it any more than my niece realized her peril, but we need Him just the same.

As we relax in His arms of love, we are safe. He will teach us, helping us to understand how He wants us to live. Then He will give us the strength to grow to be what He wants us to be. BECKY DADA

Watch the Peg You Choose!

It is better to trust in the Lord than to put confidence in man. Ps. 118:8.

My 5-year-old son held in his chubby hands a bright red wooden train engine he had received for his birthday. Of all the gifts he'd been given, that was his favorite.

"I want to take it to school to show my friends," he said. "Will it be all right, Mama?" His eyes sparkled with the thought of the fun he would have with the train that day at school.

"Of course you may take it," I agreed. "But look after it carefully. Don't forget to bring it home again after school."

"I will take care of it," he promised.

He carried his precious possession to school. He was careful not to drop it. When the bell rang, he entered the school and went to the row of pegs where the children hung their coats. He placed his coat on his peg, then balanced the little red engine on top of the peg so he wouldn't forget it when it was time to go home.

When his class was dismissed, he hurried to the row of pegs and looked for his little red train engine. It was not where he had left it. He looked on the floor, thinking it might have fallen, but no engine was in sight. He looked all around, but his toy wasn't there. He ran out of the school and all of the way home, tears streaming down his face.

"What's wrong?" I asked. "Something dreadful must have happened at school today!"

Between sobs he told me. "I—put my train—so safely—on my peg. Now it is gone!"

Tears came to my own eyes as I held him close. *The sweet innocent trust of a little child!* I thought. *Until today he didn't know about the evils in the world. Poor, poor child! His trust is shattered!*

My heart ached for him. He loved that train so much!

My son is grown now. I'm thankful to say he has learned that although you can't always trust human beings, you can always trust God. He will never let you down.

On which peg are you putting your trust? Friends, family, and church members may shatter your trust, but Jesus will never fail you! He alone is worthy of your trust!   MARJORIE DAVISON

The Bubble Gum

Be sure your sin will find you out. Num. 32:23.

School was coming to a close for another term, and I was delighted. This time we were going on holiday to visit an uncle and aunt who lived nearly 900 miles (1,440 kilometers) away.

After the long journey to Johannesburg, we exchanged greetings, then Uncle asked the children to go to the shop up the road to buy soft drinks. How our eyes lit up when he gave us pocket money, as well as money to buy the soft drinks.

We children didn't know what it was to receive pocket money. When we were bold enough to ask, we were told that Dad couldn't afford to give us pocket money, and we must not compare ourselves with other children whose parents could afford to, so we had to be satisfied.

We were so thrilled as we planned what we were going to buy with our money. As we looked around the shop, our eyes fell on all the assorted gum. But we weren't allowed to chew gum—even if someone gave it to us.

"Oh, that would be nice to try; let's buy it," I said. "We can walk extra slow and enjoy blowing the bubbles on our way home. Mother will never know."

We were very excited as we kept talking, and as we entered the gate we realized we were still enjoying forbidden bubble gum. Quickly we removed the gum from our mouths; I slipped mine into the pocket of my pretty dress Mom had made for our holidays.

The next day was laundry day. Mom called me aside and showed me the pocket that was stuck closed with the bubble gum. She asked "What's this?"

Out came the I story; I had to confess.

She said to me, "Even if you think you can hide from your mother, you cannot hide from God. 'Be sure your sin will find you out.'"

Though I was about 8 years old, I have never forgotten. I have been reminded of that story many times when tempted to do something secretly that I knew was wrong. My family and friends may never find out, but I cannot hide from God. I live every moment in His presence.

PRISCILLA ADONIS

Counterfeit Christians

*"So, every sound tree bears good fruit, but the bad tree bears evil fruit. . . .
Thus you will know them by their fruits." Matt. 7:17-20, RSV.*

Gardening is one of my hobbies. I once planted and nurtured a plant that I thought was a miniature poinsettia. But when it blossomed, it produced ugly, colorless flowers instead of the rich velvety red ones I had expected. I then realized it was a weed. I was very disappointed.

In my garden I have both the genuine and the counterfeit growing side by side. I found it difficult to tell the difference before they bloomed, so I became interested in counterfeit plants and discovered more of them. Not long ago I found a counterfeit papyrus plant. It resembled the real one except for the size.

Just as there are counterfeit plants, there are counterfeit Christians. We cannot tell, nor are we to judge, who is a genuine Christian or who is a counterfeit one. God allows the genuine and the counterfeit to grow and worship together. Jesus' parable of the wheat and the tares teaches that we are not to pull out those that look counterfeit lest while weeding the genuine are hurt. At the end-time harvest the wheat will be gathered and the tares burned. Then only will we know who is real and who is counterfeit.

At times I ask myself, "Am I a true Christian or am I a counterfeit?" How can we differentiate? Jesus said, "Not everyone who says to me, 'Lord, Lord,' shall enter the kingdom of heaven, but he who does the will of my Father who is in heaven" (Matt. 7:21, RSV). He also said, "Thus you will know them by their fruits" (verse 17).

It is important for me to bear the fruits of the Spirit which are "love, joy, peace, patience, kindness, goodness, faithfulness, gentleness, self-control" (Gal. 5:22, 23, RSV). But if the fruit is not there, does that make me a counterfeit without hope?

Unlike the weed, by the grace of God the counterfeit Christian can be changed into the genuine by responding to the transforming power of the Holy Spirit.

Lord, transform me today. Make me a true Christian, one who loves You always and bears Your fruit. BIROL CHRISTO

A New Day

This is the day the Lord has made;
let us rejoice and be glad in it. Ps. 118:24, NIV.

The alarm rang. I rolled over and shut it off, hoping to snatch a few more moments of sleep before a busy day of speaking at a Christian women's retreat in Poppi, Italy. However, nature was calling, so I threw back the covers, pulled on my housecoat, and made my way down the hall to the bathroom.

Back in my room, I noticed how stale the air smelled. The light was dim, and the bed inviting. I wanted to crawl back under the warm blankets and sleep. Instead I went to the window and threw open the shutters. I breathed deeply of the fresh, cool mountain air that flowed into the room, feeling suddenly awake and alive to the glory of a new day. Sunlight streamed across the windowsill, brightening my heart. Finches twittered in nearby trees, and from somewhere to the left a blackbird sang.

Beyond the trees a mountain mist hid farmhouses and cow pastures I had seen the day before. A small brown lizard scurried across the tiles of the sloping roof that led away from my window to a paved courtyard below, where boxes of pink geraniums bloomed.

What a way to begin the day! I thought. *Thank You, Lord, for this moment of brightness and joy!*

As I drank in the beauty of the Tuscany landscape, the mist slowly dissipated, revealing cows grazing on the hillside pasture where red poppies bloomed in profusion. It felt good to be alive, to have eyes and ears to absorb such loveliness.

Lord, this morning I throw open the windows of my soul. Your Holy Spirit comes in, refreshing me, bringing me new life and joy. Your love floods over me with its warmth, light, and energy. Your voice to me is like the singing of the morning birds. My heart echoes their songs of life, joy, and hope. Thank You, Lord, for this day! What a day to be alive!

DOROTHY EATON WATTS

Trees

Thou hast created all things, and for thy pleasure they are and were created. Rev. 4:11.

The weeping willow in the garden swayed softly in the gentle breeze. The early morning felt cool and fresh. The sun slipped above the horizon, its rays caressing the dogs relaxing in the sunshine beside me, burning away a summer haze that wrapped the distant hills.

Everywhere trees grew, filling the valley with their rich growth—birch and beech, oak and sycamore. The birds exchanged musical messages—magpies, woodpeckers, blue tits, green finches, nuthatches, and robins.

The hymn "This Is My Father's World" came to my mind. I thought, *His love is so great He created all these wonderful trees and birds for our pleasure. He gave them to help us escape from the tensions of modern life.*

A footpath nearby led to the woods, where bluebells bloomed. Beyond, a field displayed a riot of buttercups, daisies, cowslips, and clover. Butterflies flitted happily in the sun.

When my problems make me feel tense or preoccupied, I take a walk to the woods to be near trees. Even one tree can give great pleasure and respite. In the strength of its rough bark I feel security; under its green branches I stop in its dappled light and wonder how long these trees have been standing here. The seasons come and go, but these gracious trees still stand.

When we compare these great gifts of life with human-made forms of leisure and entertainment, we realize how superior the trees are. Tiny seeds grow and grow from strength to strength. What stability there is in a tree!

The left side of my face is quite warm now with the sun's rays. I can hear a cow and the sounds of sheep. A dog barks! I close my eyes and feel the peace and serenity permeate my entire being as I say, "Thank You, dear Lord, for another gift of life, a gift of peace. How good to have even these few moments away from any worries and cares! These trees have been to me like a healing refuge. Thank You for creating them for my pleasure." PHILIPPA MARSHALL

The $50 Wedding Dress

"Ask and you will receive, and your joy will be complete." John 16:24, NIV.

I was just 22 when I walked down the aisle with a young man who held a much different belief system from my own. One year later I was broken—physically, emotionally, and spiritually—and the marriage had dissolved. With the help and encouragement of my parents, I recovered, but I felt alone and that I was a total failure. But I know that I was not alone; God was with me all the time.

Two years later I met a wonderful man who shared my Christian background. He too had tasted the bitterness of divorce. We started sharing and healed together. I made wedding plans again and began searching for the perfect wedding dress. Driving down the street one afternoon, I told the Lord, "I simply do not have the money for a new wedding dress!"

Another girl on campus who was also planning her wedding was having the same difficulty. We were sharing our woes one day when I realized I might offer her my old wedding dress. She was delighted. "How much do you want for it?" she asked.

I knew she was in the same financial situation as I, so I asked, "How much can you pay? Make me an offer."

"Fifty dollars is all I can afford," she said. "But I know it's worth much more than that."

I accepted her offer, knowing that small amount would not cover the cost of a new dress for me, but it would put her mind at ease about her upcoming wedding. I started praying that the Lord would help me find a dress that fit and looked nice, but would cost only $50. A pretty tall order!

Then I discovered a bridal shop that had a closetful of beautiful second-year wedding gowns. I chose five and began the tedious job of trying them on. The fifth and final dress fit wonderfully and required only a few minor adjustments.

The moment had come. I flipped the price tag over—exactly $50. Tears streamed down my cheeks as I thanked the Lord for this answer to prayer. He has promised to fill all of our needs if we just ask.

CATHY L. SANCHEZ

A Dandelion Gift

My little children, let us not love in word, neither in tongue; but in deed and in truth." 1 John 3:18.

My little son came bounding into the house one day.
The blush of early summer's sun had kissed his cheeks at play.
And then I saw them—tightly clutched within his little fist—
A bunch of wilted dandelions I could not resist.
　　And as I hugged my precious boy,
　　His childish voice rang out with joy,
"Here, Mom, I picked these flowers just for you!"

Their yellow heads were drooping, but I used my choicest vase
And put them on the mantle in the very nicest place.
Oh, they were beautiful to me! I cherished every bloom.
Their golden heads spoke love and scattered joy throughout the room.
　　I told him that I loved him so!
　　Forever in my heart would grow
Those dandelions he had picked for me!

I thought about the gifts I thrust into my Father's hands—
My deeds of love, my triumphs—and His great heart understands.
He takes my dandelions, and a smile lights up His face;
And just because He loves me so, He gives them special place.
　　These wilted presents that I bring
　　Are not rejected by my King!
He tells me that they brighten up His day.

No costly gift of blossoms from the florist would I trade
For my son's dandelion gift his little hands had made.
No gift that we can give the Saviour dimly can compete
With His great sacrifice for us—His life full and complete.
　　And as I talk with Him I see
　　His nail-pierced hands reach out to me
To tell me, "Child, this is My gift for you!"

LORRAINE HUDGINS

Snake in the Night

*At the brightness that was before him his thick clouds passed,
hail stones and coals of fire. Ps. 18:12.*

While I was in my senior year of college, I received an invitation
to teach homemaking skills, English, music, and other subjects
in Ghana, West Africa. I was excited about the idea, but my mother
didn't want me to go.

"God, would You please change her heart if it is Your will that I
go?" I urged.

Almost overnight Mom said, "Why aren't you getting ready to go
to Africa? I thought you wanted to go!"

It was truly a miracle as I observed the change in her. God had
answered my prayer.

And several months later I was in my African home in the heart of
Ghana. One night as I lay in my bed, I became restless. With my
kerosene light in hand (our lights were turned off at 9:00 every evening)
I slipped out of bed and walked through my dark living room. As I
looked toward the screened porch, a long black snake slithered through
a hole in the screen. Barred windows opened on both sides of the
porch, so it was easy for the snake to enter the living room.

I'm sure the snake was just as frightened as I when it heard me
scream. I put on my housecoat and ran across a dark field to find the
night watchman. I could have stepped on many snakes as I ran
through the wooded area to get the watchman, but I was thinking
only of getting the one out of my house.

The watchman came running, his long blue gown flowing behind him and his pillbox hat askew, shouting "Mama, I come!
Mama, I come!"

With his bagful of sticks he followed me into the house. He found
the snake and killed it. What a relief! I thanked the watchman and
thanked God for keeping me awake to find the snake before it had
hidden in my home.

Our God is a wonderful deliverer. Truly He delivered me from
the snake, and I'm sure He has delivered me from many other dangers, seen and unseen. I will continue to trust in Him, my Strength
and my Deliverer.   RUTH F. DAVIS

Of Sparrows and Eyes

"Do not fear therefore; you are of more value than many sparrows." Matt. 10:31, NKJV.

The first time it happened I was sitting at my desk writing: clear 3-D shapes appeared in front of my eyes. I blinked and wondered what was happening to me. A few seconds later they disappeared, and I sighed with relief.

However, during the next few weeks the forms came back several times. I should have gone to the doctor, but I didn't want to hear bad news (as if not hearing it would make it go away).

My daughter was visiting me one Friday afternoon when I had another episode. Because she is a registered nurse, I decided to tell her what I had been experiencing.

"Mom," she exclaimed, "I am taking you to an optometrist immediately!"

He had never heard of shapes such as I described, but he checked my eye pressure and decided to do some more definitive eye examinations. He told me I had glaucoma. "You must get to a specialist as soon as possible," he urged.

As is common when one learns about a serious medical disorder, my initial reaction was a feeling of embarrassment and shame. But I knew untreated glaucoma causes blindness, and I knew I had to obtain medical help.

Several months have passed since that day of truth, and now I can face the facts with gratitude. I know God could have prevented the increase in eye pressure, but He chose to allow a human malady to become part of my life. In some ways it has proved to be a blessing as I meet others who share the same problem. I have even learned to look at some of the medical procedures with a bit of humor as I chat with other eye patients.

In Matthew 10:29-31 God tells us He cares about His little sparrows, and He cares even more about you and me. This is true when we see His leading in our lives, and when we cannot understand why some unfavorable circumstance befalls us.

Dear Lord, who watches over the sparrows, thank You for caring for us in the past. Help us to remember You will continue to love and care for us in the days ahead. Amen. MILDRED C. WILLIAMS

Friends

*May the God of hope fill you with all joy and peace
as you trust in him, so that you may overflow with
hope by the power of the Holy Spirit. Rom. 15:13, NIV.*

I sat alone in the sanctuary of a beautiful church. Usually worship was a happy occasion for me, but this time was different After 18 years of overseas service we were back in the United States to stay. And I was scared.

We were on our way to visit family and friends in the East, but an old-time buddy had persuaded my husband to speak to a congregation that was without a pastor. In fact, my husband had already been enthusiastically approached by the officers of the conference to think of it as a permanent position. What a challenge!

To be truthful, he wasn't so sure this was what he should do. Certainly we had been praying, but I was really fearful, nervous, very unsure of it all! After so many years in a different culture, different language—yes, even different occupation—could I fit into a place so cultured and sophisticated in America, especially into this church? Could I adjust to this new occupation and environment?

Then I thought, *Is this really my decision to make? Isn't it my husband they are calling?* Of course, I was part of the package! Oh, yes, I was really praying for help and direction.

The auditorium filled quickly. I didn't see anyone I knew. Then the room was hushed. The organ began to play softly as the elders filed in and knelt. In the silence a feeling of reverence surrounded me. My wildly beating heart quieted as I too bowed before the Saviour to whom I had dedicated my life. Hadn't He directed us all this time? Would He desert me now? Would I say no to His call? Then the Lord spoke silently to my fearful heart, *These are all My children! Friends, waiting to be made!* Peace flooded my soul.

The audience stood to sing. "Praise God, from whom all blessings flow." As the organ music swelled, my heart responded with joy and hope. *Yes, I can sing that song!* I gazed around at those beautiful, waiting-to-be-made friends. I was home again! And my fear was gone. My heart was filled with joy and peace. LOIS MAY WATTS

The Rosebush

The desert shall rejoice, and blossom as the rose.
It shall blossom abundantly, and rejoice even with joy and singing. Isa. 35:1, 2.

S omeone planted a rosebush in our garden some years ago. I don't know which tenant planted it, but I'm amazed how sturdy this plant is to have stood through all kinds of weather.

To start with, it is not growing in the right type of soil. It's dry, dusty sand that the water runs off instead of soaking into. We have fertilized it, but only a few pink buds rewarded us. But there was much foliage that grew longer and longer. Aphids kept pestering the rose bush, so every so often we had to spray it.

Then I decided to prune the bush. I'd never done a job like this before, but how hard could it be? I snipped off all the long branches just above the eye or bud. I cut out dry canes and split bark. I cut out the weak spindly canes and branches that were crossing each other in the interior, and all the candelabra type of growth. When I thought I had cut enough, the bush looked rather dwarfy, but I knew that a pruning was for its good.

I don't know types of roses or their names; I only know that mine yielded a beautiful pink rose. You can imagine my joy and excitement when, after three months, my bush was full of pink buds.

I thought of the Master Gardener and His job to prune me. He wants me to be beautiful with perfect blooms; but pruning is so painful. I get hurt in the process. The Master Gardener has to cut out the cancer of sin in my life.

I also need the right fertilizer to grow healthy. I need the rain of the Holy Spirit to refresh me, and the sunshine of God's love in my life as I come into contact with others. Gardens need weeding every so often. My life needs weeding too, to rid me of all the things that are un-Christlike in my life.

As I admire my pink roses, I thank the Master Gardener for working in my life, for pruning me to make me beautiful so that others can see Jesus in me.

Even though I may not like the pruning, Lord, keep on doing Your work as the Master Gardener. I want to bloom beautifully for You!

PRISCILLA ADONIS

Of Houses and Payments

In my Father's house are many mansions. John 14:2.

Our whole family sat listening to the real estate agent and answering her questions. As she showed us various homes listed in her multilisting book, it became increasingly apparent that there were not many in the price range we could afford. But there were a few, and soon we were off to choose our perfect new home.

Then came reality. The houses simply did not match up to the descriptions. We learned that the real estate business is full of euphemisms, descriptive terms that don't mean exactly what they say. Instead of glowing anticipation we experienced frustrated disappointment.

That night as I opened my Bible, I read John 14. It started me thinking about looking at houses and dreaming of mansions. We have bought and sold several homes since that first discouraging day, but the reality remains—what we can pay for is not the home of our dreams.

I am once again thinking about house plans and building. This will be the first home we have ever planned and had built just for us. It is exciting, but scary too. The ideas easily outpace the funds. And what if I forget something really important, or plan something I won't like later? There will be no one else to blame!

My heavenly real estate agent/builder, however, has a listing to suit every taste. And none are out of our price range—He has personally paid for each in full, in blood. No down payment is even required. And there will be no waiting, no remodeling, no disappointment, no frustrations. He already knows what I want and need, and He has promised that I can have it. Every detail will be perfect. He will even help me with the moving!

Our Father has promised that you can have your perfect home too. On the street of your dreams. I like thinking about these mansions. Will they have walls of leaves and a waterfall Jacuzzi, or will the walls be of gems and the windows of crystal? Will our homes be open to the outside, or will we bring the gardens into the home? It is all just too wonderful to contemplate.

So why is it we are so hesitant to accept the deed?

ARDIS DICK STENBAKKEN

The Chickadee

"Even the hairs of your head are all counted. Do not be afraid; you are of more value than many sparrows." Luke 12:7, NRSV.

Summer camp was in full swing with campers everywhere. We staff members worked nonstop as the days and nights blended together. For sure, home duties were last on the list. Even the birds had gone elsewhere to look for food.

Late one evening I hunted down the lawn mower. With high determination I headed for the knee-high overgrowth that was supposed to be a lush lawn. Soon the sweat rolled down my face. My shoes turned green and my ankles and legs ached as I pushed the mower up and down my yard. I was alone with the lawn. I wondered if I should pass out whether anyone would even notice.

I struggled onward and finished the lawn, returned to the house, and collapsed on the couch to cool off. A look at the clock reminded me that I had only a few minutes left before the camp's evening program began. *I could just stay here alone. Nobody would even miss me,* I reasoned. *Why, the birds don't even care where I am anymore.*

As I walked up the stairs to the kitchen to get a drink of water, I expressed out loud my frustrations to God. It wasn't really a prayer; I was just sounding off, as one would to a friend. As I got a glass from the cupboard and stepped over to the sink, a movement outside the window caught my eye. In utter astonishment I watched as a little chickadee landed on the empty feeder. My knees buckled and tears of joy came to my eyes. I felt humbled, and awed at the same time, to realize that God had heard me, even in my irreverent tone! He sent a simple bird to show me that He knows where I am at all times, even when I think I am alone.

A favorite Bible text I had learned as a child came to mind: "Even the hairs of your head are all counted. Do not be afraid; you are of more value than many sparrows."

No earthly friend could have filled my longing for companionship quite the way God did that day; I will never forget it. God sent a simple chickadee and His own words from His Book to remind me that I am never truly alone. He is always there.   DARLYN TOWNSEND

How to Walk in Glory

*Those with good sense are slow to anger, and it is their glory
to overlook an offense. Prov. 19:11, NRSV.*

I don't think she likes me."
  "No one asked me to participate."
  "Why wasn't I asked to attend?"
  "Did you notice the way he looked at me?"
  I fear I have voiced every one of these sentiments many times.
And I know I have heard them a thousand times from others—accompanied with the self-depreciating little shrug of the shoulders and
huff of the voice that goes so well with self-pity put into words.
  Is there no way to chase self-pity out of my life? It makes me so
miserable. What do I do about the times I am overlooked or neglected, either consciously or unconsciously? How can I avoid the
hurt that accompanies even the slightest rejection?
  I was excited one morning as I was reading my Bible to discover
that the wisest man who ever lived had counsel about this very subject.
(I suspect these words came out of Solomon's personal experience.)
  The wise woman, Solomon states, is patient enough not to react
immediately, but to consider before responding. After a time of consideration she realizes that it is actually to her glory to overlook an
offense, just to let the whole experience fade into insignificance.
Understanding this almost made me eager to receive an offense so
that I would have the opportunity to overlook it!
  I don't know exactly what kind of glory Solomon had in mind,
but I know the glory it gives me. It is open friendliness instead of self-protecting carefulness. I can reach out to everyone, not stopping to
consider if they will respond in kind or not. My smiles are free and
easy. I believe this glory is the glow that shone on the face of Jesus.
  This verse from Proverbs has made a real difference in my life,
and I hope it will make a difference in yours as well. After purposefully overlooking an offense a few times you may discover you don't
even notice offenses anymore! Then you can walk in easy glory all
the time, making the world around you a happy, peaceful place,
bathed in God's glory.   CARROL JOHNSON SHEWMAKE

A Daddy's Love

"For God so loved the world that He gave His only begotten Son,
that whoever believes in Him should not perish
but have everlasting life." John 3:16, NKJV.

I was walking around our farmyard one warm summer morning, doing whatever it is a 2½-year-old does. The screen door slammed, and one of my brothers ran past me toward the barn. I followed to see what the excitement was about. Before I reached the barn, I met my mama and brother racing back toward the house.

The next moments are a blurred memory. At some point I realized there was a fire. And at some point Daddy lifted me into the back of a pickup truck. I remember being pulled by my arm as another brother carried my sister and forced me to walk up our lane, away from our home. Then I heard something. I turned around to see flames shooting out the top story window of our home. The rest of the day is fuzzy in my mind. I see a fence, a gate, my aunt, the twins, the window. We sat for a very long time, perhaps hours, watching the smoke billow above the treetops.

Finally the door of the house where we had taken refuge opened, and there stood my mama and daddy and brothers. I ran to my daddy. He lifted me up and threw me in the air, and we laughed. How good it was to see him, to be in his arms, to hear his voice!

Then someone asked, "How can you laugh? You've just lost everything."

I cringed and leaned into my daddy. He cradled me in his arm, and with the other arm he reached around my mama, who was holding my sister. He called to my brothers. They came and stood with us. His voice was so sure and confident. "I have lost nothing today that cannot be replaced. My family is safe."

How thankful I am to have been given such a father to be my daddy on this earth—a man who didn't mind losing his earthly possessions as long as his family could stand with him. How much more grateful I am to know that my heavenly Father gave His most prized possession, His only Son, so that one day I can stand with Him in heaven.

NAOMI BABB

Daddy's Girl

*"I will be a Father to you, and you will be my . . .
daughters, says the Lord Almighty." 2 Cor. 6:18, NIV.*

June has always been a tough month for me because of Father's Day and my dad's birthday. I take forever finding a card that says pretty much nothing. It's painful wading through cards that say "You've always been there for me" or "We have so many happy memories together."

My parents divorced when I was 9, and my dad, though a good man, hasn't been in my life much. Oh, yes, he's attended all my graduations and my wedding. And he remembers my birthday and Christmas, but that's not the same as having a dad who is really interested and involved in my life.

So over the years I have looked to God as my Father. I know He is always available, always interested—even in the minutiae of my life. I seek from Him the affirmation that every girl wants from a father. I feel special and cherished in His presence.

My heavenly Father tells me that I am precious in His sight (see Isa. 43:4). He whispers that I am the apple of His eye (Zech. 2:8) and that He will never forsake me (Deut. 31:6). He wants me to call Him *Abba,* Father (Rom. 8:15), and vows that nothing will ever separate me from His love (verses 38, 39). When I'm troubled, He envelops me in His peace (John 14:27). When I'm brokenhearted, he binds up my wounds (Ps. 147:3) and comforts me (2 Cor. 1:3, 4). My heavenly Father longs for the time when I can stay at His house forever (Ps. 23:6).

My heart has usually been content—except when June rolls around. After years of bemoaning my situation, I determined to talk to my dad about our relationship. I figured I had little to lose and everything to gain. It took a bit of courage. I emphasized that I want him more involved in my life, that no matter how old I get, I will always need a father's love and affirmation. I was amazed at his response—he was elated! I became more special in his eyes simply by telling him I needed him.

My dad isn't perfect—no father has it all. But I know in my heart that I have a dad again. And between my heavenly Father and my father I'll cherish many happy memories.   HEIDE FORD

Circle of Glory

Look up at the sky! See how high the clouds are?
Yet, God is above them! Job 35:5, Clear Word.

My father needed surgery—a rather complicated operation that the doctors had scheduled immediately. I quickly booked a flight to Orlando to be with my parents at the appointed time. My job (or so I imagined) was to hold my mother's hand, bring a smile to my father's face, and keep my brothers in phone contact.

"Who'll be there for you?" my friends worried.

"I'm strong," I assured them as I settled the mantle of self-assurance securely on my shoulders and packed my bags.

During the flight that rain-swept afternoon the pilot advised us he was flying high above the clouds to avoid the impending storm. Idly I looked out the window. It was then I spotted the most fantastic sight I had ever seen. I blinked. They were still there. Reaching for the glasses I rarely wore in public, I noted that the beautiful blend of colors was even clearer. There on the quilted cottony clouds were two brilliant rings of light in the six colors of the rainbow.

These ovals are also symbols of God's covenant. It was God's sky-writing in color. "I am with you, My beloved daughter," I sensed Him saying to me.

The Creator-God had sent me a personalized symbol of His unfailing love just when I needed Him most. Virtual postcards from heaven, laden with messages of His reassurance. I relaxed, only then realizing how tense I had been. A text I had read earlier that week came to mind: "There is one ray of hope: his compassion never ends" (Lam. 3:21, 22, TLB). I couldn't help smiling. I had seen more than one ray of hope.

The next day my cousins and their friends came to the hospital in droves. They encircled my mother and me with their love and prayers during the long hours as we sat waiting for news. Their circle reminded me of God's celestial note the day before.

While my dad recuperated, I browsed the Web to find an explanation for what I had seen on the plane. I learned that the circular phenomenon was the effect of refracted light on the moisture-laden atmosphere around the plane. Physicists call it *aureole,* or *glory.* I was enchanted. Mine eyes had seen the glory, and it was very good.   GLENDA-MAE GREENE

JUNE 15

Let Go of the Branch!

"I am the true vine." John 15:1, NKJV.

After my first year of college I was given a job working for a summer camp in north Georgia. Part of my job included being the assistant counselor for a canoeing trip.

Before leaving, the campers were instructed in safety procedures. When we were ready to begin our trip, Tim, the head counselor, took the first canoe, while I was in the last of five.

The first part of our trip was uneventful. Then we encountered what seemed like a minor obstacle. In front of us, in the middle of the river, was a small island. Tim decided it would be easier to navigate to the left of the island. The lead canoe made it through fine. The second canoe followed and became stuck on a branch sticking out from the island. No amount of pushing would free it. Knowing that the other canoes could end up in the same predicament, I handed my oar to one of the campers, got out, and easily waded to the island. Once on dry ground, I was able to push the canoes away from the branch.

When my canoe arrived, it too became stuck. I had to stay on the island to push it free. Then to reach my canoe I had to wade to the next island, where Tim and the others were waiting. I stepped into the water and realized too late it was over my head. Instinctively I grabbed the branch and held on for dear life! The water rushed past me so fast that I couldn't pull myself back to dry ground. I knew I was going to die!

At that moment I heard Tim's voice calling, "Cyndi, let go! Let go of the branch!"

I thought he was crazy, but decided to trust him. As I let go and kept my eyes on Tim, I floated safely to where he waited.

More than once I have related this experience to my life. What am I holding on to that I think is helping me when in reality it will cause my eternal death? Bitterness? Hatred? Resentment? Fear? As I turn my eyes toward my Saviour, Jesus Christ, and hear His tender voice calling, "Cyndi, let go!" I find all of those feelings falling away. But Jesus doesn't leave me empty-handed. He replaces the empty branches in my life with the only true vine—Himself!

CYNDI STEPHENS

Eternity Now

He has also set eternity in the hearts of men. Eccl. 3:11, NIV.

I long for heaven, don't you? And when you get there, what do you want to do? Harps and golden crowns don't interest me nearly as much as having time to enjoy the beauty of the universe, time to spend with my family and friends, and time just to lie in a hammock, close my eyes, and smell the lilacs and the pine trees. Ah, that's eternity!

But wait a minute! Time is something God gives to us each day: 24 hours of time. We don't have to wait until tomorrow to enjoy eternity. Let it begin today. You can tuck a little heaven in your heart by doing something you really want to do.

I did that today. I put my computer to sleep, picked up a book I'd been wanting to read, slipped out the door, and sat in the lounge chair by our little pond. I fed the goldfish and nourished my soul with the beautiful words from Ruth Senter's book *Longing for Love*. Now, that's living!

I don't know what living means to you, but I urge you not to be like the crowd, merely existing to become "another day older and deeper in debt." That's not God's plan! He planted a little piece of eternity into each day if we'll only look for it. A friendly smile, a caring word, a whisper of fog, a shimmer of sun—it's all here on earth for us to enjoy today. If we'll take the time to enjoy and appreciate it.

For all those who believe, eternity can begin today. For those who are willing to take the time, eternity can begin now in our hearts.

Consider the words of the wise man: "What does the worker gain from his toil? I have seen the burden God has laid on men. He has made everything beautiful in its time. He has also set eternity in the hearts of men" (Eccl. 3:9-11, NIV).

Father, help me to find the little piece of eternity that You have planted in today. Help me to take the time to enjoy the beauty You have placed in the here and now. Share with me Your eternal peace. Help me to experience heaven in my heart. KAY KUZMA

Common Loon Sense

Do not enter the path of the wicked,
and do not walk in the way of evildoers. Prov. 4:14, NRSV.

My husband and I were camped by a lonely lake in the northern wilderness of North America. As we sat by our campfire watching the sunset, we suddenly heard a weird, peculiar cry come from the darkness of the lake. Because of the deep forests surrounding us, this unearthly cry sent chills down my spine.

"Sounds like the crazy laughter of a lunatic," I exclaimed.

My husband laughed. "You're about to meet a black-and-white goose-sized bird called a loon."

My husband explained that the loon is a great diver. Its legs, set farther back on its body than most birds, enable it to dive like a flash as far as 200 feet under water. Then while still under water, using its large webbed feet, it can outspeed the fish on which it feeds. The loon has one enemy—human beings.

"Do people hunt the loon for food?" I asked.

"No, but those who fish often shoot the loon because of the large number of fish they eat. When a loon sees a human, it usually dives instantly. It can actually dodge bullets from a gun. When it sees the flash, it flips its paddlelike feet and dives to the safety of deep water before the shot reaches it."

The next morning while we swam in the lake, two curious loons watched from a distance. Convinced we meant no harm, they swam closer, chattering in "loony" language. Finally, assured we were friendly, they joined us, swimming only a few feet away.

As we watched those beautiful birds, we learned a valuable lesson about friendship. Choose slowly and carefully. Watch your new friend's actions; listen to her words. If it meets the standards of Jesus, move in closer. Can you trust her? If not, that friendship could be more deadly than the hunter's gun. Dive into the safe arms of Jesus and stay there.

Later we watched a loon leave the water. Because of the position of its legs, it moved slowly and awkwardly. Good loon sense says it's never safe to venture into territory where it's impossible to dive to safety. Thanks, little loon. May we be wise like you and "not enter the path of the wicked."

EILEEN E. LANTRY

My Joy Day

I will sing unto the Lord as long as I live:
I will sing praise to my God while I have my being. Ps. 104:33.

It was summer, and time for green beans. So we drove to a U-pick farm north of town to get our winter supply of green beans to freeze.

The beans were plentiful, and the farmer's kittens played hide-and-seek with our hands among the bean bushes. They seemed to think it was a great game, and we did too. Before we knew it, we had more than a bushel of green beans. After paying the bill, we scurried home.

"What will we do with all these beans?" my husband asked as he carried them into the kitchen. "Why did we pick so many? It's more than two people need."

"And it's Friday!" I reminded him. "So we had better get started. If I sing and praise God perhaps we can get it done faster."

With my husband helping me as much as he could, I sang joy songs all day to keep my mind off the impossible and focus on what God can do with willing hands and heart through His Holy Spirit. I sang all the songs I could remember that had the word joy: "You may have the joy bells ringing in your heart"; "I have the joy, joy, joy, joy, down in my heart"; "Oh, there'll be joy when the work is done."

The work went well as we filled the freezer cartons with blanched and cooled beans, handling every one of those bean pods to cut the stems off. By midafternoon we could see we weren't going fast enough. We weren't going to get the job finished; there were still piles of beans, and evening was approaching. It was then that the Holy Spirit whispered, "Give them away."

The neighbors gladly accepted bags of green beans, and beans went into the fridge for present use or later distribution. Finally the kitchen was cleared of the last bean!

Tired but triumphant, we sat down in the living room to relax, our hearts filled with thankfulness and joy. Our whole day had been filled with joy—the joy of picking, the joy of playing with the kittens, the joy of singing, the joy of a job done, and the joy of a gift shared with friends.

MAE E. WALLENKAMPF

My Unusual Alarm Clock

Then shall ye call upon me, and ye shall go and pray unto me, and I will hearken unto you. Jer. 29:12.

As I lingered in that dreamy state between sleep and full consciousness, my ears fixed on a familiar tune. The music turned over in my mind as I awoke. I began to smile, then giggle, and finally to laugh out loud.

The music was coming from a push-button music book given to our 23-month-old daughter, Hanna, for Christmas. And there she was at 6:00 a.m., playing it for me, in answer to my prayer. "Lord, You have a thousand, maybe a million, ways to answer my prayers, but how I doubted!"

A few months earlier we had moved, and we were still getting settled. Between that and preparations for the coming holidays I had been busy, and my early-morning worship time had been crowded out. Then during the holidays we traveled to the West Coast to be with family, and I was too busy for time with God. Upon returning home, trying to adjust to the three-hour time change, I began to sleep late every day.

That is, until the morning of this story. I had felt several gentle reminders during this time that I needed my morning worship, but kept pushing these thoughts aside. Then one night I added something to my prayer. "Please, Lord, I need our morning time together and I just can't seem to get up. I turn this need over to You."

Even as I prayed I thought to myself, *Of all the nights to ask this. It's almost midnight, and I can't imagine waking up early.*

Then the song at 6:00 a.m. coming from the crib in the next room had awakened me. It was playing for me in answer to that prayer. I sat up, still laughing, and said, "I got the message, Lord, and thank You for waking me. Thank You for our quiet time together this morning. Thank You for Your tiny servant who followed Your bidding from her crib. Thank You for answering my prayer for time with You."

If you are struggling to find time to spend with God, why not invite Him to help you? He longs for these moments even more than you do. With your permission, He will help you find time. He may even awaken you early, and who knows what unusual alarm clock He might choose for you?

DAVA BENTON WHITE

A Cup of Cold Water

Silver and gold have I none; but such as I have give I thee. Acts 3:6.

I was about 9 years old when I first heard the story of Peter and
John and the lame man at the gate called Beautiful. The teacher
who told me that story really made it live. She said that a man, lame
from birth, was hoping for some money. Instead he received only
what the disciples had to give—the ability to walk in the name of
Jesus. I was very impressed with the story.

Later that week, on a hot summer day, a blind man and his companion came to our house selling brooms. My older sister and I answered the door. My sister said, "We're sorry, but we don't have any
money to buy a broom."

As we closed the door I remembered the Bible story and suggested that we offer what we could—glasses of ice-cold water. The
steps of the two men were slow, so we easily caught up with them
and made the offer. Their faces lit up as they accepted the glasses of
ice-cold water. "Thank you so much!" they said.

I was committed then and there to giving "such as I have." That
hot day's experience many years ago has been repeated again and
again. It may have been simply sharing a bulletin with a visitor or a
new member at church, or helping a frustrated mother soothe a crying child. It is wonderful how a card dropped in the mail will arrive at
just the right time to encourage and cheer the receiver. Sometimes I
may have given more—a listening ear for a grieving friend, a late-
night hospital visit, or a change in my already committed schedule to
help someone in need.

Often we may believe that having silver or gold available makes it
easier to give "such as I have." But Peter took the lame man by the
hand and lifted him up. That really is the essence of "such as I have I
give." It is the personal touch of each of us looking for and finding
our own special "such as I have" to share.

I'm asking every day for an opportunity to reexperience the joy
and excitement of the 9-year-old who identified with Peter of old. I'll
never forget that special thrill I felt as I shared what I had with those
blind men.   JUDITH WARREN HAWKINS

The Crocheted Wedding Dress

*To her was granted that she should be arrayed in fine linen,
clean and white: for the fine linen is the righteousness of saints. Rev. 19:8.*

One morning Cameron knocked at our door. "I'd like to show you something."

Cameron and his wife, Colleen, had just returned that fall from a two-year term as missionaries in a remote part of Alaska. They often showed us souvenirs of that place—knives, trays, even a bearskin.

I found myself looking not at an Alaskan souvenir, but a bride, Cameron's bride, wearing a beautiful wedding gown. This dress, although fashioned like many others, looked very different. No store ever displayed such a lovely garment!

"Colleen always admired her grandmother's dainty crocheting," he began. "One day when she was a little girl she said, 'Grandma, when I get married I'd like you to crochet my wedding dress.' Colleen had forgotten this request, but her grandmother hadn't."

When her grandmother knew Colleen was to be married, she sat with a crochet hook in her hand for more than 650 hours, week after week, month after month. Piece after piece took shape until an exquisite dress lay finished for the wedding day.

After Cameron left, I thought of another wedding garment, one provided by the King of kings for His own wedding. We are all not only invited, but given a garment to wear. This garment represents the pure, spotless character Christ's followers will possess. As we unite our lives with Christ's, we become one in Him. When God looks on us, He sees not our polluted life, but the perfect life of Christ.

Colleen's grandmother crocheted that wedding dress out of love for her only granddaughter. How disappointed she would have been if Colleen had refused to wear it. Christ lived a sinless life so He is able to offer us the robe of His righteousness, our wedding garment! How disappointed He will be if we don't accept it.

MARGARET I. CAMPBELL

Thief in the Night

The Son of man cometh at an hour when ye think not. Luke 12:40.

The doorbell disturbed my sleep at 3:30 a.m. I crawled out of bed as the doorbell rang again and again. I cautiously peered out of a window but saw only dark haze. The bell continued to ring. Tiptoeing to another window, I pressed my face to the glass to see who was there. My stomach knotted as loud banging on the door began.

"Yes?" I said.

"Ma'am, can you help me?"

I peeked through a small window in the door and saw a woman. I strained to hear her through the closed door. Her parents, new neighbors, lived on the next block and were out of town. Her maintenance man had locked her out of her apartment that was miles away. She didn't have the key to her parents' home. She had seen our porch light on and had decided to ring my bell for help.

"Move away from the door," I said. Then against my better judgment I opened the door and quickly locked the screen door.

"I need money. Do you have $20?" she asked emphatically.

"Do I have $20?" I repeated. "No, I don't." I really didn't.

The woman turned hastily, walked to a car, and entered on the passenger side. The car sped off.

I slammed the door and stumbled back to bed. Hard as I tried, I couldn't go to sleep. The nerve of that woman! Preying on innocent people like me at 3:30 in the morning, trying to make a fast buck. A thief in the night!

As I tossed and turned, I began thinking about my sleepy stupor when the doorbell rang. I was certainly unprepared for whoever was at my door at that hour. And the thought of who it was, or why, had sent me into a panic.

Suppose that when Christ knocks at the door of my heart or rings my doorbell I'm in a stupor—irritated, anxious, distraught because of the interruption. He isn't a thief in the night, though his arrival may make him *appear* as a thief. Will I give Him what He asks for? Or will I slam the door and stumble back to my comfortable bed and miss the opportunity of a lifetime?

IRIS L. STOVALL

Great Is Thy Faithfulness

The steadfast love of the Lord never ceases, his mercies never come to an end; they are new every morning; great is thy faithfulness. Lam. 3:22, 23, RSV.

My day in court was as bad as I had anticipated. I waited about three hours with the other traffic violators in the crowded courtroom. When it was my turn, I admitted my guilt and the judge lowered the fine from $99 to $50. However, that bit of grace did nothing to lessen my feelings of humiliation and shame. I was sad, tired, and discouraged when I returned to work at the medical center.

I was in no mood to see the last patient going to surgery. I was far too aggravated and tired. Yet I felt the distinct impression to go and visit her. I argued with the Spirit's prompting. "I'm too tired. I am in too bad a mood to be available for anyone," I insisted. "I need to slow down and regroup. Please, Lord, I'm not ready."

But the prompting persisted. "Go! Now!"

I reluctantly trudged up to the third floor. Dianna presented a bright and infectious smile when I introduced myself as the chaplain. And I remember clearly her opening remark. "I was just reading about angels. Such a good book. It points out that not all angels are God's. There are evil angels too. Not every book about angels says that."

I smiled back at her, genuinely delighted to meet her. We talked about God's amazing grace and our love for Him. We sang "We Are Standing on Holy Ground" and had prayer.

Finally she said, "What church do you attend?" When I told her, she said, "I want to join your church!"

I laughed for joy. When we are discouraged, instead of chastising or ignoring us, Jesus pulls us close to Himself and gives us a present. And Dianna has become my dear friend, my present. Shortly after our first meeting, Dianna and her roommate, Elna, joined my church. Their enthusiasm and outstanding musical talents are a blessing to the congregation. They also come faithfully to a support group I facilitate where their intercessory prayer gifts have been a lifesaver for the women in the group.

Thank You, heavenly Father, our encourager, our healer, the lover of our souls, for Your grace, which is new to us each morning. Great is Thy faithfulness!

WANDA GRIMES DAVIS

The Stalled Van

The Lord will keep you from all harm —
He will watch over your life. Ps. 121:7, NIV.

"Man, did you see that!" our teenage boys exclaimed as several cars, swerving to avoid hitting our stalled van, whizzed by.

I pulled our sleeping 6-year-old twins close to me. I watched the headlights of oncoming cars in the rearview mirror as they zoomed around the curve, praying that we wouldn't be killed.

We were on our way to the dealership that night, hoping to trade our decrepit van for more reliable transportation. At the most inopportune time the van stalled just beyond the curve on the busy interstate highway.

My husband pushed the van against the curb and left the children and me sitting inside while he went in search of help. We watched him walk beside the fence until he found a place where he could climb down the steep embankment that led to a distant service station.

A police car passed us going in the opposite direction. He soon returned and asked why we were parked there. After I explained our plight and told him my husband had gone for help, he promised to come back later and help if we hadn't received any by that time.

Just as the officer drove away, the headlights of a truck and car, traveling side by side, came into view. Fear overwhelmed me as the two vehicles came closer. The car suddenly increased speed and screeched in front of the truck just in time to avoid hitting our van.

"Lord, help us, please!" I cried in anguish as the van rocked in the wind created by the passing vehicles."Come, boys, let's try to push the van out of the way before more cars come and we are killed!"

We quickly pushed the van onto a narrow strip of turf bordering the highway just as a line of cars sped by. Back in the van, we thanked God for protecting us and sought continued protection. Sometimes we realize we are in imminent danger and sometimes we don't, but we felt certain that angels of God watched over our lives and kept us from harm that Monday night.   MABEL ROLLINS NORMAN

Rose Garden Interlude

He restores my soul. Ps. 23:3, NIV.

E very minute of my day was planned, including the 30-minute break from work to pick up my teenage daughter and take her to tryouts for a play. After dropping her off, I would return to work and put in another 45 minutes before picking her up and going home to make dinner.

After leaving my daughter, I realized that I needed a restroom, so I stopped at a public garden. I parked at the far end and had to walk through a rose garden to reach it. As I walked back to my car, I couldn't resist the roses. A water fountain splashed in the center of the garden, and near the edge of the roses was a row of redwood trees and a few benches. I sat down. *This is just for a minute,* I promised myself.

To my back, on the other side of the redwoods, about 80 people sat on an elevated open-air stage that faced a broad stretch of lawn. Someone was speaking to them, but I couldn't hear what he was saying.

I relaxed as a breeze caressed my face and someone on the stage behind me strummed a guitar. The people began to sing "Amazing Grace." I let the melody whirl around me as it filled the garden and rested on my heart. When the last few notes faded into the afternoon, I stood and headed for the car.

The path took me by the gardener, who was at work clipping the fading flowers and tossing them into the back of his pickup truck. On an impulse, I scooped up an armful of rose petals and carried them to the car. When my daughter got into the car a few minutes later, I showered her with rose petals. They fell on her hair, on her face, and over her shoulders into her lap. She still has some, pressed into the book she'd brought with her to read.

I never did make it back to work, and I don't remember what I had to do that afternoon. But I won't forget the time in the garden. The people singing "Amazing Grace," rose petals free for the taking, and the laughter of my daughter as the flowers cascaded over her are precious treasures in my memory.

Restore my soul today, Father, helping me to create memories of time spent with You.
ALICE HEATH PRIVE

The Broken Tie

"It is more blessed to give than to receive." Acts 20:35, NIV.

My husband and I have had the privilege of traveling to various locations in the former U.S.S.R. on humanitarian missions. On one occasion we were visiting a seminary. Many of the students had come to the school without even the bare necessities.

Even though the students attend their seminary classes in a beautiful historic building with marble floors, their living conditions are extraordinarily humble. We found many living in huge cylinders of about 10 by 30 feet. A door was cut in one end, a flat floor laid down, and then the space divided into three rooms. With the addition of windows, the cylinder was a home. It was amazing to see what the women did to create the sense of home even in these primitive conditions!

At the close of our visit with one young couple we were impressed to give them money. Tears slipped down Maria's cheeks as she confided they were down to their last rubles. The only food they had in their cupboards was tea and rice. What joy we had in sharing with them.

On another visit to the seminary we carried letters, pictures, and gifts from members of our church to students they were sponsoring. One sponsor sent his Russian friend, Vadim, a third-year seminary student, a pair of dress socks and a tie.

Upon receiving these gifts, Vadim looked at me in amazement and said in his limited English, "My tie was broken and I needed a new one. I just made a trip to Moscow. I needed new socks, but they were too expensive, and I could not afford to buy them. How do my sponsors know what I need? Why do they care about me when they have never met me and have only seen a picture of me?"

My immediate response was "God tells them what you need."

What a thrilling opportunity I had to assure Vadim of God's love and care, even in the small things of life. Won't it be wonderful when we get to heaven and can better understand the workings of the Holy Spirit and how He impresses and uses us to fulfill the needs of others?

GINGER SNARR

Choices

There is a way that seems right to a person,
but its end is the way to death. Prov. 14:12, NRSV.

I was driving down Interstate 95 the other day in a relatively unfamiliar part of the city. Traffic was really moving along, and I was
"going with the flow." I wasn't paying attention to the big green road
signs, so when the road suddenly divided—one branch flowing off to
the left, the other to the right—I was caught by surprise. If I hadn't
known the general direction I needed to go, or if I had been in a lane
too far from the correct side, it would have been easy to allow the
traffic to pressure me into traveling down the wrong road.

Many times, as I come up on a dividing road, I've thought of the
way even some of my own friends and relatives have traveled along
the highway of life, seemingly doing quite well spiritually. Then they
have chosen, been pressured, or just drifted onto the "wrong road,"
ending up going completely in the opposite direction from their spiritual destination. In a very short time they became separated from
God's people by a great distance. Even if they want to return to the
right road, it appears hopeless.

But spiritual wrong turns can be avoided. Choosing to take time
each day to study God's Wrd helps one get the big picture of life, a
clear sense of God's priorities and direction. As someone has said,
"If we don't know where we're going, we'll probably end up somewhere else."

We've all experienced the hassle of trying to get back on the right
road after literally making a wrong turn on a highway. Leaving the
right road is comparatively easy; getting back on the right road requires
a choice, a U-turn, and quite a bit of backtracking. But there is hope!

Is your life leading you in the right direction? Have you been following the road signs that lead to life eternal? If not, remember that
God allows U-turns. In fact, He encourages them. Ask Him this moment to help you make the right choices, and He will gladly guide
you back onto the right road that leads to life!

NANCY CACHERO VASQUEZ

In Everything Give Thanks

Giving thanks always for all the things unto God and the Father in the name of our Lord Jesus Christ. Eph. 5:20.

My best friend and sister, Linda, was diagnosed with breast cancer. A month later she was operated on. Then she faced chemotherapy, radiation, and more tests. This was tough for Linda and for all of us who loved her. It was especially hard for me, since I was in Cyprus and she was in the United States. I longed to be close to her during her time of difficulty.

"Why don't you fly over to be with Linda?" my husband asked. "I know you would feel better if you could be there."

As soon as we could arrange the ticket, I was on my way. As much as I wanted to be with her, I worried about what I would say when I met her—I wasn't sure I could handle my emotions.

It was even harder when I actually saw her. She looked very pale under her red turban. Yet she greeted me with a smile of reassurance. We hugged, but my heart was too full for words. I just held her close and knew that she understood my love for her.

I watched her for several days, not knowing what to say. Then one night I tiptoed to her room and looked down at her slim, fragile figure. Overcome with thoughts of death, separation, pain, hurt, and loneliness, I began to cry and awakened her.

"Don't cry." Linda spoke gently. "It's not the end of the world yet. God is still on His throne, and I know everything has a purpose. I just thank God for this experience because I know my relationship with Him has become closer. Because of this experience I feel so much love from my family and friends. Because of this experience I can relate better to others who are suffering. God's love and care have become very real in my life. I feel His presence very close to me."

I didn't know what to say. She had taken her difficulties and had found in them an opportunity for thanksgiving!

Since then God has worked marvelously in Linda's life. She was soon back to her work, still praising the Lord!

Lord, please help me to see You in every difficulty. Help me to look beyond my troubles to see Your power at work in my life. Help me to trust You more and to thank You more! JEMINA DOLLOSA ORILLOSA

Playing Church

"Nevertheless I have this against you, that you have left your first love.
Remember therefore from where you have fallen;
repent and do the first works." Rev. 2:4, 5, NKJV.

One evening while on duty at the hospital, I helped lift a male patient who had collapsed on the floor. As I did so, I partially ruptured three cervical disks in my spine. I was in charge of the orthopedic unit at the hospital, and this painful injury, which lessened my usefulness, was very frustrating.

One afternoon I opened my Bible to Romans 8:28 and claimed the promise: "All things work together for good to them that love God." In deep earnestness I cried out, "Lord, I do love You! What is the lesson that You want me to learn through this valley experience?"

The Holy Spirit spoke these words so plainly: "Kay, you have been taking your relationship with Jesus for granted."

I had never seen myself in the light of Calvary's cross—a condemned sinner who was guilty of the murder of the Son of God! In brokenhearted repentance I prayed, "Jesus, I want You to come into my life and be my personal Saviour. Please reveal the sins in my life that caused You to be crucified, agonizingly separated from Your Father, and finally broke Your heart."

My mother had given her life to the Lord when I was a 4-year-old child; therefore, I had the privilege of being taught by a godly mother to love and trust Jesus. I always had a deeply spiritual nature; I never desired to rebel—to taste of the fruit of forbidden pleasures. My young heart had a longing desire to serve the Lord and to live to make Him happy.

As a child I had two bouts with rheumatic fever and had to spend several months in bed. During this time I read and memorized Scripture passages. Jesus was very precious to me. I shudder to think what my life would have been like if it had not been for Jesus!

Tenderly the Holy Spirit helped me to realize that my worship of God had degenerated into cold formality. I had been playing church. It dawned on my soul that true religion is a loving relationship with Jesus. In that hour I was forever changed. Jesus is now my best friend, and sharing His love with others is my greatest joy.   KAY COLLINS

Special Delivery

*"Whatever you ask for in prayer, believe that
you have received it, and it will be yours." Mark 11:24, NIV.*

I was sitting at my desk that last day of June, that last day on a job I
thoroughly enjoyed. The decision for me to stay at home and care
for our soon-to-arrive firstborn had been made. Tomorrow the doctor
would induce labor.

As I was completing those last-minute tasks, an acquaintance
stopped by my door. "Haven't you had that baby yet?"

"I'm being induced in the morning," I responded.

"You don't want that to happen!" she exclaimed. "Pray that the
baby comes tonight!"

No one, not even my closest friend, had ever been so bold. I
couldn't get her words out of my mind.

Before retiring for the evening, and with no signs of beginning
labor, I prayed more humbly, more earnestly, and with deeper faith
than ever before. *Please, Lord, if it is Your will, help my baby to come
tonight!* As I closed my prayer, I truly believed God would allow our
daughter to enter this world on her own, without the use of needles
and medicine.

At 2:00 a.m. my prayer was answered. We arrived at the hospital
just three hours before I was to be induced. God's timing was perfect!

Nearly two years later I prayed the same prayer: *Please, Lord, if it is
Your will, help my son to be born tonight.* Once again there were no signs
of beginning labor. I wasn't being induced. In fact, it was one week before my due date. Three hours after my prayer we left for the hospital.

Unquestionably, God answered my prayers. Not only was I
blessed with God's presence, but He gave us two beautiful healthy
children. I know God won't always answer my prayers with such im-
mediacy, but He will most certainly answer them in His time. And
He'll do the same for you.   LYNN BEST CONNELLY

The Wrong Airport

What a God he is! How perfect in every way!
All his promises prove true. Ps. 18:30, TLB.

My heart beat faster as I walked up the ramp from the airplane. I scanned the faces of those waiting at the gate for loved ones. My husband was not there. *He's had a hard time finding a parking spot,* I reasoned. *He'll be waiting for me in the baggage claim area. I know he'll be there because he promised me for sure he'd meet me.*

"I'll be at Dulles Airport at 4:00 to meet your flight," Ron had promised the night before. "I can hardly wait to see you!"

I hurried along the corridor. From the escalator I scanned the baggage area, looking for Ron's welcome smile. He wasn't there. I sighed and took my place by the conveyor belt thinking, *The traffic is heavy this time of day, but he'll get here by the time my luggage arrives.*

My suitcases finally came, and I heaved them onto my waiting cart. *Where is Ron? I hope he hasn't had an accident. Maybe he's waiting in the wrong area.* I pushed the cart up and down, alert to anyone who was arriving. My husband didn't show. After 45 minutes I decided to call his office.

His secretary answered. "You're at Dulles Airport? Ron was just there, but they said there were no flights from Florida today! He's on his way to National. I'll call him on his car phone."

After another 45 minutes he arrived with apologies and the explanation. In his rush, he had left my flight schedule at home. However, he wasn't concerned because he was certain I was coming in on an American Airlines flight due to arrive at 3:59 at Dulles Airport.

I was on a United flight, but so sure was he of his facts that he didn't bother to check with another airline. Learning that an American flight was due at National at 3:58, he rushed over there, only to have to return to Dulles. We had a good laugh and enjoyed what was left of the evening.

He had tried to keep his promise to be there the minute I got off the plane, but he failed to do it. Because he is human, my husband sometimes fails me, but Jesus never fails! He always keeps His promises, every one of them!   DOROTHY EATON WATTS

Accepting Grace

Grace to you and peace from God our Father
and the Lord Jesus Christ. Rom. 1:7, NKJV.

I wasn't feeling good. I just wanted to go to bed. But there were dishes to do and the kitchen to clean up. The boys needed to be reminded to take showers, clean up, brush their teeth, and all those other things I reminded them of each night.

"Don't you feel good?" Tim asked as I sat at the table.

"Not really." Why is it so hard sometimes to say no?

"Why don't you go lie down?"

That was nice of him. But look at the kitchen and all the things that needed to be done.

"The boys will do the dishes. You go to bed."

Protesting only slightly, I made my way to bed. The boys protested a little more than I had, but were soon doing the dishes. Tim came and tucked me in. "Want a cup of tea?"

I did, but I didn't want to trouble him. I started to say no, but finally said yes. I let him take care of me that evening, pampering me, tucking more covers around me. It's hard for me to let others do things for me, to accept kindness and love. I always feel as though I'm the one who should be doing and giving. Many times when someone offers help, I'm quick to say no, even if I really want their help. I'm not sure if it's because I don't want to bother people or because I like doing it all myself.

Many times this attitude spills over into my relationship with God. I'm quick to do, to serve, to find another project. But I'm slow to enjoy a sunny day that He's given, or to stroll quietly through the woods. Sometimes when we're hiking, I'm so intent on getting to the top or to the end that I forget to enjoy the beauty on the way. I put more effort into what I do "for" God than I do in my relationship "with" Him. It's hard for me to accept His grace, to relax in His love. Yet God offers me grace, His righteousness, His strength, and His peace.

I need to learn to say "Yes, God," and then allow Him to snuggle me down and rest in His love. I don't need to do it all myself. He wants *me,* not my effort or my work.

O Lord, teach me to accept Your grace and peace, to abide in Your love and presence, to be and not do—and to let others do for me too. TAMYRA HORST

Cloud Cover

*By day the Lord went ahead of them in a pillar of cloud
to guide them on their way. Ex. 13:21, NIV.*

One Thursday I received a phone call from my mother telling me that my dad had had a heart attack and was in intensive care in the hospital. Of course we wanted to go be with him and to support Mom. It was too expensive to fly a family of seven from Virginia to California, so we decided to make the trip in our van.

There was just one problem: the air-conditioner in the van was broken. It would be absolutely miserable to make the trip in midsummer with five young children complaining about the heat, but we couldn't afford to fix it.

That evening for family worship we read the story of the Israelites' 40-year journey through the desert and how God had sent a cloud to shield them from the sun during the day. Since God tells us that He is the same yesterday, today, and forever, I decided to ask Him to send a cloud to cover our family on our five-day drive across the country.

At church that week I asked for special prayer that God would send a cloud to cover us. One person stopped me after church to say, "God doesn't do things like that anymore. You're wasting your time to pray for it."

The day came to leave for California. It was already hot and muggy by 8:00 a.m. We loaded up the van, buckled everyone in their seats, prayed for safety, and started down the road.

All the way to California and all the way home we had a cloud that hovered over us, shielding us from the brightly burning sun. Besides that, California experienced the mildest two-week period in June in many years!

When we got back home three weeks later, I was so happy to be able to report to the church that God still answers prayer! Praise the Lord, He is still the same today!

Father, as You led Your people in the desert long ago, lead me today. Help me to be always aware of Your presence as I go about my work today.

CELIA MEJIA CRUZ

I Saw a Miracle

*Call upon me in the day of trouble: I will deliver thee,
and thou shalt glorify me. Ps. 50:15.*

It was July and a very hot day in sunny southern California. My husband and I had attended a church service in Glendale and were heading home toward the east San Gabriel Valley on the 210 freeway. We had decided not to stop for lunch, but to continue on home, where we knew a tasty meal awaited us. So though hungry, we motored on.

We approached the area of Pasadena, where it seems as though all the avenues of the world converge onto the freeway, making at least eight lanes going in one direction at one time. The traffic situation at that point can be quite unnerving. Huge tractor-trailers, all seeming to head for the same destinations, trying to use the same lanes at the same time, rush past.

And that is when it happened.

Suddenly, on the right side of me as I sat in the passenger seat, towering above me, was the most monstrous, double tractor-trailer I had ever seen. Just as it sped by, the driver seemed to lose control. I could see the truck start to jackknife. In an effort to avoid the jackknife, the driver swerved into our lane, right in front of us, causing his trailer to tilt.

This is it! I thought. *We are going to die under this mountain of metal.* I cried out, "Dear God, please save us!"

Then a miracle unfolded before my eyes. The trailer lifted gently back into place as if an unseen hand had pushed it there. The whole spectrum of traffic continued on as if nothing had ever happened.

My husband and I were speechless. I would love to know what that truck driver thought about that experience. Did he realize that God had saved him and perhaps many others, too?

For the rest of the day we praised God for His wonderful care in answer to prayer. We have been praising Him ever since.

Lord, every day You protect and save, even though we do not always see it. Thank You. May we always give You the glory and the praise.

ALBERTA BENNETT CICCARELLI

The Peanut Butter Sandwich

Inasmuch as ye have done it unto one of the least of these my brethren, ye have done it unto me. Matt. 25:40.

The two slices of bread oozed with sticky peanut butter and jelly. Carefully placing the sandwich on a small plate, 5-year-old Katie stepped back to admire her handiwork. After filling a glass with milk, she placed a paper napkin over the sandwich and hurried to the front porch.

There sat the hobo. That's what her mother had called the unshaven old man who had knocked on their door during the evening news. He'd asked for food. "Before we know it, our house will become a diner for every indigent riding the rails," she warned darkly.

"But Mama, he's hungry," Katie pleaded. "My Bible teacher says when we feed people, we may be feeding angels unawares."

Katie's mother sighed. "Go ahead. Make the man a peanut butter sandwich if you want to."

Katie ran back to the door to tell the hobo to wait, then dashed to the kitchen to prepare her masterpiece. After giving the man the sandwich and milk, Katie had another idea. She ran up to her room and dumped the contents from her yellow plastic duck bank onto her bed. Gathering the change into one of her favorite cotton handkerchiefs, she ran back down the stairs and out onto the porch.

"Here," she said. "This will help get your next sandwich."

The man mumbled a thank-you. Suddenly feeling shy, the child rushed back inside. Later, certain the man was gone, Katie went outside to retrieve the empty saucer and glass. She found the paper napkin and her handkerchief carefully folded beneath the plate.

Delighted, she ran inside to tell her parents. "See? I told you he was an angel! He folded his napkin!"

Her mother and father smiled at one another, then at their daughter, neither one wanting to dampen her innocent faith. Time passed and Katie grew up. She never saw her hobo friend again, but she never forgot him. As she matured, the girl came to realize that her hobo was probably not an angel at all. Rather she realized that by feeding the hobo she had fed the Son of God.   KAY D. RIZZO

Something Even Better Planned

"For I know the plans I have for you," declares the Lord,
"plans to prosper you and not to harm you,
plans to give you hope and a future." Jer. 29:11, NIV.

My housemate had moved out at the end of April, and I hoped to find a new one as soon as possible to share rent expenses. I hung up signs and waited hopefully. Several calls came, but for one reason or another none of the applicants worked out. As May slipped into June, I began to get discouraged. I tried to leave the matter in the Lord's hands but still fretted over how I was going to meet upcoming financial obligations.

At the end of June I received a call from a quiet Japanese girl. I was excited to talk with her, since I had once lived in Japan, but tried not to get my hopes up. At the appointed time she met me and looked over the empty room. Not saying much, she agreed almost instantly to move in the following Monday. As I lay in bed that night I wondered, *What have I gotten myself into? After all, she is a total stranger. How do I know we'll be compatible housemates?*

Looking back, I thank God for bringing Sumako into my life. She has become a true friend and a sister in Christ. We have prayed, laughed, and cried together. We've swapped clothing, stories, and recipes. She listens patiently, offers Christian insights, and is a quiet, sure companion. Now I know God knew what He was doing when He sent Sumako. I marvel when I think of all the roommates I almost had, and how each one fell through. If one of them had worked out, I might never have met Sumako.

So many times we experience frustration when our hopes don't materialize. Whether a job, marriage partner, or new venture, we tend to envision one result and are greatly disappointed when things don't go as we had planned. However, we can be sure that God has not forgotten about us and the future He has promised. The next time your cherished plans go haywire, pause for a moment to consider that God may have something even more spectacular planned, more than you could have asked or imagined.

KATHRYN GORDON

Kitchen Love

Do not neglect to show hospitality. Heb. 13:2, RSV.

One frazzled Friday disaster struck at my home in Molokai. Right in the middle of typing the church bulletin, our ancient electric typewriter gave out. The nearest repair shop was in Honolulu, 30 miles away by sea. I knew of no one who could help.

Then I remembered a number someone had given to me. A phone call produced a vague promise that Ken, a former IBM repair technician, might be able to work on the typewriter next week.

"Would it help if I were to bring the typewriter to you? I really need it this afternoon," I pleaded.

There was a pause, but he finally agreed. "Look for a pink hibiscus hedge at the four-mile marker east of Kaunakakai."

If I had been expecting a neat, businesslike repair shop, I was in for a surprise. What I found was a shack with a rusty tin roof. Barking dogs swarmed around as I mounted the sagging steps into the tiny kitchen Ken indicated. A small girl sat eating her breakfast at the oilcloth-covered table. Ken placed the typewriter on the opposite side and began checking for broken belts or other problems.

As he worked, my eyes roamed around the small room. The few open shelves held an assortment of items that aroused my interest. Ken's wife must have had a real bent for cooking, for there were wire whips, colanders, spatulas, a Dutch oven, frying pans in several sizes, and a variety of honest, do-it-yourself equipment that predated electric food processors and blenders.

The few food supplies on the makeshift shelves and cluttered counter spoke of a limited budget. Then a small plaque on the wall caught my eye: "Bless my little kitchen, Lord, and warm it with Your love."

Are there times in your house when there's too much month at the end of the money? Do you hesitate to invite someone to share a meal because you fear what you have to offer is too plain?

I left with a repaired typewriter—and a determination to be more hospitable. Warmed by the sweet Spirit of our Lord, my little kitchen can be a blessing to my family and to many others. *Bless my little kitchen, Lord. Warm it today with Your love.*   DOREEN KITTO CLARK

Why Grow More?

God has given each of you some special abilities;
be sure to use them to help each other. 1 Peter 4:10, TLB.

The clear sky promised lots of sunshine as another hot summer day dawned. It was a splendid Tuesday, which, according to my schedule, was the day to wash clothes. Everything went quite routinely until the afternoon. As I looked out the window at the clothesline full of dry clothing, I noticed it was beginning to rain. It would be enough to undo all my hard work!

"Come help me!" I called to the children as I ran to snatch the clothes off the line. My husband heard my distress call and immediately joined us. Priscila Emile, only 4, held the basket of clothespins and a few smaller pieces. My husband and I were gathering the large articles of clothing when we realized that 8-year-old Paulo Fernando was jumping to reach the clothesline so that he could take clothing down.

When we were finished bringing the dry clothes indoors, Paulo said, "Sorry, Mom, I couldn't get as many clothes as I wanted to. I can't reach the clothesline very well. I think that I have to grow more so that I can help more!"

I hugged him. "You did as much as you could, and that was enough," I said. "I am happy with the wonderful help you gave."

He was satisfied with my answer, but I continued to think about the phrase "Grow more to help more."

How many times we nurture the desire to grow intellectually, professionally, and even spiritually, for selfish reasons so that we can gain something in exchange, or to call attention to ourselves. How often is it that we desire to grow more in order to help more?

We have heard about not hiding our talents; however, when we decide to use them, it is often for our own benefit. How many personal growth projects are being laid on the altar before God to be blessed?

There is nothing wrong with wanting to grow, investing time and money to develop our abilities, to widen our horizons, to study, and to become specialized in some area. But have you asked yourself, *Do I want to grow more in order to help more?*

NELLY PIAGENTINE DO PRADO SOUZA

The Skinny Plant

*Withhold not good from them to whom it is due,
when it is in the power of thine hand to do it. Prov. 3:27.*

I stared in horror at the plant my coworker was holding. She looked so pleased, all smiles at her accomplishment. My once-beautiful plant that had draped its green-and-white fingered leaves on my rich, golden oak cabinets now reached for the ceiling with skinny branches.

I noticed she had not trimmed this plant in the way I had in mind, although she had volunteered to water and trim my office plants as I worked to finish a deadline on my computer. Now I looked beyond the injured plant at the others nestled on top of the oak credenza. Ninety percent of her work was beautiful; perhaps this one too would recover.

"Thanks," I said, "for all the trimming and watering you did. They look nice." And I thought of the many times I've done mostly good work, but people have noticed only my mistakes.

So many times we don't comment on the major part that went right, looking instead on the part that went wrong. We often withhold good words of praise to whom it is due. I had heard this principle explained many times at the Toastmasters club I attended. Commenting on what a speaker did right could help build her conference as well as help her improve her skills.

With those new insights I decided to sit down with my friend to share about all the things we had in common. She did the same with me. Then we mentioned our differences. We had 20 items we liked, and only five that we didn't like. Focusing on what we liked about each other, the good we saw in the other, strengthened our friendship.

The plant sits on my credenza, its skinny little leaves reaching for the ceiling rather than copiously draping toward the floor. I still hope that it will one day regain its former beauty. Meanwhile, it's a reminder to focus on what is right and good instead of what goes wrong.

EDNA MAYE GALLINGTON

When God Shouted

I have learned to be content whatever the circumstances. Phil. 4:12, NIV.

I was too content. My husband and I were very, very happy with our work in Minnesota. We had lived there for 15 years, so we knew, understood, and loved our people. We were perfectly content to continue working there until retirement.

One summer day we drove to our youth camp, two hours away, to attend a retreat for pastors and their families. During the song service of the first meeting I left the hall to use the telephone. I found that a woman was already using the phone. When she finished, she turned and said, "Please call your neighbor. There has been a storm, and a tree has fallen on your house."

After getting more details, I went to where my husband sat, waiting to welcome the pastors and start the meeting. Instead of welcoming the pastors, he told them we would be leaving immediately to take care of our house.

We found that the tree had made a 4' x 6' hole in the roof of our bedroom. It then rolled off and fell to the ground, missing another building, landing in a clear place in our yard. There had been eight inches of rain, so everything in our bedroom was dripping with water. Soggy insulation from the ceiling was scattered throughout the room. There was also damage to the ceiling in other parts of the house, and water had started to run downstairs.

The insurance company gave us a wonderful settlement, and in a few weeks we moved back to the fresh, clean quarters. We had new carpet, a new roof, and fresh paint. I remember asking my husband, "Do you think we will be able to enjoy our 'new' house, or do you suppose God is getting it ready to sell because He wants us somewhere else?"

A few months later we got the call to Moscow, Russia. Five days after we put the house on the market, it sold. We were able to pack up quickly and move.

It's true that we should learn to be content. It's also true that we can become too content. God often speaks in a still small voice. But sometimes He has to shout at us to get our attention! BARBARA HUFF

Stars or Mud?

Whatsoever things are lovely, whatsoever things are of good report; if there be any virtue, and if there be any praise, think on these things. Phil. 4:8.

The view was magnificent as we climbed the last few feet to the top of the 7,200-foot (2,200-meter) peak, Arvaniti, one of the highest in Greece. Hot and sweaty, our legs aching from the two-and-a-half-hour ascent, we sat down on the rocks to absorb the beauty. We could see snow-covered Mount Olympus, Greece's highest mountain, towering three mountain ridges away.

As far as the eye could see, wooded hills and rocky mountains, sparsely studded with vegetation, spread in a glorious patchwork of greens and gray. Behind us our ascent route wound giddily through a riot of wildflowers—tiny, delicate, snow-white stars, purple pansies with smiling faces, yellow buttercups and cowslips, forget-me-nots, and bird's-eyes of brightest blue. Here and there large pockets of snow still remained, framed by thousands of orange crocuses, while tens of thousands more waited patiently under the snow for the thaw that would free them too. There is still so much beauty left in this old world of ours, so many reminders of the creative power of our loving God.

Oh, yes, the clouds of flies were irritating, and the insect stings made my arms so swollen that I had to remove my watch, and my legs felt like lead. My face was sore and red from too much hot spring sun. And only the speedy intervention of my husband saved me from being stung by a scorpion crawling up my back.

But that is life! Beauty and ugliness, joy and sorrow, good and evil coexist, and we must choose, moment by moment, what we are going to think about, discuss, and store in our memories. We can dwell on the positive—or the negative. The choice is ours, and to a great degree our happiness is the direct result.

As a teenager I once wrote a derogatory composition. The principal called me into her office, gave me a reprimand for my negative thinking, and summed up with these words:

"Two men looked out through prison bars,
The one saw mud, the other stars."

Fifty years have passed since then, but I have never forgotten her lesson.

REVEL PAPAIOANNOU

Trixie's Missing

Rejoice with me; for I have found my sheep which was lost. Luke 15:6.

My 6-month-old cat was missing! I had taken her outside on her leash and fastened her to the tie-out, as usual, and gone back into the house. She had romped and frolicked in the yard, combed the grass for insects, and finally settled down to rest. When I checked her shortly afterward, she was gone.

"Trixie!" I called out as I searched the yard and surrounding neighborhood. *Did someone steal her? Did her leash loosen accidentally?* The thought of her trotting along with her leash dangling from her neck upset me. *What if she tried to cross a street or climb under a fence? What if she shimmied up a tree?*

One hour. Five hours. Nine hours. No Trixie. *My sweet kitty, where are you?* I wondered.

As sunset approached, my fears turned to great sorrow. Perhaps Trixie wasn't coming home. I grabbed a flashlight and headed out the door. I couldn't give up! Shining the light about I called out, "Trixie; mama's girl!" I turned a corner and continued walking. "Trixie baby; mama's gi—"

"Meow. Meow."

I followed the sound, shining the flashlight into the darkness. There, in a tree, was my cat, leash and all.

Trixie meowed anxiously, standing spread-eagled on two wooden posts. I stretched to reach her, and after careful maneuvering untangled the leash and retrieved her. I hugged her tightly as I walked home, rejoicing. Trixie, already eager to jump down and venture off again, had no idea how happy I was. At home, my family celebrated with me. Trixie was home!

I thought, *How precious our pets are to us! And how much more precious are our family and friends. Many have wandered into dangerous territory. They need concerned Christians who will search for them, never giving up, finding them before it is too late. They need loving friends who will never give up until they are safely home.*

That's what I did for Trixie. That's what the Good Shepherd did for the lost sheep. Will I do that for my family and friends?

IRIS L. STOVALL

Think HEIRS

If children, then heirs; heirs of God, and joint-heirs with Christ. Rom. 8:17.

W hen faced with an overwhelming situation, I think HEIRS, an acronym for Have Every Imaginable Resource to Succeed. When I face a problem that seems frustrating, I tell myself, *I am a royal heir and the person I am interacting with is one as well. Together we have every resource needed to get through the situation at hand. At least one of us must ask for the provision needed.*

Once, in a motor vehicle office, I encountered an official who did not see eye-to-eye with me regarding my signature. You'd have to see my signature to understand. I felt that I should have the liberty to sign as I pleased. The official insisted that I do it differently. I argued with her, determined to do it my way. To say that the officer was not at all pleased with my tenacious resistance would be an understatement.

My body temperature and blood pressure rose. I heard sighs and muffled murmurs from others in line. I was about to explode when I thought, *I must demonstrate qualities of respect and humility if for no other reason than to make God proud. I was born with the specific purpose of bringing Him pleasure. How can I bring God pleasure in this situation? Should I give in, or continue to insist on my way?*

As I waited for the officer to decide about my signature I suddenly thought, *Lynn, you are supposed to be thinking HEIRS! Remember, that's what you rehearsed before getting in line.* Immediately I felt calm. My perspective changed as I remembered that the officer and I are both children of God. I decided to treat her as an heir and to carry myself as one.

I am happy to tell you that the HEIRS idea worked! Yes, I got the license, and at the same time I left with everyone's dignity intact, I hope.

In the most stressful situations God wants to give you whatever you will need to get through. Today, when faced with a difficult situation, think HEIRS. We are royal heirs! We have every imaginable resource needed to succeed.

LYNN MARIE DAVIS

Gaining God's Perspective

Blessed are the poor in spirit: for theirs is the kingdom of heaven. Matt. 5:3.

I was listening to my husband as he read the morning devotional. Suddenly my ears tuned to the words "poor in spirit," sensing that the message was especially for me.

My spirits regarding my mothering skills have caused me to feel bad lately. Two days ago what should have been a 10-minute stop in the mall turned into a 30-minute nightmare. I got my children to sit down, but as soon as I turned around they were off in three different directions. From then on it was a desperate attempt to concentrate on what I was doing, while telling the two oldest to stop running on the chairs, retrieving baby Carolyn from the hall, and begging Stephen to "please set a good example by sitting patiently." I hissed at Kathryn to quit running in front of people and set baby down so she'd stop fussing. I told Stephen to unwind his sister's coatstring from the chair, while wildly looking down both corridors in a search for my baby. I wondered to what lengths I could go physically before someone called child protective services.

Poor in spirit? I'll say! Who trained these kids anyway?

Then there's my role as homemaker. I've been attempting to help financially by baby-sitting, but it's not enough. I may have to go to work full-time out of my home. I don't want to leave while my youngest is little.

Poor in spirit? You bet!

My self-image as a whole is in dire straits. In spite of the fact that my exercise equipment collection could handle three women at one time, and the fact that I've had the best health education possible, I'm still not winning a battle to lose 60 extra pounds. How low can a woman's spirit go?

Poor? No doubt!

But maybe this spirit I'm feeling is actually pity. Lucifer had a pity problem of sorts, didn't he? And didn't sin begin with his desire to exalt himself? Perhaps when Jesus talked about being poor in spirit, He meant having less of the spirit of self-sufficiency and less self-reliance, less exalting of my own ideas about what life should be. Perhaps it's in relinquishing my hold on my life and letting God have control that I am blessed.

Yes, I'm feeling better already. I praise You, Lord, for Your faithfulness to me!

DENISE HANCOCK BENNER

What Kind of Light?

"You are the light of the world." Matt. 5:14, NKJV.

The Bible is God's Word. More important, I'm learning the Bible is God's Word for Marian. I continually reinforce this concept by inserting my name into verses. When I read Matthew 5:14, it says, "Marian is the light of the world." There are no qualifiers, of course. God has made me a light; how I shine and whether I glorify Him depends on my choices. What kind of light am I?

At Christmastime I noticed the little white lights sometimes flicker on and off. Am I that kind of light, I wondered? Do I just attract attention and not let God use me to glorify Him?

The other night I came to some road construction and saw a large arrow light up, one light at a time, directing traffic away from a big ditch onto a detour. As each separate light came on, it caught my attention; together these lights made the big arrow that pointed the safe way to go. *I'd like to be that kind of light*, I thought. Together with other Christians, I can help point the way to those who don't know the danger ahead.

I'd like to be a black light. Plain rocks and pictures become beautiful when a black light is turned on. Especially for children with low self-esteem, I would like to be God's black light, showing them their beauty, their qualities, their talents that they may not have seen.

I'd like to be a big searchlight that attracts attention. I'd like to be the light that points people to Jesus.

Unfortunately, sometimes I'm a heat lamp. A short time in my presence and you become uncomfortable.

Sometimes I'm a spotlight, critical, pointing out faults I find in others. Too many times I use this on pastors, teachers, or other church members. God must weep at my using my light in this way.

My first choice is to be a grow light. This light will encourage people to die to self, as a seed must, in order to become what God intends it to be. I want to share with new Christians, to give aid in growth, yet turn off at the right time so that in their private devotions they may establish a good root base in Christ.

God needs my light. God needs your light. God needs our lights here and now. What kind of lights are we? MARIAN M. REIBER

The Lost Purse

Oh, give thanks to the Lord! Call upon His name; make known His deeds among the peoples! Sing to Him, sing psalms to Him; talk of all His wondrous works! Glory in His holy name. Ps. 105:1-3, NKJV.

As I pulled to a stop at our destination, I asked my husband to please bring my purse from his side of the car.

"Purse? There isn't any purse here," he answered.

I took a quick check through the car but was forced to admit the obvious. "I must have left it in the restroom of that minimart where we stopped two hours ago."

"Let's see, that's twice now!" my husband mused.

I objected. "Honey, it's been 10 years since I lost my purse!"

To myself I thought, *I'm really ashamed to ask the Lord to watch over that purse when I've been so careless again.* But I prayed anyway. "Lord, I know I don't deserve Your love and kindness. Please forgive my carelessness once more. Even if the money is taken, let them leave the credit cards."

We decided to call the minimart. My husband talked. "Hello! Has anyone turned in a purse that was left in the ladies' room? It was black, with a lavender wallet inside. . . . Oh, wonderful, you do have it! We can't thank you enough. Do you have a safe place to keep it until we come back by there tomorrow? Again I want to thank you so very much." He put down the phone with a smile.

I collapsed in a nearby chair, and we both praised the Lord for this unbelievable answer to our prayers.

This experience started me thinking about my reactions. Why did I doubt that I could come to the Lord with another lost purse problem? I was seeing Him through my own human frailties, judging Him by my feelings. How often have I been impatient with others' mistakes? Do I feel I must measure up before I come to the Lord with my petitions? If His actions toward us depend on what we deserve, there isn't any one of us who would have hope.

I like the way Oswald Chambers puts it in *My Utmost for His Highest*: "We have to realize that we cannot earn or win anything from God; we must either receive it as a gift or do without it. The greatest blessing spiritually is the knowledge that we are destitute; until we get there our Lord is powerless."

MARIANETTE JOHNSTON

God in the Skies

The heavens declare the glory of God;
and the firmament sheweth his handywork. Ps. 19:1.

I've traveled from the west to east
    And from the east to west,
And seen in God's great changing sky
    A glorious treasure chest.
As clouds and sunshine march across
    His heavenly esplanade,
I find in every form and color
    Attributes of God.

The azure skies reflect His peace;
    The gray skies—His concerns;
And with each morning sun His smile
    Of love on me returns.
The storm clouds mark a troubled God;
    The rain—His pitying tears;
The rainbow—promise of His care
    Until the tempest clears.

His flashlight is the lightning's burst
    That pierces night and shower;
The thunderclap that rolls across
    The heavens is His power.

And so His presence stays with me
    through every changing day.
Both His approvals and denials
    Guide me along life's way.
He bids me lift my eyes toward heaven
    That I may daily see,
In storm or calm, God's love unfailing
    For the likes of me.

LORRAINE HUDGINS

Genealogy: Do I Have One?

Jesus himself was about thirty years old when he began his ministry.
He was the son, so it was thought, of Joseph, . . . the son of Enosh,
the son of Seth, the son of Adam, the son of God. Luke 3:23-38, NIV.

I knew her name. I had her address. I had her phone number. But we had never met. We lived several states apart, so I was filled with great anticipation the day we would actually meet. Her name is Jane Anna; my name is Roxanna Jane, and I had mused to myself about this interesting similarity.

I have very few living relatives and have felt sad through the years to know so little family history. I never met my grandparents, and my parents are gone now too, so my quest to learn about my past started a little late. I have one older cousin who I thought might fill in some information, but her mother died when she was a baby, and she knew very little other than that there was a woman in Tennessee she thought had done some research into our family history. Her name was Jane Anna.

I was delighted to meet this sweet white-haired woman in her 80s and find out that we share the same great-grandparents, making us second cousins. She showed me a couple books in which I found my name and my mother's and grandmother's names. Until that moment those were the only three generational names I knew on my family tree. But the best was yet to come. I found names back to the 1500s in England, and the name of the ancestor who landed in Virginia in 1674. I was so excited! I couldn't believe I really had those kinds of roots—I had spent my entire life thinking I was sort of a genealogical orphan.

Fortunately, I learned long ago that earthly heredity is not a factor in salvation. My accepting Christ is what makes me a child of Abraham. However, the Bible does give a number of lists of genealogy, because being able to trace their family line was important to the Jews. The one I like best (and the one I want to belong to) is the list in Luke 3 that traces Jesus' ancestry back through the generations to Seth, the son of Adam, the son of God. Being a daughter in the family of God is the only family record that really matters!   ROXY HOEHN

How God Answered Our Prayer

He will listen to me and answer when I call to him. Ps. 4:3, TLB.

We had recently moved to a larger city and were still unfamiliar with it. On our way home from an appointment our old station wagon performed well until I reached a stop sign. Immediately the engine stalled. Smoke and steam poured out from under the hood. The engine was dead.

My husband, blind and very feeble, could be of no help. I left him in the car while I went to a service station across the intersection and inquired, "Do you have a mechanic available?"

"No," the attendant replied. "Sorry."

"Where could I find one?" I persisted.

"A little farther down the way." He pointed in the direction from which I had come.

A couple young men helped roll the car to the side of the highway out of the lane of traffic. I appreciated that. They raised the hood and looked around but could do nothing. My husband and I didn't know what to do except pray.

Only a few minutes later a car going in the opposite direction pulled off the highway. I recognized the treasurer of our church and his wife! He came over to our car and assessed the situation. "I'll go find a tow truck for you," he offered.

He was gone quite a while. Soon another car, also going in the opposite direction, pulled off the highway and stopped. The driver of that car was our daughter-in-law, Myrna! I told her our mutual friend had gone for a tow truck, so she waited with us.

Myrna, who was well acquainted with the area, knew an excellent mechanic not far away to whom she directed the driver of the tow truck. We followed in Myrna's car. He had just finished a job and could repair our station wagon immediately, and at a reasonable price. Our car was ready the next day.

We thanked the Lord for sending our friends and Myrna to help us just when we needed them. Surely the Lord heard and answered our earnest prayers. MARTHA MONTGOMERY ODOM

Good Days, Bad Days, God Days

"Your strength will equal your days." Deut. 33:25, NIV.

Going to work was the last thing I felt like doing. Fatigue and stress from a variety of sources had taken its toll, and for some reason I felt particularly fragile. *If anyone says "boo" to me today,* I thought, *I'll just crawl into a corner and cry. I will have quite enough challenges finishing the draft of a 20-page report, printing off copies for the administrators to check, and completing any necessary amendments in time to meet the publication deadline. I don't need any added difficulties.*

"Lord," I prayed, "I can't handle any extra problems today. Please give me a good day."

No sooner had I set to work on my report than the whole computer network "crashed." After a considerable period, during which harassed-looking information systems personnel scurried back and forth under the eyes of frustrated would-be computer users, we were able to access the word processing program again. But by then, of course, all the printers linked to the network were obstinately refusing to print. It was not a good day!

The day was proceeding pretty much as it had begun when it occurred to me that although God had not done what I asked, I hadn't ended up in a corner crying—and didn't even feel the need to. He hadn't given me a good day, but He had given me the strength to cope with a bad one.

Not long after—and quite out of the blue—came a really good day! It was a Friday, and I was mentally prepared for the usual sort of "Friday thing" in which I start out at 8:15 in the morning with a plan of what I want to achieve for the day, but by 9:30 the plan has been abandoned in favor of just keeping ahead of a tide of chaos. This particular Friday the traffic was manageable, my worship presentation went smoothly, a colleague actually volunteered to take a tricky project off my hands, and the shoe store was both able and willing to replace a pair of faulty shoes on the spot.

On the way home I was feeling so good I nearly panicked, in case this was all to make way for something totally awful. But I shook myself and said, "Thank You, Lord, and keep reminding me to 'let every word and each desire and all my days be Thine.'"

JENNIFER M. BALDWIN

Busy Signal

Listen to me; pay attention to what I say. Prov. 7:24, NIV.

I had really great news, and I wanted to share it with a friend. So I dialed her number, anticipating that she would share my excitement and joy. The phone rang several times before she answered.

"Hi, this is Roberta," I said. "How are things going?"

"Oh, fine," she responded. "How about you?"

"Great!" I almost shouted. "I have something really exciting to tell you!"

"Can you hold on a second?" she interjected, the last two words fading away. I heard the sounds of children's voices but could not make out the words.

She came back. "I just feel frustrated sometimes," she said. "My children were playing so happily until I picked up the phone."

I sympathized and inhaled to start my news. But it was a half second too late.

"Oh, I've been wanting to talk to you," she cut in. "My son is starting voice lessons next week. The teacher says he's a musical genius. He is very excited and practices every day." She continued to tell me about the lessons and her baby-sitting problems, concluding, "In fact, I need to let you go. There is an important phone call I need to make right away."

"I understand," I sighed. "Talk to you later."

It wasn't a satisfying call. I felt ignored, unimportant, not valued, even put down. But it made me think. I probably sound a lot like my friend when I am all caught up in my problems and the important things I am doing. Moreover, I know I have given God the very same treatment.

He has impressed me with the feeling that He has something great He wants to share with me. But I have allowed myself to be distracted by little details and disturbances. I have told God how many problems I am facing and how busy I am doing all kinds of important things. He has heard that final click, ending a conversation in which He never got a chance to talk.

I want to give God a chance to tell me His exciting news. I know that what He wants to share with me is the most important thing of all!

ROBERTA FRANKLIN CLAUSEN

Hand in Hand With Jesus

The Lord your God is with you, he is mighty to save. He will take
great delight in you, he will quiet you with His love,
He will rejoice over you with singing. Zeph. 3:17, NIV.

I walked into the ladies' room and entered the closest stall. We were out with friends that evening—one of many nights out that week, savoring one last time with special friends before we bid them farewell.

We had just accepted a call to Red Deer, Alberta, Canada. I was excited to go. My husband and I had made the decision together after much thought and earnest prayer, carefully considering all the pros and cons of this move and its effect on our family and the church we were currently pastoring. We could really see God's leading in our lives, so we had decided to go. In only a few weeks we would be leaving all that was familiar to us and entering a foreign land.

Suddenly I had a *big* knot in the pit of my stomach. I felt ill, and it wasn't the food or the flu! I broke down and began to sob. Now I was really in a fix, because I had to go back out and face my friends, and I was falling apart.

"Lord, help me!" I prayed. "You know I want to serve You, and I will go wherever You want me to go, but I am afraid. Please forgive me and help me to trust You more. Please comfort me and help me. I am tired and vulnerable right now. I need Your strength, Your comfort. Please bless me and help me."

Instantly the words to a song interrupted my thoughts and calmed my fears. It was as if the Lord were holding me in His loving arms and singing to me like a mother sings a lullaby to her child. (See Isaiah 66:12, 13.)

As I stopped my crying and focused on the words of the song, I recognized the sweet love song. It is often sung at weddings. "Walk hand in hand with me through all eternity, have faith, believe in me, give me your hand."

God quieted my fears with His song and embraced me with His love. In faith I took hold of His hand and reverently went back to my friends, knowing that God was with me and would keep me in His care. KATHY JO DUTERROW YERGEN

My Way

Trust in the Lord with all thine heart; and lean not unto thine own understanding. In all thy ways acknowledge him, and he shall direct thy paths. Prov. 3:5, 6.

He was such a little boy, this grandson of ours, but as he saw it, he was "all grown up." He always wanted to do just the right thing. His blue eyes looked at the world with such innocence and would fill with tears if he thought he had done something wrong. His question was often "Grandma, did I do good?"

One balmy spring day his mom and I went into town to do some shopping. Marlene was carrying the new baby, so I felt responsible for the safety of my little grandson. We were ready to cross the street and, as most grandmas do, I cautioned, "Honey, hold my hand while we cross the street so you will be safe from the cars."

He looked at me with just a hint of independence and said with a voice as grown-up as he could muster, "Grandma, I'm big enough now to hold my own hand." He promptly folded his two little hands in front of him and started to cross the street by himself.

Many times have I said, "God, I just cannot solve this problem. Please help me." My heavenly Father never refuses my request. But there have been times when my attitude has been, "Lord, things are going better now; why don't we just let me do it. I'll call if I need You." There are so many occasions I have wanted to "lean unto my own understanding," to hold my own hand instead of His.

When I was younger, one of the popular songs was "My Way." The words aptly described how the singer had survived by living his life "my way." At that age I didn't see the emptiness of that theory. Now I know how senseless life can be when we abandon trust and try to do things "my way." We humans are blessed with a healthy amount of independence. But unless it is balanced with trust, God cannot speak to and through us.

Lord, today I really do want to trust You. I don't want to be like my little grandson, who wanted to do it all by himself. Thank You for the promise that if I acknowledge You, You will direct my paths. JEAN REIFFENSTEIN ROTHGEB

Love's Proof

These three remain: faith, hope and love.
But the greatest of these is love. 1 Cor. 13:13, NIV.

I'll know it's love when:
You ask me how I am and really want to know.
You ask me to share a meal with you.
You squash gossip about me and others.
You pray with and for me.
You care about my kids.
Your eyes fill with tears because of my problems
    and frustrations.
You rejoice with me when things go right for me, even
    when things are going wrong for you.
You believe in me when I don't.
You squeeze me on the shoulder when you could have
    ignored me.
Your friendship is something I can count on.
You share spiritual insights that excite and yet steady
    my growth.
You visit me when I am sick and cook for my hungry family.
You give me a small plant or cuttings from your garden.
You cover my social inadequacies.
You send me a card or call me for no special reason.
You make me feel I can be a success.
You are genuinely kind to my difficult relatives.
You never leave me feeling shredded in public or in private.
You always have time to talk.
You never try to bully me into your way of thinking.
You know my limits and don't embarrass me by pushing me.
You always think the best of me and are patient.
You are willing to risk your safety physically, socially, or
    materially for me.
I know that your love comes from your relationship with God.
Your demonstration of love helps me understand God better. I know
that your love for me shows that you are a true Christian. Thank you
for your love.
URSULA M. HEDGES

I Will Not Forget Thee

*I will not forget you! See, I have engraved you on
the palms of my hands. Isa. 49:15, 16, NIV.*

Leo, Nikki, Jason, Andy, Emily, Buster, Jimmy, Kari, Kayla, Tasha,
Tori, Tyler. They are the names of our grandchildren, unique and
fitting for each precious child. Ranging in age from 16 months to 16
years, each has created within me a very special love. Each day their
names are found upon my lips and in my heart. My daily prayers as-
cend to heaven for them.

From their first little drawings to their greater scholastic achievements, we have followed their progress. With their gifts of pretty
stones, clover blossoms, dandelions, and artistic creations, they have
shown their love to me. I dream big dreams for them. I pray long
prayers for them. I long to keep them safe from danger, from temptation and harmful influences. They bring me sadness and hurt on occasion, but joy and pride more often.

Often Grandpa has joked, "Had I known grandchildren were so much
fun, I'd have passed up having kids and gone straight to grandkids!"

Everyone laughs, but in our hearts we love those "kids" in adult
bodies whom we call our children with a love as intense as when
they were our "little kids." Each of our original five Burnetts has developed into a unique strong individual, with talents, capabilities, and
aptitudes developed personally. Each selected a marriage partner who
has brought into our family more capabilities and love to share.

Is it likely I can ever forget my children or grandchildren? Hardly.
My love for each is so great it often brings a tightness in my chest because my heart feels so full. This is my family.

And Jesus Himself loves them much more than I can ever love
them. I believe I would do almost anything for them, but I cannot do
what Jesus has done. As much as I love each member of this precious
family, I cannot save them from hurt, from death, from sin. But our
Saviour has graven them upon the palms of His hands; He will do for
them what I cannot do.

*O, my Father, today I seek Your loving-kindness, Your protection, and
Your Holy Spirit. Please, Father, save each one. May our circle of love for
each other extend into eternity together.*

BETTY R. BURNETT

You Can't Bother God

Casting all your care upon him; for he careth for you. 1 Peter 5:7.

I was visiting with a recently converted young man and asked him how his business was getting along.

"It's going well. I'm about to close one deal that is worth $14,000 to me." He paused and looked embarrassed. "It's so important that I've even prayed about it."

"Why not?" I responded. "Prayer is talking to God about everything."

"I pray about other things," he replied, "but I didn't feel it was quite right to bother Him about money matters."

My young friend voiced a common concept—God is interested only in our souls. He sent His Son to save us from the penalty of our sins; He offers us power to overcome sins; He promises forgiveness if we fall into temptation. He guides us in every aspect of our spiritual lives, but His interest stops there.

This is not so. God is interested in us as persons. He knows all about us—even to the number of hairs on our head (Matt. 10:30). He has promised to supply all our needs (Phil. 4:19). We can talk to Him about everything that concerns us. We can ask for help and guidance in everyday life, and He will give it.

Are you studying and in need of help with an exam or an assignment? God will give you wisdom (James 1:5).

Are you having health problems? James 5:14-16 tells us that "the prayer of faith shall save the sick."

Do you have cares and worries, unsolved problems, insurmountable difficulties? Tell God about them, ask Him for help. You'll be amazed at how He solves your problems if you hand them over to Him.

Matthew 6:28-32 and Luke 12:22-31 tell us that God cares for ravens and lilies. How much more He cares for you. Talk to God about your concerns. He loves you; He wants to be your confidant.

A noted Christian writer has said, "Keep your wants, your joys, your sorrows, your cares, and your fears before God. You cannot burden Him; you cannot weary Him. He who numbers the hairs of your head is not indifferent to the wants of His children" (Ellen G. White, *Steps to Christ,* p. 100). GOLDIE DOWN

One More Day

The angel of the Lord encamps all around those who fear Him, and delivers them. Ps. 34:7, NKJV.

W e're going to die," my husband stated as he calmly looked into the rearview mirror of our 1994 Corvette. I turned toward him to see what he meant. At that moment a 25-foot produce delivery truck hit the side of our car, sending debris past the window and onto the busy four-lane highway.

My husband and I had, on a sudden whim, decided to surprise my niece, who was working at summer camp in the beautiful mountains of Colorado. As we drove up the last stretch of road to the camp, we found her and several friends leaving for a drive to Pike's Peak. We joined the young people, leaving in two cars for the drive to the peak. Somehow we managed to become separated. As we traveled, my husband and I speculated whether the others were in front of us or behind, concluding they must be behind, so we pulled off the edge of a very crowded four-lane highway to wait.

We hadn't been there for more than three minutes when my husband looked into the rearview mirror and announced, "We're going to die!" He watched the large truck advancing down the narrow highway edge toward us. Suddenly, and without a moment to spare, the truck veered away from the back of our car, but struck the side of our car, strewing wreckage over the road, and sending two propane tanks into the ditch beside the highway.

We sat in silence and in awe of the miracle we had watched unfolding in our behalf. The car hadn't moved an inch; it had remained absolutely still. Why didn't it spin out into oncoming traffic? Why didn't the propane tanks from the shelf on the truck hit the large back window of our car, possibly causing an explosion or coming through the window? Why was the puncture on the full tank of gas so small? What did it take for our guardian angels to move that huge truck from our path and onto the highway lane?

We will forever be grateful that the Lord gave us the gift of another day. *Thank You, Jesus, for this day too!* KARON SCOTT

Good, and Ready to Forgive

For thou, Lord, art good, and ready to forgive;
and plenteous in mercy unto all them that call upon thee. Ps. 86:5.

A sad thing happened at our house recently. Peanut, my daughter
Holly's pet mouse, had died and had to be buried. I still remember her wailing from her room.

"Mommy, Swan ate Peanut!" Her pain went through my heart.
Then, while she was yet crying, she yelled, "I hate Swan!"

Since I am blind, Swan, my guide dog, aids me in my daily travels. She had not eaten the mouse, but while Holly was talking on the phone, Swan brought her catch to us, as if she had done us a favor. Since this was the second time she had brought us a mouse, we took it with the usual mixed emotions. Once we discovered this was no ordinary mouse, however, we all felt bad.

Then a wave of judgment and blame swept through the house. Holly had left her aquarium on the floor without its protective lid. I had not punished Swan for the first mouse she had caught. My husband recalled a period of time when he was concerned about Swan's location. And my oldest daughter had ordered the removal of the aquarium from her bedroom because of its smell. The blaming went on and on.

After a time, however, Holly repented of leaving the aquarium where she had. And I promised to get her another mouse. Yet it was still difficult to see Swan as anything but a nasty beast.

The next afternoon I was amazed to find my daughter petting Swan and saying to her, "It's hard to stay mad at you, because you're so cute." What a wonderful quality God had placed in this child. And this quality was not unlike His own. It was because of the goodness in Holly's heart, and her readiness to forgive, that the rest of us were also free to forgive. Swan was restored to her place of affection in our household once more because Holly was willing to forgive.

Lord, make me more like Holly and more like You—good and ready to forgive and plenteous in mercy to all who wrong me. Take blame and judgment from my heart for this new day.   NANCY BEZANT

Grace at Midnight

He who watches over you will not slumber; indeed, he who watches over Israel will neither slumber nor sleep. Ps. 121:3, 4, NIV.

A nd, Retta, don't lose any sleep over this."
So ended my phone call to my boss. Never mind that it was the middle of the night and I had awakened her. Never mind that the news I had shared involved a mistake I had made, a stupid mistake that would cause her hardship. Never mind all that. Her concern was for me.

The irony of my supervisor's words was almost amusing. For now that I had verbally handed the problem over to her, it was she who would go without any sleep. I could go home and get some rest. She, on the other hand, would have to struggle to find a solution. Because she was my authority, my foibles had become her ultimate responsibility. The buck stopped on her end of the phone.

It's not hard to care for those who make us look good. It's another story when someone makes life difficult. On those occasions grace is not the usual response. To experience undeserved grace in the face of our own blundering can be all but shocking. Grace from a supervisor is an unexpected gift to be cherished.

There is Someone else who has authority over me. With Him I have come to expect grace. But though I can rely on it, His grace still fills me with awe, especially when I've really messed up.

My failures do not bring Him any joy. In fact, they mar His reputation. They make life difficult for Him. But even when I call Him up in the night to tell Him what I've done, He is never short with me. It seems He is always alert and waiting for my call. Morning, noon, or midnight, His response is predictable. "Let's throw this incident into the bottom of the sea. It's history. And Retta, don't lose any sleep over this. That's My job. The buck stops with Me. You see, I never slumber nor sleep."

RETTA MICHAELIS

A Modern-Day Good Samaritan

Which now . . . thinkest thou, was neighbor unto him? Luke 10:36.

It was nearing the end of our visit to London. Bart and I decided to do one more museum, the Imperial War Museum.

Enid and Bill, our bed-and-breakfast hosts, had invited us to go with them to the All Souls Church of England on Regent Street for the Sunday evening meeting. I assured them we would try our best to be back by 5:30.

Enid said, "We always go early, as 1,000 people might attend, and we like to sit in a special pew."

We were back in time for a short nap before leaving at 5:30. The traffic was heavy, and Bill seemed to be driving erratically as I watched the white line flash by. We were no more than a mile from their house when Enid noticed it too and kept calling to him, "Billy, Billy, turn in, turn." He paid no attention to her, and when we got to the traffic light the car stopped.

We then realized something was seriously wrong. It appeared that Bill was having a stroke. Cars rushed by, horns honking.

A man in dress clothes came running over and asked, "Anything I can help you with? I am a chauffeur, and maybe there is something I can do for the car."

I quickly explained the situation to him, and he helped Bart lift Bill out of the driver's seat.

Enid said to Bart, "I have never driven this car. Could you drive us to Charing Cross Hospital?"

My husband hesitated, since he wasn't used to driving on the left side of the street. That's when John, the chauffeur, offered to drive to the hospital. John parked at the emergency entrance and said to Enid, "You call me when you're ready to go home. My friend and I will come and drive you."

Bart and I spent the evening in the hospital with Enid. Bill regained some of his faculties and could smile and talk a little with us before we left about three hours later. John cheerfully picked us up and drove us home.

Later, as we sat with Enid eating warm lentil soup, we gladly labeled John "a modern-day good Samaritan." He was there when we needed him.

DESSA WEISZ HARDIN

Too Many Flowers!

Let your moderation be known unto all. Phil. 4:5.

I love growing flowers in my garden, and before last summer I never thought I could say I had too many. But because of an abundance of rain and a shortage of sunshine, my perennial plants grew into a profuse abundance of spindly stems that mounded up and began to fall over onto the lawn. When I discovered that my beautiful white drifts of daisies were killing the grass beneath them, I knew I had to snip them off.

Reluctantly I brought my shears and began trimming back the overgrown plants. Soon we had enough cut flowers to arrange a bouquet in every room of the house. Then we gave bouquets away to neighbors. Finally I found myself doing what I never thought I could: throwing away fresh flowers. I simply had too much of a good thing!

We sometimes find ourselves "overdoing," even on the good things. We want to be involved in church work, care for our families, clean and organize our homes, study, exercise, and spend time with friends. Our days are filled with good things we want to do. Our to-do lists are like overgrown gardens.

How can we keep all this in perspective and maintain a healthy balance? One way is by scheduling frequent priority checks. I regularly ask myself: Am I really doing the most important things, or just the seemingly urgent ones? Am I allowing myself to be buried under something that has become too much of a good thing? What activities should I snip off?

A friend of mine actually practices saying no graciously to non-family requests for her time and energies. She also maintains a habit of giving three no answers for every yes. We just can't do everything, no matter how good it would seem!

Striving for the moderation necessary for a healthy lifestyle, I am reminded often of Proverbs 3:5, 6: "Trust in the Lord with all thine heart; and lean not unto thine own understanding. In all thy ways acknowledge him, and he shall direct thy paths."

Lord, help me today to set priorities, cutting those activities that need to be cut. Help me to learn to say no to the good so that I can say yes to the best.

BRENDA FORBES DICKERSON

Cable Car Ride

When I am afraid, I will trust in you. Ps. 56:3, NIV.

Three carloads of us left Bern, Switzerland, for Interlaken. From there we drove through a lovely green valley, at the end of which tourists could take a cable car to the top of Schilthorn.

"We thought you'd like a cable car ride up the mountain," our host said. "The view is magnificent!"

"Count me out," I said. "I prefer to keep my feet on the ground. I'll watch birds down here in the valley."

"You really should come," my friend Ruthie urged. "George and I have taken this ride, and it's worth it."

"I'm afraid," I admitted. "What if the cable snapped?"

"They are really very safe," Ruthie assured me.

Our host came back with a ticket for me. I didn't want to disappoint him after he had already paid for me, so I followed the others into the car. I positioned myself by the glass and held tightly to the metal rail. As the car was pulled slowly up the cable, I gasped at the beauty. Below me cows grazed beside colorful Swiss cottages. We passed mountain meadows bright with flowers. Goats munching grass looked up as we passed. An old man and a dog walked a winding alpine trail. It was a picture right out of the book *Heidi* that I remembered reading as a child.

We got off at a small village part way up the mountain. We sipped juice while sitting on a patio overlooking the valley. A chaffinch lit on a pine tree nearby and sang its heart out. It was a magic moment, and I wanted to stay there forever.

I followed a footpath to a meadow outside the village where field-fares called to one another. Engrossed in the discovery of a new bird, I missed the cable car going down and had to wait another half hour. Meanwhile, I sighted a second new bird, a ring ouzel, handsome in his black coat and white collar. I was so glad I had gotten courage to take the cable car ride. My fears had been unfounded, and the reward at the top was great. I wonder how many other mountain-top experiences I have missed in life because I was afraid of the unknown, unwilling to step onto the cable car of faith.

Lord, when You invite me to experience something new, help me to overcome my fears. Help me to trust You and not be afraid.   DOROTHY EATON WATTS

Rejoice Always

Rejoice in the Lord always; again I will say, rejoice! Phil. 4:4, NASB.

L ast summer while camping in Maine our family decided to leave our camper at the campground and venture seven and a half miles away by boat to a remote site for a night of tent camping.

"It will be a great experience for the boys," encouraged my usually not-so-adventurous husband.

My boys, ages 5 and 8, agreed. With some reservations, I packed up our gear, and we started off. After settling in, enjoying a campfire-cooked supper, and reading by flashlights, we squeezed into our three-person tent. Aside from the primitive bathroom arrangements, I was actually enjoying our experience.

Then we awoke in the night to the sound of rain. It was falling softly, but I began to worry. My fears mounted as the sky remained dark and threatening after dawn, suggesting more than gentle rain. We decided to break camp quickly and eat breakfast back at the camper.

As we loaded the boat, I kept looking at the sky and remembered the admonition from the old camp manager to keep our eyes on the sky. "I've seen three-foot waves come up on that lake in a matter of minutes," he had said.

We piled into the boat and steered toward the darkest part of the sky. *What if a storm arises? David can't swim.* I gripped the sides of the boat, praying that nothing would happen during the 25-minute ride back to the campground.

Then I heard Daniel singing. Over the noise of the motor and the wind blowing in my face I caught pieces of the tune. "Rejoice in the Lord alway, and again I say, rejoice." What a sermon that taught me about trusting in God!

Yes, I had been praying—but I never gave up the fear and worry. It was as if I really didn't believe that God was taking care of us. God, in His gentle way, used Daniel's cheerful song to refocus my attention on Him and to remind me that true rejoicing means I'll be content to know that everything is in His hands.

Dear Father, please keep that tune running through my head today and every day so I can learn to trust You completely in all situations and to rejoice in You always. LILLY TRYON

Broken Hydrants

I will bless those who trust me. They will be like trees growing beside a stream — trees with roots that reach down to the water, and with leaves that are always green. Jer. 17:7, 8, CEV.

When I was a child, we lived in New York City on 180th Street. Summertime was hot and muggy. There was no air-conditioning and no gentle breeze. One apartment we lived in faced the street. Only our living room and one bedroom had windows. In another apartment we lived on the back side of the building with a view of the alley and the dirty red brick building next door. To see the sky we had to open the window, stick our heads out, and crane our necks to look up.

Nevertheless, I loved the city. Aunts, uncles, and cousins lived on our block, so I always had family around to watch over me. We didn't have trees or grass, just concrete sidewalks, asphalt streets, and a fire hydrant on every street. To see grass and trees we had to walk several blocks to the park, so our front steps, sidewalk, and street were our playground. On really hot muggy days the teenage boys would open the fire hydrant and let the water gush into the street. My brother, two sisters, and I would take off our shoes and run through the water, squealing with delight. We didn't care if our clothes got wet—it felt great! There must have been 40 to 50 of us, including the children from the next block who came over and played with us. The fire hydrant on their block looked fine, but the underground pipe connecting it to the water supply was broken.

Those two fire hydrants remind me that the world is full of people whose lives are barren and empty. Broken hydrants—disconnected from the source of water—Living Water. When we're not connected to Christ, when our eyes are not focused on Him, something happens to our relationships with each other and with God. Sometimes the change is so gradual that we don't even notice it, but in time it leaves us dry and barren.

Lord, help me to stay connected to You so my life will be pure, friendly, gentle, sensible, kind, helpful, genuine, sincere, and filled with exuberant joy, even in the midst of conflict.   CELIA MEJIA CRUZ

Lesson From a Map

Thou shalt guide me with thy counsel. Ps. 73:24.

While teaching Vacation Bible School, I decided to encourage my children to look to the Bible as the guide to their lives. A map of our city seemed to be a perfect illustration. I enlarged map sections around the church to ensure that the children could see the street names and, with my assistance, locate their homes.

The point I wanted to emphasize was that just as a map gives us directions from where we are to where we want to go, so the Bible gives us directions from where we are now to where we can find God.

"Children," I began, "I want you to find your house on this map of our city. Draw a line from it to the church."

The task seemed simple enough to me. Each child finally located his or her home on the map. They all found the church. The problem came in drawing the line from home to the church. The children soon discovered that there was more than one way to get from their house to the church. In fact, some of them found many ways to reach the church.

H'mmm, this is very interesting! I thought. *I think there is a spiritual lesson here for me!* So often I read the directions from the Bible and expect everyone else to move in unison the way *I* think we should go, making right and left synchronized turns. I've not stopped to realize that people may come from different perspectives, traveling different routes to the same destination.

Too often I have used the Bible like a cookbook: to get the correct outcome I must follow the recipe, step by step, doing the same thing in the same way every time. Perhaps the Bible is more like a map, showing us where we are and where we want to go and the different routes we can take to get there. It is possible for each of us to arrive at the same place, but we may have to take different routes. Some may need to travel north, others south. Still others need to take detours. Some find the road easy, others find it rough. That's because we aren't all on the same road, though our destination is the same.

Our circumstances are different from each other's, but God is still leading each of us on the road to the kingdom. He knows our starting place and how to get us to where we want to go.

ELIZABETH DARBY WATSON

God's Flower Arrangement

*As God's chosen people, holy and dearly loved, clothe yourselves with
compassion, kindness, humility, gentleness and patience. Col. 3:12, NIV.*

I searched the flowers and branches laid out on the tatami mat floor
by my ikebana flower arranging teacher. I rejected one after another. That twisted branch would be difficult to work with. That
stem was so misshapen. I wouldn't want that lopsided flower in my
creation. I finally made my choice of materials and knelt at the low
table to create an arrangement from the most nearly flawless stems I
could find.

Our class was studying a Japanese art form developed through
centuries. We painstakingly bent branches to their prescribed angles.
Broken stems would have been the result of impatience. We cut out
distracting foliage, fearing that we might have cut out too much. We
moved stems a little more forward, then a little more back, then just a
bit to the side. We positioned the flowers again and again until we
thought we had a form of art—or until we gave up!

Then the master teacher studied our creations. She snipped a
branch here and moved a stem there. We were awed by the difference her touches made.

As I moved around the low table admiring the others' arrangements, I was fascinated by Miss Kondo's creative use of misshapen
stems I had rejected. I was amazed that the twisted branch I had
passed over was the highlight of Mrs. Kusayama's arrangement. The
lopsided flower I had not chosen was the stunning focus of Mariko's
creation. My arrangement with its nearly flawless materials was simple, maybe even beautiful, but it somehow lacked character.

Ultimate assurance is knowing that I, like a flawed branch, am
chosen by God. Because I have often been rejected, I treasure His ab-
solute acceptance. He doesn't reject me because of my blemishes and
imperfections. He sees what He can make of me. He knows my potential to glorify Him.

Being chosen is wondrous. But more astounding is God's desire to
make each of us into something beautiful, like a flower arrangement
displaying His character.   ELAINE HAGELE

In His Name

There is no other name . . . by which we must be saved. Acts 4:12, NIV.

I seldom rent a car, so I was a bit excited about the prospect. As I was flying to a familiar place for only a short visit, it seemed more logical to rent a car than to depend on someone else to get me to and from the airport. So I had reserved a compact.

After deplaning I headed straight to the car rental concession. Yes, I could see my name on an envelope in the waiting rack. As the clerk asked my name and picked up the envelope, she asked which model I preferred. *This is going to be a snap,* I thought. *What model sounded the most fun?*

"Credit card and driver's license, please."

I had them ready. The clerk studied them a moment and handed them back. "You have to have a driver's license and credit card in the same name. Do you have one with your own name?"

No, I didn't. I had been using a credit card in my husband's name for years. However, I knew I should have one in my own name and had applied for a Visa card of my own. It had been approved, but the card had not yet arrived.

What to do? I tried showing identification with both my husband's name and mine on it. No good. I went to another company. No luck there either—they all required a driver's license and credit card in my own name.

My own name. A very special and precious identification. It is me, not an extension of someone else, even a relative.

Like my character and my identification with God. I can't take credit for what my husband does, and I don't have to take blame either. God looks at *my* record, *my* name. Even a special relationship with someone like Moses or David or Daniel will do me no good. No one else can gain salvation for me.

With one exception. I must claim the name of Jesus. In fact, that is the only way I can be saved, for "Salvation is found in no one else, for there is no other name under heaven . . . by which we must be saved."

Thank You, Jesus, for looking at me as a unique individual. But most of all, thank You for giving me a special name and covering me today with Your goodness and Your name. ARDIS DICK STENBAKKEN

Why Me, God?

Praise be to the God and Father of our Lord Jesus Christ,
the Father of compassion and the God of all comfort,
who comforts us in all our troubles. 2 Cor. 1:3, 4, NIV.

This can't be happening to me!" My mind reeled as I sat in the doctor's office waiting for him to confirm what I had already guessed from seeing the sonogram. Dazed, I listened as he came into the room. His voice softened as he told me the unthinkable.

I had miscarried for the third time.

The rest of the day passed in a blur as I sank into the deepest depression I had ever experienced. After the second miscarriage my husband had taken a day off work. We spent the day at the park with our 3-year-old. It was so comforting to talk about our dreams for our unborn child, to cry together, to grieve together. Healing was slow, but it did come.

But things were different after the third loss. A person can process only so much grief at one time before the brain says "No more!" For my husband that translated into pouring himself into his work, where things were not so depressing. For me it meant trying to skip the grieving process. I was tired of being sad. Desperately I wanted to forget what had happened.

Friends unknowingly helped me stay in the denial stage. After all, what does one say to someone after three deaths? Society barely acknowledges the event. Nothing had ever tried my faith to such an extent before. Where was God? Why did He allow me to face such sorrow and disappointment? Could I ever trust Him again? It was especially difficult to struggle with my core beliefs about God when, as a pastor's wife, I didn't want to shake anyone else's faith.

Praise the Lord, He still speaks to us today! He is our source of comfort. Looking to the cross, I realized that Jesus asked the same question I was struggling with: *My God, My God, why have You forsaken Me?* His path in life was not easy. How did He deal with His trials? Simply by trusting God, moment by moment.

As I learned to give my pain to Jesus, I stopped denying my feelings. I allowed myself to cry if I felt like it. You know what? The Great Comforter cried with me, and then He dried my tears. WILMA BURTON KING

Cherishing Chickadees

That is what is meant by the Scriptures which say that no mere man
has ever seen, heard or even imagined what wonderful things
God has ready for those who love the Lord. 1 Cor. 2:9, TLB.

My husband moved the food boxes from our van to the picnic table at our campsite below the Ancient Bristlecone Pine Forest. Suddenly he called excitedly, "Come quickly!"

I hurried to the picnic table and was awestruck at what I saw. Little mountain chickadees were edging close to the boxes.

"Try putting some granola in your hand and see what happens," he urged.

I had known the thrill of a brilliant western tanager resting briefly on my shoulder and a bridled titmouse landing for a few awesome seconds on my finger. But I was totally unprepared for the experience that came to us that evening and the next morning.

One after another those delicate creatures curved their tiny claws over my finger and grabbed a grain or two of oats, barley, or rye and flitted off to enjoy each savory morsel. Word must have gotten around, because birds began flying in from behind and in front of us. In fact, at times there was a lineup in the piñon and junipers above us. As soon as one finished, another came in for a landing on my out-stretched hand.

One I dubbed Mrs. Aggressive. She seemed to have no fear what-soever. As I spoke lovingly to her, she seemed to respond to my voice by cocking her head in understanding. In fact, she became a bit of a nuisance during breakfast the next morning. Even though we had left some grains on the top of the ice chest, she kept coming in to survey the whole lay of the land. She decided the food in my cereal bowl looked more enticing than the grains on the ice chest. I held my breath as she landed on the edge of my bowl, snatched some break-fast, and flew to a nearby branch. It wasn't long before she was back—this time on my whole-wheat raisin-nut bread. When her bill was full, she took off again.

How I look forward to heaven! The creatures of the wild will be my friends. We can interact without fear. Thank You, Jesus, for this blessed hope!
DONNA LEE SHARP

Grandpa's Song

*And he carried me away in the Spirit to a mountain great and high,
and showed me the Holy City, Jerusalem,
coming down out of heaven from God. Rev. 21:10, NIV.*

This text takes me back to a hot, still summer day when I was 9 years old. It was not a time for work. Boiled potatoes and new roasting ears of corn had satisfied the noon hunger of my grandpa. By now the milk was on its way to town on the big creamery truck, and the separator was washed and shrouded with its dish towel protection. The farm activity gave way to the lull of the after-dinner hour. Even the shaggy farm dog's usually perpetual-motion tail was still, and he rested his muzzle on his paw as he slept under the hay wagon.

I raced out the door to see where everyone had gone. I found Grandpa resting in a chair under the box elder tree. Passing Grandpa I headed for the windmill tower. I retrieved a tin cup from its nail and pumped a cup of cool water from the well. Mmmm, that tasted good!

Then I heard a familiar sound—Grandpa was singing. "'Just over the mountains in the Promised Land, lies the holy city built by God's own hand.'"

I plopped down on the grass near his feet as he sang on.

"'As our weary footsteps gain the mountain's crest, we can view our homeland of eternal rest. We are nearing home! We are nearing home! See the splendor gleaming from the domes afar . . .'"

My eyes wandered to the weathered roof of the barn, and then beyond to the shelter belt of trees just below where the gentle slope of the hills climbed upward. No domes near here. Just the sun beating down on the cornfields and pastures that swept away from this simple farmstead.

"'See the glory streaming through the "gates ajar" . . .'"

Our gates were simple screen doors that squeaked when we opened them, and barbed wire gates with movable posts. Not too much glory about these gates.

"'There we soon will enter, nevermore to roam. Hear the angels singing! We are nearing home! We are nearing home.'"

That day I caught a glimpse of my heavenly home through my grandpa's song. It is a vision of glory that is still in my heart.

VIRLYS MOLLER

Moving

Thy will be done in earth. Matt. 6:10.

I dreaded moving. I loved my home, school, church, country living, and having all my family within a day's drive. And this move was not just to another city, or even to an adjacent state. This move was across the country—about as far as one can move and still remain within the United States.

I had prayed for more than two years about this move. I didn't want to go. But when God finally made it clear that now was the time, I accepted it. On one hand it was difficult; on the other I found peace as it became clear that this was God's plan for our family.

After being listed for nine days, our home sold to the first person who looked at it. A beautiful home in the new area was quickly located. In fact, we were on a plane flying to our new home in just five weeks.

Although we were following God's plan, this was still the most difficult move of my life. The people were different—they spoke differently, ate differently, and even dressed differently from what I was used to. I was used to the clouds and drizzle that are so prevalent in the Pacific Northwest. In Florida I suffer from the heat and humidity, though I find the constant daily sunshine a blessing. It was a challenge to find the grocery store, a beautician, a dentist, a Christian bookstore, and even K Mart. I had to deal with lizards and insects. Through it all I had an assurance that I was where God wanted me to be.

Everything has not gone smoothly since this move. We've had some challenges in adjusting to our new world. But still I have the assurance that I am where God wants me, and this now comforts me. Through it all I have felt God's blessing on our family. We are here for a reason.

Even though I would not have chosen to make such a major move with all the adjustments that came with it, I purpose to lean on Him daily. I will strive to make certain that each day I am saying "Thy will be done, not my will."

CARLENE WILL

Women Praying in the Night

Let us then approach the throne of grace with confidence, so that we may receive mercy and find grace to help us in our time of need. Heb. 4:16, NIV.

It was morning, and our prayer group had been in the presence of God all night. We'd each had a turn sitting in the "prayer chair, encircled by the group as each one laid hands on us and prayed over us for our needs.

> Women praying in the night,
> Gathered together by God's leading,
> Hearts hurting, overflowing, needing,
> Hearts bleeding, wanting to touch the hem of
> Your garment.
>
> Women praying in the night,
> Hearts talking, singing, laughing,
> Sharing, caring, understanding,
> Wanting to receive Your Spirit's outpouring.
>
> Women praying in the night,
> Claiming the power for healing, guidance, forgiveness,
> faith, wisdom, prosperity,
> Claiming the power for our families, ourselves,
> our friends,
> Claiming the power for deliverance.
>
> Women praying in the night,
> Coming together to give thanks,
> Feeling at peace, feeling blessed,
> Receiving answers, seeing signs,
> Remembering the power of praying all night.
>
> Women praying in the night,
> A force of power, a force for change.
> We praise and thank You, we adore and love You.
> O Lord Most High! Our King of kings.

LUAN CADOGAN

Catfish and You

We also rejoice in our sufferings, because we know that suffering produces perseverance; perseverance, character; and character, hope. Rom. 5:3, 4, NIV.

Many of us have come face-to-face with difficulties. In trying circumstances and difficult situations, great discoveries are made about ourselves, our capabilities, and our ability to survive. Somehow we find ways to endure the inconveniences and deprivations.

I learned a lesson in survival from codfish. It was a time when the industry faced financial disaster unless a way was found to ship codfish from the East Coast to the West Coast successfully without its losing flavor in transit. As it was, the industry was losing a lot of money.

Then a creative person solved the problem: the codfish were placed in a tank with their natural enemy, catfish. During the trip west the catfish chased the codfish all over the tank. At their destination the codfish were still as fresh as when they were first caught, with no flavor loss.

In most of our lives God-appointed "catfish" give chase, causing just enough tension to keep us striving, alert, and growing spiritually.

Tuberculosis claimed my father's life, leaving my mother at age 33 with five small children to raise. She determined that welfare assistance was not the solution and managed to keep gainfully employed as a cook, laundress, or maid.

At age 13 I worked in a bakery, where I shelled nuts eight hours daily, six days a week, for $5 a day. We eventually opened our own home-based hand laundry. With perseverance, hard work, and thrift, we survived.

I developed talents that led to my learning to design and sew, and making what we couldn't afford to buy. Thus self-sufficiency, trust in God, contentment with what we had, and appreciation of God's bestowed blessings enriched our lives.

I think the God-appointed "catfish" of poverty, though an inconvenience, added a dimension to our lives that built character, strengthened faith in God, and gave hope. If there are "catfish" in your life, perhaps God is leading you to spiritual growth.

MABEL ROLLINS NORMAN

The Baby's Prayer

We know not what we should pray for as we ought: but the Spirit itself maketh intercession for us. Rom. 8:26.

My husband and I and our two little girls were living and working in Johannesburg, Transvaal (Gauteng). We decided to take a weekend break and go up north about 225 miles (375 kilometers). At that time gas could not be bought between 6:00 p.m. and 6:00 a.m. Neither was it sold on weekends.

We enjoyed our short vacation, visiting friends we hadn't seen for years. Early Sunday morning we started home. My husband thought he'd be able to get home on a tank of gas, but then we took a wrong turn somewhere and wasted much time and precious fuel. We ran out of gas in an industrial area that was fairly dangerous. We could see no cars on the road, no houses, nor were there any people in sight—only factories and more factories. Everything looked so dismal.

Our only help was to commit our case to God. I prayed first, then our 6-year-old daughter, then my husband. Then our 2-year-old daughter decided to pray. Now, she couldn't talk well. All she said was "Au-au, au-au, au-au. Amen." But you should have seen the expression on her face as she prayed in her own way! She was so serious and so sincere.

When we opened our eyes, there was the direct answer to prayer. A young couple from the church we attended had come all that way for a drive. And where we were parked is where they decided to turn around to go back home. They willingly siphoned enough fuel out of their car to put into our van, and we were on our way. We felt this was an answer to all our prayers, even the prayer of our 2-year-old.

Like babies learning to talk, we also come to God with inadequate vocabularies to express our need and our dependence on Him. Still, He hears and understands. What a wonderful God!

PRISCILLA ADONIS

Look for the Gift

Every good and perfect gift is from above. James 1:17, NIV.

Hot flashes! Those inconvenient, irritating, unpredictable hormonal fluctuations that seem to be wired directly into one's internal thermostat. Those moments when suddenly, for no logical reason, your personal furnace blows seven times hotter, your face breaks into a vivid pink flush, your ears flame bright red, and perspiration oozes from every pore. Talk about feeling out of control. At best they are mildly inconvenient, dictating a need for layered clothing. At their worst they make one want to don a bathing suit and fly into the teeth of a cold wind.

Some years ago I made the decision to develop the habit of looking for the gift in every situation. Even though I had learned that identifying and focusing on the gift could make a positive difference in my life, no amount of discussion with my friends had resulted in our defining even one gift in hot flashes.

Soon afterward I attended a lecture on women's health. One of the participants brought up the topic of hot flashes. In response the presenter chuckled and suggested that we try thanking our bodies for the protective hot flashes. I sat up straighter in my chair, ears alert.

"You know the role of fever in the body," the woman said. "Many harmful organisms cannot survive in the presence of increased body temperature. By periodically raising body temperature, hot flashes may protect us from some illnesses by killing off harmful viruses and bacteria. It may even contribute to women's longevity."

I could hardly wait until the break to call a couple of my friends. "Guess what?" I asked as each in turn answered the phone. "I've just discovered the 'gift' in hot flashes!"

This perspective has not stopped our hot flashes, but it has made them more tolerable. Viewing this piece of physiology as a gift from above dissipates some of the resulting stress.

I've made a renewed commitment to look for the gift in every aspect of life, even in those situations when identifying a positive aspect seems so elusive. If there is a gift in hot flashes, there must be one in everything! ·

ARLENE TAYLOR

I'll Call Her Back

*"They would search for God and perhaps grope for him
and find him." Acts 17:27, NRSV.*

W hen I call my daughter, Linda, occasionally I chat with her
young boys. I enjoy hearing their childish voices chattering
about the things they are doing. When their mother says, "Do you
want to talk to Grandmother?" they usually come running.

Several months ago, after talking with Cody, I asked to talk to
Ryan, the 8-year-old. I could hear Linda speaking to him, as he was in
the same room. Imagine my surprise when, instead of the joyful
sound of small steps bounding to the phone, I heard this grown-up
little voice say, "Tell her I will call her back."

I found out that Ryan had been given a new book and just couldn't
be interrupted at that moment.

How many times, when the Lord calls us, have our actions told
our best and dearest Friend that we have something more important
to do than spend time with Him? Jesus longs for communion with us.
We've heard a lot about prayer; we've read and memorized quotations about prayer. But do we really know, experientially, what
prayer is? Do we talk to Him, listen to Him, grope to find Him?
When we seek the Lord, we will find Him, for He is waiting close by.

Why, God, do we have to grope for You when You are right here
beside us?

*Because, child, it takes the seeking and the groping to clear the darkness
from your eyes so you can see I'm right here beside you.*

One game our grandchildren love is hide-and-seek. We make it
easy for the boys to find us, even giving obvious signals to ensure
that they are victorious in the search.

God is not playing games with us or trying to hide from us to
make it difficult for us to find Him. This is just an illustration of how
He loves to be involved with us and is giving us signals and directions
to find Him any time we sincerely seek Him.

*Lord, may I seek Your presence today. Help me to be available and eager to
commune with You. Thank You for telling me how to find and enjoy You today.*

JODI EULENE DODSON

231

Manna From Heaven

*Our fathers did eat manna in the desert; as it is written,
He gave them bread from heaven to eat. John 6:31.*

After my company closed down and I had to face unemployment, I didn't know what to do. Every job I applied for had hundreds of applicants, and even filling out the application forms presented problems. They asked for personal references, along with current jobs held by these references. Naturally, my references were all coworkers who were also out of work. Even my out-of-town friends were out of work.

Prospective employers remained unimpressed, and interviews were few and far between. As the months wore on and money got tighter, I had nowhere to turn but to Jesus. I remembered the words of Paul: "My God will supply all your needs" (see Phil. 4:19). I needed a job. Where was it?

I also recalled the words of David: "I have not seen the righteous forsaken, nor his seed begging for bread" (see Ps. 37:25). I wasn't begging yet, but I did need food. I remembered how the wandering children of Israel had survived in the wilderness on manna, bread from heaven.

"I'm doing my best to find work," I prayed. "Can't You help me out? Isn't it time You sent a little manna from heaven?"

The answer was quick in coming. "What did you think the tomatoes were for?"

I had forgotten about the tomatoes. That very afternoon a friend had given me a bag of tomatoes from her garden's excess and had promised me some eggplant. She knew things were hard for me, and she was happy to help. I had already received my "manna" that day, but because it had not dropped out of the sky, I hadn't recognized it.

When things go wrong, it's easy to ignore the blessings that are all around us. We search for angels with wings and overlook the kind that walk on human feet. Miracles are no less miraculous just because they don't come with Hollywood-style special effects. "Angel food" was delivered by human hands belonging to neighbors and friends. A friendly word of encouragement, a phone call from a neighbor, a simple bag of tomatoes—all are blessings from heaven.

GINA LEE

In a Sun-scorched Land

*The Lord will guide you always; he will satisfy your needs in a
sun-scorched land and will strengthen your frame. You will be like a
well-watered garden, like a spring whose waters never fail. Isa. 58:11, NIV.*

Take two people in their late 40s, transplant them from the
wooded northwestern United States to the Sahara in northeast-
ern Africa, and you have the potential for shock—culture shock,
weather shock, diet shock, and every other possible type of shock.

In Khartoum there are daily power outages, with no fixed schedule of time or length. Temperatures during the summer don't drop
below 85° F day or night, and housing construction of concrete soaks
up the sun's rays. Our generator was undependable. I feared contract-
ing malaria. I always boiled water, bleached vegetables and fruit. I
had no E-mail contact with family. Why did we come to this desolate
land to live under these conditions?

We had moved into our brand-new home just a year and a half
earlier. It had been so much fun watching the house grow and sensing God's presence throughout the building process. Then suddenly it
was up for sale. The day after Christmas we walked through the
rooms one last time. After a prayer of thanksgiving and seeking God's
guidance, we locked the doors, climbed into our car, and drove out
the driveway that wound through the woods.

A few weeks later, on the other side of the globe, I kept reminding myself that this earth is not my home. I must not be attached to
places, things, or even countries. *But Lord, I miss my sons. I miss the
green forests and fields. I miss the ocean and the mountains. I even miss seeing clouds in the sky. Lord, we felt You were leading us here, but . . .*

And then one morning while I was studying the Bible, God
pointed me to the promise I have cherished from that day to this:
"The Lord . . . will satisfy your needs in a sun-scorched land and will
strengthen your frame. You will be like a well-watered garden, like a
spring whose waters never fail."

The Lord has satisfied my needs in this sun-scorched land. When I
feel that the garden of my soul is running dry, I realize I need to spend
more time drinking from the Spring whose waters never fail.

SHARON STADDON

Rest for the Weary

My soul finds rest in God alone;
my salvation comes from him. Ps. 62:1, NIV.

While down on my hands and knees, scrubbing the kitchen floor, I reviewed the long list of things yet to be done. A pile of laundry beckoned from the hall, bills needed to be paid, and bare cupboards signaled it was time to buy groceries. And that was only part of the list. There were sheets to be changed and baking to be done. Houseguests coming for an extended visit promised to be fun, but in preparation for the fun there was work to finish. I was exhausted, but I had to keep going.

As I bent over my work, pondering my plight, a shadow fell across the floor. I looked up to see my husband and teenage daughter. *Now what?* I thought.

"We came to ask you if you could use some help." The words began to soothe the moment they were spoken. What a wonderful thought! My to-do list did need to be done, but I didn't have to do it! I had help! As it turned out, my husband and daughter helped me finish the kitchen floor, and then bought groceries while I started the laundry. That finished, I crawled under a quilt to pay bills and even got to enjoy a little rest at the same time.

I am currently working on another to-do list. This list has eternal consequences and includes fruit I can't buy in the grocery store—fruit such as patience and love and long-suffering, exotic fruit not often seen. At times I become overwhelmed with the length and difficulty of the list. Will I ever get it all done?

Other times when I'm on my knees I sense a shadow falling across the floor. In my mind's eye I look up to see my Father with an outstretched hand. He's motioning for me to give my list to Him. He wants to help me by taking care of the list for me. Not just some of the items, but all of them.

Lord, You know that I can't do everything on my own. You have offered to bear my burdens today. What a relief! What a way to live! Know what? I think I have time to rest! Thank You.   RETTA MICHAELIS

Seeing With God's Eyes

"The Lord sees not as mortals see; they look on the outward appearance, but the Lord looks on the heart." 1 Sam. 16:7, NRSV.

Y ou look like you've been dragged through a hedge backward!" she exclaimed, eying my hair suspiciously. "Your hair is absolutely wild." She paused to get a closer look. "What have you done to it?"

All the women in the office had raved about my hair that day. Now I was nonplussed by my friend's response. "It's the style!" I said defensively. "Haven't you seen anyone wear their hair this way?"

"I don't have to like your hair to love you!" she laughingly chided.

She was right. One doesn't have to like everything about another person in order to care for them. Nor can one determine the value of another person by her appearance. We often get so distracted by an outward feature that we fail to see the person for who they are.

My mind wandered to Val, the girl who came to see me wearing a different fashion atrocity each week. Today it was a black-and-white blouse, tucked into a pea-green paisley miniskirt over plum-colored ribbed tights. The hiking boots were an added bonus.

I couldn't fathom her sense of fashion. "Help me know how you choose what goes together, Val," I said, scratching my chin. She spent several minutes trying to explain rave dress to me, but in vain.

"It's OK, Barbara," she laughed. "But if you have to understand it to work with me we'll be here for a while!"

Over the weeks I'd developed respect for Val's ability to face her problems with determination. Anyone else would have wanted to curl up and die. She was a strong, courageous woman.

I'm so glad God isn't thrown off by things such as our looks or styles. He simply looks at me with a warm heart and moist eyes and says, "You're My child, and I love you."

Lord, may I always look beyond the outside layer to the hearts of others.

BARBARA COUDEN

Holy Spirit Money

"Just as you did it to one of the least of these
who are members of my family, you did it to me." Matt. 25:40, NRSV.

I was on a two-week speaking itinerary in Russia. During a three-hour drive to an isolated campsite almost on the border of Finland, I heard incredible stories of hunger, poverty, and need.

I had money that friends had donated for the needy of Russia. I called it "Holy Spirit money," since I had not specifically asked people to give it. Many knew I was going and had slipped me cash donations to give away.

Now young people sat on logs in a U-shape around me before a blazing campfire. Their eyes barely left my face as I presented the fascinating subject of pair bonding. At the conclusion these bright, inquisitive youth asked questions. It could have gone on all night, but I had money for them in my pocket. Ten to 15 of the most needy had been selected to tell me their story at the close of the meeting. The time had come.

Natasha was 20 years old. She and her younger brother lived with their mother, who subsisted on a pension of less than $17 per month. (To put this in perspective, a loaf of bread cost 60 cents.) From this pitiful amount they had to pay for the rent on their flat, a phone, food, and clothing. They had just lost their phone and were living on bread and potatoes.

"Natasha," I asked, "when was the last time you had a banana?"

"I have never tasted a banana in my life," she replied.

Never tasted a banana! At home I have a banana on my cereal every morning. My heart was incredibly touched to meet a 20-year-old who had never tasted a banana. I couldn't hold the tears. When the tears subsided I explained to her that I didn't have a lot of money to give away. But I had a little money to give, especially for fresh fruits and vegetables to supplement her diet. I explained that this money was a gift from friends far away who loved the Russian people.

That night I discovered that it is infinitely more fun to give than to receive.

Look around you. Is there someone who has a need? Can you give something of yourself to someone today? NANCY VAN PELT

Christiana's Rest

*Come unto me, all ye that labour and are heavy laden,
and I will give you rest. Matt. 11:28.*

"Give me wisdom today, dear Lord," Christiana prayed. "Make me a good wife and mother." In spite of her daily prayers, some days went as she wished, and some didn't.

Minutes later she surveyed the carefully laid breakfast table. She had done her best again. Was it good enough?

"Good breakfast, hon," John mumbled, his mouth still half full.

The day wore on. Christiana performed each duty carefully. But a vague cloud of dissatisfaction hung over her.

A happy squeal from Leah drew her into the living room. She dropped to her knees beside the little girl and her dolls. With her elbows on the floor in front of her knees she cupped her chin in her hands. "Krissy looks like she might roll off that box. I bet she's scared," she pointed out to Leah.

"That's not a box, Mommy," Leah protested. "It's her diaper table; she's not worried. She knows I'm taking care of her."

Christiana looked at the trusting face of Krissy on the diaper table, and the doll's serene smile spoke of rest. She looked at Amy and Dora being dressed by their "mommy," and their faces also said "rest."

As if in a daze Christiana rose, her gaze falling on a painting on the far wall. Jesus was calling a boatload of fishermen to shore for breakfast. "Rest," it called out to her. The shaft of sunlight falling to the living room floor breathed "rest." Her own carefully tended plants smiled up at the sun and nodded "rest." Yes, the whole house, tastefully decorated and carefully tended, called "rest." Why hadn't she seen it before?

"Come unto Me, . . . and I will give you rest."

I taught the verse to Leah, but she had to show me what it meant.

Now each time the cloud settled over a duty, Christiana stopped and listened. "Don't worry. I am taking care of you," God whispered. "Each thing you attempt is the right thing for this moment because you have asked Me to take care of you. I won't leave you. Stay close by Me, and I will lead you unto rest."   SUSAN SCOGGINS

A Night at a Blind Camp

"I am the light of the world. Whoever follows me will never walk in darkness, but will have the light of life." John 8:12, NIV.

One summer I volunteered to serve as a blind camp assistant counselor. Since I am bilingual, I chose one of the adult cabins where I could assist the women from Brownsville and Laredo who did not speak English. That summer I learned that most of the blind are very capable of doing whatever needs doing. But like the rest of us, if they haven't acclimated themselves to their surroundings, they get a bit turned around—only they are far more graceful about it.

It was not unusual for some of the women to wake in the middle of the night for a trip to the restroom or to get a drink of water. On our second night together, a faint voice woke me. In a Spanish whisper she said, "I can't find my way back to my bunk. Please help me."

In my sleepy stupor I whispered back, "It's OK to turn on the light." Suddenly I realized what I'd said. I had just asked a blind woman to turn on the light so she could see where she was going! The stupidity of my suggestion caused me to sit up, now fully awake. Tumbling out of my top bunk, I apologized profusely all the way down. "I'm sorry! I wasn't thinking! How stupid of me!" I stammered.

She laughed, and by then some of my other truly good-natured campers were also awake. Our cabin filled with hysterical laughter when everyone heard our story. From then on the women and I became friends and shared many more memorable moments.

It was utterly absurd for me to suggest that my blind friend turn on a light to get back to the comfort of her bunk, wasn't it? But how do we respond when the Light of the world invites us to turn to Him? It seems we would rather stumble around in the darkness, especially a darkness of our own making, than to turn to Him for light and help.

When asked if there was anything worse than being blind, Helen Keller emphatically replied, "Yes, having sight but no vision." I would add having a Source but not turning to it. Why do we stumble alone in the darkness when the Light is there waiting to guide us?

ROSALYNDA KOSINI

No U-turn

Narrow is the way, which leadeth unto life. Matt. 7:14.

One dark night I found myself driving on a steep narrow highway with no shoulder on the road. Suddenly my headlights caught the sign with the international emblem for "No U-turn!" I could instantly imagine how hazardous it would be to try to make a U-turn on that winding narrow grade.

My next thought was of a popular bumper sticker that reads "If you're headed in the wrong direction, God allows U-turns." This was in direct contrast to the no U-turn sign I had just encountered. What was the difference? In silence and darkness I drove on in deepest thought. Finally the difference became apparent to me.

Yes, if we're headed in the wrong direction, God indeed not only allows U-turns, but very much encourages such action. In fact, God is continually seeking ways to woo us back to the right road, much the way I imagine an ardent suitor courts the one he desires to marry. But God is far more loving, attentive, creative, and persistent in the way He goes about winning us to Himself.

Furthermore, God has given us a good road map in both the living and the written Word so we can know we are on the right road. With heaven as our goal, once we are on the right road, there is no reason to make a dangerous U-turn. But if we are on the wrong road, a quick U-turn can save us much disappointment and heartache farther down the road.

Once we're secure on His vantage ground, headed toward heaven, I picture God fervently encouraging us to make no U-turns but to keep going along that narrow, steep upward grade with all the power and protection He's eager to give us.

Since seeing the no U-turn sign that night on the narrow highway, I've made a commitment to make no spiritual U-turns on my way to heaven. We're just too close to the end of earth's history to turn back now.

Won't you join me in a firm resolve to stay on the path that leads to eternal life?

Lord, I'm on my way. I don't want to make any U-turns or backtrack today. Guide, guard, and bless my path this day. JUDY COULSTON

Letting Go

He will command his angels concerning you
to guard you in all your ways. Ps. 91:11, NIV.

My husband's brother, Vernon, invited our children to ride with his family on a trip to California, where they planned to spend a few days. Our children would then fly back to Nashville by themselves. The thought of their flying home alone caused me to worry. With the exception of a few days' visit with grandparents or camp, our children had not been anywhere without us since birth. We were particularly concerned about our son, who has a chronic medical condition that requires constant monitoring and medication.

My husband approved. The children were eager to go. So we arranged a flight. I knew my brother-and sister-in-law would care for our children as if they were their own, but I still hesitated. My prayers did not decrease my worries.

Would our son take care of his medical situation as he should? He emphatically declared that he would. His older sister promised to keep a watchful eye out for him. Still I hesitated.

"Please sit down, Elaine; I want to talk you," my husband said gently. "If we are all here in Nashville, can you prevent any one of us from getting sick? Can you prevent an accident here in Nashville? Can their guardian angels protect them as well in California as they do in Nashville? Isn't God watching over them in Nashville? Can't He do the same in California, on the airplane, or wherever they go? No matter where they go, God cares for them as much as you do. What can you do in your own power? God is more than able."

As he spoke, my worries drained away. With a greatly lightened heart I agreed to let them travel.

Are you a mother facing a frightening separation from your child because of school activities, camp, college, divorce, illness, or just the fact that your children are getting older and more independent? As the suitcases and bags are being packed with clothes, pack all of your worries, your fears, your anxieties, and give them to Jesus. In return He'll give you a package full of freedom from worry. And He'll give you joy, peace, and comfort that no one else can give.   ELAINE NORMAN

Friends

A friend loves at all times, and kinsfolk
are born to share adversity. Prov. 17:17, NRSV.

The church service had just ended when someone touched me on the shoulder and said, "I am Angelica." It was then that I remembered we had agreed by phone that we would talk. So we went to a small room.

She looked very young—I couldn't imagine she might be married and have three adolescent children. She was dressed inappropriately for church. Her hands shook constantly, and her eyes were red, the result of a sleepless night full of weeping. She told me she was taking 28 pills a day. She told me she had been baptized as an adolescent and that she normally attended the church meetings, though I had never seen her.

I listened carefully, and we agreed to meet again. After prayer, I asked if I could give her a hug. I wanted to let her know as much love as possible and that I understood her tragedy and that she could depend on me.

She began to cry uncontrollably. When we separated she said, "I am 49 years old and cannot remember that anybody has ever given me such a loving embrace."

Many years have passed. Angelica is my friend to this day. I learned to love her and accept her as she is. She no longer dresses as she did, and she helps those in greatest need.

I have never been able to forget what she said after that prayer. Constantly I think of how many people around me need a friendly hug, a smile, acknowledgment, or a simple act of empathy. From the contacts that I have with so many, I've concluded that behind almost every face there is a tragedy, even those faces that are always smiling. Many times these are the ones who suffer the most. How important it is to have a friendly hug and an attentive ear during the difficult moments of life.

You have given us this opportunity today, Lord. More than an opportunity, it is a privilege. In helping others we forget ourselves with our problems, small or large. I place myself in Your service, God, to be an instrument in Your hands to bless others. CRISTINA FERNANDEZ

Kitt's New Shoes

My God shall supply all your need according to his
riches in glory by Christ Jesus. Phil. 4:19.

My mother, a single parent, worked hard to support her five children. She had great faith in God and imparted this faith to us. With her meager salary she had to feed, clothe, and educate each one of us. It was a hard struggle, but through faith in God we survived.

The case of my brother's torn shoes illustrates Mother's trust in God. Kitt's shoes were torn so badly that his toes were sticking out. The shoes were beyond repair, and there was absolutely no money for new ones. A friend made fun of Kitt's shoes and said to my mother, "Instead of paying your tithe this month, why don't you buy your son a decent pair of shoes?"

My mother replied, "I would rather see my son with torn shoes than to rob God. My God will supply my every need."

Her friend scoffed. "Do you think God is going to drop a pair of shoes from the sky?"

"Sea, land, or sky, my God will supply my every need," Mother replied firmly.

On Friday of that week Nazim, a Muslim boy, asked my mother to allow Kitt to come to his house for half an hour. Mother agreed. Within 15 minutes Kitt came running home, carrying a big brown paper bag, shouting, "Look, Mommy, what God has given me!" He opened the bag, and out fell three pair of new shoes. Nazim's father had ordered shoes from Oxendale, England. After nine months the shoes had arrived, but not one pair fit Nazim. The shoes fit Kitt beautifully. All three pair were a gift from Nazim's father.

Mother immediately sent word for her friend to come to see Kitt's new shoes. When the woman saw the shoes and heard the story, she was speechless.

Later my mother called us children together. We thanked God for this evidence that Mother served a living God who supplied our every need.

WINNIE KURIAN

We Are Not Playing Horseshoes

Then Agrippa said unto Paul, Almost thou
persuadest me to be a Christian. Acts 26:28.

L iving close to Atlanta the summer of 1996, our family took advantage of the Olympics, going twice to see world-class athletes strive to go faster, higher, and be stronger. What we didn't see in person we saw on television, vicariously living with the competitors the ecstasy of victory and the agony of defeat. What could cause more anguish than to miss a medal by fractions of a second?

Gwen Torrence, defending gold medalist in the 200-meter event, missed even qualifying, coming in a discouraging one thousandth of a second behind third place. Likewise, long distance runner Mary Decker Slaney, a crowd favorite because of her having been tripped in a previous Olympics, missed qualifying for her event by the same thousandth of a second. What a crushing blow! To come so very close, yet to be excluded. Being close counts in the game of horseshoes, but not in the Olympics.

I teach a class in twentieth-century authors. One of my favorites is Alexander Solzhenitsyn, the Russian Nobel laureate who lived in the United States for years before deciding in 1994 to go back home. As coincidence would have it, my husband and I flew into Anchorage, Alaska, on the same day as did Solzhenitsyn on his flight back to Russia. But we missed seeing him by a few hours. What a disappointment! Being close is great when you're playing horseshoes, but not so great when you miss seeing someone you hoped to encounter.

Missing an Olympic event and missing seeing a famous author pale in comparison to King Agrippa's situation—coming so very close, yet missing salvation. "Almost thou persuadest me to be a Christian," he told Paul. So close, and yet missing by an eternity.

When I was a child, I would ask my friends, "Would you rather be almost saved or almost lost?" Those who answered too quickly would say, to my delight, "Of course, almost saved." Too late they would realize the error of their choice.

And too late some of us will comprehend the choice we've made—almost saved. Being close counts in horseshoes, but not in life.

WILMA McCLARTY

Security

Then the eyes of the blind shall be opened, and the ears of the deaf shall be unstopped. Then shall the lame man leap as an hart. Isa. 35:5, 6.

I lean my cane against the wall, for I'm a bit unstable;
My hearing aids and teeth and glasses all go on the table.
I go to bed a helpless soul, stripped of friendly aids,
And soundly sleep till early morning light my room invades.

Then I put on my glasses (for I can't see very much),
And don my hearing aids (because I need to keep in touch).
My appetite is fine, and so my teeth I'm glad I've got;
And since I totter in my steps, the cane helps out a lot.

But when I get to heaven, I won't need my walking cane.
My hearing aids and glasses I no longer shall retain.
My dentures—I'll just toss them. Perfect pearls I then will wear!
And I'll have all my faculties when Jesus takes me there.

Yes, these are all a nuisance, and they slow me down a bit,
But since they're temporary, I'll endure them with a wit.
So when I close my eyes at night, I'll thank my heavenly Friend
That when He comes these artificial things will have an end.

I just can't wait to *see* Him, and to *hear* Him speak to me!
With confidence I'll *walk* with Him and *eat* from heaven's tree!
Transformed, I know when He confers upon my head a crown,
That Jesus—and my faculties—will never let me down!

"He who was seated on the throne said, 'I am making everything new!'" (Rev. 21:5, NIV). *Lord, I praise You that someday soon You will make all things new, and that includes my eyes, my ears, my heart, my lungs, my legs! What a joy to think of the totally new person I will be! With that hope I can get through today.*
LORRAINE HUDGINS

A Tent Unmoved

You surely know that your body is a temple where the Holy Spirit lives. The Spirit is in you and is a gift from God. 1 Cor. 6:19, CEV.

All night long the windstorm beat upon us. Our small nylon tent seemed frail in its tenuous perch on the rocky ridge. As the ferocity of the tempest increased, every seam and cord were strained to the limit. Gust after gust tore at the rain fly, pummeled the walls, and whipped the floor around us into a billowing frenzy. Only the weight of our presence inside prevented the tent from being snatched helplessly away by the force of the gale.

During the long sleepless night I thought of the tent that was God's first earthly temple and remembered that I too am called a temple. What a fragile tent-temple I am. I am prone to physical frailty, emotional instability, mental dullness, and spiritual weakness. I'm forced to face all sorts of storms in my spiritual life. Personal winds of strife may result from broken relationships, natural disasters, religious persecution, physical affliction, career disappointments, personal failures, or a myriad of other perversities. Winds of false doctrine or of human passion may come.

All alone, empty, I would be as formless folds of cloth driven before the prevailing gust of the moment. I could be tossed into the treetops of emotion one instant and hustled into the rocky chasm of doubt the next. Soon I'd be torn and useless.

Whatever the current tempest or storm, I need a presence in my life to anchor me to Jesus, the rock of salvation. What a precious gift the Holy Spirit is! He comforts and enlightens as needed. He brings conviction, and with it strength and stability. With Him inside I can be found standing when the tests and trials are through, a credit to my Maker, counted worthy of His presence through eternity.

Lord, I don't know what storms I may face today. I need the presence of Your Holy Spirit that I may be a tent unmoved, anchored on the rock of my salvation. KATHLEEN STEARMAN PFLUGRAD

Italian Angel

In all thy ways acknowledge him, and he shall direct thy paths. Prov. 3:6.

My husband and I were enjoying the beautiful countryside of northern Italy while driving from Bellagio, Lake Como to Lake Maggiore. The roads were narrow and winding, and the town piazzas were filled with residents enjoying their friends.

Our knowledge of Italian was limited, and we became confused by the signs at an entrance to the *autostrada.* Nothing on the sign resembled any of the city names on our map. The choice was to enter the *autostrada* to the left, or to continue on the same road to the right. If we chose wrongly we could go miles out of the way before realizing our mistake. The sun would soon be dipping behind the mountains, and traveling unfamiliar roads was not where we wanted to be after sunset.

We pulled over and parked to the side of a tollbooth. Surely someone could help us in making our decision. There was a narrow ramp leading to the *officina,* and seeing a man come out the door, I decided to inquire there.

As I tried to open the door of the office, the man called to me. "May I help you?"

My husband and I, with map in hand, explained that we were heading for Stresa. He pointed in the direction of the *autostrada* and showed us the name of the town where we should exit to continue on our way toward Stresa on Lake Maggiore.

Thanking him, we headed toward the car. Before getting in, we turned to wave a final thank-you, but the man was nowhere in sight. The only other vehicle besides ours was a motorcycle, so we had assumed it was his. The motorcycle was still there, but the man had vanished. We were perplexed. If the office was closed, why had we seen him coming out the door?

We concluded that we had encountered an Italian angel. And why not? Hadn't we asked God to guide our path this day? We pulled away from the curb, paid the toll at the booth, and resumed our course to Stresa. As we drove we praised the Lord for sending help to guide us on our way. ALBERTA BENNETT CICCARELLI

It Is Love

Dear friends, let us love one another,
for love comes from God. 1 John 4:7, NIV.

I'm terrible about stuffing things under my bed. If I don't know
what to do with something, it goes under the bed to be dealt with
later. This habit of stuffing disagreeable things out of sight has carried
over into my emotional life. Having a sensitive nature, I have accumulated hurts like a dog acquires fleas.

With the passing of time the old hurts served as a foundation for
new ones, and they were stored right down there with everything else.
Even after accepting Jesus as my Saviour I wrestled with the garbage I
had stuffed away to be dealt with later. Feelings of low self-worth prevented me from experiencing the joy God wanted to bestow.

I've prayed long tearful prayers. *Teach me, Lord. Be my counselor and
help me to know why I feel the way I feel. Help me to grow up emotionally
and spiritually!* God held me in His arms and cried with me. Many of
the answers I sought came as one item at a time was pulled out from
under my emotional bed, talked about, and put in its place.

Yet I could tell there was still something under there. I planted both
feet against the bed frame and tugged with everything I had, but the
emotional garbage would not yield. Then a woman cared enough to
reach out to me, determined to crumble my wall of reserve. Another
sister joined her. They brought their flashlights, got down on their
knees with me, and facilitated the total clearing process I needed. They
were women who were not shocked by what they saw. They were
women eager to be God's love with skin on, willing to teach, to pray,
to encourage, and to love me. An entire transformation took place in
my heart and life because these women were on the watch for someone in need of sincere and lasting friendship.

Women are tremendous nurturers. We're made that way. We can
make a dramatic difference in someone else's life today. It isn't hard
or mysterious. It is love.   JOELLA BROWN DAVIS

Boxed In

"Lord, help!" they cried. And he did. Ps. 107:6, TLB.

M y husband and I were driving two cars from British Columbia to Maryland. On the fifth day we drove through Chicago rush-hour traffic. I tried my best to keep up, leaning forward, gripping the wheel, straining to keep Ron in view.

Coming out of a construction zone, I found myself on a six-lane freeway with the vehicles bumper to bumper. I was boxed in by huge tractor-trailers going 65 miles an hour. I couldn't see Ron's red Suzuki, and panicked. Tears blurred my vision.

I screamed aloud my fears. "I can't do this! I'm lost, and I'm losing control! Help me, Lord! Help!"

Seeing an exit coming up, I put on my right blinker and tried to ease into the turning lane. No one gave way. I pulled onto the no-drive wedge separating the freeway and the exit ramp. The cars flowed by on either side of me in solid lines.

Should I take this exit? I wondered. *Or should I keep going straight?* Ron had the map; I had been depending totally on him to guide me. I felt so helpless.

"Help, Lord! What shall I do?" Just then a space appeared in the line going onto the ramp. I swerved into the line and found myself on another freeway headed east. Two minutes later I saw the red Suzuki waiting for me near the turnoff of a travel plaza.

We parked, and I collapsed in Ron's arms, bawling from relief. My whole body ached from the tension of the past half hour.

Sometimes life is like that. We get boxed in by circumstances beyond our control and we don't know what to do. We want to stop and do nothing, but the traffic of life just keeps pushing us forward, and disaster seems certain.

Perhaps we have depended heavily on someone else for direction—a husband, a mother, a father, or a friend. Then death snatches the loved one from us and we are left feeling helpless, not knowing which way to turn. We can depend on no one but ourselves, and we feel unable to cope. Our eyes blur with tears, and we can't see a way out of the crisis.

We cry, "I can't do this, Lord! Help me!" And He does.

DOROTHY EATON WATTS

Class in Patience

Ye have need of patience. Heb. 10:36.

While we lived in the mission field, my husband and our two boys fell ill with the same sickness. Then one of the boys developed a swollen gland on the right side of his face. It was frightening to watch it alter the shape of his face. I felt lost without my husband to advise me, yet I didn't want to bother him when he had such a high fever himself.

Each morning the gland became bigger. Finally I decided to take my son to a pediatrician who had come to the nearest town to do relief work. It was a time when we had a gasoline shortage and were allowed only five liters at a time, just enough to make a one-way trip to town. To make matters worse, there was a leak in our petrol tank.

After waiting for an hour to get our five liters of petrol, we drove into town, only to learn that the doctor had left two days before. A surgeon was expected later that afternoon, but no one was sure of the time.

There I sat in the heat in the corridor of that less-than-ideal, developing country hospital with a sick boy in my arms, a sick husband at home, and another toddler who was having a difficult time sitting still. "Help, Lord!" I cried out silently.

"You have need of patience"—the words of Scripture came to mind. *Yes, Lord, I do need patience, but what I need more is help for my child and his father, and that soon, please!*

The doctor finally arrived after three long, desperate hours. Taking a quick look at the gland, he sent me home with a five-day prescription. If the swelling didn't disappear in five days, the doctor would have to operate.

Four days later the gland was as big as ever. With a heavy heart I prepared for the fifth day. When I awoke the fifth morning, however, the swollen gland was back to normal!

I felt overwhelmed with joy and gratitude. Waiting had been so hard for me, but I feel that during that time the Lord did help me to make progress in learning patience.

Lord, thank You for being with me in the difficult hours when patience seems so hard. Give me patience today when I need it most.

VERENA JAGGI-RECHSTEINER

Energize Me, Lord!

To be mature is to be basic. Christ! No more, no less. That's what I'm working so hard at day after day, year after year, doing my best with the energy God so generously gives me. Col. 1:28, 29, Message.

Energize me, Lord;
fill me with
faith,
love,
hope—
Change me, for Your sake,
so that I no longer grope.

Energize me, Lord;
fill me to
glorify Your name—
Change me, for Your sake,
so that I live shed of shame.

Energize me, Lord;
fill me with
Your Spirit sweet—
Change me, for Your sake,
so that I can be complete.

Energize me, Lord;
fill me to share
Your Word—
Change me, for Your sake,
so that Your great name be heard.

Energize me, Lord;
fill me with
the way to pray
for others' needs—
Change me, for Your sake,
so that I may do the deeds
that You would have me do.

BETTY KOSSICK

Foggy Times

Great peace have those who love Your law,
and nothing causes them to stumble. Ps. 119:165, NKJV.

Our trip was almost over. Soon we would be touching down in Fresno, California. The flight attendant, however, had told us when we boarded that it might be impossible to land because of the fog in the area.

During the short flight I thought of the similarities between the fog in Fresno and the fog in my life. For weeks I had been praying, yet God's voice seemed silent. I was looking for direction in a couple matters, but nothing was clear. I couldn't seem to feel God's presence. I still kept my quiet time, praying and studying my Bible. I prayed and talked with friends. I did all the things I knew I should. Yet God seemed far away, as if there were a fog between us.

I peered out my window; outside everything looked clear. *Where is the fog?* I wondered. Then all of a sudden we were in it. I could see nothing but fog. The plane kept going. Suddenly we broke through the clouds and were practically on the runway. The pilot had relied on his instruments and the control tower to get him through. He brought us safely through the fog to a safe landing.

The message was clear to me. God was telling me to keep going, to keep relying on my controls—the Bible, prayer, godly friends, and His control tower—the Holy Spirit. And even though I couldn't see or feel His presence, I would soon break through the fog and be where He wanted me to be.

Have you gone through foggy times? Maybe you are going through those times now. Hang in there. Keep heading in God's direction, relying on the controls: His Word and prayer. Soon He'll bring you through the clouds into the place He wants you to be.

That weekend in California I broke through the clouds. God's love wrapped me in such a way I felt I could touch His love like a blanket. He was with me all along; I just had to keep trusting. He gave me the peace to keep trusting and also kept me from stumbling spiritually.

TAMYRA HORST

Snowball

How great is the love the Father has lavished on us, that we should
be called children of God! And that is what we are! 1 John 3:1, NIV.

When my daughter was in seventh grade, she was assigned to
do a science project of her choice. She was to do the experi-
ments, record the results, and display her work at the science fair. She
had no idea what to do.

"I saw a project several years ago in which two rats were fed
good food and two rats were fed junk food, and the results were as-
tonishing," I suggested.

"I love that idea!" my daughter said.

We purchased four rats that soon became pets, and at the end of
the project we kept them. One of the rats was an albino my daughter
named Snowball. About six months later, when she took Snowball
out to play, we noticed the rat was having difficulty breathing. She
would not even eat the cheese we offered her. Snowball was definitely very sick.

I struggled with what to do. I knew that if I didn't do something,
she would die, but I didn't have any money in my budget for a veteri-
narian bill. After waiting a couple hours for a vet to call me back for a
phone consultation, I called a pet emergency center in a city 25 miles
(40 kilometers) away to ask their advice. They told me the best thing
was to bring Snowball in, but it would cost $47 to see her. That
seemed like a lot of money for an animal that had cost only $2, but
because of my daughter's love for Snowball I decided to take her to
the vet. The vet said Snowball had pneumonia and gave us antibiotics
for her. On the way home I glanced at Snowball to see how she was
doing, and a sense of God's lavish love struck me.

Jesus was more willing to die for me than I was to take Snowball
to the vet. He knew He wanted me in heaven, and He would have to
die to make it possible. He did not consider the cost. While I lost
sleep, He lost His divine form and accepted the form of humanity for
eternity. Most people would not want anything to do with a rat; He
should not have wanted to have anything to do with me, but He died
to save me. What love!   CAROLYN HURST

The Bus Stop Bully

The Lord shall preserve thee from all evil:
he shall preserve thy soul. Ps. 121:7.

We had just moved to military housing in Frankfurt, Germany, and my fourth grader, Lora, had not had time to make friends. On the first day of school she hurried off to the bus stop a block from the house. She felt strange. Everybody else seemed to have friends. Suddenly she noticed a bigger girl yanking at the sweater of a small boy and yelling at him. The boy was crying, and his face was smudged with dirt.

This went on for a while, and no one seemed to care. Lora wasn't very big either, but she marched over and said bravely, "Hey, you shouldn't do that. He's only a little kid!"

The girl turned on Lora then, pushing her backward. Her dinner pail fell to the ground and spilled the contents in the dirt. She leaned over Lora and puffed hot, threatening words into her face. Just then the school bus roared around the corner, and the children raced for a place in line. In a few long strides the big girl pushed to the front of the line.

Lora didn't mention any of this to me that afternoon, but the next morning she hesitated at the door. "Mom, there's a big girl at the bus stop . . ." Then the story tumbled out.

I knew she wouldn't let me walk her to the bus stop, but I was sure she would believe her guardian angel would go with her. I took her in my arms, and we both prayed. Then I felt her little body straighten up, and her usual smile returned. She quickly waved goodbye.

That afternoon she raced into the house. "Mom! I got to the bus stop this morning and Barbara, that big girl, gave me a dirty look and headed my way. Just then the bus came, and she turned and ran for the front of the line. I know God was protecting me."

From that day on we took a minute to pray. Lora would ask for help for remembering her spelling words or for anything else that was on her mind. Never again did I hear tales of Barbara, the bully at the bus stop. MARY C. EDMISTER

Going the Wrong Way

Ponder the path of thy feet, and let all thy ways be established. Prov. 4:26.

It was the first day of school. My 14-year-old son, J.T., was entering the ninth grade. He had decided he would rather take public transportation than have me drop him off at the school. The bus he was to take was just one short block from our house. Several days before he had called the bus company, gotten the departure schedules, and decided which bus would get him to school on time. Everything was set for his first experience with the bus system.

He said goodbye and walked out of the front door, headed for the bus stop. I was sure he was pleased with himself and feeling very grown-up, especially since I had finally relinquished my parental right to drop him off at school "like a little kid." I was practically ready for work when J.T., looking quite dejected, came back into the house.

"What happened?" I asked.

"I don't know," he responded. "I stood at the bus stop, and the bus came. I saw it across the street, but it was going the wrong way."

"The wrong way? Where were you standing?" I inquired, trying to hide the irritation in my voice as I realized I would have to be late to work to drop him at the school.

When he told me exactly where he had stood waiting for his bus, I knew that despite his earnest efforts and careful planning in deciding the route he needed to travel, he had been standing on the wrong side of the street. So yes, the bus had been going the wrong way. He'd missed the one connection he needed to take him to his destination on time.

Sometimes we map out our plans, check our schedules, and decide the best routes. We get everything set, but still success in life isn't guaranteed. Nor is our entrance into the kingdom assured. And woe to us if, when our heavenly Father comes to give us the ride we've been waiting for, we are standing on the wrong side and miss the connection to our heavenly home.   Iris L. Stovall

The Beauty of Bristlecone Pines

Consider it pure joy . . . whenever you face trials of many kinds, because you know that the testing of your faith develops perseverance. Perseverance must finish its work so that you may be mature and complete. James 1:2, 3, NIV.

The constant gurgle of rain through the gutters on our house didn't help my spirits. It had been only three weeks since we'd been evacuated because of the dangers of breaking levees on both sides of us. Rains were threatening another storm watch because the soggy land could hold no more moisture.

My heart was heavy also because of an unknown physical condition that had my husband's doctors concerned. Coping seemed difficult. I began reminiscing about our travels just a few months before, and a vivid picture came to mind.

We had stood on an 11,000-foot (3,350-meter) mountainside in the Ancient Bristlecone Pine Forest in eastern California. At the time I tried to picture the galelike winds that had hurled hail, snow, and sleet at these gnarled, twisted pines. For 4,000 years the blizzards of winter had battered them on these windswept heights. Fires had blackened the grain of some, but in the process had produced an incredibly beautiful design—a golden luster framed in black.

What etched itself on my mind was the way those barren twisted limbs reached up toward the azure blue sky. They seemed to say, "We've fought the elements on this stark mountainside for thousands of years, and now nothing can destroy us."

Somehow as I relived our September adventure, I too looked up, lifting my heart to God, and the day seemed much less foreboding. In my heart I knew I could accept whatever this day might bring. I could use the trials to help me gain the perseverance I need. With God's help I too could endure the battering winds of life's afflictions.

Today, Lord, give me the peace of knowing that You are taking care of me and that with Your help I can weather anything that comes my way. Please stay with me and help me to gain strength and endurance from the winds of trial. DONNA LEE SHARP

The Just-in-Case Bag

Preach the Word; be prepared in season and out of season;
correct, rebuke and encourage—with great patience
and careful instruction. 2 Tim. 4:2, NIV.

Our latest overseas assignment brought us to Russia. It was not without anxiety that we accepted this call. However, the love to serve the church, the prospect of living in a country rich with history, and the chance to immerse ourselves in another culture provided us the incentive to answer positively.

Living in the metropolis of Moscow is a challenge to us. We have had to learn many new ways to cope with life, but these new things have only contributed to making us more capable and efficient. One thing we have learned to include in our daily preparation is what we affectionately call the just-in-case bag. It has become as important as dressing before going to work.

It could be any kind of bag—a ladies' purse, a tote, or a shopping bag. In it is an umbrella (just in case it rains), three or more plastic bags (just in case we would pass by the grocery store on the way home, since they don't give free plastic bags), my passport (just in case I'm asked to identify myself), bus tickets, subway tokens, and the usual contents of a purse. In winter add to that a pair of mittens, a scarf, and a hat.

At first my husband resisted the idea of carrying a bag. He'd been used to going to the office with only his wallet safely in his pocket. Whatever office materials he had with him usually went in a folder and were tucked under his arm. But several unwelcome experiences later, he finally carried his own bag.

Oftentimes I have also resisted doing what is good for me. The Bible admonishes, "Be joyful always; pray continually; give thanks in all circumstances, . . . avoid every kind of evil" (1 Thess. 5:16-22, NIV). "Let us love one another" (1 John 4:7, NIV). "Avoid godless chatter" (2 Tim. 2:16, NIV). "Submit yourselves, then, to God. Resist the devil" (James 4:7, NIV). There are hundreds of these instructions that could only benefit me.

Today, God, help me to make Your wise counsels part of my life, that I may be able to draw from my life, as I do from my bag, the precious truth of Your love anytime, in any place, to help anyone. MERCY M. FERRER

Imaginary Lions and Tigers

Surely God is my salvation; I will trust and not be afraid. Isa. 12:2, NIV.

When our older daughter, Krysta, started school, our 2-year-old daughter, Shelby, was left at home alone with me. Midafternoon of the first day of school, Shelby came to me and said, "There is a lion in my room."

"Is it a big lion?" I asked.

She giggled and then said decidedly, "No."

"Is it a little lion?" I asked.

She nodded and giggled some more. "It bites!" she said matter-of-factly in a soft voice. Then she asked me to read to her, and the subject was forgotten.

The next morning I discovered the bedroom and bathroom doors closed. When I asked Shelby why, she quickly and seriously explained, "There are lions and tigers in there." I asked if it would be all right for all the animals to stay in the bathroom so I could open the bedroom doors. She agreed and ran off to play.

That afternoon she came to me again. "I want to read my books in my room, but there are lions and tigers in there."

I wondered if I could deal with these creatures. I asked if it would work if I went into her room and told the lions and tigers to leave. She said it would. And it did!

Then later that day an alligator moved into the basement when Shelby wanted to play with her basement toys. This time the creature left when I went down and spoke loudly to it. The rest of the week these invisible visitors came and went frequently. Every time I asked them to leave, Shelby said they did. During the next several weeks the visits became less frequent until we ceased to hear about them at all.

How easy it was for me to solve Shelby's problems. First she believed I could. Then she trusted that I did. Her problems weren't real, but she believed they were.

I wonder how many times my anxieties are like Shelby's imaginary predators? The things that are stopping me from freely enjoying life aren't even real sometimes. But I can take my real and my invented worries to God and know He will deal with them. And He does!

ROBERTA FRANKLIN CLAUSEN

A Time to Love

*For everything there is a season, and a time for every matter
under heaven: . . . a time to love, and a time to hate. Eccl. 3:1-8, RSV.*

Scene 1: She sat close to him, her hand resting gently on his knee.
They said nothing, only stared into space. Suddenly they gazed
into each other's faces and smiled, bumping foreheads. He stretched
out his feet and noticed that his shoelaces were untied. In a quick second
she was down on her knees, tying them. His disability made him
incapable of tying his shoelaces.

Scene 2: They strolled hand-in-hand along the pathway strewn
with the rust-colored leaves of fall. The scenery was breathtaking,
and they seemed to be savoring every aspect of it. They had probably
led busy and fulfilling lives in the past, but now that they were in the
sunset years of their life they had no intention to hurry. He spotted a
bench at the edge of the lake and guided her there gently. Their conversation seemed animated, and I could hear the melodic blend of
their laughter. Moments later he embraced her and kissed her gently
on her forehead.

Scene 3: One of my most joyous recollections of baby-sitting my
niece, Aviella, was kissing her and observing the sparkle in her eyes
and hearing her chuckle with delight. Of course I had to allow her to
reciprocate those feelings as she drooled all over my face. After she
learned to talk she would say, "Do it again, Auntie."

The language of love is as universal as a smile. It is understood by
everyone—young, old, or those with physical or mental disabilities.
Daily we are bombarded with scenes of hatred, and our senses are
numbed as we look at the television, read the newspaper, or surf the
Internet. The world is in dire need of love. All around us we see faces
starving for the gestures of love—a hug, smile, a kind word, or a kiss.

Show love to someone today. This is a time to love.

ANDREA A. BUSSUE

The Roommate

Do not be anxious about anything, but in everything, by prayer and petition, with thanksgiving, present your requests to God. Phil. 4:6, NIV.

L ord, what am I going to do now?" My prayer was far from the faith-filled request for help it should have been. Within a few months I would be starting as a freshman at college. All my friends had already paired up with roommates. I had been left out. A day seldom went by without my pleading with God to work it out so that I could have a "good" roommate.

I was not an independent and confident person. On top of that, this was going to be my first time living away from home, and I knew I would be homesick. Besides, it seemed everyone I talked to related a horrid roommate experience. One friend had a roommate who talked to herself and never washed her clothes. Another girl had gone through four roommates in just one year. I started imagining the horrible experiences I would encounter.

When the dreaded day finally arrived, it was almost as awful as I had imagined. I began moving into the room while my new roommate-to-be was away. I'm a real "neat freak," and the room was a mess—clothes flung from one side to the other, and the sink counter top cluttered with hair products, makeup, and dishes.

"She could have at least cleaned up before I came!" I commented to the friend who was helping me move in. This poor roommate had no chance. I had decided that we probably wouldn't get along before I had ever met her.

However, after a few weeks of getting to know each other, we got along wonderfully. We were complete opposites in many ways, but God knew our individual strengths would complement each other. Today she is still one of my best friends and as close as a sister.

It would have been so much easier if I had put my full trust in Christ. He was taking care of my "roommate dilemma" from the moment I first asked Him. When I have concerns now, I think about that experience and try to put my faith in Christ, knowing He will take care of me. SYNNOVA HILL

Reluctant Singer

I will praise you with my whole heart; . . .
I will sing praises to You. Ps. 138:1, NKJV.

One Monday morning I rolled out of bed still half asleep. Grabbing my towel and toiletries, I went downstairs to the first-floor shower room. The sounds of splashing water, squeaking door hinges, and morning greetings awakened me fully.

As I entered a shower stall I heard the outer door burst open, and a singing voice grabbed my attention.

" 'Oh, how wonderful! Oh, how marvelous is Jesus' love to me,' " she sang.

Stifling the urge to join her in singing, I quickly showered and left the room.

Throughout the day that song haunted me. God had been wonderful in allowing us to travel through more than 16 hours of dense fog and occasional rain showers to Hagerstown, Maryland, for a writers' workshop. Most of us were fatigued from travel and would have welcomed the opportunity to remain under the warm covers, but we had to be at the publishing house on time for the first meeting.

There are times in our experience when tiredness, discouragement, worry, and cares could be banished with song, but we are too tired, too busy, too sleepy, or too forgetful of God's care, mercy, and loving-kindness. Oh, that we would remember to lift our voices in praise and worship often, for singing lifts the burdens and bonds us closer to God.

Henry Ward Beecher wrote, "Sing evening and morning . . . lift the voice of praise against cares. Praise God by singing."

Several times throughout the morning I caught myself singing snatches of the song. It was infectious and had etched itself in my mind.

A Christian writer, Ellen White, suggests that Jesus, in His childhood, was taught by His mother to sing and often lifted His voice in song. He sang while at work in His father's carpenter shop. Before His companions knew it, they were cheered by His song.

Unknown singer, I join you now. Let's praise God together, for God's love is wonderful!   MABEL ROLLINS NORMAN

Your Son

For God so loved the world, that he gave his only begotten Son. John 3:16.

We gave our last hugs and quick goodbyes. My son started the old truck we had given him to take to college, and he was gone. But I couldn't go back inside the house. I watched him drive down the driveway. When he was out of sight, I strained my ears to pick up the last sounds of the motor chugging up the little hill through the woods. I followed him in my mind-sight: he was driving down the hill, waiting for the traffic at the highway, turning right to head west for his new school.

He had left before, but this time it was different. Oh, yes, he was going to attend a Christian college. There was nothing to worry about, really. But inside I knew he would never be truly home again, not to stay.

He was a young man. He would come home again to visit, but the comfortable days of hearing him whistling down the path toward home, of living as a complete family, those days were forever gone. Home would not be the same again; home was empty. I missed my son.

Then I remembered another Parent who sent His Son away on a long journey. How did the Father feel? His home would be empty too! He would miss His Son!

God, once You said "Goodbye."
You sent Your Son over a long hill.
He was a good Son.
But He would not be with Christians
In a good college.
As You turned back home,
Was Your house empty too?
God, I never knew before!
You missed Your Son!

"For God so loved the world . . ." Thank You, Father.

RUTH WATSON

Spot Remover

*"If you remain in me and my words remain in you,
ask whatever you wish, and it will be given you." John 15:7, NIV.*

My 12-year-old daughter, Amy, wanted a permanent wave put in her waist-length hair. I purchased supplies and dug out my old hairdressing equipment. We chose a Sunday afternoon when her daddy would be out of town.

Before I started the wrapping process, I suggested we have special prayer. I explained to her that this had been my custom when I had been a hairdresser. My patrons didn't always know that I prayed over their hair, but I always gave the Lord the credit for any compliments I received. So we bowed our heads together, and I asked the Lord to help me to do a good job and to give me a happy and satisfied customer. Amy giggled!

Five hours later the job was completed, and her hair turned out beautifully. Although I had been careful to make certain that every perm rod received the proper amount of perm solution, I had been careless about covering my clothes. The peroxide from the solution left big bleached spots and streaks running down the legs of my nice green slacks. I was sick! I had just purchased a leather vest to go with those pants, and now they were ruined.

That evening at family worship I knelt and thanked God for the success He had given me on the permanent and prayed for forgiveness and for help in knowing how to wash my pants. Suddenly I had a thought: *Put on some spot remover and wash the pants in "safe for color" bleach.* It seemed like a really silly idea to me, but then I thought of Naaman, the man with leprosy who was told by the prophet Elisha to wash seven times in the muddy Jordan River and he would be healed. *The wisdom of God is often foolishness to us. God asks for faith and obedience,* I reasoned.

I put on the spot remover and placed the pants in the washing machine with the bleach. I wish you could see my pants! There are no more spots. I went to bed praising God for His goodness, even when I messed up!

It's true that in answer to our prayer God sometimes says no. But if we don't ask we might miss out on that special blessing, because He just might say Yes!   KATHY JO DUTERROW YERGEN

Life's Maze

"I know the plans I have for you," declares the Lord. Jer. 29:11, NIV.

While waiting in the South Bend airport for my flight back to Washington, I talked with God. "Father, please send Your angels to protect our plane and keep it from crashing. You held off the destruction of Sodom for the sake of 10 righteous ones. Would it be too bold for me to ask for extra-special care for the sake of one righteous—and for all the others on this plane? Amen."

I boarded the small plane and found my seat. I'd had window seats before, so it was nothing new for me to gaze down at the earth. I was used to seeing cars and buildings appear as miniature toys. But this time the earth's layout caught my attention. It had never occurred to me before that streets and highways have been planned out like a jigsaw puzzle with all the pieces fitting together. Sometimes when I'm driving, the street layouts seem so ridiculous that I think to myself, *How could anyone have planned this?* But looking on the maze from a higher sphere I could see that every street, parking lot, building, and field was part of a plan.

God has a perfect plan for our lives, too, but because we're living in a lower sphere and cannot see the whole picture, we don't always understand or follow His plan. I can hear God saying, "If only you could see the whole picture, My child. Follow My plan. I'll be with you and give you strength and patience to reach your destination without your being led off the perfect path onto a side street of Satan's."

How do I find God's plan for my life? I must study the Master's plan book, the Bible. I must communicate with the Master Planner. The instructions are useless if I don't know the Master Planner who wrote them. And I need to talk to people who have had the Master Planner build their lives. They've had experience in reading His instructions and can help me understand.

I arrived home safely that day with a new appreciation for my Master's planning book—and with a determination to follow His perfect plan through the maze of my life.   BONITA SHIELDS

A Treasured Card

And he said unto me, My grace is sufficient for thee:
for my strength is made perfect in weakness. 2 Cor. 12:9.

Not long ago I pulled out my keepsake box that is filled with treasured greeting cards. Some were made for me by my children when they were in school; others were special ones of encouragement from friends. But one little postcard is by far the most special card I ever received. It's worn and faded now from age and handling, but it is priceless. I remember well when it came.

I had been in the hospital with a major illness that made me feel as if my whole world had spun out from beneath me. I was experiencing despair. The pencil drawing on the front was of a little boy and his puppy. It was such a sweet picture. I thought how wonderful it must be to draw like that, and I was somewhat envious of the artist. Inside, the card said the usual "Hope you get better soon." At the time, though, I was just too weary to read the handwritten message.

A few days later I picked up the card to examine the drawing again, only this time I flipped it over to read the note my cousin had written. I read that the picture had been drawn by Ann Adams, a polio victim who drew by holding a pencil between her teeth. I couldn't believe it—the drawing was so beautiful! The little note on the card said it had taken her two months to complete the drawing. What perseverance and patience! I thought she must have had peace and hope in her heart to draw of such innocence.

Ann Adams had not let polio stop her from being a blessing to others. I was blessed by that little card because it managed to find the secret place I had hidden my hope. When my recovery seemed impossible, I would think of Ann Adams. She could have given up and been miserable as an invalid; instead she chose to be creative and productive with the talent she had. Through her weakness she was made strong. Her little card is one of my greatest treasures.

Lord, thank You for hope for this day. Help me remember that through Your grace our strength is made perfect.   JO ANN HILTON

The Lake of Fire

The Lord is not slack concerning His promise, as some count slackness,
but is longsuffering toward us, not willing that any should
perish but that all should come to repentance. 2 Peter 3:9, NKJV.

We had flown into Hilo, Hawaii, just a few hours before when we learned that a volcanic fire pit in Hawaii Volcanoes National Park had become very active. Eagerly we inquired, "How do we get there?"

With less than an hour of daylight left, we began the hike over the rugged lava bed. Sharp, jagged lava rocks, narrow fissures, and difficult terrain slowed us down. The safe area was marked off by white poles pounded into the uneven black rocks. On either side steam erupted from unseen vents. Stooping down, we could feel the heat. The smell of burning sulfur filled the air.

A light drizzle of rain made our slippery path more hazardous. As darkness came on, the red glow in the sky ahead became brighter. We felt a tingle of excitement as we neared the roped-off area. We could hear a cracking sound, as if the surface of the earth were being torn apart.

As we climbed up to the rim, which was guarded by ropes, we gasped at the spectacular scene below us. A seething lake of fire ebbed and flowed, exploding in golden-orange flames. The chill of the black rainy night at our backs contrasted sharply with the intense, brilliant heat from the boiling caldron of liquid fire before us. Endless fire patterns formed as the molten mass boiled and broke into fragments. Frequent explosions sent molten rocks and fire many feet into the air. Horribly beautiful, it struck both terror and wonder in our hearts.

Adding this unforgettable view of the earth's interior forces to "whosoever believeth in him should not perish, but have everlasting life" (John 3:16) brought joy and happiness. Our thankful hearts knew we would never need to know the terror of those who choose to turn away from following Jesus.

Oh, the wonder of God's love! As we listened, saw, and felt the heat from the terrible lake of fire, we were so thankful for the promise that we all can enjoy everlasting life.   EILEEN E. LANTRY

A Day of Deliverance

*Cast thy bread upon the waters: for
thou shalt find it after many days. Eccl. 11:1.*

It was 1944, and war was raging. My mother and I were in a labor camp deep in Germany. Food was scarce, and the hunger pains were ever present and in abundance. Not wanting us to die yet, the guards allowed us to go to the neighboring villages and beg for something to eat. The main gate would swing open, and we were given an hour of freedom.

As we walked past an orchard, Mother and I saw a one-armed man breaking off dry branches from the trees. Apples, glorious apples, littered the ground. Though ill-dressed, emaciated, and dirty, we gathered the courage to ask for some. The man turned to us and smiled. Waving with his one hand and pointing to his house, he said, "Please, come in and meet my family."

The kitchen was bright and clean. A friendly woman and three young girls sat at the table. We struggled against the aroma of food. We learned that the father had lost his arm on the Eastern Front. We shared that we had lost my father in the camps. Awkward silence followed. We ate simply but in plenty. As we left we were laden with food and old dresses. "Please," they said, "return when you can." Throughout 1944 this family saved us from starvation. They themselves were poor, but oh, how rich in spirit!

Winter was nearing, and all my mother had for warmth was a torn woolen blanket. From it the oldest daughter in the farm family, an accomplished seamstress, fashioned a coat. For my head, gray with lice, she made a woolen cap.

Deliverance came in May 1945; the American soldiers with the white star on their vehicles drove straight to the camp and tore down the main gate and barbed-wire fence. We were free, free from hunger and fear! The guards had disappeared the night before; the commandant had been murdered by some of the prisoners.

And the German family who had cared for us? Now Mother and I began carrying food to their home. American generosity was at full throttle, and whatever was given us we shared with the family—the family who had a small home, orchard, and hearts large enough to encompass two refugees so very far from home.　　　　ALLA CZERKASIJ

God Hears Our Cry

Fear thou not; for I am with thee: be not dismayed; for I am thy God: I will strengthen thee; yea, I will help thee; yea, I will uphold thee with the right hand of my righteousness. Isa. 41:10.

I can remember the day as though it were yesterday. My husband was hospitalized in very serious condition, the victim of an automobile accident. It was a Sunday, and as always I had spent several hours at the hospital with him.

That evening our friends, Dr. Carlos Waldir, who had rescued my husband, and his wife, Lucia, were with me. While Carlos went to the hospital, Lucia stayed with me, giving me support and trying to relieve my distress. Then they left, and I was alone again. My older children were out with their friends, and the youngest was at my sister's house.

I realized that my husband's situation had worsened, and he would face another surgery the following day. I felt great anguish as I paced around the house. I went to my children's room and looked out at the deserted street. My despair and loneliness deepened.

I tried reading the Bible, but its words brought no comfort to me. Distraught, I fell on my knees in my living room and wept. "Lord, have mercy on us," I whispered. At the same time I had an unexplainable sensation. I felt as though a hand patted my head and a voice said, "Daughter, be of good cheer! Fear thou not; for I am with thee: be not dismayed; for I am thy God: I will strengthen thee; yea, I will help thee; yea, I will uphold thee with the right hand of my righteousness."

I do not know how long I remained kneeling there, but when I got up I felt the greatest sensation of peace and comfort that I have ever known in my life. I had the certainty that the Lord was with me.

Praise You, Lord; in spite of our being sinners, You hear and listen to our cry. When I fear, help me to remember again how You have upheld me in the past. Give me peace and assurance for this day that You are with me always.

NICEA FERREIRA TRINDADE

Night of Terror, Night of Joy

The Lord himself shall descend from heaven with a shout. 1 Thess. 4:16.

The year was 1967. The Nigerian civil war had started in the eastern part of the country a few months before my admission to a church-sponsored college. I lived in the western part. The war was only on paper as far as I was concerned. Occasionally I saw army lorries carrying soldiers along the highway, but my life continued as if nothing serious were going on in my country—until the last day of our orientation week.

That Friday the college students and faculty had planned a get-together for Saturday night to welcome the newcomers. I went to bed early that night, but was jolted awake at 1:00 in the morning by a loud *bang! B-O-O-M!* The explosion shook the very foundation of our dormitory. I jumped down from my bunk bed, quickly putting on my housecoat as I ran from my room, my roommate running behind me.

Suddenly the electric lights went off, leaving us in darkness. By that time there had been many booms, one following the other. I could hear people from all directions, shouting and crying. Nobody knew what had happened. By the time we reached the open street, the explosions had stopped. Later that morning we were told that a rebel plane on a bombing mission to Lagos had been discovered and shot down before it could cause any havoc.

I was shaken by that experience. If ordinary earthly explosions could produce such heart-shaking situations, how will it be when "the Lord himself shall descend from heaven with a shout"? That will be a fearful time for those who are not expecting Jesus to come. They will cry for the rocks and the mountains to fall on them. The sounds of the mighty hosts coming will be a dreadful experience for many. For them it will be a night of terror.

I am comforted, however, that this same Lord is my Lord, and I shall not be afraid at His appearing. For me it will be a night of joy. I will look up and say, "Lo, this is my God. I have waited for Him, and He will save me" (see Isa. 25:9).   BECKY DADA

War Against Worry

*"Which of you by worrying can add
one cubit to his stature?" Matt. 6:27, NKJV.*

My husband was at a school board meeting that had started at 7:00 p.m. and was supposed to end at 9:00, or perhaps 10:00, at the latest. While waiting for him, I read to pass the time.

Ten o'clock came and went, and he hadn't come. I continued to read to quiet my fears. I should have gone to bed by 11:00, but I knew I'd never sleep if he wasn't home. So I continued to read.

When I looked at the clock and found that it was already 1:10, I couldn't concentrate any longer. My mind raced. My throat felt tight. I paced the house, my face pinched with worry. I expected any moment the phone would ring, informing me of the accident. *Maybe he's dead! What shall I do with all of his books? How will I arrange the funeral? How can I pay for the house mortgage? Where should I live? They will repossess the house.* A thousand and one thoughts galloped like wild horses through my mind.

Finally at 2:35 a.m. I heard the door open.

"What happened, honey? Why so late? Any problem with the car? Are you all right?"

"Everything is OK. We had to grapple with a big problem at the school. We couldn't leave until it was solved."

My worries had been unfounded.

I have never learned my lesson about fully trusting God. Did my worrying help me at all? I worry about things that never happen. And even if an accident had occurred, would my worrying have helped ease the situation? My worrying never added anything to my stature or to my spiritual growth. Therefore, why worry? It is wasted energy.

I have decided to proclaim war against worry! I am determined to say with the prophet Isaiah, "Behold, God is my salvation, I will trust, and not be afraid: for the Lord Jehovah is my strength and my song; he also is become my salvation" (Isa. 12:2).   OFELIA A. PANGAN

Classroom Disturbance

And it shall come to pass, that before they call, I will answer. Isa. 65:24.

It was a typical sultry, tropical morning in Fiji. All was silent in my small, one-room school as the pupils tried to solve a math problem in a given time. All heads bent over their papers. I smiled at their intense concentration.

The quiet was suddenly broken when Tim banged his desk. All eyes were on him as he began to flail his arms violently. We were stunned. Tim was usually a well-behaved student. Normally I would have quietly spoken to such an offender; a word was usually enough to bring a student in line. However, instead of behaving in my usual controlled manner, I rushed to his side, unceremoniously yanked him out of his seat, put my foot on his chair, and turned him over my knee. With his head down, his legs and arms still flailing, I repeatedly thumped him on his back. The other children stared at me, their usually placid teacher seemingly gone berserk.

Suddenly there was a soft ping on the wooden floor. Tim gasped and stopped waving his arms and legs. I stopped thumping his back and helped him to an upright position. I picked up the object that had fallen—the end of a ballpoint pen. Tim had been sucking on the end of his pen as he concentrated. When the top had come off unexpectedly, he had sucked it into his throat. There it lodged in his windpipe, blocking the passageway so he couldn't breathe.

At the time I had no idea that he was gasping for breath. In fact, I had no time to think. It seemed I was propelled by an unseen hand across the room to do what I did, not even understanding why I did it.

For a few minutes we all sat silently in a state of shock. Then I began to ask questions and we reviewed the drama. We discussed the seriousness of the situation. I was alone with the children. There was no other help nearby. We believed God had worked to save Tim's life, even though we had no time to voice a prayer for help. Before we called, He heard and came to our aid.
JOY DUSTOW

Flight to Siberia

I am persuaded, that neither . . . height, nor depth, nor any other creature, shall be able to separate us from the love of God. Rom. 8:38, 39.

The plane winged its way across the darkened Siberian landscape. The plane was full, but I felt very much alone. I had not been able to find my evangelistic team in Moscow, so now I was headed for Siberia alone, and no one knew where I was. How it would work out, I had no idea.

I prayed earnestly as we began the six-hour flight to Siberia. "Lord, help me. We will arrive in the middle of the night. What if no one is there to meet me? What will I do?"

Immediately I thought of two Bible promises: "My God shall supply all your need" (Phil. 4:19), and "I will never leave thee, nor forsake thee" (Heb. 13:5). As I silently repeated these verses, peace came to my frightened mind. I sensed the presence of Jesus and knew He had a plan for my rescue.

During the flight I discovered one English-speaking businessman to whom I could talk. When I told him of my predicament, he assured me, "If no one meets you, I'll help you. So don't worry."

No one met me. The businessman was true to his word and asked his driver to take us to the hotel where he would negotiate a room for me.

"What brings you to Siberia?" my benefactor asked as we drove through the dark streets.

"I want to share the good news of God's love," I said. I shared a little of what our team would be doing.

A smile lit his face as he assured me, "You will be a blessing to many people."

I hope we were a blessing. I know that I felt greatly blessed by God's tender loving concern given through a stranger who took care of me until my colleagues arrived.

Nothing—not the vast expanse of Siberia nor the height of a jet airplane—can separate me from Your love, Lord. Please send Your peace and Your assurance for this day. LONNA TACHENKO MILBURN

White Stone Hearts

*"I will give you a new heart and put a new spirit within you; and
I will remove the heart of stone from your flesh and give you
a heart of flesh. And I will put My Spirit within you." Eze. 36:26, NASB.*

God showed me His incredible love and two precious promises
during a family vacation to the New Jersey shore. Early one
morning I walked the beach alone to spend time with the Lord. How
I longed to draw closer to Him! I longed for my walk to be deeper. I
was tired of dealing with the same weaknesses and habits. I wanted
to be changed on the inside, and I knew I couldn't do it.

Out of habit my eyes looked down as I walked, searching for a
pretty shell. Usually I am disappointed—New Jersey beaches can't
compete with the sand dollars, conch shells, and shark's teeth that I
had found while living in Florida. However, that morning my eyes
caught a glimpse of a small white stone, very tiny and smooth and in
the shape of a heart.

Immediately the Spirit brought to my mind the verse in Ezekiel
36:26: "I will remove the heart of stone from your flesh and give you
a heart of flesh." The stone became a visual reminder of God's
promise to change me—to remove my hard heart and give me a soft
heart, full of His love.

Two years later, after a prayer of intense desire to know God as a
friend (as Mary Magdalene, Enoch, Noah, Abraham, and Isaac knew
Him) God showed me another precious promise: "And I will give
them a heart to know Me, for I am the Lord; and they will be My
people, and I will be their God" (Jer. 24:7, NASB).

My desire to know God is His desire too. And He plays an important part in the process. He doesn't wait for me to get my act together
first, but He gives me a heart with the capacity to know, love, and
obey Him.

Now when my family walks the beach collecting shells, I collect
little white stone hearts. Each is a reminder of God's precious
promises and His incredible love for me. LILLY TRYON

Nameless, but Significant

Follow my example, as I follow the example of Christ. 1 Cor. 11:1, NIV.

We'd spent the weekend camping at Mason-Dixon Campground in western Maryland. Now we were winding our way to the Youghiogheny River in Pennsylvania to go white-water rafting. We were pumped!

The six in our raft made a great team, deftly maneuvering through catapulting rapids—usually going forward, but sometimes backward. We paddled furiously to avoid rocks, and occasionally had to grab an arm or leg of a teammate to keep them from being jettisoned out of the raft.

The day was half spent when I saw her. I'd jumped in at Swimmer's Rapids and was bobbing through the swirling waters when my eye caught sight of something white. I looked again. I'd seen numerous kayakers running the rapids throughout the day, but this one was different. This kayaker was a she, and she had white hair. As I floated by her kayak, my curiosity was at a peak. I just had to know. Gathering courage, I brazenly asked, "How old are you?"

Not at all offended by my forwardness, she answered, "Sixty."

Wow! Kayaking at 60 years of age! What an inspiration! I decided right then and there that if she could kayak in her 60s, then I could do it in my 30s. And I have.

The power of example is amazing. Many people besides your immediate family and friends notice your actions. Speaking patiently to your child in a trying situation can be a gentle nudge to another mother. Bowing your head to say grace in a restaurant can encourage another Christian to be more open with her faith. Returning to school later in life can inspire other women to develop gifts to the fullest potential. And whether you kayak in your 60s or walk regularly in your neghborhood, your silent example can motivate a younger person to value her health and add zest to her life.

So whether you are prominent in your church and community or feel nameless, remember, your actions are noticed and your example is significant.   HEIDE FORD

Love Completed

Acquaint now thyself with him, and be at peace. Job 22:21.

My daughters are two years apart in age, and both are adopted. When Amy passed her eighteenth birthday, she became curious about her roots. Several years later Sara followed suit. I gave them my blessing, as I had always been grateful to their mothers for having given them up for adoption. I knew in my heart that God had directed these precious babies to us.

When Amy contacted the agency through which we had adopted her, she was told that at about the time of her last birthday Janice, her birth mother, had contacted them. She wanted them to know where she was in case her daughter tried to locate her.

Since Janice knew where Tom, the birth father, was, the agency arranged for them to meet Amy together. We soon learned that Janice's love had been like God's love, steadfast and always seeking. Whenever Janice had returned to our city, she wondered if any of the little dark-haired girls she had seen were her "Laura." For 18 years she had always wondered where Amy was and what she was doing.

Janice died at age 40, just two weeks after Amy's wedding. What a shock to all. Amy treasures the five years they had. Janice was a true example of God's open arms desiring to receive the lost child. Amy and Janice found a completeness.

Sara's search was not the "dream come true" that her sister's was. Not all birth mothers want to be found, and their wishes need to be respected. However, to the child it comes across as a second rejection. Sara then sought her birth father, only to discover he had died eight years earlier. His three sons, her newly found half brothers, assured her that Jimmy would have been delighted to have known a daughter. Sara found answers, but not the completeness her sister had found.

Earthly parents can be birth, adoptive, or foster. Some will disappoint us, but most do the best job of parenting they can. How fortunate we are to have a heavenly Father who will never disappoint us. We can find completeness in Him when we seek Him. His arms are always open and waiting.

JUDY HAUPT JAGITSCH

The Contact Lens

Seek ye first the kingdom of God. Matt. 6:33.

It was the early-morning rush in our house. There were lunches to make, children to get to school, husband to send off to work, and a quick burst of house tidying before going off to work myself. This particular morning—a glorious sunny morning—I decided I had just enough time to hang out a load of washing on the clothesline.

As I quickly pegged up the sheets, the wind suddenly flapped one in my face. I blinked, and out fell a contact lens. Crouching, I started looking in the grass on the side of the path I'd been facing. In New Zealand it rains a lot, and the lush grass is very thick and very green. Every sparkle I thought was my lens was really the early-morning sun shining on the wet grass.

Precious minutes passed. Finally I straightened up and prayed, "Lord, I don't have time to search. Please show me where my contact lens is; I have to get to work."

Instantly I was impressed to look on the other side. I stooped down—and there was my lens in the grass on the opposite side of the path! Again I prayed, this time with a thankful heart.

There are many things we are instructed in God's Holy Word to look for, things so much more important than a contact lens.

Psalm 34:14—Seek peace and pursue it.

Amos 5:14—Seek good and not evil.

Psalm 27:8—Seek God's face.

And the most important of all, Matthew 6:33—Seek first the kingdom of God.

A word study of "seek" could be an interesting devotional activity. *Young's Analytical Concordance to the Bible* lists Hebrew words that are translated as "seek" and informs us this word is used in about 300 Old Testament texts. There are a number of Greek words used for the concept of seeking. The word appears more than 100 times in the New Testament. Some questions you might ask yourself as you study are: What am I to seek? What am I not to seek? What Bible characters sought for something? What parables of Jesus have to do with seeking?

Lord, today we seek Your face. Be gracious to us. Amen.

LEONIE DONALD

Get Yourself Ready

Then the Lord reached out his hand and touched my mouth and said to me, "Now, I have put my words in your mouth." Jer. 1:9, NIV.

There was little air in the recording studio. The two camera operators, sound technician, and production manager were all busy with individual tasks. Props and clutter were scattered about out of sight from the cameras.

I had flown more than 6,000 miles (9,700 kilometers) to film one of my most important seminars. Every minute of filming was extremely expensive. What added to the incredible pressure was the humidity. The studio was not air-conditioned, and we had to stop every 15 to 20 minutes to wipe perspiration from my face. Since this was Brazil, a Portuguese crew was putting this on film to dub into Portuguese. The director could speak only one English word: "Action!"

Doubts of my ability to carry on under such difficult circumstances crowded my brain. Yet my mind had to remain focused; I had to smile and note which camera to look into. Could I handle this? So much money was going into this project. I was weak with apprehension and fear the first of four days of filming. How could I carry on?

Suddenly I recalled a scripture I had read that morning: "The Lord . . . said to me, 'Now, I have put my words in your mouth.'" Encouraged by it, I had read all of Jeremiah 1. It was as though God knew in advance how difficult these next four days of filming were going to be. He knew I was going to need strength to meet the challenge when I was alone halfway around the world.

Throughout the ensuing days of filming, I carried on like a pro, they said. Not because of anything I did within my own strength, but these verses from Scripture gave me peace and confidence when I most needed it.

Is God calling you to a task you feel is beyond your abilities? Maybe you too need to read the words of Jeremiah. "Get yourself ready! Stand up and say to them whatever I command you. Do not be terrified" (verse 17). God can do great things with a little talent that is totally dedicated to Him.   NANCY VAN PELT

September Snow

"If you do not forgive others, neither will your
Father forgive your trespasses." Matt. 6:15, NRSV.

In anticipation of the arrival of my brother-in-law and nephew, my mind whirled with a multitude of questions. It had been more than 20 years since we had seen each other. My sister had died from alcoholism when she was 49, and I blamed her husband. As the years passed, my anger toward him persisted, regardless of his efforts to remain a part of the family. Four years earlier I had rededicated my life to Christ. I knew, however, that I still had some unfinished business. I desperately wanted to forgive my brother-in-law as Christ had forgiven me.

We scheduled a visit, and my brother-in-law and nephew finally arrived. My heart pounded as I looked at my nephew. His actions, speech, and gestures reminded me of his mother. The memories came flooding back, and all my best-laid plans were crushed as the anger again became insurmountable. I could not forgive my brother-in-law.

During the next day and a half I wrestled with my feelings and with God. "I cannot forgive; but if I do not forgive, I cannot become like You, Lord. I cannot experience that peace of forgiveness." On retiring that night, I put all my fears, hurts, and anger at the foot of the cross. It was now in God's hands. I asked that a way be opened so I would have peace.

When I awoke the next morning, the tumult that had been raging inside was now a calm feeling of peace. I felt contentment. Then I looked outside and saw snow. I felt that God, in His wisdom, gave us this snow in answer to my prayer. We had planned to spend the day touring, but instead found ourselves snowbound in September—a perfect opportunity for God to work.

As my brother-in-law and I talked, the walls began to crumble, and the floodgate of tears opened up on both sides. We prayed together and thanked God for giving us a forgiving spirit.

As I gazed upon the snow it reminded me of God's love and His righteousness. He tells us in Isaiah 1:18: "'Come now, and let us reason together,' says the Lord. 'Though your sins are like scarlet, they shall be as white as snow.'"

PHYLLIS ALEXANDER

Embraced by Beauty

Bless the Lord, O my soul, and forget not all his benefits. Ps. 103:2.

Beauty enfolded me in her arms this morning as I walked in Paint Branch Park. The golden woods seemed set afire by the rising sun, blazing against a bright-blue October sky.

Leaves crunched beneath my feet, a lavish carpet in shades of red, gold, burgundy, and brown. A soft breeze added fresh leaves, shifting the pattern of my royal carpet. I followed it to a bridge, arching a creek where mallards floated with the leaves.

The leaves, like miniature rafts of red and gold, whirled in the eddies, emerging to float quietly on. How fragile they were! Released from the safety of the branch to which they had clung all summer, they set loose into the rushing stream, soon to be far beyond my reach or sight. Profound thoughts lay in my mind. I longed to sit a while and let the thoughts come with the wisdom and understanding of my own frail "raft," sometimes floating, sometimes whirling frantically through life.

The pungent odor of the leaves underfoot brought back memories of walking to school in Jackson, Ohio. I felt transported back in time, away from the struggles and trials of my adult life, back to the awareness of beauty and joy I had known as a child.

At this moment I saw the playground swings, and like the 7-year-old child I had been, I ran for the swings. With a push of my feet I sailed through the crisp air, the sun on my upturned face. My golden retriever, Matt, did not approve. He jumped up at me, trying to stop the swing. The experience held no memories for him. He wanted to move on, and so we did.

But I took with me a moment of joy, a memory of happy times and a home that was no more, except in my heart. I felt revived by a return to childhood, the experience of abandonment to beauty, and a sense of oneness with all creation. I felt strengthened for my journey on the stream of life.

I bent to pick up three burgundy leaves to paste into my prayer journal, a reminder of my morning with God. "Thank You, Lord, for the golden delight of this day," I whispered. "I promise to take time more often to let You embrace me with beauty, kiss me with sunshine, and fill me with joy." DOROTHY EATON WATTS

The African Violet

*Our light and momentary troubles are achieving for us an eternal
glory that far outweighs them all. So we fix our eyes
not on what is seen, but on what is unseen. For what is seen
is temporary, but what is unseen is eternal. 2 Cor. 4:17, 18, NIV.*

I stood in front of the window that sunny autumn day soaking up
the sunshine. With my eyes closed against the brightness I could
practically see the life-giving blood flowing through my eyelids. The
warmth was enough to carry me through the mundane task at
hand—cleaning the house.

As I cleaned the kitchen counters, I was reminded by my patient
African violets that I was behind in their monthly watering. For years
I've had a couple plants that bloom five or six times a year. A third violet had been included in a beautiful houseplant bouquet we received
when my husband's mother passed away three years before. It had
never produced a single blossom, and I had been inclined to throw it
out the past few months. But much to my surprise, there was a beautiful grouping of blossoms. I had all but given up on this plant.

*God never gives us up for lost when we are lifeless, in need of His life-
giving water,* I mused. *I should fix my eyes on His promise of eternal life, not
on my day-to-day troubles.* It's easier to do this some days than others.
There may be squabbles with family members, worries about taxes,
and concerns about a serious illness or a death.

God is always looking for ways to remind us that He is in control, I
thought as I finished up the watering chore. Suddenly tears came to my
eyes as I remembered it was my mother-in-law's birth date. I probably
wouldn't have realized it until the day was past, but her love of flowers
and the fact that her death brought us this plant were too much of a
coincidence. It was another reminder that God cherishes life more than
anything, and He wants so much for us to spend it eternally with Him
in a place where death will no longer have a hold. *Lord, pour Your living
water upon me this day.*   PATTY KNITTEL

OCTOBER 3

Interruptions

*"Call to Me, and I will answer you, and show you great
and mighty things, which you do not know." Jer. 33:3, NKJV.*

M y husband, Tim, was attending a seminar, and I was elsewhere
presenting a seminar. Our boys were with me, so I had brought
things for them to do. They were supposed to be sitting quietly, creating books about nature and Bible stories. I was in the middle of my
presentation when I felt a tap on my arm. There was Zachary.

"Mom, how do you spell *animals?*"

Quickly I spelled the word for him and told him he needed to
stay at the table till after the seminar. A little frustrated, I went on
with the presentation.

A few minutes later I felt another tug on my sweater. Zachary
had another question.

Later, in the car, I shared my frustrations with Tim. "He kept interrupting right in the middle of the seminar. I didn't know what to
do. He should've known better."

"We don't need to talk about this right now," Tim replied.

I became quiet and my thoughts turned to God. *Does He ever get
frustrated with my interruptions, my constant questions and prayers? He has
a lot more important things to do than I have. If I interrupted with a prayer as
He was addressing the angels, would He get frustrated with me? No! God is
always there for me, always willing to listen. He is always willing to stop and
take care of me, no matter what.*

"You know, maybe it's good that Zachary felt he could interrupt
me, no matter what I was doing," I told Tim. "I'm glad that he felt
that nothing was more important to me than he is. Isn't that how
God sees us? Nothing is more important to Him than us. We're not
an interruption to Him; He invites us to talk to Him, to ask Him questions." I was smiling. The frustrations were gone.

*Thank You, Lord, that You're never too busy to hear me when I call.
Make me a parent like You. You're willing to drop everything for Your children. Help me to do the same.*   TAMYRA HORST

Heavenly Presents

*There are varieties of gifts, but the same Spirit. And there are
varieties of ministries, and the same Lord. 1 Cor. 12:4, 5, NASB.*

I have sometimes hesitated to open a present because I didn't want
to ruin its beautiful appearance. I stop and admire the carefully
chosen wrap and the shimmering ribbons. After opening the present,
I contemplate its beauty and show appreciation for the token of love.

I find it exciting to watch the reactions of those who receive gifts.
The greater the excitement in the receiver, the happier the giver is for
having given the gift. I enjoy looking for a special gift for someone I
love. I get excited as I anticipate her reaction.

I once responded to a call for volunteers to help in a home-based
ministry for divorced or separated people. On my first assignment I
spent many hours wrapping presents. I had fun looking for just the
right gift wrap to go with each gift. I noticed how special and unique
the gifts were. Soon I heard that many of the gifts had been donated
by people who had been blessed by that ministry before; this was
their way of giving something back in appreciation. It was their way
of making someone else feel special too. Some of the gifts were personalized and laced with lots of love and prayers.

I was glad I had volunteered. Other gifts that could not be purchased or wrapped were given that weekend: gifts of hugs, kindness,
encouragement, acceptance, healing, time, and much more. How do
you wrap those?

Later I helped out in Caring for Marriage weekends. Both of these
ministries still continue to provide many gifts that cannot be purchased, wrapped, or tied with pretty ribbons. What a privilege to be
involved in gift wrapping, table setting, cooking, cleaning, and whatever has been needed! I have praised God many times during those .
long, tiring hours for the gift of helps and the reward that comes after
the guests express the blessings they receive, and for the way God
touches their lives through the selfless, dedicated leaders who minister to them.

*Thank You, Lord, for the spiritual gifts You have given me. Help me to
find ways to use those gifts to bless others.* CARMEN O. GONZALEZ

The Bottom of a Well

Who forgiveth all thine iniquities; who healeth all thy diseases;
who redeemeth thy life from destruction;
who crowneth thee with lovingkindness and tender mercies. Ps. 103:3, 4.

I wanted to die. I felt as though I were at the bottom of a deep dark well from which there was no escape except by death. For many years I was a victim of depression. I had no apparent reason for my sadness. Friends tried to help, but their efforts seemed to make no difference. Only those who have experienced this situation will know what I went through.

Friends recommended a well-known doctor. I went, but could only cry. I couldn't answer the doctor's questions. Everything was fine at home. I had three beautiful healthy children and a husband who loved me. What could I tell him?

He prescribed some medicine and scheduled me for another appointment. I continued in this way for three years, sometimes getting a little better, but sometimes returning to the depression.

"Lord, free me from taking this medicine," I begged. "I feel like an addict." I claimed the promise of Matthew 8:17: "He Himself took our infirmities and bore our sicknesses" (NKJV).

Immediately I sensed the Lord was healing my mind and body, but I continued my regular appointments with the doctor. Little by little, I improved. Finally the doctor said I had recovered enough and would no longer need to take the medication, nor would I need to return for visits with him.

"I have been cured by the Great Physician," I told him on my last visit. I knew that a dramatic change for the better had occurred when I gave the problem completely over into His hands, letting Him bear my burden and my illness.

It's been 20 years, and I never tire of witnessing to the power of such a wonderful God. He is our greatest friend, one who is concerned with our needs of body and mind. He is a God who answers prayer. He brought me out into the joy and light of health and wholeness.

Lord, help me to remember today that no matter how dark life may seem, You are still with me. You have an answer for my problems. You can lift me into the light.　　　　　　　　　　　　　　NICEA FERREIRA TRINDADE

Contentment

*I have learned the secret of being content and in any and
every situation, whether well fed or hungry,
whether living in plenty or in want. Phil. 4:12, NIV.*

Some of the disadvantages of growing up in a family of 16 children
during the Depression years were the hand-me-down clothes,
sleeping three in a bed, and the almost continual gnawing in the
belly. But some of the advantages far outweighed any lack we may
have experienced through the years.

There was no TV and sometimes no radio, so we made our own
fun by playing school, jacks, hopscotch, and tag. With our large family
we even had our own baseball team. In the evenings we'd sit
around the dining room table by the light of the flickering oil lamp
and listen to Mother tell stories of her life on the Dakota plains.

Our mother was one of the most nearly perfect women I ever
knew, but I can't remember her ever asking the blessing on our food
before our meals or teaching us to say prayers at bedtime. The only
time we heard God's name uttered was when our father cursed during
his frequent encounters with the bottle.

When I was about 5 years old, I was invited to a small neighborhood
Sunday school that I attended regularly for several years. During
this same time my aunt Fern came to visit. She taught me to kneel by
my bed and say my prayers before I went to sleep each night.

I gave my heart to the Lord when I was about 12. Even though I
had little encouragement from my parents, I grew up knowing right
from wrong. It was this special relationship with my heavenly Father
that kept me from some near scrapes during my teen years. I was
married with two small children before I had a real conversion experience
and was baptized.

More than a half century has passed since those early days.
Although those times were hard and I had many disadvantages, I also
received many blessings. Out of those early experiences came stamina
that neither poverty nor a depression could stifle. I learned early on to
be content, come what may.

*Lord, today help me to be content in spite of my circumstances. Help me
to be content as You guide and sustain me.* CLAREEN COLCLESSER

Lost Ring

God is our refuge and strength,
an ever-present help in trouble. Ps. 46:1, NIV.

One October morning I was returning from a walk to my mailbox when I noticed my young neighbor. She seemed to be searching through the grass by the front of her home. As she has multiple sclerosis, I called to her to see if she needed help. She slowly made her way over to me. I could see that she was crying.

"Oh, I am so upset!" she said. "I walked my daughter to the school bus this morning, and when I returned home I noticed my wedding ring wasn't on my finger. I've lost weight recently, and my ring keeps slipping off. I've looked everywhere, but I just can't find it! What am I going to do?"

Embracing her, I asked if she would mind if we prayed about her problem. She consented. Taking her hands in mine, I prayed right there in my driveway, asking God to help us locate Lisa's ring.

"I feel much better now," she said when we had finished.

She turned to go home, and I went into my house. As I worked in my kitchen, the phone rang. It was a very excited Lisa. She explained that after she had returned home her husband had decided to search for her ring. He retraced the route she had taken that morning, and in a place that she had searched earlier, nestled under a golden leaf, was her ring.

"It seemed he was led to look in that spot," she said, her voice almost singing. "It's a miracle we found it!"

And we agreed it was God doing the leading. Within 10 minutes of the time we had offered prayer the lost ring had been found. A ring is such a small thing, but it was of great concern to Lisa, and God took notice of her prayer and answered it. What a marvelous God! What a friend!

Lord, I thank You that nothing that in any way concerns my peace is too small for You to notice. Help me to turn to You every day for strength and guidance. I know You care!   ROSEMARY BAKER

A Sweet Savor

Walk in love, as Christ also hath loved us, and hath given himself for us an offering and a sacrifice to God for a sweetsmelling savour. Eph. 5:2.

"Why don't you buy an electric breadmaker that mixes, kneads, raises, and bakes one luscious loaf at a time?" my friend asked me. "It makes breadmaking so easy!"

I shook my head and smiled as I brought out my old-fashioned breadmaker. I had gotten it at an antique shop. It was an answer to an ad my friend Linda had placed in a local paper in an effort to find a breadmaker like hers for me.

Made of tin, the breadmaker has changed color and has a dent here and there. The necessary parts are intact—the kneader, the crosspiece, the handle and the lid. It still operates, even though it is minus the clamp to hold it to the table while I turn the handle.

The breadmaker must have been a very welcome invention that took a lot of work out of bread preparation. No more tedious kneading, only a few turns of the handle. I can almost see the old farmhouse kitchen where everything was homegrown and prepared from scratch. What a time-saver the breadmaker must have been!

The directions for making wholesome bread, printed right on the lid of the mixer, are very simple. Turn the crank for three minutes, let rise, turn the crank again, turn the dough out on a floured surface, cut in four equal pieces, roll out with a rolling pin to get the air bubbles out, fold, and place each roll in a greased pan. When the dough has risen to the proper height, the pans are popped into the oven. What a sight to see four golden-brown loaves cooling on the countertop! The heavenly fragrance that lingers through the whole house makes every mouth water.

Our lives are like a loaf of fresh-baked bread. There is a certain amount of preparation in getting ready to meet our Lord and Saviour. God has given us every needful part and directions in His Word to turn out a completed product.

God Himself has provided the "clamp" to keep me on the right road. If I follow His directions, the end result will be a sweet savor that will fill all heaven. LAURIE DIXON-MCCLANAHAN

Tree of Faith

The apostle said unto the Lord, Increase our faith. Luke 17:5.

During October nature's dress in eastern Africa is made of rather dull shades of yellow, brown, and gray. From time to time a mango tree provides a green spot on the landscape, but the earth is dry and dusty.

When my heart is heavy, I feel like I too am dry, dusty, and colorless, a part of my drab surroundings. Then overnight appear the lonely violet blossoms of the jacaranda tree, clothing it in a brilliant spring gown. Its flowers bring beauty into the lifeless countryside. I call it the tree of faith. The jacaranda tree is the first sign that rain will come to eastern Africa. I wonder where it gets the strength to blossom when all nature seems dead?

I've seen people like that. When times get rough, when the situation seems hopeless, they draw strength from deep inside, from the long roots. They pull themselves together and start anew.

I've seen the same faith in little children. They take their confidence to face life from the love and security they experienced in their home. But I've also seen children who never developed the faith in their ability. They are not wanted, not loved, not cared for. No dazzling light of blossoms is in their eyes. It makes me angry and sad.

In our garden there is a beautiful old jacaranda tree. Termites chew on its old bark; we had to cut down some branches. But it brings each year its faithful blossoms.

I love my tree of faith. It must have long roots to reach water, the water of life. Does the Lord sometimes give me a dry season so I can grow long roots? As the jacaranda tree blossoms in a difficult season, so I pray my tree of faith will blossom, bringing promise of better days.

VERENA JAGGI-RECHSTEINER

You Have God

God is able to provide you with every blessing in abundance,
so that by always having enough of everything, you
may share abundantly in every good work. 2 Cor. 9:8, NRSV.

The lunch table was cleared, and we moved into the living room. Soon it was time for everyone to leave. As the goodbyes began, the doorbell rang. A bright-eyed 4-year-old burst into the room in a flurry of petticoats. "Where is my grandma?" she wanted to know.

"I'm right here, sweetheart." My friend enveloped her in a hug only grandmothers can give.

"Well, let's go." Her hand firmly clasping her grandmother's, the little girl strode to the door, beginning the exodus of all the other guests.

"But how can you take your grandma away?" I asked in mock despair. "I'll be all alone." My mournful tone was doing nothing to change her decision.

"You have God," she reminded me crisply. "That is enough." With that she escorted her beloved grandparent to the waiting car.

Later that afternoon as I walked down to the lake, I realized anew that she was right. I saw His eye for color in the ruby red of the fall dogwoods. He appeared in the apricot kiss of the setting sun reflecting on the water. I heard Him in the glorious evening bird song. I tasted Him in the tangy crunch of the apple from my neighbor's orchard. I felt Him in the cooling breezes that gently caressed my cheek. Yes, I had God, and it was more than enough.

Meditating on His goodness on that waterfront park bench, I turned the pages of my mind's catalog of blessings. God was my environment. And it was good. Everything was charged with His grandeur. I was so thankful for life's beauties.

With David I exulted, "I'll be the poet who sings your glory—and live what I sing every day" (Ps. 61:8, Message).

Dear Lord, on my discipleship journey, help me to be so attuned to the fact that You are always with me that others looking on will notice the glow and see You too. Thank You for masking my frailties and imperfections in Your purity. I have You, God. It is indeed enough!

GLENDA-MAE GREENE

Mystery Keys

"I have set before you an open door,
which no one is able to shut." Rev. 3:8, RSV.

When I moved into my mobile home, I was handed a set of keys. Because the original home had been added onto, I had a total of five doors with locks on them, plus a shed. I tried the keys in the various doors and made a startling discovery—I had a key for the front door and one for the shed, but none for the other four doors. I also had three leftover "mystery keys" that didn't open anything at all!

A key is no good without a lock to match it. Likewise, a lock without a key is of no use. In order for a lock to perform its vital function and protect people and property, it must have a key.

So it is with reading the Bible. Some passages seem mysterious to me because I don't understand the historical background and customs of the Holy Land. Then I search through a reference book I have on biblical times and can place the passage in the proper context. Other texts are symbolic and present problems in translation.

When I started studying my Bible, I used to feel like I did when I was exploring my new home, frantically trying to match up the keys and the locks. Even the disciples were sometimes confused with the sayings of Jesus. Now before I open my Bible I first pray for understanding.

I also use any extra help I can get by consulting with older Christians and perusing Bible commentaries. Often one text becomes the key to understanding another text. I know that for every locked door in my study, Jesus will provide the key. He will give the Holy Spirit to guide me, to open the door of my understanding.

Lord, I am sometimes lost as I walk through Your Word. There are doors of understanding that seem closed to me. As I open Your Word just now, give me Your Holy Spirit. Help me to find the keys that will match each locked passage. Give me the message You want me to learn today. GINA LEE

God's Reception Room

The Lord is good unto them that wait for him. Lam. 3:25.

Vivid memories spring to mind when I recall the hours I spent in my physician father's office, filling in during his nurse's summer vacation each year.

"Doctor Daddy," as I affectionately called my father, always made time for those who really needed him, so the waiting room was always bustling. In those days the reception room was usually called the waiting room, where his patients waited their turn for treatment. (I much prefer to call it the reception room, for patients are there to receive.)

A couple months ago a loved one sustained a serious injury; it has proved to be a long, very painful road to recovery, and she's still far from being completely healed. Others who have experienced similar circumstances can relate to how utterly disheartening this can be. So I was trying recently to encourage my loved one by telling her that God had placed her in a very special room for a while—His reception room.

I reminded her of a thought a friend of hers had shared in a letter: whenever she was allowed to go through a great disappointment, God always brought a great blessing to her afterward so she would know He still loved her.

Seeing the great struggle with pain my loved one was suffering, I tried to indicate to her that if she'll patiently wait upon the Lord, trusting that He knows what He's doing, a great blessing will come from this excruciatingly painful ordeal. Hard as it may seem, she now needs to position herself in God's reception room to receive.

This experience has taught me that God gives us "faith days" to remind us that we've chosen to be led by Him. When you're in the crucible of a health crisis, dear soul, remember that Jesus is still tenderly caring for you, longing to see you come out victorious on the other side.

If you are currently in God's "reception room," don't give up! Cling to Jesus in your pain and suffering. Rest in Him, wait for Him, for it is still true that "the Lord is good unto them that wait for him."

JUDY COULSTON

Look for the Beautiful

*I'd say you'll do best by filling your minds and meditating
on things true, noble, reputable, authentic, compelling, gracious —
the best, not the worst; the beautiful, not the ugly; things to praise,
not things to curse. Phil. 4:8, Message.*

My husband and I take a three-mile (five-kilometer) walk around our neighborhood each morning. Brisk walking not only invigorates us, it also gives us the opportunity to enjoy the beautiful landscaping in our community.

One morning my husband found a nickel. Two days later I found a treasure of two pennies. A week later we found a quarter. We found these on different streets. What do you think we did after those great finds? You guessed right! Instead of enjoying God's creation, our eyes almost always focused on the streets. Why? We were looking for more pennies! We no longer looked for the beauty of flowers and well-manicured lawns. Our pace also slowed.

"Don't you think we're getting ridiculous?" I asked my husband. "We now search for pennies instead of enjoying the flowers."

In our Christian life, don't we sometimes get our priorities wrong? God has given us intelligence so that we may put things in proper perspective. But we focus our attention on mundane things. We become preoccupied with insignificant things of this world. We look for things that may not lead to Christian maturity. We indulge in experiences that stunt our spiritual growth.

Our experience reminds me of two people who stepped from their homes. One saw the garbage on the street, while the other saw twinkling stars up above. Sometimes we look at people and see the negative and ugly in their character instead of seeing the beauty. We perceive them as offensive, whereas in reality they can help us grow in grace. There is something positive and praiseworthy in everyone if we will but look for it.

Help me today, Lord, to focus on the noble, the lofty, and the praiseworthy things in life instead of the ugly and the mundane. Help me to lift my eyes from the sordid things of earth to the beautiful things above.

OFELIA A. PANGAN

A Great God

Behold, what manner of love the Father hath bestowed upon us. 1 John 3:1.

W hat did you do today?" I asked my 6-year-old daughter. "I did math, I read a book, and I played with my friend," she began. (The objective of this conversation was to try to recount all of our activities, stretching our memories to remember everything.)

"And what did you do today, Mommy?" Rachel asked after she had recounted a series of adventures.

Now it was my turn. "I ironed your clothes, helped you get dressed, fixed breakfast, packed a lunch for you, took you to school, brought you home again, helped you with your homework, made dinner, and read you stories from your Bible lesson."

After realizing how much my activities focused on doing things for her, Rachel exclaimed, "You are a great mom!" It was as if she knew this all along, but these activities really proved to her that I am a great mom.

In the same way, intellectually, I know God is great, but how often do I take the time to recount all that He has done for me? How often do I actually review, item by item, how God has demonstrated His love for me? I took my journal out and read page after page of God's intervention in my life.

As I looked back at the past couple years, I was reminded anew that there was not a day when God was not near and concerned about what happened to me. I realized how God had been my Comforter, Provider, Sustainer, Companion, Strength for the day, Shepherd, Lord who heals, Bread of Life, Prince of Peace, Alpha and Omega, and so many other things.

Then I sat back in awe like Rachel and exclaimed, "You are a great God!"

Why not take a few minutes to enumerate all that God has done for you during the past 24 hours? I guarantee you'll agree with me, "God, You are a great God!"

VICKI GALLON-CLARK

Family Resemblance

A new heart also will I give you, and a new spirit will I put within you: and I will take away the stony heart out of your flesh, and I will give you an heart of flesh. And I will put my spirit within you, and cause you to walk in my statutes, and ye shall keep my judgments, and do them. Eze. 36:26.

I stood in the hall of my friend's house looking at a wall full of pictures. There were newborns wrapped in blankets, children smiling, wedding and graduation scenes, and family portraits by the Christmas tree. It was a wall full of memories.

As I looked over the many faces, I couldn't help but notice a family resemblance. "It's no secret they are your children," I remarked to my friend. "They look just like you."

Instead of agreeing with me she began to laugh. "Oh, Retta, you know our kids are adopted!"

It was true, of course. I had been present when all the papers had been signed and those children had become her own. I had been among those who had prayed for that day to come. But somehow I had forgotten. And adopted or not, the similarities were undeniable. I guess people just start resembling each other when they live together.

That incident in the hall of my friend's house has given me reason to ponder the fact that I too have been adopted. As God's adopted daughter I share His name and am heir to His riches. But do I dare hope to be His daughter by resemblance as well? Is it possible that when others look at me they will see a reflection of Him? What a transformation that would be—to act as He would act, to think thoughts He would find attractive, to speak words He's been heard to utter. There is nothing I want more, but what are the chances?

The truth is that as with my friend's children I can expect to resemble my Father by simply spending time with Him. How can I be so sure? Because He has promised it. The One who created me in the first place has promised to re-create me with a new heart, a heart like His.

RETTA MICHAELIS

Seesawing

The Lord maketh poor, and maketh rich;
he bringeth low, and lifteth up. 1 Sam. 2:7.

Do you remember seesawing as a child, and the way the wind would rush through your hair as you were lifted up? Going up seemed magical compared to the going down, which always happened automatically and sometimes abruptly. Life is very similar to see-sawing—there are lows and highs, and thankfully, neither lasts forever.

Ironically, it is the person on the bottom who has the most choices. The person on the top can only sit still and hang on tightly. But if you're the one on the bottom, you can use the ground for leverage to push up, or you can stay put. You can even give up and quit for good. We all know what will happen if you stay put—nothing! And if giving up altogether is the choice, there is a definite problem. Life is not a game you play by yourself, so your decisions will determine others' directions also.

I grew up with the idea that if we do everything right, everything will turn out all right. This is just not true. As children we never questioned the ups and downs of seesawing; we just accepted it as part of the game. But as adults we have a very difficult time with the lows.

Is it wrong to question God when we are perplexed about our situations? There really is no doubt about God's love for us and His concern for our well-being. He knows what we are going through, and He has promised to make provisions for every circumstance. So if you are on the down side of life, sit tight until you are ready to push. Then ask God for the strength and push with all your might. When you are up again (and you *will* be), encourage those who need to be lifted up.

Lord, I don't know if today is going to be an up day or a down day, but with You by my side, I can know it will be all right. Thank You for the blessings today holds. JO ANN HILTON

The Inner Sign

I will imprint My laws upon their minds, even upon their innermost thoughts and understanding, and engrave them upon their hearts. Heb. 8:10, Amplified.

Kim hefted her book bag onto the couch and plunked down beside it. "I made a commitment to personal growth this weekend," she announced proudly. I sat forward expectantly. She eyed me over the top of her glasses as if to determine whether or not I could be trusted with this new information. Her anxious hands smoothed her long white dress down over dark, combat-style boots. "Do you want to know what it is?" she demanded.

"Of course I do!" I replied. (I really did like Kim.)

"Well," she started mysteriously, "I decided that I needed some inner sign that I'm trying to turn my life around."

"And?" I encouraged.

"I didn't want anyone to know about it, but I wanted it to be something that I was always aware of." Kim brightened. "So I did this!" And with that she thrust out her tongue. Gleaming off to one side of her tongue was a small steel rod. "See it?" she happily asked.

"I sure do!" I said, feeling a pang of weakness shoot through my knees. "Didn't it hurt to get your tongue pierced?"

"Only at first. But," she triumphed, "every time I feel it I know that I need to make better choices." She rolled her tongue to show me what she meant.

Oh, please don't, I anguished inside. Collecting my fading wits, I exclaimed, "Now that is—creative." We both howled with laughter at my obvious loss of words.

I thought about Kim's need for an inward sign. She didn't know that Jesus will write His law on our hearts and send us the Holy Spirit to prompt us to make good choices. Piercing her tongue was the best she could do, given her experience. She was willing to have pain and inconvenience so she could improve herself.

And what of me? The Holy Spirit is a free gift, and so is most everything else that heaven has to offer. But I keep forgetting to ask. Jesus made it simple. I don't have to be a certain way or like certain things, or undergo painful procedures. I just need to ask, and God provides it.

BARBARA COUDEN

Blessed Assurance

Thus says the Lord: . . . I will contend with those that contend with you, and I will save your children. Isa. 49:25, NRSV.

I stood at my kitchen sink one morning, looking at magnificent snow-capped peaks while I washed the breakfast dishes. I never see them without saying in my heart, "Thank You, Lord, for giving us such beauty." This morning I added, "And thank You for watching over my husband as he helped a friend push his ailing car on a lonely road, and for helping them find the car's problem quickly so it can be fixed and they can be on their way."

Then I heard His still small voice in my heart: "I'm glad you're thankful when I answer your prayers for these small things. But why do you not trust Me with the big things in your life?"

I was shocked! "Lord, I do trust You with the big things! I trust You with every part of my life. What have I not trusted You with ?"

Again I heard that quiet, calm voice: "You do not trust Me to take care of your children. You get up in the night and worry and pray for their salvation. Why don't you trust Me to take care of their lives, both spiritual and physical?"

I thought of the nights I had gotten up in the wee small hours to pray for my children, and the nights I had been aware of their father getting up to pray for them. I thought of our concern over what will happen to our grandchildren.

Tears filled my eyes, and I realized that I had disappointed my Lord in lacking faith. "Oh, my Father, why could I not see that? I am so sorry. I know You promised that You will save them. But somehow I thought I had to remind You."

The words of Isaiah 59:21 came to mind: "My spirit that is upon thee, and my words which I have put in thy mouth, shall not depart out of thy mouth, nor out of the mouth of thy seed [my children], nor out of the mouth of thy seed's seed [my grandchildren], saith the Lord, from henceforth and forever." What a blessed assurance He has given me!

I still pray for my children and grandchildren every day, but now I pray, "Lord, You have promised that You will save my family. This day I give them to You, for I know You love them far more than we do."

JEAN REIFFENSTEIN ROTHGEB

Influence

Come, ye children, hearken unto me:
I will teach you the fear of the Lord. Ps. 34:11.

Please sit down, Susan," Miss Kohler called from the front of her first and second grade classroom.

I looked up, surprised to find myself standing.

"Please sit down, Susan," she said again.

I sat down.

This scene repeated itself several times, and every time I was dumbfounded at how I could be standing beside my desk, working diligently, not realizing that I had stood up. I remember it coming as a total surprise each time.

Finally the teacher came to my desk. "Why do you stand beside your desk to work?" she asked kindly.

I had no idea.

"Maybe your desk is too tall for you," she decided. "We'll have somebody adjust it and see if that makes a difference."

The maintenance man lowered the desk, and the problem disappeared.

It wasn't until I was a mother myself and had dealings with the teachers of my own children that this incident came back to me, and I said a little prayer of thanks for teachers like Miss Kohler. This teacher could have hounded me, punished me, scolded or belittled me for being such an "uncooperative" child. It could have made a difference in my entire educational experience if this teacher had allowed herself to believe that I was a "bad" girl. Instead she studied the problem, asked sincere questions, and found an answer.

Doesn't it happen often that when we recall insignificant memories of our childhood they are memories of something that influenced our entire life, for better or worse? The people who performed the small act probably don't remember having done it at all. I'm sure Miss Kohler didn't know I would remember the incident for years. I'm sure she didn't consider it a life-influencing situation.

More often than we know, it's the smallest, most insignificant act that has the most lasting impact on a life. When all of our actions are taken in kindness and gentleness, coming from the source of kindness and love, then our actions will be an influence for good.   SUSAN SCOGGINS

Hope

I wait for the Lord, my soul doth wait, and in his word do I hope. Ps. 130:5.

Sometimes the smallest acts of kindness and thoughtfulness are truly our greatest gifts. In the fall of 1996 I received a birthday card from my dad. That may not seem like a big deal to you, but my father had never sent me one before. And here one was on my thirty-eighth birthday.

At first I thought it was from my mom. She is my greatest fan. In fact, it wasn't until I read "Love, Dad" that I realized that this message was from him. God's timing was perfect, and He gave me this love message when He knew I needed it the most. God's like that.

I gave my dad a poem on soft pink parchment mounted in a picture frame. I had been inspired to write it the day I received this most precious gift of love. I would like to share it with you.

Hope is born in heaven
In heart, in hand and pen
It speaks to you in silence
When all alone you've been

Hope is all there is
When nothing's left to give
It creeps in slow and quiet
Then screams a soul to live

Hope lives in the darkness
Dispels the clouded grip
It swells and grows so slowly
It quivers, through soft red lip

Hope is born in heaven
A gift to humankind
Wrapped in love and mystery
Free, for all the world to find

May these words give you the courage never to give up on what we need the most, hope!

CATHY O'MALLEY

Leaves and Bottles

*He who began a good work in you will carry it on
to completion until the day of Christ Jesus. Phil. 1:6, NIV.*

I love the maple trees in my backyard. I love them in spring when
bright-red "helicopter" blossoms are on the branches. I love them in
their full green beauty of summer. Even fall isn't bad with the crunching
of leaves underfoot. But in winter I can't say I'm too grateful for them.

In winter the leaves are blown over the house and end up in my
front garden and on the sidewalk leading to the front door. They
leave horrible stain imprints on the walk. Today I raked the leaves
and thought, *One day soon I'm going to scrub this sidewalk clean again.
My job won't be complete until every stain is removed and my sidewalk looks
like new. I've started this project, and I am determined to finish it!*

Then my thoughts turned to my life. My sin is like these leaves. It
comes and stains my heart, leaving horrible stains that only Jesus can
take away. Then sometimes after Jesus does the miracle of cleansing,
the enemy comes with more leaves, and I need Christ's cleansing
power once more. It's a job that needs repeating every day until
Christ comes. He started the job in me, and He will complete it!

The other morning at breakfast my youngest son asked if he
could open a new jar of strawberry jelly. "Please use up the apricot
first," I said. "We need to finish the old before beginning the new."

A few days later as I took my shower I realized that I had not
one, but three types of conditioner bottles in the shower rack. None
of them was empty! Looking around some more, I found two kinds
of hair spray, half-finished.

These half-full bottles remind me of my spiritual life. *How patient
He is with me. He waited 23 years before I accepted Him as my Lord and
Saviour. He has consistently been loving, forgiving, long-suffering, and merciful.*

He will not leave me like a half-finished bottle, propped up in a
corner. Nor will He leave me like a half-swept walk, the stains still
visible. He began this project, and He will finish it!

MOIRA BARTHLE

Snakes

*The great dragon was hurled down —that ancient serpent
called the devil, or Satan, who leads the whole world astray.
He was hurled to the earth, and his angels with him. Rev. 12:9, NIV.*

If we see a snake today, we shudder and wonder how this creature of the dust could have been so very exotically beautiful in the beginning. Some people keep snakes as pets, but living in the country exposes one to snakes—and not by choice. Such was my case.

One fall day I was in the garage putting clothes in the washing machine. In my peripheral vision I saw something move. Looking down, I saw about 12 inches of a black snake's tail disappear under the machine.

Through the winter I watched my step carefully so as not to step on the uninvited guest. It kept carefully hidden in a warm spot and thrived on mice. When spring arrived, friend snake told us thanks and goodbye with a thin layer of skin that it shed in a prominent place. But this was not the last of the snake.

A pair of eastern bluebirds nested near our woodshed. The snake sensed a good meal in that nest and tried to get to it by climbing up the metal woodshed. It got caught on a protruding piece of metal and couldn't free itself. The birds were frantic, and by their actions I knew there was either a cat or a snake nearby. The snake must have fought for its life, because it was drained and limp when we found it. My husband removed it and tossed it out in the woods.

Soon it returned to take up residence near the house again, and we encountered it in and around the flower beds. The poor creature finally met its Waterloo when it tried to exit from under our patio through a hole too small for its body. Half in and half out of the hole, it dehydrated and died.

It was a reminder to me that someday Satan will meet his end also. He has gotten himself into something he cannot get himself out of. He has passed up the opportunity for redemption.

Another snake was once lifted up in the wilderness, representing the Son of man, lifted up to draw all people to Himself to be saved. For that I am most grateful.   DOTTIE O. BOWEN

The Birthday Cake

Be ye kind one to another, tenderhearted, forgiving one another, even as God for Christ's sake hath forgiven you. Eph. 4:32.

We had just moved to a new neighborhood, and I greeted our next-door neighbors warmly. But they didn't return my greeting. Each time I tried, my efforts were met with hostility.

They were a young couple with two young children whom they left in the care of a maid while they worked all day. I found the maid to be very pleasant and willing to talk, even though she knew little English. I decided to give her some things for her home that we were unable to use. She seemed grateful.

The maid was busy much of the day, cleaning house for the young couple, so I asked her if she would like me to watch the children while she worked. She agreed. I love children and enjoyed telling them Bible stories. The length of time they spent with me increased until they were spending most of the day with me, even having lunch at our house. They went home each day just before their mother returned.

"I'm going to have a birthday," the boy told me one day.

"How old will you be?" I asked.

"Four years old!" He looked very proud as he held up four fingers. "I'm a big boy!"

"Indeed you are!" I agreed. I decided to make him a birthday cake in the shape of a boat. I decorated it and put it on a platter set on a sea of chopped lime jelly. His eyes sparkled with excitement when he saw it. I was sure he had never seen anything like it before.

Later that evening the children's mother knocked on my kitchen door. She was weeping as she stammered her thanks for the cake. "You have made my little boy so happy," she said through her tears. "I feel ashamed for the way we treated you. We have hurt you many times, but you have been so kind to us."

"It's all right," I said. "We can still be friends."

Jesus was not welcomed either when He came to this world, but He loved anyway. That has made all the difference.

PRISCILLA ADONIS

Lost in the Night

The Lord will watch over your coming and going both now and forevermore.
Ps. 121:8, NIV.

Late one Friday afternoon my four boys, ages 9 to 16, asked to ride their bikes to the corner to meet their father and race him home. I agreed. I knew that this race with their dad was a cherished activity.

After they left I lit candles, put on my favorite gospel music, and relaxed in my glider rocker to read while waiting for them to return. I expected my five men to burst through the door within minutes, filling my home with energy. Thirty minutes later I glanced out the window. It was much too dark outside, so I decided I had better go get the boys, since their dad was late.

I found the boys where they were supposed to be, at the corner riding their bikes. But only three of the four boys were there. "Where's Matthew?" I asked.

When they didn't know, I became alarmed. Matthew is a special needs child. We had just moved into the neighborhood after a major move across the country. In addition to his other disabilities, Matthew had a poor sense of direction. At school he sometimes had difficulty finding his desk.

We began a search for Matthew, but first we paused to pray for his safe return, each of us praying a short prayer. Friends joined the search; we stopped and talked with anyone we saw on the street. No one had seen a boy on a bike.

When 20 minutes had passed without our turning up even one clue, I knew I had to call the police. I was giving them photos and a description when a jogger, the last person I had stopped and asked about Matthew, rode up on her bike with Matthew in tow.

She had spotted him around the corner and down the street, looking confused. He was staring blankly at a street sign, trying to figure out how to get home.

Matthew had been missing for an hour, the longest hour of my life. I praise God for His tender watchcare over my very special son, who frequently needs His help.   CARLENE WILL

Ant Invasion

Go to the ant, . . . consider her ways, and be wise. Prov. 6:6.

A nts are very wise creatures," I told some students. I had been studying Proverbs 30:24-28, which speaks of ants, conies, locusts, and spiders. "My research has proved to me that they are not only wise, but prudent and cautious," I further stated.

The ants must have heard my words of praise, because they visited my kitchen not long after that. When I saw the long procession of ants marching along the floor, I decided they must really appreciate me a lot! However, the feeling wasn't mutual. I was horrified to see them invading my kitchen. I ran for a can of insecticide and sprayed them.

The next day another procession moved across my kitchen floor. At that point I began doubting their wisdom. "Wise beings don't annoy others," I grumbled. "If you were wise you would know I don't like ants in my kitchen." I got the insecticide and sprayed again.

The next day the ants returned. I sprayed. They returned the next day, and the next. For one week I had ants invading my kitchen every day. Why were they so intent on coming where they were not wanted?

I decided to stop a moment and watch them. What was the object of their search? Why would they risk death to enter my kitchen? It was then I noticed that the procession ended at the small dustbin near the sink, where I put bread crumbs, fruit peelings, and other bits of garbage.

I got their message. If I didn't want to see the ants, I needed to get rid of the reason for their trip. After that I tried not to leave any dirt or trash in my kitchen. I washed everything before sleeping at night, and I made sure we cleaned the floor and sponged the table and chairs after every meal. There would be no more superficial cleanliness in my kitchen. I would have total cleanliness. There would be no reason for the ants to come again.

The ants never returned. They had finished instructing me! I realized that the ants were exceedingly wise. It was I who lacked the wisdom.

JEANNE D'HARIMALA RASOANINDRAINY

Night-lights

The heavens declare the glory of God;
and the firmament shows His handiwork. Ps. 19:1, NKJV.

Sometimes in the darkness of night, when I'm unable to sleep, I confidently walk through our home, guided by the softly shining night-light. The dim glow of the bedroom clock appears bright in the wee hours of night. I move from room to room, checking out my little world. As I approach the window behind the kitchen table, I see lights in the homes of two neighbors and wonder why they are awake at this hour. Across the fields I see the security lights of nearby farms, shedding their protective glow for the families who reside there.

Opening the draperies in the living room reveals more beauty of the night. Far in the distance I sometimes see the lights of an iron ore freighter on beautiful Lake Michigan. Occasionally I notice the flicker of the lighthouse on Beaver Island.

Focusing on my garden, I strain to see the deer whose hoofprints I found during the daylight hours. A car drives past, its headlight and taillights blinking along the winding country road.

Pulling a chair before the bay window, I scan the heavens for stars. There is such beauty in the nighttime sky. Orion glistens, beckoning me to explore its velvety depths. In my mind I hear my youngest grandchild singing "Twinkle, Twinkle, Little Star." The Milky Way stretches across the heavens, its beauty causing me to catch my breath. The moon moves slowly along, casting long shadows on the yard.

I think of Bible verses that speak of the heavens, of light, of love, of protection. Psalm 8 is one that sings in my heart: "When I consider thy heavens, the work of thy fingers, the moon and the stars," "O Lord our Lord, how excellent is thy name in all the earth!" (verses 3, 9).

I feel my body relax, the tension of the day draining away. God's night-lights have brought peace to my soul. I close my eyes a moment to thank God for putting the stars in the firmament, night-lights to guide us to Him, to rest. I then rise and follow my own night-lights back to bed. I can sleep now.   BETTY R. BURNETT

A Little Teamwork Goes a Long Way!

*Give instruction to the wise, and they will become wiser still;
teach the righteous and they will gain in learning. Prov. 9:9, NRSV.*

When my brother John and I were in elementary school, my father instituted a plan in our family that must have been a wonderful boost to my working mother's spirits. Even though my father wasn't a church member at the time, he respected the fact that the other three members of his family kept the Sabbath, and that it was important to my mother that the house have a thorough cleaning in preparation for this special day.

Coming from a family of 10 children had taught my father how to sling a mop and polish bathrooms until they shone. So every Thursday evening, when our parents returned from work, the four of us moved into action. Dad gave the assignments, and he, along with my brother and me, would charge into cleaning the house. Stripping beds, vacuuming, cleaning bathrooms, polishing mirrors, emptying trash, and dusting the furniture were tasks shared among the three of us.

While we cleaned, our mother went to the grocery store to purchase the week's supply of groceries. Somehow each week we managed to complete our tasks at about the same time. And when Mom would pull up to the curb with the groceries, we'd run out to help her carry them in and put them away as quickly as possible.

As I think back over the years, I marvel that although we all would have rather been doing something else, we were usually in good spirits. Perhaps it was the reward that made the tasks lighter. For when the house was clean and the groceries had been put away, we'd all pile into the car for a trip to our favorite ice-cream store. Double-dip cones of our favorite flavors and time together as a family—how could you beat it? We'd sit in the car, relishing the ice cream and chatting about the week's events.

I respect my father for his initiative to lighten the load of our working mother and for the fact that he gave my brother and me a lesson in family teamwork. Little wonder that I still reward myself for tasks completed—with my favorite ice cream! ROSE OTIS

Yindi, the Last Koala?

"Your Father knows what you need." Matt. 6:8, NIV.

I watched a television program that featured Yindi, a tiny koala whose mother had been hit by a car when he was still in her pouch. Yindi was still hairless, and his eyes were still closed. My heart warmed as I observed the dedicated care the mother and baby koala received. Concerned people provided constant love, medicines, and support until the mother could fend for herself. Yindi was coached to behave like an animal raised in the wild and was eventually released into a eucalyptus forest as a healthy, mature male koala.

Yindi will not be the last koala living on the eastern coast of Australia. It is believed there are at least 40,000 others, but they face grave dangers from dogs, cats, and foxes, as well as humans who run them down when they try to cross highways.

Brushfires are another danger to koalas, for the fires destroy the eucalyptus trees that provide their food. People clear the land for new developments, removing still more koala habitat. Koalas are also plagued by a disease that blinds them. Incapacitated, they have to remain in the tree tops and are unable to escape when danger comes. Australia without koalas would be unthinkable, so there are organizations dedicated to their preservation.

Christians are in a similar position to the koalas, I mused. This world holds many dangers for us, too. Metaphorically we have foxes, cats, and dogs that would destroy us. There are vehicles of circumstance that can maim or kill us. The fires of trouble come to burn us. A multitude of diseases, such as discouragement, can take away our spiritual vision.

Just as I believe it unthinkable to have Australia without our much-loved koalas, so God must feel about His world and His much-loved children. Because He is concerned about our preservation, He shelters us when we are hurt. He provides us an environment without sickness, predators, or destroying fire.

Yindi is now enjoying a koala refuge. It has all he needs for survival. Soon I will be enjoying the refuge God has prepared for me. Meanwhile, He provides everything I need to survive.

URSULA M. HEDGES

Tattling

Jesus said to him, "If it is my will that he remain until I come, what is that to you? Follow me!" John 21:22, NRSV.

When I taught first grade in the public schools of San Bernardino, California, many families in our school neighborhood were transient. By the end of the year I had 70 children on my class register, of whom only 20 had been there all year. Most weeks I had about 35 children in my class. Each week new students arrived and others left.

It was difficult trying to integrate new students into the class every week. Six-year-olds are real sticklers for the rules, and they are the world's worst tattlers. You can imagine what my life was like with new children coming every week who didn't know the rules. Thirty other children would tell me, "Susie isn't doing it right, Teacher!" or "He doesn't know how to write his name!" and point accusing fingers at one of the new children.

"Teacher, Teacher, Teacher" all day long, all year. It was my first year of teaching, and I wasn't at all sure I wanted to do this another year. But by February I had sorted it out and decided to give teaching another try. Those transient children taught me something very valuable.

As I think about it, I can clearly see that my class was a lot like people in my church. Always looking around to see if others are following the rules. Tattling. "I can't believe it, but I know that was a double Big Mac the youth pastor was eating!" "How much do you suppose she paid for that dress? You know how she is when the church needs money—always opposed." "Don't you think she wears too much makeup? Aren't we supposed to be plain?" "It's awful how they raise their kids—they must watch six hours of TV a day!" Tattling, tattling, tattling.

Jesus had a quick answer for Peter when he wanted to be responsible for someone else. "What is that to you? You must follow Me." Good advice. I don't want to be like my tattling first graders. I want to keep my eyes on Jesus and follow His direction for my life. He can take care of the other people without my tattling. In fact, He can take care of them better if I don't tattle. DONNA J. HABENICHT

A Sparrow and a Song

*"Are not two sparrows sold for a penny? Yet not one of them will fall
to the ground apart from the will of your Father. And even the
very hairs of your head are all numbered. So don't be afraid;
you are worth more than many sparrows." Matt. 10:29, NIV.*

I drove to work frustrated and angry. Self-pitying thoughts tumbled through my mind like children shoving and pushing to be the first in line. At work an abundance of responsibilities kept me under an unbelievable amount of pressure and stress. At home the burden of housekeeping, cooking, driving the children to school, and paying the bills were not helping. Grief from the recent loss of my mother felt like an ever-tightening grip.

"God," I cried, "don't You care?"

God had continued to bless me in many ways, but my attention seemed focused on the "No," "Not yet," and "Wait" answers I was receiving. "I don't want to wait, Lord. Help me now!"

"Even the radio won't cooperate," I muttered angrily. My favorite gospel station was filled with static. Restlessly I pushed the buttons. The button came to rest on another Christian station. At the red light a little sparrow flew past my windshield to the sidewalk and began feasting on the remains of a fast-food meal someone had tossed out. Seeing the bird obviously enjoy its unexpected meal brought a smile to my lips. As the light turned and I drove on, the words of the next song swirled around me like a healing salve: "His eye is on the sparrow, and I know He watches me."

Warm tears poured down my face, releasing the pain and washing away the bitter thoughts. I pulled over and just let the cleansing tears flow. God was working to heal my wounded spirit. He arranged for me to hear a comforting song just when I needed it. That incident gave me courage to face each succeeding trial patiently. And because I knew that His eye was on that sparrow, I knew He was watching and caring for me.

Are you overburdened, stressed, angry, impatient? Just know that today, tomorrow, and every day—Jesus cares for you.

ELAINE NORMAN

Goose Sense

Behold the fowls of the air: for they sow not, neither do they reap, nor gather into barns; yet your heavenly Father feedeth them. Are ye not much better than they? Matt. 6:26.

I saw some geese one autumn day, high-flying in the sky.
They looked like they were headed south; I knew the reason why.
They flew in V formation, and I wondered as they flew
How scientists had learned so late what geese already knew.

They've learned that as birds flap their wings in V configuration,
An uplift is created for the next bird in formation.
By flying thus they nearly double each one's flying strength,
And that means fewer rest stops as they travel greater length.

When on occasion one goose falls from out its V location,
It feels strong wind resistance till it gets back in formation;
And when the lead goose tires and falls behind, then, in transition,
The next goose following assumes its turn in lead position.

If any goose is wounded by gunshot and drops below,
Two geese drop with it to protect till it can safely go.
If it survives, they speed to join their comrades in the sky,
And honk encouragement ahead to teammates as they fly.

Perhaps we all should learn from geese who glide the same direction,
And pool our strength on common goals by keeping good connection.
Let's use a little goose sense and proceed in tight formation.
By pulling all together, we will gain more inspiration.

It makes good sense to stand beside our sister and our brother,
For we will soar much higher on the thrust of one another.
Let's take our turn at tedious tasks, if we would be succeeders,
And like the geese, honk reassurance to our fellow leaders.

LORRAINE HUDGINS

Passport Control

They were longing for a better country—a heavenly one. Heb. 11:16, NIV.

I took my place in one of the long lines of passengers waiting to present their documents to the immigration office at Washington, D.C.'s Dulles International Airport. In one line were women from India in shimmering saris. Behind them stood a gray-haired woman wearing a flowered scarf on her head, tied under the chin Russian babushka-style. In yet another line several women wore brightly patterned dresses with matching turbans. I guessed they were from western Africa. Several lines over, a number of Muslim women wore black burka dress that revealed nothing but their eyes. Mixed among these were businesswomen with briefcases and backpack-carrying young people in blue jeans.

I wondered about these women. What were their thoughts as they entered this country that was not their homeland? Were they tourists or immigrants? What had they left behind, and what lay ahead of them? In their faces I read excitement, apathy, sorrow, fear, impatience, and anticipation. Each woman grasped her passport in her hand, the precious document that would allow her to experience life in the United States.

I too held my passport firmly. I was in one of four lines for those holding United States passports. I was coming home to the land of my birth. My heart beat a little faster at the thought of home. A sense of pride and patriotism was mixed with my joy of return. This was my country, my home, my native land!

As I moved closer to the immigration counter, I thought ahead to another homecoming to a country I have never seen but often dreamed of entering. My heart beats with anticipation of golden streets, walls of jasper, a river of life, and a reunion with friends and loved ones. I haven't been there, but it is my country, my inheritance, my birthright as a daughter of God.

Then it was my turn to hand over my passport. The officer opened to my photo and smiled at me. "Welcome home!" she said.

Lord, I hold tightly to another passport, one stamped with the blood of Your Son. It guarantees my entrance to my heavenly country. I can hardly wait until I hear Your voice speaking those long-awaited words, "Welcome home!"

DOROTHY EATON WATTS

Parts of the Whole

All these are inspired by one and the same Spirit,
who apportions to each one individually as he wills. 1 Cor. 12:11, RSV.

I had always thought every home should have a set of plain white dishes. They're basic, sensible, long-lasting, and blend with every color of tablecloth or kitchen decor. So soon after I established my own home I bought a set. However, they looked stark and monotonous on my table. They were boring. I gave them away.

A friend purchased a set of white dishes at a factory outlet store. On her table they look elegant, pristine, gracious. She loves them, and her guests rave about her beautiful table.

Another friend dislikes sets of anything. Versatility and possibility—not uniformity—are her favorite words. As I was setting her table for supper one evening, there were no two place settings alike. She ate with the shell-patterned fork; another guest used an old English piece. And I got Italian steel. It suited her personality and style. It was fun at her house, but it wouldn't work at mine.

Driving home from that visit, I stopped at a roadside pottery shop known for its fine work. I noticed a blue-green pitcher on display. It had streaks of teal blue on the rim, deep azure blue in the center, and thick streaks of turquoise poured down the handle to the base. I was immediately attracted by its vivid colors and texture. As the potter wrapped it for me, she grinned and said, "These pieces are all unique, just like people are, you know?"

I reflected on her words and my friends' table preferences. I had tried for years to be a white-plate Christian—smiling, sensible, soft-spoken. Well, everyone isn't the same, and I felt like I was in a straitjacket. My pitcher is a visual feast to me, useful and handy. To others it may be overwhelming, or even ugly. As Paul says, if we are all the same, then the body of Christ will have missing functions. "Now you (collectively) are Christ's body and (individually) you are members of it, each part severally and distinct—each with his own place and function" (1 Cor. 12:27, Amplified).

Every time I reach for my pitcher, I'm reminded that what the potter said was true—we are all unique, and it makes the world so much more interesting. BARBARA COUDEN

The Road Taken

Since we are surrounded by such a great cloud of witnesses, . . .
let us run with perseverance the race marked out for us. Heb. 12:1, NIV.

Not long ago I felt discouraged and downhearted. *Dear Lord,* I prayed, *please give me something to help bring me out of this semi-depressed state I'm in.*

I wandered about the house, looking for some words of comfort and hope. I came across a poem written by my friend Sonya Cameron. Sonya is a young mother of two who has a flair for using words that touch the heart. And she's had her own struggles. Reading her poem inspired me with hope and courage. I felt uplifted as I thought of un-fallen worlds cheering me on in my struggles. Here's her poem:

The Road Taken

The road oft taken is sometimes the road less trodden.
Overgrown with our doubts and fears—it's almost forgotten,
For its way is not smooth from thorns, stones, and holes.
There is no map of guidance to steer our souls.
The path is oft crooked and hidden from plain sight.
It is mostly an uphill path many travel in the night.
Even though its way seems hard,
This road is well traveled by a faithful cloud of
witnesses,
To show us how and what to do.
If we could just endure till we see the end of the road,
Our gift, our reward, our crown is waiting at Christ's door,
And no bother the way the road may seem to be—
Travel it, my sisters—
Take heart, God be with thee.

Single parents, weary mothers, caregivers of aging parents, we are all sisters traveling the road oft taken. We are not alone as we travel the road; we have a great cloud of witnesses. Take heart, as I did, for God is with us.   BEVERLY SAWYER KINSEY

Unsaid Goodbyes

I am with you alway, even unto the end of the world. Matt. 28:20.

The morning I left for Africa was hectic. Mom helped me recheck everything I needed to take, then we loaded up and headed to the airport, arriving around 5:00 a.m. Our flight was scheduled to leave at 6:30, but we didn't want to take chances. I wandered around the airport with my family, killing time. We ended up back at gate C to wait for my plane.

I sat in silence, afraid to talk lest my voice betray the emotion welling up inside me. I already had a lump in my throat and a tight knot in my stomach. I knew I should say my goodbyes to my family, but I couldn't. Not yet.

Suddenly Lisa, a classmate also bound for Africa, came running up to us. "Brianna, they've switched our flight to a different plane, and it's boarding now!" My parents and I each grabbed a piece of luggage and hurried toward gate A. I followed Lisa through the metal detector, then turned to tell my family goodbye. I started to walk back to hug my parents when a guard appeared. "No!" she ordered. "You can't go back."

"I'm just going to tell my parents goodbye," I explained.

She said something about smuggling things. I don't know what else she said because my sobs drowned out her voice. My head started throbbing, and the knot in my stomach tightened. I yelled to my parents, but my voice got lost in the drone of the crowd. "I love you! I love you!" I shouted through my tears.

"This is the last call," someone announced. "All passengers should be on board the aircraft."

I took one last look over my shoulder at my family waving to me, turned, and boarded the plane. My eyes were swollen and my heart ached. It was bad enough that I was to leave them for a month, but I hadn't even said goodbye! Lisa did her best to comfort me, but she hadn't been able to say goodbye to her parents either. But God was there. He was listening that day as two 14-year-old girls boarded a plane to Africa. He gave us the promise "I will be with you always."

He was. Twenty-eight days later we returned. Our parents gave us an extra big welcome to make up for lost goodbyes.

BRIANNA RENEE WALKER

Miracle Trip

*My God shall supply all your need according to His
riches in glory by Christ Jesus. Phil. 4:19, NKJV.*

M any important events took place in 1993, but the most exciting
was that I had the privilege of seeing my mother that year. I
had been praying for this for some time.

Our church had an annual council scheduled for Bangalore, India,
that year. My boss recommended I go as support staff, because he
knew I wanted to see my mom. For some reason it did not work out.
I felt quite disappointed but continued to ask God to open a way, if it
was His will. I told Him how much I longed to see my mother,
whom I had not seen for two years.

One morning Rose Otis, who was then the women's ministries
director of our world church, walked into my office and very calmly
asked, "Stella, would you be willing to help out with women's ministries seminars in Bangalore?"

I couldn't believe my ears. I asked her to repeat it, because it
seemed too good to be true. I was so ecstatic that I gave her a great
big hug and squealed so loudly with excitement that my boss rushed
out to see what was going on. I composed myself and told him that
Rose had just asked me whether I'd be willing to help her out with
the Bangalore women's ministries seminars.

This is how my God works. Rose was wanting someone to travel
with her and help her with the seminars. She had asked one of her
friends to go with her, but that person was unable to do so and offered to give her ticket to anyone who could. While Rose was praying, asking God who should go with her, my name came to her mind.
The very next day she came and asked me. This was an answer to
my prayer too. I was able to get my passport in just one day, although it usually takes at least six weeks.

I was thrilled when my mother told me that God had also answered her prayers by bringing me to India. Immediately I thought of
the promise in Philippians 4:19 that my God will supply my every
need (even to send me to India!), according to His riches in glory in
Christ Jesus.

STELLA THOMAS

Just Looking

Ye are bought with a price: therefore glorify God
in your body, and in your spirit, which are God's. 1 Cor. 6:20.

Business was slow at the card shop where I worked. The beautiful day seemed to belong to everyone except me, and I was feeling somewhat down to be inside working. The bells on the door announced the arrival of a young woman, and I gave the usual "Hello. Let me know if you need any help." As she came closer to the checkout counter, I could tell she was distraught and had been crying.

"You're a Christian, aren't you?" she blurted out.

I was somewhat shocked and wasn't sure if she was going to like my answer. "Yes. How can you tell?"

"Oh, I just can," she said with a tone that still did not give me any indication why she had asked. She didn't share what problems she was having, but she did talk about how life was really hard for her at the time.

I told her that God knew what she was going through, and He would see her through it. She agreed that it was wonderful that His love and forgiveness were always there for us.

She left a little more composed than when she had come in, but now I was the one who was frustrated. There was so much more I wanted to tell her, but with only a few minutes, what could I have said? I should have invited her to our church to hear the message in detail. There she could have met a whole family of Christians to love and nurture her. I wanted to give her a free sample that would show her what she was missing. I didn't have anything to give her. All I had was me.

I realized how important our outer packaging can be, because we may never get a chance to give our sales pitch for Jesus. How did she know I was a Christian? I hope it was the peace that had shone on my face and the happiness displayed in my smile. I want people to see enough of Jesus in me to want to know more about Him. I want them to know that the price has been paid. JO ANN HILTON

Of Checkbooks and Garment Bags

God is our refuge and strength,
an ever-present help in trouble. Ps. 46:1, NIV.

David, Kerry, and their two children were going to Alaska to spend a week with David's parents. I had agreed to take them to the airport. We loaded the car and left to pick David up at the school where he taught.

As we drove along, Kerry mentioned, "We need to go by way of the bank so I can make a deposit and cash a check." As she started writing the check, she suddenly exclaimed, "Oh, Anna May, we have to go back to the house! I have only one check, and I don't want to go so far away for so long with just one check. I always put a spare book of checks in my purse when I begin to run low, but for some reason I hadn't noticed I was needing more. Now we're losing time by going back."

I waited in the car while she ran into the house. I was surprised when she soon returned, toting a big garment bag. As we loaded it in, a big smile spread across her face. "Can you believe it? If I hadn't forgotten to put in another book of checks we would have arrived in Alaska with no clothes to wear to church. I don't know how I could have missed it before. Wow!"

I believe that God cares about every little thing that concerns us. We just need to ask Him to guide and direct us each day. Sometimes He uses very simple things to show us how much He cares about us. Perhaps He allows "little troubles" to come along to save us from bigger ones.

God, there are many things to do and to remember this day. Please take care of me and help me when I miss some of the important things. I know You love me. Thank You. ANNA MAY RADKE WATERS

Examination Results

"If you believe, you will receive
whatever you ask for in prayer." Matt. 21:22, NIV.

We were waiting for our daughter's medical school final examination results. Late one night we received a telephone call from the pastor of the church where our daughter had been studying, informing us that she had passed the examinations. We were thrilled. "God has answered our prayers," I told my daughter.

My daughter was not satisfied. "If it is really true, why didn't my best friend call?"

Yes, why didn't her friend call? I began to wonder about this too. If the message were true, she would have been the first to call. Within the next two hours we made several calls in an attempt to contact her friend to confirm the news. Unfortunately, we could not reach her, and spent a fitful night of sleep.

Early the next morning her friend called, saying the results had been announced the previous evening. She had tried to contact us but could not reach us.

At 5:00 that evening several of my daughter's friends got together and thanked God for her success. We all rejoiced. How good God had been to our family. But I had been anxious about my daughter's success. I had fasted and prayed every morning for nearly two years because she had problems with her eyes. Her tear glands were dry, and she had to use eyedrops. I believed that God would give her success in her studies in spite of her problem. But where was my faith now when we received the good news?

I was ashamed of my little faith. Why couldn't I tell my daughter not to worry, that God was in control? Why could I not accept the answer when it came? Why had I made all those phone calls? Why had I worried all night?

Lord, help me to trust You more, believing that You will always do what is best for my family and me. Give me faith in Your promise and peace in Your presence.   HEPZIBAH G. KORE

Living the 20/80 Rule

"Everything is all right." 2 Kings 4:26, NIV.

I t had been a tough month. I had made a decision that was unpopular with a close friend. My optimism withered under her glare of disapproval. I reviewed the pros and cons, yet came to the same conclusion. Others took notice when I couldn't seem to pull out of my lethargy and sadness.

As I drove to work one morning, I shared with my heavenly Parent. *God, I don't seem to be able to climb back up the emotional scale to enthusiasm. Please impress me to make a different decision, or help me find the courage to proceed, letting go of my internal conflict.*

I waited in silence. Nothing. I sighed as I slipped a Bible in Living Sound cassette into the tape deck. The Shunammite woman came to life. Her only child had suddenly died. Setting out by mule, certain that the man of God could help her, the bereaved mother went in search of Elisha. When the woman met Elisha's servant, he asked, "Is your child all right?"

She replied, "Everything is all right."

Wait a minute, I thought. *In the midst of personal disaster and grief, everything was all right? Her only child was dead. Her husband didn't want her to go to Elisha. What could she possibly have meant?*

A stress-management equation known as the 20/80 rule flashed into mind: "Twenty percent of the effect to our mind and body can be attributed to the stressor; 80 percent to our perception of the stressor." Obviously the Shunammite woman had learned this. Her son was dead (20 percent), but she was in God's hands and, while willing to work toward a preferred outcome, was content (80 percent). That made everything all right.

Well, Arlene, I asked myself, *is everything all right with you?* Yes, everything is all right. True, I still regretted that my decision had been misunderstood, but I could climb back up the emotional scale to enthusiasm.

I now carry a 3 x 5 card. On it is written, "Remember the 20/80 rule and the Shunammite woman! Everything is all right!"

ARLENE TAYLOR

A Standing Invitation

God . . . hath raised us up together, and made us sit together in heavenly places in Christ Jesus. Eph. 2:4-6.

Early one morning I looked out the kitchen window. It had snowed the day before, unusual for our southern city of Nashville. Only a week earlier we had basked in 70°F weather.

I checked the outside thermometer. It registered just above zero! The snow lay cold and heavy upon the ground. As I gazed upon our beautiful winter wonderland, the lights from the outside pole in our yard created myriads of beautiful sparks that flitted about on the surface of the snow like summer fireflies.

I shivered just thinking about the homeless people and God's creatures out there in the intense cold. With a prayer of thanksgiving for warmth and shelter, I began my quiet time with God.

These moments fill me with a warmth that people cannot create. Years ago I received a gilt-edged invitation to spend precious intimate time each day "in heavenly places" with the royalty of the universe. This special encounter includes my Father God, my dear Jesus, and the magnificent Holy Spirit. I am certain there are also myriads of heavenly angels with us in this encounter, for I have felt their presence. There is no better way to start the day, no matter what the temperature outside. I can assure you, there is nothing to compare with being in this sacred circle, surrounded by the majesties of heaven. Love fills my heart as I review God's abundant love and mercy in saving me for these precious hours with Him.

God has not only pulled me out of the miry clay and set my feet on a rock, He has pulled me all the way up to sit with Him in heavenly places with Jesus in order that in ages to come, He might show the mystery of the riches of His grace.

My standing heavenly invitation also includes the royal banquet at the conclusion of the earthly race that will honor the heavenly King and open the way to perpetual "heavenly places" with Him.

JODI EULENE DODSON

Our Homeland

Our homeland is in heaven, where our Savior the Lord Jesus Christ is; and we are looking forward to his return from there. Phil. 3:20, TLB.

In 1979 I studied abroad at a Christian college near Valencia, Spain. Along with my fellow American classmates, I gradually learned the Spanish language, began to understand the people, and started to feel a part of their culture.

After I married a Brazilian, my new husband and I decided to serve the Lord in his country of origin. Of course, no one is ever prepared completely for a new culture. Language was not a problem for me, since Portuguese is somewhat similar to Spanish. As the eight years have passed since we arrived in Brazil, the unknown has become familiar. Many times I forget that I am living in a foreign country.

The Brazilians accepted me as one of their own. There have even been times I have been asked, "What part of Brazil are you from?" In spite of their total acceptance of me, there is one recurring occasion that reminds me, with a tug at my heart, that I am not—and never will be—completely a part of this culture. When I hear the happy and delightful melody of the Brazilian national anthem, the awareness is accentuated when those around me begin to sing. I feel completely foreign to my surroundings. Feelings of not belonging flood my whole being as my heart and thoughts return to my beloved America. My lips remain silent as those around me enthusiastically express their patriotism.

Each time this occurs I realize the Lord is helping me understand the true meaning of patriotism. The sadness and longing for my country becomes a valuable lesson in true citizenship. I am reminded that we are not Americans or Brazilians, or citizens of any other country, for that matter. We are citizens of another homeland who are temporarily residing on this earth. One day we will live together with the King of the universe as inhabitants of the same celestial nation.

I long for that day, don't you?   BETH VOLLMER CHAGAS

White Bread and Moldy Mattresses

"Give us today our daily bread." Matt. 6:11, NIV.

What would you like for supper? Two or four slices of white bread?"

It didn't sound exciting, but it did fill our stomachs when there were not a lot of other choices. Carole Ferch-Johnson and I were visiting a very small South Pacific atoll nation as part of our women's ministries work. Our hosts had explained that they were afraid to prepare food for us because someone in the last American group they had fed had become sick. She didn't want that to happen again. We answered that we would be fine—"Just take us to a grocery store." So here we sat, making the best of what we could find in the little 10-shelf, one-stop "supermarket."

I thought this might be the opportunity I'd been looking for to lose a few pounds, but all the food available was high-calorie and low-fiber. As we ate our bread and drank our bottled water, though, I thought of many who had only moldy bread and water after a hard day's work in a place they had not chosen. Nor were they free to leave. And neither did they have cheese, Marmite, and peanut butter for their bread as we did.

Lord, give us this day our daily bread. Thank You that mine is usually whole-wheat and is in addition to an abundant variety of good food. Thank You for the reminder.

That night I tossed and turned; I couldn't sleep. Although it was very warm, the ceiling fan helped. My back hurt from either the firm mattress or the wooden slats under it, I wasn't sure which. But every time I turned on my stomach, the smell of the moldy mattress became overwhelming. Even putting my hand between my face and the sheet didn't help much. But as I lay there, I thought of all the people sleeping on the wooden or cement platforms in the village nearby. They had only a woven mat to give any comfort. And no ceiling fan—only an open thatched roof. A soft, salty sea breeze picked up, and soon I slept well.

You make me lie down in green pastures. My waterbed, my home with automatic heating and cooling—all blessings I take for granted every day. Help me, Lord, to have a grateful heart and a willingness to share of myself and my abundance today. ARDIS DICK STENBAKKEN

Tree Theology

*They are like trees planted by streams of water, which yield
their fruit in its season, and their leaves do not wither.
In all that they do, they prosper. Ps. 1:3, NRSV.*

I didn't know much about bonsai trees until we received one as a gift. "Bon" refers to a small pot, and "sai" to a tree or plant. The ancient Eastern art of growing and cultivating miniature trees is a living, ever-changing, never-finished art form. When properly cared for, the trees live and continue to grow for hundreds of years.

I took careful notice of the particulars regarding proper sunlight, watering, fertilization, preserving the cultivated shape, soil change, and repotting for the eight-year-old *Eugenia compacta*. I proceeded to follow the instructions in detail—or so I thought.

One day I was horrified to see that some of the lush green leaves had dried and were falling. As I hurriedly put the tree in water, I noticed new shoots had popped up, blurring the original shape of the foliage. How had this happened? The tree had been in good shape just a couple days before.

As I pinched off the new chaotic growth to restore the contour of the tree, I thought of my spiritual "tree." It too had been in good shape a couple days before, but today I had been too busy to pray and read God's Word. Little wonder the psalmist used a tree as a symbol of spiritual growth. My life "tree" needs spiritual sun, water, nourishment, pruning, and shaping just as the miniature tree does. As I read God's Word, pray, and spend time with Him, I soak up His light, water, and nourishment.

Jesus, my designer, keeps me trimmed and sculpted. He prunes my life of the old dead branches of routine that stunt my development. He also pinches off the new shoots of selfishness that mar the Christlike shape into which He is molding me.

Just as the bonsai needs new soil and a larger pot over time, Jesus changes my circumstances, bringing a variety of experiences to me so I can learn new things and grow faster. To make me into a more symmetrical form of His art, He may change my location.

Thanks to the bonsai, I am constantly reminded to invite Jesus to shape my "tree," to cultivate and to sculpt me. Properly cared for, my "tree" should last forever.   JOYCE NEERGAARD

From a Cross to a Crown

Fear none of those things which thou shalt suffer: . . .
ye shall have tribulation: . . . be thou faithful unto death,
and I will give thee a crown of life. Rev. 2:10.

Every daughter of Jesus Christ
shall have a cross to bear in this life.
In divine love the Lord makes each different in design,
    but all will require total surrender, faith, and self-sacrifice.

From the sheer weight of this seemingly cruel cross,
    alone and in agony, to her knees the disciple falls.
She cries out in fear for compassion and help.
    And by grace the Saviour yokes her to Himself.

They journey on together on life's dreary road,
    longing for the Promised Land
    and struggling under the load.
Then something awesome happens
    somewhere along the way.
With tears of gratitude her joyful heart begins to sing.

That ugly cross becomes lighter, and even begins to shine.
    Behold! It's been solid gold all the time.
From that painful cross one glorious day
    will come the crown of life.

The magnificent brilliant gems adorning it
    are for she who once was lost, but now is saved
Because she came to know the Saviour, Jesus Christ.
    Seeing Him in the humble life of one woman,
A precious enduring saint.

I wrote the above words as a gift for my grandmother, Feryl G.
Moore, for her eighty-sixth birthday. Her life of surrender, faith, and
self-sacrfice has led me to know my Saviour, Jesus Christ, better.

DEBORAH SANDERS

Details

"The very hairs of your head are all numbered." Matt. 10:30, NKJV.

I was on my way to work the other day when I overheard the following conversation on the bus intercom.

"The road to Navy Medical is closed, so the bus will be delayed," radioed a bus driver.

"Can you see what's happening? Is it an accident?" questioned the dispatcher.

"A helicopter is coming in to Navy Medical Center. It's nobody important," replied the driver.

"Well, I hope that person is not badly hurt and will be feeling well soon," responded the dispatcher.

"'Nobody important'? Excuse me!" I muttered.

"That's serious. What does he mean, 'It's nobody important'?" asked my bus driver, shaking her head.

In the other bus driver's eyes it was not the president of the United States, a head of government, or any important official or dignitary, hence no need to block the traffic. How myopic our perception of who is important!

Like the bus driver, we go through life consciously or unconsciously categorizing people into two groups—important and unimportant. But we are all important in the sight of God, regardless of our ethnic or racial origin, place of birth, education, or socioeconomic status. The psalmist David says that my God loves details. "You formed my inward parts; You covered me in my mother's womb. I will praise You, for I am fearfully and wonderfully made; marvelous are Your works, and that my soul knows very well. My frame was not hidden from You, when I was made in secret, and skillfully wrought in the lowest parts of the earth. Your eyes saw my substance, being yet unformed" (Ps. 139:13-17, NKJV).

Yes, God loves details. We are so important to Him that He has even numbered our hairs. He knows how many are missing each time we pull a comb through it. He knows which ones have split ends and are breaking.

Lord, I feel a sense of importance that You, the omnipotent God, care for me. I'm so happy to know that You are aware of the details of my life. Help me to show others that You care for them, too.   ANDREA A. BUSSUE

A Reason to Praise

"I will be with you and protect you wherever you go
and I will bring you safely back home.
I will never leave you or forsake you." Gen. 28:15, Clear Word.

Note: When my brother and his family had a car accident, I called them. I told my 12-year-old niece, "I feel less stressed when I put my feelings on paper. Maybe writing will help you, too." Two weeks later she sent me the following story. I asked her permission to include it in the devotional book.—GLENDA-MAE GREENE

It was a foggy, gray evening. My dad was driving my mom and my brother to a church meeting. Suddenly a van went through a stop sign the driver did not see. It crashed into my family's car just inches in front of where my brother was sitting. The dashboard fell in. Glass was everywhere. The car spun all over the road and landed 130 feet (40 meters) from where the collision occurred. It was a wreck. Blood dripped down my dad's face. My mom was squished by the seat belt she was wearing. My brother was really scared. Everyone was badly shaken.

When my mom arrived at the church where I was helping with the children's program and told me of the accident, I could not hold back my tears. My friends put their arms around me to comfort me. Then the pastor took us into another room to pray together. I wanted to ask why God had not sent His angels. Then I realized that He had.

I have always loved my family, but since the accident they are even more special (although I still can't seem to resist teasing my brother). My grandparents, aunts, uncles, and cousins, who called to praise God for sparing us, are my family too. The people at my church are also part of my family. Even my angel (I call him Luigi) is part of my heavenly family. It makes me feel so special.

Last Christmas I got a card from a great-aunt. It seems to say exactly how I feel. It reads:

Praise the Lord 'cause we're healthy!
Praise the Lord 'cause we're here.
Say a prayer of thanksgiving,
And then say one again!
Praise the Lord for His blessings,
Hallelujah! Amen.

CHRISTINE GREENE

Lasting Joy

Set your affection on things above, not on things on the earth. Col. 3:2.

It started out as the best year of my life. Everything was going my way. My life was like a fairy tale, a dream come true. I couldn't ask for anything more.

First of all, in April I graduated from college, president of my class. All my family sat in the bleachers, cheering for me as I came down the aisle. What a thrilling moment! Then in August I was married to a wonderful Christian man. Oh, how excited I was! I could not wait to see what else life had in store for me.

In September my husband and I moved to Berrien Springs, Michigan. I started looking for a job as a school teacher about a month after school had already begun. To my surprise I practically walked in and got a job on the spot. My life was wonderful! What more could I ask for?

Then it happened. Thanksgiving weekend, while I was thanking God for all the good things He had done for me, I received a phone call that my sister had been killed in a car accident. The news drove a knife through my heart. It seemed as if my life were over.

How could this happen, Lord? She had a husband and a 4-year-old daughter. She was about to graduate with her master's in education. And what about her ministry in the singing group Joy? Surely You needed her here. We needed her here. I needed her here.

I couldn't understand it. I started hating other people's testimonies about how God changed their trials into blessings. This could in no way work together for my good.

Then one night I heard a song that reminded me that I would see her again. I imagined catching a glimpse of my sister running across heaven with open arms. Heaven became even more precious to me.

I've always wanted to go to heaven to see Jesus, but I was never in a hurry; life was going so well for me down here. Now I realize the joys of this earth can easily be taken away. My sister's death has reminded me to build my hopes on things eternal instead of the things of this world. He has promised that lasting joy will come when He returns!

JENNIFER GILL FORDHAM

A Job Well Done

I have glorified thee on the earth: I have finished the work which thou gavest me to do. John 17:4.

One blustery cold November morning my husband and 3-year-old daughter were donning their warm clothing in preparation for going outside. Jennifer was excited—she had obtained permission from Daddy to "help" him work in the detached garage. They would be moving things out in preparation for the cement workers, who were to arrive shortly.

After sending them off, I continued my work in the warm house, caring for our 8-month-old daughter. A knock at the back door came a few minutes later, and an anxious voice called, "Mommy, Mommy!" Worried that perhaps she had gotten hurt or too cold, I went quickly to see what she wanted.

"Daddy needs a pencil and a tape measure," she told me with an important air.

"OK," I replied, proud that she had been able to keep the request in mind during the walk from the garage, at the back of the property, to the house. I found the requested items and sent her on her way.

"Daddy!" she called as she neared his location.

"Did you bring the pencil and the tape measure?"

"Yes!" was her jubilant reply.

Jesus has given us a task to do. As His children we have a mission to spread the gospel to all the world, sharing His love with others. Are we as proud to do His bidding? Or have we, in the long wait for His return, gotten sidetracked, occupied with other important things? When He comes, will we be able to look up and joyfully tell Him that we have finished the task He gave us to do?

What is Your special task for me today, Lord? Please give me the strength and commitment to accomplish with satisfaction what You want me to do for You and for others. Help me keep my mind on the goal.

SHERYL A. CALHOUN

Heaven's Power Source

I am the vine, and you are the branches. If you stay joined to me,
and I stay joined to you, then you will produce lots of fruit.
But you cannot do anything without me. If you don't stay joined to me,
you will be thrown away. John 15:5, 6, CEV.

The lights went out unexpectedly. I stuck my head out the door and saw several neighbors staring up and down the street in surprised wonder. *Oh, well,* I thought. *I'm not inconvenienced. I'll just find something else to do until the electricity is restored.*

I was wrong! Everything I thought of doing while waiting for power restoration—cooking, washing, ironing, typing, or sewing—required electricity. Being abruptly disconnected from the power source was aggravating and troublesome. Finally I retrieved my trusty old kerosene lamp from its place on the shelf and decided to crochet until the electricity was restored.

Until emergencies arise we usually take for granted our labor-saving devices and modern conveniences. We believe they'll always be there for our use. When the inevitable occurs, we're caught off guard momentarily and tend to become impatient or angry. Work plans for the day must be altered, some of them at great inconvenience. If the electricity is off for several hours, refrigerated and frozen food must be monitored to avoid spoilage.

About a week ago our neighbor cut a large limb from the oak tree in her front yard. New in the neighborhood and unsure what to do with it, she laid it beside the clothesline in the backyard. A week later the leaves were dried and shriveled because the branch was no longer connected to its power source.

We have a power source in Jesus, the True Vine. When prayer, Bible study, and regular church attendance are given low priority or discontinued, our connection with the power source is gradually weakened and may be severed. Jesus warns that unless you and I stay joined to Him, we'll be thrown away like the tree limb.

Lord, help me today to be connected to Your never-failing power source.

MABEL ROLLINS NORMAN

Waiting on the Lord

Wait for the Lord; be strong, and let your heart take courage;
yea, wait for the Lord! Ps. 27:14, RSV.

Most of the time flying excites me. I think about my family and the new adventures we will share. But this trip was different. Because of limited finances and work and school schedules, I was traveling alone. Also, this time there was great sadness in my heart because I was traveling from Seattle to Pittsburgh to attend my precious grandmother Sarah's funeral.

It was a cold, frosty morning with sleet coming down. My husband's loving embrace and prayer soothed me as I entered the gate. He stayed long enough to watch the plane proceed to the runway before he left. But a failure with the plane's deicing equipment forced the pilot to turn back. The temporary delay became hours of waiting inside the plane. Finally we were permitted to exit the plane and return to the terminal.

I tried many times to reach someone in my family to let them know, but received only busy signals, endless ringing, or answering machines. We were given few options: wait for our plane to be repaired, wait for a later evening flight, or return the next day. I had no choice but to wait. I prayed for patience, comfort, and guidance.

Funerals are especially difficult in my family. For many of my relatives, who are unbelievers, death is so much more painful and without hope. I remembered the scripture "O death, where is thy sting? O grave, where is thy victory?" (1 Cor. 15:55). I remembered my grandmother's love and wrote about her qualities on scraps of paper, using the time to compose a tribute to her.

Almost 20 hours later I arrived at my destination. I was able to present a loving tribute at my grandmother's memorial service on the theme "Grandmother was a lot like Jesus." In suffering, in mercy, and in grace her life demonstrated God's love. I thank God for my grandmother and the seeds of love she sowed in my life. The delay was a blessing, allowing time for reflection and prayers for renewed strength in the Lord.

CAROL J. SMITH

Ordinary Things

It is good to give thanks to the Lord, to sing praises to your name,
O Most High; to declare your steadfast love in the morning,
and your faithfulness by night. Ps. 92:1, 2, NRSV.

During this Thanksgiving month I choose to focus on what I have to be thankful for. Here are a few thank-yous from this week.

On Monday I had lunch and an hour of sharing with a dear friend.

On Tuesday I received a letter from another friend I had not heard from since we walked to school together 43 years ago.

On Wednesday I completed a sewing project that had been under way for many months. Also, I received a visit from two of my grandchildren.

On Thursday I went shopping and did the laundry.

Friday I cleaned the house and prepared for Sabbath.

All week I cooked meals, choosing food from a well-stocked cupboard and refrigerator. Every evening my husband was by my side. I spoke to my parents and children on the phone. There was enough heat to ward off the chill from our unseasonably cool weather.

All of these are very ordinary things. But ordinary things make up the bulk of life. And ordinary things are most apt to be taken for granted.

I want to praise God and thank Him for all the ordinary—and extraordinary—ways He has blessed me. I ask Him to open my eyes to the privileged way I have been permitted to live my life. I want my gratitude to spill over into the lives of those who are filled with physical or spiritual hunger. I want my thankfulness to wrap warmth around those who are either physically or spiritually cold. For that is the mission given to me by the One who is author of every blessing, both ordinary and extraordinary.

Something to do: Make a list of at least two or more ordinary things for each day of the past week for which you are truly thankful. Or keep a thank-you jar on your kitchen table. Write on a slip of paper at least one new thing each day. At the end of the month take out the pieces of paper. Count your blessings!

BARBARA ROBERTS

I Was Spared

*The angel of the Lord encampeth round about them
that fear him, and delivereth them. Ps. 34:7.*

My dad worked at the WeetBix factory, not far from our home in Wynberg, Cape Town, South Africa. He rode his bicycle home for lunch. On his way back to work he'd often give me a ride on his bicycle as far as the corner. I looked forward to that ride.

One day, though, he said he was in a hurry to get back to work so he couldn't give me my usual ride. I was very upset over this. While Mom and Granny engaged in their household activities, I decided to slip away and walk to the factory. I was only 5 years old, but I knew the way.

I had to cross the train tracks, cross the busy main road, and then go up to Court Road, where the factory was situated. When I reached the factory, my dad was shocked to see me.

"Why did you come here? How did you get here?" he asked.

"I walked all by myself. I came here because you didn't give me my ride," I replied.

He asked the boss if he could be excused from work for a while to take me home.

In the meantime my mother and grandmother had started searching for me. I was nowhere to be found. When they heard the screeching of a train's brakes, they knew there had been an accident. Quickly word flew around that a little girl had been killed. My mother and grandmother thought it was I. When my dad and I arrived back home, how relieved they were that I was well! It could have been me, had I been a few minutes later. The victims were two sisters who lived down our road. The little sister was killed instantly, and the older sister survived the accident with terrible scars to her legs and her body.

My parents didn't scold me, but all knelt down to thank the Lord for sparing my life.

I wonder, Lord, how many times You have spared my life, times when I didn't even know I was in danger. Thank You for life today. Help me to live it for You with joy and gratitude. PRISCILLA ADONIS

Divine Preoccupation

He said unto them, I have meat to eat that ye know not of. . . . My meat is to do the will of him that sent me, and to finish his work. John 4:32-34.

I have always known that one of the big differences in the genders is that a married woman's time is generally regulated by the needs of her family—mealtimes, bedtime, getting-up time. A man can become so absorbed in the task at hand that he becomes oblivious to the passage of time, mealtimes included.

This was recently brought to my mind more forcefully as I accompanied my salesman husband on one of his trips to sell homegrown citrus. We had our usual hearty breakfast before leaving home, and as we made our various stops, Bill enthusiastically engaged in his selling.

Around 1:00 I began noticing the various eating places and mentioned several as we passed them. But my suggestions fell on deaf ears. On and on we traveled with Bill immersed in the joy of selling.

Finally, with all the fruit gone and our vehicle headed for home, Bill said, "I'm hungry!" By this time it was 4:00, and I had long since decided to take a drink of water and wait for dinner until we got back home.

This brought to mind the words that Jesus spoke to His disciples that day He visited with the woman of Samaria: "I have meat to eat that ye know not of."

I gained a new appreciation for Jesus' dedication to the task given Him by the Father of saving humanity. As Jack Blanco paraphrases it in *The Clear Word:* "Jesus, overhearing their conversation, said, 'The food I'm talking about is the happiness that comes from doing God's will and accomplishing what He sent me to do.'"

Dear Father, this day I would like to know the happiness that comes from doing Your will and accomplishing what You want me to do. I lay all my plans at Your feet. Show me rather what You want me to accomplish today. Only then will I feel satisfied when the day is done. RUBYE SUE

Cooking for Jesus

"Then these righteous ones will reply, 'Sir, when did we ever see you
hungry and feed you? Or thirsty and give you anything to drink?' . . .
And I, the King, will tell them, 'When you did it to these
my brothers you were doing it to me!'" Matt. 25:37-40, TLB.

My friend Joyce loves to talk about her granddaughter, Heather.
One evening little Heather and her mom had started to eat
supper when Heather suddenly shouted, "Stop! We have to pray!"

"Thank You for this food," Heather prayed. "Someday I want to
cook for You. Amen."

What a wonderful response! Heather has learned the importance
of taking time to thank God for His blessing and to offer Him a gift of
appreciation in return.

I want to be like Heather, stopping often to spend time with Him,
to thank Him for His blessings and His goodness. How often do I
stop to make time for God in my life? I make time for hobbies, projects, and service to others, but too often these good things crowd out
my personal time with God.

I've apologized to God, embarrassed for my neglect. Then I
hastily read a verse or two and make a quick list of thank-Yous and
requests and hurry on my way. At such times I rush out the door
feeling unsatisfied, still needing my Father's blessing. Like Heather, I
need to say, "Stop! I have to pray!"

I must spend quality time with God. I need to linger in His presence. I must guard my time with Him. My personal time with God is
more precious than gold and diamonds, and more to be desired than
my daily food.

In gratitude Heather offered to cook for God. Like Heather, I can
"cook" for Jesus by inviting a lonely person home for a meal, taking a
single mother and her children to a concert, sponsoring a needy child
to camp, or providing childcare for a worn-out mother. I could host a
social for singles, youth, or seniors in my church. Whatever I do for
others I am in reality doing for Jesus.

Lord, help me to stop often today to thank You for Your blessings, to re-
member Your goodness. Then out of my gratitude, help me find a way to
"cook" for You today.   CARMEN O. GONZALEZ

Her Gift of Love

Thanks be unto God for his unspeakable gift. 2 Cor. 9:15.

Have you ever yearned for something so desperately that it created an aching heart? You didn't even think about asking God's will; you just knew that you wanted something very special.

When I was a teenager, my family was very poor. My sister and I were latchkey kids, going home to an empty house after school every day. Mother worked hard for necessities, and there was never money for anything extra.

There wasn't much to do when school was out, so I would wander around downtown Bay City, looking at all the beautiful things in the store windows, things we could never afford. And then I saw it—the most elegant coat in the window of Sam's Brothers Women's Shoppe. It was fashioned of soft rust-colored material, fitted with a slight flair at the hemline, wide fashionable lapels, and leg-of-mutton sleeves. In my mind's eye I could see myself whirling around in that beautiful coat, dancing gingerly down the broad sidewalks of town.

How I yearned for that coat! I knew that the price was far out of reach for a family who wore donated clothing. We never got anything new. Nevertheless, every day after school I pressed my nose against the glass of Sam's window and suffered an aching heart.

One day my mother walked downtown with me, right into Sam's Brothers exclusive shop, so I could try on that magnificent coat. It was just my size, and it fit perfectly. I don't know how long it took my mother to pay for that coat. It was her sacrifice—her gift of love.

In the many years of my Christian walk I've thought about a Father who sent His Son as the greatest sacrifice of all. He understands all about our heart's yearnings. He responds with His blessings too numerous to list. The coat is long gone, but God's beautiful sacrifice fills my heart with peace and contentment.

I don't know if I ever thanked my mother for that coat. It is too late to express my heartfelt feelings for her, but I can thank my heavenly Father for His tender mercies as He takes care of every need on a daily basis. *Thank You, dear Father.* LAURIE DIXON-MCCLANAHAN

Homeward Bound

*In my Father's house are many mansions: if it were not so,
I would have told you. I go to prepare a place for you. And if I go
and prepare a place for you, I will come again, and receive you unto myself;
that where I am, there ye may be also. John 14:2, 3.*

As I petted our family cat, my heart ached. We knew she had recently given birth, but try as we might, we couldn't find her kittens! Where had she hidden them? It was raining, and I worried that the kittens were cold and wet. An empty box awaited them in our family room, a box lined with soft warm blankets. Food and water had been placed nearby. If only she would bring them home!

But this stray cat who had adopted us was not yet sure of our trustworthiness, at least not with her little ones. Over the course of time she had learned that we were not going to hurt her, and she did come around for food and stroking. But allowing us access to her precious litter was another matter entirely. She kept her brood hidden.

As I watched her head off across the neighborhood, I longed to be able to speak "cat" with her. I could explain that we wouldn't hurt her babies, and that we had prepared a home for them where they would be safe and warm.

The cardboard box in our family room is not the only home that stands empty. I'm told of a place that has been prepared for me in my Father's house. And to date it's still vacant. I wonder if His heart aches as He watches me go out into the cold. Does He long for words with which to woo me toward home? Come to think of it, why do I keep wandering around this neighborhood? It's chilly and dangerous and lonely.

I'd like to trust my Father enough to stop my aimless meandering and head in a direction that will lead me home. I don't want His heart to ache on account of me.

Father, I want to go home to that beautiful place You have prepared for me. Even so, come, Lord Jesus.
RETTA MICHAELIS

He Gave Me a Plate

Do not be anxious about anything, but in everything, by prayer and petition, with thanksgiving, present your requests to God. Phil. 4:6, NIV.

Bring Stephanie's plate, dear!" I called to my husband as I followed our daughter's two little children out to the garage. We were headed for my son's house.

My husband helped to buckle the children's seat belts, closed the door, and we were on our way. Down our steep paved driveway and around about 10 corners we came to Uncle Dwane and Aunty Stephanie's house, where my little passengers were to spend a couple hours playing with their cousins. As it was rainy when we arrived, we hurried them into the house.

"Goodbye, Grandma!" they called.

Just as I was about to drive off, my son said, "Mom, did you know that you have a plate on the back of your car?"

"No!" I replied, bewildered. "It can't be."

Dwane came back and picked up the glass platter, now filled with water, and showed it to me. When we realized what had happened, we were astounded. The force of gravity should have dashed it to pieces, having drawn it off the back of the car and onto the ground. Centrifugal force should have hurled it to the ground as the car went around corners. The rain should have provided a surface slippery enough to dislodge the plate. But none of these natural laws operated in this case. Something, or Someone more powerful, had taken control of that plate and kept it safe on the journey.

In relating the story to my husband, I said, "Just before I left, I had been praying about a situation in the church. I feel as if I have been on holy ground. I did not put out a fleece like Gideon, but God has given me a plate!"

Although I had no solution to the church situation, it was safely in God's care. If He could keep that plate from breaking, He could handle the difficulty in our church.

Lord, today help me to remember that nothing is impossible with You. You have a thousand ways to take care of my needs of which I'm not even aware.

URSULA M. HEDGES

It Is Cold!

"As long as the earth endures, seedtime and harvest, cold and heat, summer and winter, day and night will never cease." Gen. 8:22, NIV.

As I write, we are experiencing very cold weather here in northern Minnesota, with temperatures dipping well below zero. And don't forget the windchill factor. Winds blowing from five to 40 miles an hour make it feel much colder. There is more snow than I have seen since the March blizzard of 1966. It's a soft fluffy snow that looks so pretty when it falls and covers everything, truly making our area a winter wonderland.

But when the winds blow, the snow is whipped into the air, causing visibility to be very poor. Several travelers have become disoriented and lost their way in the storms. Often they run off the road and have to spend time waiting to be rescued. Cellular phones have been the saving factor for several. Sitting in a car or truck for hours, often through the night, is not pleasant, and those who have survival kits with them are fortunate. They have planned for emergencies.

Unfortunately, lives have been lost when people venture out during the storms. All are warned to stay with their vehicle when it stalls or becomes stuck in the drifts. Their vehicle becomes their safe haven.

In Jesus we have a safe haven. Our survival depends upon our close walk with Him. When we choose to stay with Him, we are safe. He cares for us in every emergency.

As long as time lasts we will have seasons. The cold and snow will come every year. We will need to take every precaution to protect ourselves and our families from the storms and the snow that drifts around us.

Storms occur in our spiritual lives too. Just as snow and cold make traveling difficult, so sin clutters our lives and makes traveling the Christian pathway difficult. Our only safety is to ever stay in the safe haven of Jesus' presence.

Lord, keep me close to You today, no matter what storms of life beat upon me. I will be safe in Your presence. Thank You, Lord, for Your promise never to leave me in the storms of life.

EVELYN GLASS

The True Gifts of Christmas

The star . . . stopped above the place where the child lay. At the sight of the star they were overjoyed. Entering the house, they saw the child with Mary his mother, and bowed to the ground in homage to him; then they opened their treasures and offered him gifts. Matt. 2:9-12, NEB.

There are 26 days left until Christmas. This information is constantly being updated because my son asks me every hour. If he had his way we would have gotten our tree the day after Thanksgiving, but I tried to explain to him all the reasons we should wait until at least December. Any reason I came up with was lame to him, I'm sure.

I guess I'm getting older, and this time of year seems to point out this fact more than any other. It seems like it was only last week that I put the decorations away. For another thing, I'm looking for shortcuts in the areas of decorating and shopping. Then there's the desire to cut down on the spending and give everyone something practical. At any rate, it's good I have the children to remind me that this is the season for giving, and sometimes that also means giving in and giving up.

For the kids' sake we will get a real evergreen tree for the family room. I will hang lights outside again this year and might even do more than just drape them from the porch railing.

It seems so appropriate that children bring the Christmas season back into focus. We adults sometimes forget to stop and notice the joy and wonder in children's eyes as they look at a lighted tree in a dark room or excitedly wait for you to open their gift to you.

It was a little child many years ago who brought adults to their knees in wonder and joy. They brought gifts; they brought adoration; but they took home more than they could ever have given. They took back a promise, a hope that life would one day be eternal and full of joys with no sorrows.

This Christmas watch your kids (or borrow some if you have none at home) as they decorate the tree and the cookies. Capture some of the joy and enthusiasm we tend to lose as we get older and more sophisticated.

PATTY KNITTEL

The Blizzard

"Fear not, for I am with you; be not dismayed, for I am your God. I will strengthen you, yes, I will help you." Isa. 41:10, NKJV.

I awoke early Sunday morning and looked outside. A blanket of snow stretched away from my window in every direction. The snowstorm that had been predicted for two days had finally arrived. The children and teen group homes, where I was scheduled to dispense medications that day, were the focus of my attention. I quickly prepared myself for the day and weather.

Traveling to the first group home was easy and smooth. The snow was falling, but driving visibility was good. I was feeling very confident about my driving in the snow and continued traveling to the next home.

By noon the pattern of the snow began to change. Before I left one of the homes, a worker commented, "I hope you don't get stuck in the snow."

Confidently I replied, "I have a van; don't worry."

Before driving off, I asked the Lord for His protection. The driving visibility had changed, and the snow was mixed with ice. My windshield wipers quickly coated with ice, making the clearing of the windshield impossible. I began to panic. Being unable to see, I pulled to the side of the road—and right into a snowdrift. My van was stuck with all four tires in the snowdrift. I was frightened. What would I do now?

"Jesus!" I shouted. "Help me!"

The words "Fear not, for I am with you" seemed to echo in my mind, quieting my racing heart. The promise of His presence always with me gave me hope. Calmly and slowly I pressed the accelerator. My tires began turning, and out of the snowdrift they rolled. I removed the ice from the wiper blades so the visibility was good again, and I arrived safely at my destination. The Lord had been ever present in my time of need.

What a comfort it is, Lord, to know that no matter what problem I face today, You will be there with me. You will keep me calm and give me strength. You will be my helper. With You by my side I have nothing to fear!

SHARON MARSHALL-RANDALL

My Second Translator

God has revealed it to us by his Spirit. 1 Cor. 2:10, NIV.

I had been in Italy for less than 24 hours when I came face-to-face with my inability to communicate. I had already tried to talk with some of the 150 women attending the Christian women's retreat, but it was a lost cause. I couldn't make any sense of their rapid-fire Italian.

"Your study of Spanish will help you understand Italian," a friend had told me. It wasn't happening. To be among a group of vivacious, talkative women and be unable to join in the conversation was frustrating.

On the morning of the second day I recorded in my journal a prayer for help. *Lord, please bless the ears and hearts of the women who listen to my talks today. Help them to understand not only the words but also Your message of love. Bless the one who translates for me. Help him to choose words that will touch the women's hearts.*

It seems to me that I need two translators here. I need one who speaks Italian, but I require another who will translate to the women's hearts Your love and power. Please, Lord, send Your Holy Spirit to be my translator today.

I continued writing. *Although we cannot speak to each other, help me to communicate love to these women through my eyes, my facial expressions, and my touch. Even without the use of words, reach their hearts through me today.*

At supper that evening a woman across the table from me spoke to me with the help of a friend. "Your message touched my heart," she said. "We all feel that you love us. We just look at you, and we can know your love."

"Thank you for sharing that," I replied. "That's exactly what I asked God to do this morning!"

Later I wrote, "Wow! I feel so humble. Even though I am unable to speak their language You have been able to use me to reveal Your love. I'm so glad. Thank You, Lord!"

Send Your Holy Spirit to be my translator today, Lord. As I go about my work, meeting people in the marketplace, or interacting with family members, I want to communicate Your love. DOROTHY EATON WATTS

Not Alone

*"Do not fear, for I am with you; do not be dismayed, for I am
your God. I will strengthen you and help you; I will
uphold you with my righteous right hand." Isa. 41:10, NIV.*

Most people were skeptical and said it couldn't be done. A
flower festival lasting 10 days? Impossible! The flowers would
never last that long, especially since it was December and there
would have to be heat in the church.

My reasons for wanting to hold a Christmas festival were twofold:
to remind the public of the real meaning of Christmas, and to raise
£5,000 to equip a room in the local hospice. So with a prayer in our
hearts we began to prepare for our Joy to the World Festival of Flowers.

As the time approached, I became fearful. This was the seventh
Festival of Flowers I had organized, and I had always relied heavily
on the backup of Alf, the church's indispensable deacon. But Alf had
died earlier in the year, and I didn't know how to face the festival
without him. Then God reminded me, "Do not fear, for I am with
you. I will help you."

And He did. I missed Alf every single day, but Alf left us a legacy
in his daughter, Pat, and her husband, Peter. They, along with others
the Lord sent, helped ensure the smooth running of our festival. God
gave me the strength to be at the church for 15 hours a day and still
have the energy to enjoy every program. As the children presented
the Nativity, the age-old words brought tears to many eyes. The
choir programs were a taste of heaven, and the Carols by Candlelight
service was moving. The mayor and his wife, who attended the day
we presented toys for the disadvantaged children, kept their driver
waiting an extra 45 minutes. Hundreds flocked to the church.

And we raised the £5,000 to help the hospice. The flowers? Two
hours every morning and two hours every evening were spent in watering and spraying the 35 exhibits that told the Christmas Story,
from the Incarnation through the dedication in the Temple. It was
nothing short of miraculous that the flowers looked almost as fresh
on the last day as they did on the first. God's promises are sure!

AUDREY BALDERSTONE

Amazing Grace

"The Lamb at the center of the throne will be their shepherd;
he will lead them to springs of living water. And God will
wipe away every tear from their eyes." Rev. 7:17, NIV.

I could count on my fingers the times we did anything together. But each time was like slipping into shoes that had molded themselves to my feet. That's why a sunny day in July turned dark when I learned that cancer had invaded your colon.

"Call if there's anything I can do," I pleaded. "Grocery shopping, cleaning, laundry, yard work, trips to the doctor." Each offer appeased my grief. Each acceptance made me feel as if I could restrain with kindness the swelling tide of runaway cells.

Too soon, however, it became evident I was a mere dinghy sailing into the storm swell alone. Too soon your body began to lag farther and farther behind your sweet, sweet spirit. Too soon my heart broke under the millstone of orphaned questions.

Then one December Sunday your husband called. You needed someone to spend the afternoon with you. Could I? And so between 1:00 and 5:00 we kept watch together. When you couldn't talk, we simply smiled at one another. And when your golden lab, Daisy, came to inquire about your status, I handed you dog biscuits to feed her. The nuzzle of her nose made you chuckle. Toward evening we sat together on the couch. I held a glass of apricot juice as you sipped through a straw. Afterward, while we were holding hands, the sun broke through the clouds, painting our silhouettes on the opposite wall. When your husband returned, we hugged and kissed goodbye.

"Until next time," we lovingly, stubbornly asserted.

Three days later you died.

Oh, I do believe God will wipe away my tears. But for now I will gladly let them fill my eyes, spill over, and run down. Their refractive lenses help me to comprehend the afternoon my orphaned questions found a Parent. The afternoon when dog biscuits and apricot juice became emblems of His broken body and spent blood, when shadows on the wall became His angels, and when a pillow-strewn sofa became His throne of grace upon which reigned our broken hearts, miraculously made whole. LYNDELLE CHIOMENTI

He Knows Me

*You created my inmost being;
you knit me together in my mother's womb. Ps. 139:13, NIV.*

I got together this past year with several longtime (but certainly not old) friends. I've known one of them from babyhood. We attended school together through high school and into college. But during the past 15 years our communication has consisted of sporadic Christmas newsletters and a few phone calls.

When we met this year, there was a familiarity, a lack of "strangerness," an appreciation founded on understanding each other's roots. She knew where I came from because she had been there.

I visited another friend I hadn't seen for more than six years. We had shared deeply through the years. Then she got married and moved away. Christmas letters became our most constant form of keeping in touch. During my visit with her we stayed up talking through two nights. The openness, understanding, and simple acceptance grounded in knowing the worst and best of each other's lives rejuvenated and revitalized me.

A third friend and I hadn't seen each other in two years. In high school we shared the turbulent teens—crushes, crises, and comedy. We were maid and matron of honor in each other's weddings. When we got together this year, we effortlessly picked up where we had left off, because we know each other.

As I savor these relationships, I feel a sense of being in touch with who I was and who I have become. These friendships have stood the test of time. Each of these friends knows things about me—and remembers things about me—that no one else in the world can understand.

I am also coming to realize that I have another longtime Friend. He remembers who I was and where I came from, and He knows who I have become. His friendship has stood the test of time. He fuses my past, present, and future.

When we meet in the greatest reunion of all, there will be a familiarity, a total lack of "strangerness." He really knows me. And I will begin to understand better just how open and honest and accepting He really is. We will pick up right where we left off—to continue on throughout eternity.   ROBERTA FRANKLIN CLAUSEN

Super Savings

*God's gift to us is the happiness we get from our food
and drink and from the work we do. Eccl. 3:13, CEV.*

I love surprises. I find it hard to understand someone who professes to "hate to be surprised." To me a surprise can be anything from the glimpse of a hummingbird to the brilliant orange of the first spring poppy in my garden to an unexpected freebie in my mailbox.

The mail has always held an element of surprise for me. Aside from bills and ads that routinely occupy our mailbox, there is sometimes a magazine, a letter from a friend, or maybe a coupon. Today it was a coupon for a free bottle of shampoo from my favorite supermarket. This is not the first "surprise" I've received from this company. And as I've said, I love surprises.

But these "extras" are not the reason I shop at this store. I shop there because I find what I need, the prices are good, the service is great, and the quality excellent. I like the people who work there, and it's in a convenient location.

I have shopped at other supermarkets. Some are closer to my home. Some promise better service and lower prices. Some claim higher quality. But when I've been taken by these promises, I always come away disappointed. It is then that I return to the place I trust, wondering why I strayed in the first place.

This is like my walk with the Lord. Just by believing in and accepting Him I have the promise of salvation and eternal life, with complete happiness forever! But like the supermarket with its "extras," the Lord blesses me with gifts and talents as I strive to grow in Him.

The daily answers to prayers, friendships garnered in the name of Jesus, fears and problems overcome, abilities recognized and utilized, unconditional love and acceptance, are all the product of a relationship with Jesus Christ. These blessings always come as a wonderful surprise to me.

Sometimes I stray from what I know is right. Sin presents itself to me in many flavors and from different directions, and I often make bad choices. But unlike the surprise coupons that I find in my mailbox, God's love and forgiveness have no limits and no expiration date.

TERRI CASEY

Signatures

This is the covenant that I will make with the house of Israel
after those days, saith the Lord; I will put my laws
into their mind, and write them in their hearts:
and I will be to them a God, and they shall be to me a people. Heb. 8:10.

Since the beginning of our marriage my husband and I have had a
guest book in our home. Over the years the signatures have multiplied, and occasionally we will take time to read over each entry. A
date, a signature, and sometimes a brief note kindly written bring
back floods of fond memories about a particular time spent with family and friends in our home.

A few months ago I was looking through a box of old letters.
Now, I wouldn't classify myself as a "general pack rat," but when it
comes to personal letters, cards, and notes, I could probably count on
one or two hands those that I've just read and thrown away. For
many years boxes of letters have accumulated in storage; sorting
through them was always on my list of things to do—later.

This particular day I decided to begin the task and cherished a
few quiet moments to sort through stacks of letters dating back to my
early school days. As I scanned through the piles, trying to decide
which ones I should open and reread, I was surprised that I could instantly recognize who the sender was on some, not because their
name was on it, but from the handwriting on the envelope.

Years had not faded the memory of the handwriting of
Grandmother, some school friends, a pen pal, and others who had
written frequent notes. It soon became a sort of test for me as I
searched through the envelopes. I surprised myself at how much I
could remember from so long ago—the unique style of the writing
gave away the secret of who had sent the message.

I was struck with the spiritual implications that day. Christ wants
to write His signature on our hearts so that when others read our
lives, they'll know He dwells inside. More important, when the
Father in heaven looks at us, He will see Christ's signature on our
character and write our name in the Lamb's book of life.

I want Christ's signature on the letter of my life—it's the only one
the Father recognizes!   SHERYL A. CALHOUN

344

Wake-up Call

Ye shall seek me, and find me, when ye shall
search for me with all your heart. Jer. 29:13.

I listened as the speaker said that the greatest need was a personal, uninterrupted time alone with God each day. I felt he was speaking to me. I felt an overwhelming desire for a daily encounter with my God. While I always respected my husband's request for time alone with God, except for emergencies, I couldn't seem to find time to do it myself. Yet I wanted such an experience.

I love to sleep, so I got up each morning only when it was time for me to get ready for work, and I went to bed early each evening. My days were filled to the brim. There was always so much to do for each waking moment. However, I prayed, "Lord, if my angel will wake me up each morning at 6:00, I will spend time getting better acquainted with You."

The next day it seemed like someone nudged me awake at 6:00, as if to say, "This is your wake-up call." I crawled out of bed, donned my slippers and robe, and found my easy chair. I placed my Bible beside me. It was so quiet; I just absorbed the peacefulness. I slipped to my knees and prayed, "God, my need for You is so great. Please speak to me through Your Word, and then give me understanding so I can know Your will for my life. I want You to perform spiritual surgery on my mind, to open it, tuck all the information inside, and then suture it up to remain intact for all my future needs."

From that day my angel has kept his part of the bargain. Every morning I awake at 6:00, eager for my time with God. I need the beautiful gems from God that are hidden deep in His Word to be unfolded as I search! His presence and the blessing He sends each day fill my heart to overflowing, in spite of what heartaches, trials, and difficulties there may be.

Our dearest Friend wants time alone with us each day. He has so much to share with us that will make each day far brighter.

ANN BLANDFORD

My Little Friend

*Are not two sparrows sold for a penny? Yet not one of them will fall
to the ground apart from the will of your Father. . . . So don't be afraid;
you are worth more than many sparrows. Matt. 10:29-31, NIV.*

One autumn morning I saw a small bird in my hedge. I hadn't
seen it before. *What a beautiful red robin you are with your brown-
green wings,* I thought as I watched my new friend. It had a pretty
head, vivacious eyes, and legs that were thinner than matchsticks.

Who are you? Where is your mother? Are you an orphan? It saw the
sparrows' feeding place and went timidly to get some food before it
flew away.

I stocked up the food, changed the bath water, and filled up the
drinking place. The next day I sat and waited. The robin flew to the
hedge at the same time as the day before and seemed to be asking,
"Have you set the table?" I thanked God as I watched my new orphan friend. It was so different from the gray sparrows and all the
other birds.

The fall turned to cold winter. For a while I didn't see my red
robin. I feared it had fallen, frozen, to the ground. From my kitchen
window I looked at the sparrows on the feeding board hanging from
a branch. I longed to see my red robin.

I talked to my heavenly Father. *Not even a sparrow will fall to the
ground without Your knowledge. Is my red robin still alive? Show me that
You care, even for the birds.*

I was still immersed in my thoughts when I noticed a shadow
pass. It was my little friend! It looked toward me and seemed to be
saying, "Here I am. What's wrong? I had to interrupt my business
when I was ordered to come to you."

I answered, "I know. You are an answer to my prayer. If our
Father in heaven has taken care of you in the frost and cold, why
shouldn't He take care of us?"

*Thank You, Lord, for sending red robin to testify to me of our Creator's car-
ing love toward His creatures. The birds who stay for the winter await spring.
We await an eternal spring. Thank You for touching my heart so tenderly.*

HELENA KLINGMAN

Punkin and Me

Awake! Be on the alert! Your enemy the devil, like a roaring lion, prowls round looking for someone to devour. 1 Peter 5:8, NEB.

Seven years ago our two daughters each received a kitten for Christmas, and the cats have been precious members of our family ever since. But this year one of the cats was poisoned and had to be put to sleep. Our younger daughter pined and pined for her cat until we reluctantly agreed to find her a new kitten. Thus Punkin entered our lives.

Our older cat, Laura, has no use for Punkin. She hisses and growls when the little kitten comes near. She has threatened to leave several times, pawing furiously at the front door and leaving with her nose and tail in the air. But she always returns, and she always gives us a look as if to say, "Why is *that* thing still here?"

Our Sheltie, Delilah, loves Punkin. In fact, we are all sure she believes that Punkin is her kitten, and her kitten alone. They play together for hours, and when they are both exhausted, Delilah allows Punkin to root around on her as if she were her nursing mother. Sometimes Delilah plays too rough, and Punkin gives a long, drawn-out meow that definitely sounds like pain. When I hear that, I come running to the rescue. I hold Punkin, scolding Delilah at the same time for being so rough. But as soon as I put Punkin down, she looks for the dog and pounces on her, starting the whole process over again.

As I was watching them this morning, it occurred to me that I'm quite a bit like that little kitten. I play with sin, run after it, and grab at its tail. Then when I'm overwhelmed and feel like I'm about to be gobbled up, I pray a pitiful prayer. The Lord *always* picks me up and holds me, at the same time sending the devil on his way. As soon as the Lord leaves me to my own choices, just like Punkin, I start grabbing for the devil's tail, and it starts all over again.

Lord, please help me to overcome the desire to play with sin. Please help me see Satan as a roaring lion who's trying to devour me, instead of as a playmate to pursue. And thank You for being my Protector, Counselor, Restorer, and God. I love You, Lord. Amen. CANDANCE GRAVES DEVORE

Plover Neighbors

He shall cover you with His feathers, and under His wings you shall take refuge; His truth shall be your shield and buckler. Ps. 91:4, NKJV.

Intrepid Park, at the corner of our street, boasts a few scraggly trees and a concrete walking path. However, it is the place a pair of plovers chose for their nesting home last spring. In November (spring-time in Australia) my husband and I watched anxiously as three tiny chicks wandered close to the road. The plover parents called out loudly to each other as we passed.

The devoted parents diligently watched over their chicks. One parent stood in the middle of the road to slow down traffic, because as the babies grew they wandered to the lawns of nearby houses looking for insects. As the weeks passed, everyone living in the neighborhood came to know the plover family.

Then came our typical Queensland summer storms with thunder, lightning, and heavy, torrential, subtropical rain. I would lie in the comfort of bed at night, wondering how the plovers were.

The next danger came two weeks before Christmas. A house in Intrepid Court is a yearly winner in the Brisbane Christmas lights competition. With that honor comes the nightly viewers—hundreds of cars bringing thousands of people to Intrepid Park. We feared for the family of plovers.

Two days before Christmas the local council came to dig up part of Intrepid Park to improve the drainage. The grass the plovers had nested in was dug up, drains laid, and bright-orange fence erected in the middle of the park. The plovers survived.

Meanwhile, the three young plovers grew and became adventure-some. In spite of their parents' warning calls, they wandered along the street into a busy road. Twice my husband chased them back into the safety of their quieter street. Early one morning we heard the adults' anguished calling. One of the young had been killed by a car. My heart ached for those birds. They looked so forlorn.

I thought of how sad our heavenly Father must be when I, His daughter, wander away into places that threaten my eternal life. How many times has He carefully watched me, protecting me from danger, when I didn't even realize it?

LEONIE DONALD

He Shall Direct Thy Paths

*Trust in the Lord with all thine heart; and lean not unto
thine own understanding. In all thy ways acknowledge him,
and he shall direct thy paths. Prov. 3:5, 6.*

December 1995 found me in Panama's Torrijos Airport ready to
return to the United States after a holiday visit with my family.
I arrived back in Spring Lake, North Carolina, and fell into my normal
routine. At work the next day I met with my supervisor for my annual performance review. It was marginal. I went back to my cubicle
upset at what I knew was an unfair appraisal. As I debated my alter-
natives, I saw a letter in my in box from the personnel office, offering
a buyout for those with 25 or more years of service. I knew God was
talking to me through these circumstances. He seemed to be telling
me, "It's time to retire and work for Me." Years before I had promised
I would serve Him through selling gospel literature.

After praying about it and talking with my children over the holidays, I—or rather, the Lord—made my decision. I requested a March
31 retirement date. With the decision made, I was filled with a new
sense of purpose and looked excitedly to my new job of working for
the Lord. I contacted the publishing department of my church to offer
my services. Unfortunately, the Fayetteville district position was
filled. I felt a keen sense of disappointment. "Maybe the Lord wants
me to do something else." I prayed about it.

One night in February, at prayer meeting, my pastor's wife asked
about my retirement plans. I told her, "I really don't know, now that
the literature evangelist position is taken."

She said, "No, it isn't; it's vacant."

This was a direct answer to my prayers. I interviewed with the
publishing director, was accepted, and haven't looked back since.

In *The Desire of Ages,* Ellen White, a gospel writer, states, "Our
heavenly Father has a thousand ways to provide for us, of which we
know nothing. Those who accept the one principle of making the service and honor of God supreme will find perplexities vanish, and a
plain path before their feet" (p. 330). Are you uncertain of the path
you should take? "In all thy ways acknowledge him, and he shall direct thy paths."   WILMA C. JARDINE

Lighthouse

O send out thy light and thy truth: let them lead me; let them bring me unto thy holy hill, and to thy tabernacles. Ps. 43:3.

We turned our backs against the winter wind and watched fish merchants clear away the remains of their unsold catch. Darkness began to descend on the dock in the gulf of Finland that December day. The twilight seemed somewhat eerie, since it was only about 3:00 in the afternoon and a gloomy daylight had been with us a mere six hours.

People collected around us, little by little, as we waited, and soon a small tub of a ferry pulled up to the dock and put down its gangplanks. In minutes it pulled away, carrying people, most of whom lived on the Suomenlinna Fortress Island, my husband, and me. The ferry made its way between several tiny islands that were nothing more than colossal smooth rocks peeking out of the water. A warehouse perched on one of them. What appeared to be a residence sat on another. As we approached our destination, the rhythmic circling rays of a lighthouse reflected through the haze.

The boat docked, and we made our way up the cobbled road between quaint buildings, arriving almost immediately at the lighthouse. A massive iron fence, fashioned in marine tradition of anchors and huge anchor chains, marked a square court around the lighthouse. I peered into a lighted basement window and there, to my amazement, was a costumed group of children, complete with angel wings and a homemade foil star, obviously rehearsing for a Christmas play.

I quickly walked around to the front of the building and looked up. What I saw struck me forcefully. This ancient stone lighthouse served a dual purpose: it also served as a church! Supporting that redeeming beam of light, someone had crafted a replica of the cross of Christ, one guiding light supported by another. And in the bowels of this structure tender children prepared for yet another revelation of the Light being introduced personally into our dark world.

It wasn't long before we had to return to the mainland. The light of day had faded, but we were guided safely through the jutting rocks by the rays from a unique multipurpose "lighthouse."

SUSAN SCOGGINS

The Gift of Giving

*Every good and perfect gift is from above, coming down
from the Father of the heavenly lights, who does not change
like shifting shadows. James 1:17, NIV.*

Christmas is a time for giving and receiving gifts. When I was a
child, I used to sit beside the Christmas tree and imagine, with
hopeful anticipation, what treasures might be contained in the colorful packages. I also thought about the pleasure there would be when
some of the presents that I had wrapped would be opened.

As I grew older, the presents that I treasured most were the gifts
that people gave of themselves. The art of giving a portion of ourselves is sometimes lost in a culture that puts so much emphasis on
possessions. There are so many ways to give of ourselves.

We can give gifts of the heart: nurturing, consideration, affirmation, empathy, and an understanding spirit.

We can give gifts of the mind: plans, poems, ideas, and dreams.

We can give gifts of the spirit: forgiveness, kindness, love, hope,
charity, and faith.

We can give gifts of the voice: encouragement, guidance, humor,
good cheer, and creative inspiration.

We can give gifts of our time: patience, personal attention, and a
listening ear.

God set an example of gift-giving by sending us a Person—the
Jesus Child. Under most Christmas trees there will be several gifts.
On Calvary's tree there was only one—but it was a priceless and perpetual gift that superseded all others. Not only that, but God's gifts
are irrevocable (Rom. 11:29). They are there for the asking, and we
are told to covet the most excellent of all gifts: love (1 Cor. 13:13).

Christ was a master in the art of gift-giving. He held children on
His lap, and they felt loved and special. He talked with women, and
they felt valuable and recognized. He washed the disciples' feet, and
they felt important and humble. Christ gave to others gifts of time,
personal attention, touch, listening, affirmation, and nurturing—perfect, incomparable, inestimable gifts. What a marvelous example for
us to imitate! ARLENE TAYLOR

Accidents and Answered Prayers

The angel of the Lord encampeth round about them
that fear him, and delivereth them. Ps. 34:7.

The last thing I remember before the crash was waking from my nap in the front seat of the car, thinking we were tailgating a tractor-trailer. But the truck had apparently stalled on the highway. I cried, "Harold, aren't we much too close?"

That's all I remember. Then silence.

The accident happened to our family of four on a vacation trip to Arizona. Before we left, Harold's parents had come over to say their goodbyes, and after kneeling and having prayer to ask for the Lord's protection, we were on our way.

It became obvious after several hours that a snowstorm was coming our way. Harold felt that since we would be traveling in a southerly direction, we would eventually get out of the snow, so we continued on. Then Harold fell asleep at the wheel.

When we came to, we were aware of the voices of motorists who had stopped to offer their help. We were taken to the nearby hospital in cars. After all the tests and body checks, we were most thankful and relieved to learn our injuries were not life threatening.

Sometime later our young son questioned why our accident had happened, since his grandpa had prayed for God's protection on our trip.

"Yes, we did pray for protection," my husband explained. "But I didn't do my part. I was wrong by driving in a snowstorm and driving when I was sleepy. Jack," my husband continued, "had we not prayed, we might have all been killed."

Not until we read a newspaper report of our accident did we learn that a tractor-trailer following our car had come upon the accident too rapidly in the snowstorm and had taken to the ditch to avoid hitting us. We could only imagine what could have happened to our family had that occurred.

When my brother went to view the wreckage, he remarked, "Someone was riding with them."

Yes, God did answer our prayer, many times over. Thank You, dear heavenly Father.   CLAREEN COLCLESSER

God's Treasure Chest

"Where your treasure is, there your heart will be also." Matt. 6:21, NKJV.

Having read that familiar text again, I suddenly found new meaning in it. We were in the throes of the Christmas celebrations, the children had taken part in their Nativity play, and our family was looking forward to the holiday season with great anticipation.

On arriving home one day, I found an envelope on the mat. Inside were two sets of house keys and a note from a good friend and neighbor who lived across the street. Ann reminded me that a few days earlier I had agreed to look after her home while she and her family spent Christmas with relatives some distance away. She also reminded me that I'd agreed to look after her next-door neighbor's home for a few days as they were away also.

I groaned. In the hustle and bustle of Christmas I had forgotten my conversation with my friend. I decided to go to Ann's neighbor's home first. As I turned the key and opened the door, I felt I was not entering a home, but a palace. Everything was just as it should be—only the best would do. These people had no children and obviously indulged themselves in life's luxuries.

Then I went to my friend's home. What a contrast! When I had negotiated the tricky front door lock, I walked into a well-lived-in home. The children's stockings were still hanging in the lounge, and the decor looked as if it had seen better days, but this was the house I would always treasure. Here lived a true friend. It was here that a surprise party was held for me when we finally adopted our second daughter. It was here that many a recipe had been exchanged and many a well-read book borrowed.

As I walked back to my home, I began to realize the true meaning of Jesus' words and asked myself where my treasure was.

JUDITH REDMAN

Better Than Christmas Slippers!

Each of you must give as you have made up your mind, not reluctantly or under compulsion, for God loves a cheerful giver. 2 Cor. 9:7, NRSV.

My sister and I were Christmas shopping together when she spied a pair of slippers. "I need to buy those slippers!" she exclaimed. I liked them too and decided to buy a pair also. Suddenly we looked at each other with the same thought: I could buy her a pair, and she could buy me a pair, and we'd have our gifts for each other out of the way!

This ridiculous slipper experience led to a revision of our Christmas gift-giving. Our family had discussed stopping this Christmas nonsense and getting involved in some worthwhile project, but no one ever did anything about it—until I went to the Philippines one year.

After I saw groups of people meeting for church under torn tarps and sitting on wooden benches without backs, I asked, "How much would it cost to build a simple church?" I learned a modest church could be built for $4,000. Would my family give up their gift-getting and donate funds for a church in the Philippines?

They did! On Christmas Eve we celebrated a Swedish Christmas with a traditional Swedish smorgasbord. We sang carols and enjoyed a candle lighting service. Only the children received presents. Then I reported on our mission project.

That was nine years ago. Since that time our family has raised money for a variety of exciting projects: pews for a church; a speaker system, mixing board, and chimes for a seminary chapel; a computer for a seminary student; a piano for a church; a mobile book trailer from which to sell books; a telephone system on a college campus. Our project this year was salary for a Bible worker, which should produce 50 to 100 baptisms. None of us is wealthy, but we each gave as we could. God blessed our meager efforts, and the results have been amazing.

Christmas as we used to know it has disappeared. Do we miss it? Never! We've found that nothing can replace the joy and satisfaction we feel as we select an annual project and do for those less fortunate than we are. Isn't this the real spirit of Christmas?   NANCY VAN PELT

A Necessary "Detour"

*I am the Lord thy God . . . which leadeth thee
by the way that thou shouldest go. Isa. 48:17.*

I had already completed most of my Christmas preparations. Shopping was almost done, packages were well on their way to parents and daughters, cookies were decorated, and so was the house. Even though I had work I needed to do in my office, I felt impelled to do some final Christmas shopping at a Christian bookstore.

Forgetting that I was more than halfway to a bookstore close to home, I took the freeway to a bookstore in the next town. After exiting the freeway, I decided to stop first at a market for some special bread, sunflower seeds, and other goodies not available at the local chain markets.

Then whom should I see right there across the bulk-food cases but a friend from several years back. After the usual "How are you doing?" she shared that she had been laid off some time before and was about to lose her home. Overwhelming depression rendered her unable even to get out of bed to go to her temporary job. I shared that a friend of mine had been through a similar experience that summer, and I believed I understood what she had been going through and how hard it was to pull oneself out of it.

After we explored the usual legal and practical options for getting her life on track and saving her home, I tried to think of some words to encourage her. I shared the Lord's recent leading in my life and how I had learned to depend fully on Him for my everyday needs. We hugged and then parted.

Later, driving home, I began to beat myself up mentally, wondering why I had gone so far out of the way when I had so much to do, and why, when I knew I had to go to that same town just two days later, I didn't wait until then to go to the bookstore.

Then I knew why: I needed to see my old friend and know her troubles and needs so I could add her to my prayer list. Furthermore, she needed the encouragement. It also made me even more thankful for the Lord's leading and blessing in my own life.

JOYCE WILLES BROWN-CARPER

A Lost Chance

Ho, every one who thirsts, come to the waters. Isa. 55:1, NRSV.
Let anyone who wishes take the water of life as a gift. Rev. 22:17, NRSV.

She was sitting on a low brick wall outside the medical building where I had an appointment. I assumed she was reading during a break in her schedule. In her lap she held an open Bible, in one hand, a lit cigarette. It was difficult for my mind to take it in.

I have wished many times, as God has brought that scene to my mind, that I had stopped and commended her for openly reading the Word of God. I remember feeling a moment's hesitation, but then pressing on to my appointment. Why didn't I respond to the Spirit's suggestion? I refused to decide to stop and speak to that soul until it was too late.

Perhaps, like the Bible story of Philip, she was the "Ethiopian" placed there by God, but I hurried on my way, missing a blessing by not responding instantly. And the blessing God had in store for her was lost. I will probably never know the name of that precious soul sitting there as people hurried by.

Even though it's unusual to see someone with the Bible in one hand and a cigarette in the other, I believe that woman is a child of God and His heart longs for a close relationship with her.

I had my opportunity. The only thing I can do now is intercede with God on her behalf, praying that He will send another someone to just the right place at just the right time. I am praying that He will.

It's a sobering thought that we cannot call back even one single moment. The only way we can show our remorse is by making the most of what time we have left by working in unity with God for the souls of others. The opportunity may never come again.

O God, make my heart sensitive to hear Your Spirit. Make me quick to respond to the cry for help, whether spoken or silent.

JODI EULENE DODSON

The Best Gift

Thanks be to God for his indescribable gift! 2 Cor. 9:15, NIV.

It did not promise to be the best Christmas ever. Quite the opposite. I couldn't remember ever before not having parents, at least one daughter, or a husband with whom to celebrate Christmas. But that was the situation this year.

I was going through a difficult divorce. Mother was still recovering from her broken hip, so my parents couldn't travel. "Grand-dog" Pallie, a sweet, beautiful collie, went into renal and liver failure and had to be put to sleep. Our daughter was celebrating Christmas in the Bay Area with her sister and father—I was not invited. Only my housemate, who was more depressed than I, was going to be around.

It wasn't all bad, but I focused on the negatives and ignored the occasional bright spots in the holidays. Despite the bleak situation, I decided to go through the motions and decorate the house.

And then a friend and her husband practically begged us to have dinner and spend Christmas Day with them. We also made a quick trip to see an elderly woman in the church who invited us in for prayer and to look at pictures of days past. Then we were off to the cemetery to visit the grave of a friend's late mother and grandparents.

All this brought the realization that gifts, a big dinner, and family are not what Christmas is all about. This year I realized that the "ideal" Christmas does not exist anymore; perhaps it never did, nor is it important. We cannot find happiness by wishing for what cannot be for many reasons. The saying "Jesus is the reason for the season" became more real.

God, did I ever thank You for Your great Gift at Christmastime? How can a robe, slippers, perfume, the love of a good man, or any of the other things I might wish for even begin to compare with that Gift that I take so much for granted? Jesus came for me before I needed Him. Thank You so much!

JOYCE WILLES BROWN-CARPER

357

Family Reunion

Behold, he cometh with clouds; and every eye shall see him. Rev. 1:7.

While I was waiting to pay for my purchases recently, I began a conversation with an attractive young woman. "Are you about ready for Christmas?" I asked.

"Oh, yes," she said. "This is the last gift that I'm going to get." Then she almost glowed when she said, "I'm so excited! My father is coming from Chicago, and I can hardly wait. In fact, he could be arriving at any moment now!"

I could see this was going to be a wonderful reunion for her. She'd been preparing for it for some time and had even put something in his room to make him feel very welcome.

How excited am I about my Lord's soon coming? Do I feel as though I can hardly wait? How diligently am I preparing for that glorious reunion? Am I really ready? It may be later than I realize for my Lord's return.

I think of the day when I was to be in charge of a morning church meeting. I had done this many times before, and I was ready to leave early. I looked at the clock. It was a long, long time before I really needed to be there, I thought, and what could I do when I got there? After all, it wouldn't take but a few minutes for me to get everything ready to start. I looked out at my sun-drenched backyard and the sparkling pool. What better thing to do, I reasoned, than to enjoy myself and walk in the warm sun.

It seemed that only a few minutes had passed before the jangling of the phone interrupted my reverie. When I picked up the phone, the frantic voice of my friend brought me back to reality. "Where are you? You are due to go on in just a minute or two!"

Stunned, I wondered if this was only a bad dream. What on earth had gone wrong? Could this really be happening? But it was. I had been so sure in my mind that I had oodles of time. So very sure.

Dear Lord, help me to look for Your return eagerly. Awaken me from my lethargy. Make me alert to the nearness of Your appearing.

PAT MADSEN

Room at the Inn

*Ask, and it shall be given you; seek, and ye shall find;
knock, and it shall be opened unto you. Matt. 7:7.*

A fter a long trip from Canada, we stopped at the first town in New York to eat supper. As we were finishing our meal, my husband asked, "Where are we going to stay for the night? We didn't make any reservations."

As there was a motel connected to the restaurant, we decided to see if they had any nonsmoking rooms.

"We have just one room left," the man replied.

"How much is it?" I inquired.

"Sixty dollars," he said. It was too much.

We drove on, passing two more unsuitable motels. We were beginning to feel like Mary and Joseph looking for a place to stay. My husband took a deep breath and stated, "We are never going to find a place to stay that suits you this late at night."

Now, I'm a person who believes the Lord is interested in all of our life events. So as we drove down Interstate 81, I bowed my head and prayed, "Dear Lord, please help us find a decent place to stay tonight."

Soon we began to see the lights of Watertown ahead. "Let's get off at the first exit," I suggested.

My husband drove up in front of the office of the first motel from the exit. "This chain will be too expensive, and they won't have a room anyway," he grumbled.

In the motel office I took my place in line behind a young woman who was talking to the motel clerk. "No," he was saying, "we have no rooms left."

This did not dampen my spirits. I put on my sweetest smile. "Sir, do you have any nonsmoking rooms?"

They did not. As I turned to leave, he suddenly said, "Oh, wait a minute—we do have one non-smoking room, but the TV in that room is broken. We'll let you have it for $50."

My husband was strangely silent as we carried our bags up to our second-floor room. When we had our devotions that night, we thanked Jesus for our lovely, reasonably priced room. For us there had been a room in the inn. ROSE NEFF SIKORA

The Runaway Car

*Giving thanks always for all things unto God and the Father
in the name of our Lord Jesus Christ. Eph. 5:20.*

Three days before Christmas I was delivering automobile parts to repair shops. With each delivery I gave a calendar and a tin of nuts in appreciation of their business for the past year. Twice I had been out to the car—first to get the auto part, then the calendar and nuts. When I returned to my car the third time, it was no longer where I had parked it—it was heading for the snowbank! My husband, Dennis, is particular about our car, so I called him to ask if he wanted me to call a wrecker to get it down from its perch. He decided to send his own truck. As I waited, more of the story unfolded.

On the console, in front of the gearshift, I had kept our automatic garage door opener. Apparently it had gotten into a position to stop the gearshift from engaging in park.

The news got worse. The owner of the shop told me that his van now had burgundy paint on it and the doors were dented. Evidently my car had first clipped his van before going forward and bumping into an old pickup that was parked to the left of it. That collision damaged the front end of our car before it finally glanced off to "rest" on the snowbank.

At first it seemed hard to find anything good about my situation, but as I thought about it, I found I had many things to be thankful for. For one thing, my husband is not easily upset when the car is damaged. For another, suppose there had been small children in the path of our driverless car. Third, I can be thankful there weren't more vehicles or property for our car to collide with. Fourth, there could have been an embankment that our car could have gone down into, instead of coming to rest on the snowbank. Fifth, there was an area ahead of the car in which there were several trees it could have bumped into if the snowbank had not been present.

Thank You, Lord, for Your protecting care. Please help me always to give thanks in all things, because in You there is always much to be thankful for!

MARGE LYBERG MCNEILUS

The Much-needed Gift

It is more blessed to give than to receive. Acts 20:35.

At Christmastime each year our four children would take $5 and divide it among the 10 people on their list: two grandmas, one grandpa, Aunt Margie, Mom, Dad, two brothers, a sister, and a Grandma Healy we had adopted.

About a week before Christmas we'd take our annual trip into town to do our shopping. My husband would take two children, and I would take the other two. Then later we would exchange children. This way they could buy for us without our knowing what they were getting for us.

One Christmas our youngest child found a glass for Grandma Healy. It was the ugliest glass I had ever seen, green with designs all over the outside. I tried very hard to get him to choose something else—a potholder, a dishcloth, anything but that glass. But the more I tried, the more determined he was that he wanted this very glass for Grandma Healy and that she would love it.

Christmas Eve we went over to Grandma Healy's so the children could give their presents to her. She was delighted, as they were, as she opened each present and exclaimed over them. Finally she opened Garry's present.

"I love it!" she exclaimed. "It is my favorite color."

A few days after Christmas I was visiting her again. She said she wished she could afford to give the children presents. I told her she did give them the greatest present—learning it was "more blessed to give than to receive." Then she confided in me, "You know, I loved all the presents the children gave me, but I really loved Garry's glass the most because my hands have so much arthritis in them that it's hard to hang on to a glass. This one has a rough outside I can hang on to. It's my favorite glass to use."

God had impressed a child with just what she needed.

Lord, help me to listen for Your still, calm voice today, impressing me with what I can do to make someone happy this Christmas season.

ANNE ELAINE NELSON

A Beautiful Gift of Love

*For God so loved the world, that he gave his only begotten Son,
that whosoever believeth in him should not perish,
but have everlasting life. John 3:16.*

One Christmas Eve a few years ago I was sitting in my daughter's
home on one end of the couch when another daughter and son
came into the house. She went back to the car for a package, and
their 9-year-old Jason walked across the room directly to me without
speaking to anyone. Keeping his head down, and never turning to
look at me, he quietly said, "I'm going to give up." He then turned
and stood by me, still never lifting his head or looking at me.

Immediately I put my arm around him and pulled him to my side,
saying, "You don't want to give up. You know Grandma loves you a
whole bunch."

He said, "Uh-huh."

I hugged him tightly then released him, but he didn't move.
When his mother came back in, he glanced at her, but no one said a
word. The room was quiet. I looked at Jason. He was very sullen, but
he wasn't pouting. He was hurting too much, and trying very hard
not to cry. He came to Grandma! He had never done that before.

I put my arm around him again and hugged him. I felt such
warmth between us. I do believe he felt the same way. I hugged and
released him several times before his cousin broke the silence and
spoke to him. He smiled and stepped away. He made no special eye
contact with me the rest of the evening. I never did know what the
problem was.

What did I get for Christmas? I don't remember. I had already received a most precious and priceless Christmas present this grandma
will cherish forever. No tinsel. No paper. No ribbon. Just a warm gift
of much-needed love for both of us.

*Dear Lord, thank You for the gift of love You gave that Christmas long
ago. Help me to remember this holiday season that of all the gifts I can give,
love is the most priceless of all—and the most welcome.*

ESTHER ARNEY LARSON SHADDAY

Christmas in Thailand

The time came for the baby to be born, and she gave birth to
her firstborn, a son. She wrapped him in cloths and
placed him in a manger, because there was
no room for them in the inn. Luke 2:6, 7, NIV.

It just didn't seem like it would be Christmas this year. My images of
the yuletide season consisted of shopping malls, caroling, cold weather,
family, and chestnuts roasting on an open fire. I, however, would be celebrating Christmas in Thailand, where I was spending a year as a student
missionary teaching English. I loved Thailand, but I wanted to see a little
snow and be with my family for just one day. Instead, I would be vaca-
tioning at some of the most beautiful beaches in the world.

On Christmas Eve, 11 other teachers and I rode down to Krabi.
We arrived after dusk and started looking for a place to stay. We carried our luggage from one resort to another, but everything was full.

The driver of a *songtow* (a pickup truck that functions as a taxi) offered help. He invited us to spend the night at his house—all 12 of us!
He was our Christmas miracle. With high spirits we loaded our stuff
into his *songtow* and got in.

We drove down a long, bumpy, dirt road and ended up in a small
Muslim village. Through the darkness we could make out wooden
houses standing on stilts. When our host showed us into his home,
his petite wife greeted us graciously, showing no surprise that 12 for-
eigners had just shown up on her doorstep.

The whole family treated us like honored guests. When it came
time for bed, they put mats on the concrete floor and gave us two
small pillows. Our host then left and returned with 10 more pillows.
(I suspect we were the only ones in the village with something to put
our heads on.)

The next morning I awoke early, got up, and slipped out of the
house to explore. As I took pictures of the neighbors' water buffalo and
the village mosque, it didn't seem like Christmas. But for the first time
Christmas felt real to me. When we had no place to go, a stranger took
us in and exhibited a spirit of self-sacrifice that embodied what the first
Christmas was all about. SARI KARINA FORDHAM

A Note of Thanks

Enter his gates with thanksgiving and his courts with praise;
give thanks to him and praise his name. Ps. 100:4. NIV.

G ood! I thought to myself. *She got them all done!* Christmas had just come and gone, and I had asked my daughter to write thank-you notes to those who had shared gifts with her. I was pleased to see that she had complied so quickly. I began to sort through the stack so that I could get them in the mail. *This one can go with my letter to Grandma, and this one I can take to work, and this one—*

I stopped and stared. The note in my hand was addressed to me.

Dear Mommy, it began. My eyes blurred as I read the one thank-you note I had not asked my daughter to write. *Thank you for giving me life and loving me and spending time with me.* I read on, and as I did, the words took root in my mother heart. After reading the precious letter through several times, I went searching for the author. A big hug was in order.

With my tears dried and a song in my heart, I resumed sorting letters to mail. But my thoughts were somewhere else. When was the last time I had sent a thank-you note that wasn't expected? I began making a mental list of those in my life who deserved such a letter. My own mother; that friend in college who had loved the homesickness right out of me by making me feel at home with her; that teacher who instilled in me his passion for learning; the coworker who offered to work for me on Christmas Day; the neighbor who found our lost cat. Then there were all the people at church who give of themselves so unselfishly all year, receiving little or no thanks. What a surprise it would be for most of these people to get a thank-you note.

And then I thought of my heavenly Father. Of all who deserved my thanks, He was the most worthy. But when was the last time I had given Him a note of thanks? I dropped to my knees. "Thank You for giving me life and loving me and spending time with me," I began.

RETTA MICHAELIS

God Sees Me

Thou God seest me. Gen. 16:13.

On a recent visit to the home of our grandchildren, my husband and I noted with pride the positive growth and development in the boys, who were now 6, 8, and 10 years of age. We noted a responsiveness and growing sense of reliability.

One day their parents were away, and we were taking care of them. They were especially good that day, helpful and obedient. The usual little tiffs between them were conspicuously absent. We commended the boys on this and noted their obedience to their parents.

The 6-year-old looked up at me with his big brown eyes and said, "Oh, we do that on weekends and when people are here." He wanted to set the record straight.

"Oh?" I queried. "And what do you do at other times?"

"Well," he replied, "sometimes we do, and sometimes we don't."

The honesty of this remark caused me to ponder. *Do I, like my grandson, do and say the right things when I'm being observed or know that my actions will impact another person's life, and at other times, when I think it won't matter, let down my guard?*

My actions and thoughts are open to my heavenly Father at all times. He knows the intent of my heart. He knows if my actions spring from true integrity of heart or from a deceitful spirit within.

"O Lord, you have searched me and you know me.
You know when I sit and when I rise;
You perceive my thoughts from afar.
You discern my going out and my lying down;
You are familiar with all my ways.
Before a word is on my tongue
You know it completely" (Ps. 139:1-4, NIV).
"You have set our iniquities before you,
Our secret sins in the light of your presence" (Ps. 90:8, NIV).

Lord, help me today to be honest with You. May all my thoughts and actions be as unto You, knowing that "Thou God seest me" at all times.

JOAN MINCHIN NEALL

Even That Year Was a Good One

Whoever loves [her husband] more than me is not worthy of me; . . .
and whoever does not take up the cross and
follow me is not worthy of me. Matt. 10:37, 38, NRSV.

I knew when my husband accepted the invitation to go into the Army as a chaplain that he would likely be in a war zone within a year. Within just six months he was already half a globe away. I had no idea what dangers he faced other than what I could surmise from the nightly casualty figures given on the news. And that was enough for constant worry.

I wasn't without challenges myself. I had a 6-month-old daughter and a 2½-year-old son. I thought it would be a terrible year, but Grandpa and Grandma were right there to help whenever I needed them. (And even those times I didn't think I needed them but probably did.) But for children, that was not the same as having daddy there to help with the good-night ritual. The war zone assignment was for 12 months. He was missing those first steps and first words and all the cute things a 2-year-old can say and do. And daddies are supposed to be there for birthdays, aren't they? And what about Christmas?

And wouldn't you know it, that was the year the Internal Revenue Service decided to audit our tax return. What next! Sometimes it all didn't seem fair.

Because I knew my husband was going to be gone 365 days, I had taken on some one-year projects. One of those was to read through one of the new Bible versions. One night as I was reading in Matthew, today's text jumped out at me. The reason my husband was not with me was that we both felt God had a special work for him to do among those facing death and chaos every day. Did I really think I needed him more than they did for this short time? For right now this was my cross. As I thought about it, however, I realized that my cross did not even begin to compare with what Jesus had suffered and done for me.

Lord, please help me to keep things in perspective. Make me worthy of what You have done for me. May today's challenges be faced with Your grace and Your power. Thank You for being with both of us that year. With You, even that year was a good one.
ARDIS DICK STENBAKKEN

Power to the Weak

He gives power to the weak, and to those who
have no might He increases strength. Isa. 40:29, NKJV.

Father, this is a tired day. I woke up discouraged and am going downhill. The pale winter sun is outside, not in here where I work. Work takes all my strength. Today bills must be paid; how much of these insufficient funds can I allot to each? My children are struggling; what can I do to help them? And when I know what to do, where will I find the energy to help them best? My heart's gas tank is empty, Father. I am running on fumes. You promised to give "power to the weak." I qualify. And You promised "increased strength" to "those who have no might." I'm Your textbook case!

Father, the load feels a little lighter already.

Father, my friend just brought me a cartoon spoofing snow and cold. You sent him, didn't You? Thank You. I needed to relax and laugh with a friend.

Father, a coworker I hardly know stopped me in the hall and asked about my children and promised to pray. Was this encounter also from You? Thank You for sending sympathy just when I needed it most.

I can't stay awake, Father. I need to go home. Please help me get home safely.

The cream of mushroom soup feels warm. Let me guess, Father. You made the half-price sale on the soup irresistible last week so it would be in the cupboard for today. I feel loved and cherished. I'm relaxed and at peace.

My son says I've been dreaming aloud, talking about sun lamps! That sleep felt so good! Thank You, Father. I feel so much better. Do You mind if I cry?

Thank You, Father, for keeping Your promises for me today. I was worried, and You brought me peace. I was empty, and You filled me. I was weary, and You gave me rest. I was weak, and You gave me strength. Thank You!

CAROL JUNE HUTCHINS HOOKER

My Psalms of Thanksgiving

*Speaking to yourselves in psalms and hymns and spiritual songs,
singing and making melody in your heart to the Lord. Eph. 5:19.*

My first psalm:

O Lord God, my Father, Creator of the mightiest atom, the tiniest delicate flower, Father of Jesus, my personal Saviour and Friend. How mysterious are Your ways, yet how loving are Your thoughts toward me.

This is Your loving daughter, who stumbles, falls down regularly, fails, and yet tries so hard to reflect Your love day by day in her life. My heart is full of humbleness at Your ever-forgiving spirit.

Thank You for this tiny seed of faith within me that is growing daily, clinging desperately to Your promises of love for me. Its tendrils reach out valiantly in trust of Your watchcare for the welfare of those I so dearly love.

Please, dear Father God, create within me the clean heart for which David prayed, that my words and acts may be a daily blessing to others. May my life be a reflection of Jesus, Your Son, my Saviour. Empty me of self and fill me with Your Spirit. Amen.

My second psalm:

Great is the Lord and greatly to be praised in the quiet of the night when stillness is upon the earth. Above me the stars glow in their pristine beauty, and the Milky Way washes the sky in majestic waves. When I look upon the constellation of Orion, my heartbeat quickens at the thought of a soon-coming Saviour.

The ground beneath my feet is frozen in the clutch of winter, but the snow glistens from the reflection of the high-riding moon. The clear wintry air fills me with exaltation as I behold the night beauty spilled from Your heavenly hand. A sudden streak of light catches my eye as a star moves swiftly through the atmosphere.

The northern lights humble me to the frozen earth in a prayer of love and gratitude to You. How great You are. How faithful You are.

Praise, all praise to You, my Father, for the nighttime and the beauty it brings to me, drawing me ever closer to You.

BETTY R. BURNETT

He Is Coming — Soon!

*This generation will certainly not pass away
until all these things have happened. Matt. 24:34, NIV.*

"Mommy, how many more days till Jesus comes?"
The question came as we checked off another day. For several months the children and I had been marking off the days on the children's special calendar and counting off the days until Daddy would come home. My husband was serving as a U.S. Army chaplain in Vietnam. My own counting and marking had started at 365. Now there were 26 more days. It was so nice to know just when Dick was coming home.

I had planned many projects to help pass the time that year and had begun many projects that needed to be done. With two small children the days were never idle, but now there was not much time left, and almost none of the projects were getting done. In desperation I had set a deadline for each day of the remaining time. There was less than one month left, and half of last month's projects still weren't completed.

Finally Dick returned. One day early. When he called from the airport, I was so excited. But nevertheless I blurted out, "You can't be home—I'm not ready yet!" After I said it I felt terrible—it really did not make it seem like he was the most important.

Which all makes me wonder just what my spiritual countdown calendar would look like if I knew how many more days till Jesus comes. God knows I have a strong tendency to procrastinate, to find things that look interesting to do first, and that if I knew just when He is returning I would put off getting ready. My guess is that all of us are a bit that way. We would probably find all sorts of worldly things that would keep us away from our spiritual growth projects until the very end. Not only is that dangerous, but we would miss all the benefits of the relationship with Jesus now, each day.

Even now there is danger of putting important spiritual things off, thinking we have more time than we really do. How fatal to say to Him, "You can't come—I'm not ready yet!"

ARDIS DICK STENBAKKEN

Biographical Sketches

Betty J. Adams is a retired teacher and the mother of three adult children. She is active in California in women's ministries, Community Services, and with her church newsletter. She has had articles published in *Guide* magazine and enjoys reading, traveling, quilting, writing, and her grandchildren. **Jan. 23.**

Priscilla Adonis, a first-time contributor, is from Cape Town, South Africa. She is a retired minister's wife, the mother of two adult children, and enjoys working with the children in her local church. Her hobbies include crocheting, flower arranging, and writing letters. **Jan. 10, Apr. 25, May 30, June 8, Aug. 13, Oct. 23, Nov. 22.**

Phyllis Alexander writes from South Dakota, where she retired after 45 years of working as a registered nurse. She is active in her local church's women's ministries department and serves as the communication secretary, chorister, pianist, church and school board member, lay evangelist, and missionary. Phyllis is a widow with two children and eight grandchildren. She enjoys writing poetry and stories, the outdoors, and witnessing. **Feb. 27, Mar. 11, May 14, Sept. 30.**

Naomi Babb is active in her church teaching a kindergarten Bible class, scheduling the children's stories for church service, and serving as a deaconess. One of her poems was in an anthology in 1994. She has been the stepparent of four wonderful young people. Among her many hobbies are sewing, crafting, drawing, painting, fund-raising, and writing. **June 12.**

Rosemary Baker, a freelance writer living in Iowa, is the author of the children's book *What Am I?* She has had contributions in *Shining Star, Kids' Stuff,* and other magazines. She is a member of the Iowa Poetry Association, is active in church and volunteer work, and enjoys working with children. Other special interests include arts, crafts, poetry, music, and painting. **Oct. 7.**

Audrey Balderstone, the mother of two sons, helps her husband operate a number of businesses in England. As president of the Adventist Business and Professional Association she is active in church and community work, runs a bimonthly home fellowship group meeting, and enjoys entertaining and flower arranging. **Jan. 18, Mar. 16, Apr. 29, Dec. 2.**

Jennifer M. Baldwin writes from Sydney, Australia, where she is the clinical risk management coordinator at Sydney Adventist Hospital. She has served in various capacities in her local church, including elder, Bible class teacher, and communication secretary. She enjoys writing and has contributed to a number of church publications. **July 20.**

Mary Barrett, a pastor's wife and the mother of two daughters, is the author of *When God Comes to Visit.* She plays an active part in her husband's ministry and particularly enjoys children's and prayer ministries. She also writes for various magazines. For relaxation Mary loves to walk, play badminton, be with friends, and make crafts. **Apr. 22, May 27.**

Moira Barthle is a wife and mother/home school teacher of two active boys. She likes walking, reading, studying, and entertaining. She has served as the women's ministries coordinator and on the executive planning committee of her church for two years. **Oct. 21.**

Pam Baumgartner is a missionary in Nicaragua. Besides nurturing her family, she supervises a project to promote family worships, counsels young people, and writes and studies for her master's degree in family relationships. **Feb. 24.**

Dawna Beausoleil, a former teacher, lives in Thunder Bay, Ontario, Canada, where her husband pastors a very large geographic district. She is a published writer, an amateur oil painter, and loves camping, crafts, and jigsaw puzzles. **Feb. 14.**

Denise Hancock Benner is a wife and mother of three preschoolers. Growing up in Indonesia gave her a love for travel, and being born into a pastor's family gave her a love for singing and music. She leads song service in her church, is in charge of the children's stories, and teaches a teens' Bible class each week. Her favorite pastimes are reading and sewing. **July 14.**

Susan L. Berridge is a registered nurse and driver's education teacher. She has a master's degree in education and teaches health occupations at a vocational school. She and her husband, Ron, enjoy living in a rural setting with their children. They have four daughters ranging in age from preschool to college. Her hobbies include painting, gardening, outdoor activities, and most of all being a mom. **Jan. 15.**

Annie B. Best is a retired public school teacher. She enjoys listening to music and shopping for her three grandchildren. Annie has worked in the cradle roll and kindergarten departments of her church. **Feb. 22.**

Nancy Bezant is a blind Christian woman with a spouse and four children. She is an active 4-H leader promoting environmental care, community service, and secret good deeds among the children. Her interests include writing, growing plants, and learning new things. **July 28.**

Ann Blandford works as an assistant to her pastor-husband. She is a freelance writer whose interests range from music to gems and minerals, birdwatching, and cooking. She spent six years in mission service, establishing the first women's ministries department in Hong Kong and Taiwan. She now directs a women's prayer meeting in her retirement community. **Dec. 7.**

Dottie O. Bowen is a widowed housewife and mother of two who lives at Pisgah Estates in North Carolina. She and her husband of 53 years worked and lived in Panama and Central America for 31 years. She is actively involved in prison ministry. **Feb. 7, Mar. 10, Oct. 22.**

Joyce Willes Brown-Carper is a professional musician, former elementary school teacher, and a freelance writer of children's stories and articles published in the *Adventist Review*. A graduate of Walla Walla College, she holds a B.Mus.Ed. and practiced law for several years, but is now pursuing her dream as a full-time writer. Her husband, Gil, is a portrait artist. She has two daughters, Elizabeth and Helena. **Dec. 17, Dec. 19.**

Rose Marie Brown is a retired schoolteacher. She is involved in her local church as head deaconess, librarian, and correspondence and bulletin board coordinator. Rose enjoys crafts and is currently creating craft kits for use in Vacation Bible School programs. **May 17.**

Betty R. Burnett, from "Charlevoix the Beautiful," Michigan, particularly enjoys the beauty of the area in which she lives. Her greatest passion is her family, and second, reading. Well-turned phrases make her glow. **July 25, Oct. 26, Dec. 30.**

Andrea A. Bussue was born on the Caribbean island of Nevis. She holds a master's degree in education and has been an educator for more than 10 years. Presently she works at a special education school in Washington, D.C. She has been a superintendent and children's choir director at her local church in Maryland. Andrea loves children and enjoys reading, traveling, sewing, cooking, and meeting people. **Sept. 11, Nov. 15.**

Luan Cadogan lives in Toronto, Ontario, Canada, with her husband and two children. She is pursuing a master's degree in worship and liturgy at Ontario Theological Seminary, and is also the children's program coordinator of her church. **Aug. 11.**

Sheryl A. Calhoun is a homemaker, wife, mother of three young daughters, and registered nurse. Her home is in West Virginia; however, the family is on temporary assignment in England. Her interests include cooking, sewing, and music. **May 26, Nov. 18, Dec. 6.**

Margaret I. Campbell has worked as an accountant, teacher, and registrar. She and her retired minister-husband have two daughters and two granddaughters. She enjoys reading, poetry, gathering materials for scrapbooks, and keeping in touch with family. **June 21.**

Terri Casey lives in southern California with her husband of 20 years. They have two children and two grandchildren. She and her husband operate an excavation business. She is the safety officer for several medical practices and teaches a Bible class for youth at her local church. Terri enjoys writing, walking, quilting, reading, and storytelling. **Dec. 5.**

Fonda Cordis Chaffee has a doctorate in educational administration and undergraduate degrees in dietetics, specializing in food systems management. She is a teacher, the mother of two children, and a widow. She has served for over 40 years in denominational service and enjoys traveling, playing Scrabble, crocheting, and gardening. **Feb. 25.**

Beth Vollmer Chagas is a pastor's wife in Brazil and enjoys her work as a translator. She writes for two denominational publications in Brazil. Mother of two children, 9 and 6, she makes time for walking, sewing, and writing. **Nov. 11.**

Shari Chamberlain is a chaplain at Ukiah Valley Medical Center in California. Answering a call into ministry in the early seventies, she has also worked as a pastor and health evangelist. Shari's hobbies include traveling, biking, gardening, and visiting with friends. **Apr. 24.**

Lyndelle Chiomenti is an editor for Bible lesson materials. She is married and enjoys writing, reading, crocheting, antiques, history, water gardening, and biblical studies. **Dec. 3.**

Helen Christian works in a laboratory doing quality control work. She has four children and two grandchildren. Her favorite activities are stamp collecting, working with young children, gardening, bush walking, and reading. **Jan. 29.**

Birol Christo is a retired schoolteacher who also worked as an office secretary and statistician. She lives with her retired husband in Hosur, India. Birol is the mother of five grown children and enjoys spending her free time gardening, sewing, and making craft items to finance her project for homeless children. **May 31.**

Alberta Bennett Ciccarelli is a published freelance photographer and writer. She and her husband recently retired to the central California coast. They have four married children and three grandchildren. Her hobbies are traveling and butterfly gardening, and she enjoys spending time with her grandchildren and assisting with church activities. **July 4, Aug. 30.**

Doreen Kitto Clark, a retired teacher and executive secretary, lives with her husband in Fresno, California. Her last teaching position was at Maui Community College on Molokai island. Traveling, writing, and reading are leisure activities she enjoys. Church and community service projects take up much of her time, as well as caring for her small great-grandson. **July 7.**

Roberta Franklin Clausen graduated with elementary education and English degrees. She works as a certified childbirth educator. She serves on two church ministry teams and edits newsletters for each. She has two young daughters. Her passions include her husband and children, friendships, reading, writing, and music. **July 21, Sept. 10, Dec. 4.**

Clareen Colclesser is a retired nurse. After being married for 54 years, she became a widow in 1994. She is blessed with two grown children, six grandchildren, and four great-grandchildren. She enjoys staying active in her church, poring through her stacks of interior decorating books, working crossword puzzles, and writing letters and short stories. **Feb. 4, May 19, Oct. 6, Dec. 14.**

Kay Collins has been happily married for 32 years. For 24 of these she and her husband have been a gospel-medical team in evangelism all over North America. She is a registered nurse by profession and gives health presentations, and is a Bible instuctor and a soloist. Personal and public evangelism are her greatest joys. **May 3, June 29.**

Lynn Best Connelly, a housewife and mother of two, lives near Springfield, Illinois. She holds a master's degree in education, has taught at the college level, and has also worked as an accountant for the state of Illinois. Lynn enjoys reading, music, playing tennis, exercising, and spending time with family and friends. **June 30.**

Barbara Couden is a marriage, family, and child counselor and directs counseling centers on two college campuses. She teaches in the School of Public Health at Loma Linda University in California. Barbara has published a number of anecdotal and professional articles, and enjoys reading, traveling, and music. **Mar. 15, Aug. 19, Oct. 17, Nov. 2.**

Judy Coulston is in private practice as a nutritionist in northern California. She hosted and coproduced a weekly half-hour television program and has been teaching pathophysiology at the University of Phoenix. She enjoys traveling and presenting health seminars. **Aug. 23, Oct. 12.**

Eva Alice Covey, mother, grandmother, and great-grandmother, was a schoolteacher before her marriage. She enjoys teaching the adolescent children in her church and is the women's ministries coordinator. She enjoys music, raising flowers, poetry, and reading. **Apr. 13.**

Celia Mejia Cruz has been the women's ministries devotional book project manager and administrative secretary in the Department of Women's Ministries at the General Conference of Seventh-day Adventists, Silver Spring, Maryland, for the past six years. A pastor's wife, local church elder, mother of five children, and grandmother of one, she enjoys people, presenting seminars, and preaching. Some of her other interests are reading, writing, dogs, and collecting Siamese cat figurines and plates. **Jan. 20, July 3, Aug. 3.**

Noeline Cutts is the mother of five and a grandmother living in New Zealand. She has written and illustrated two books of poetry and is working on a third book. She works as an accounts clerk and is a distinguished member of the International Society of Poetry, and has been nominated for the Hall of Fame on the Internet for her poem on Creation. Her hobbies are portrait painting in oils, gardening, and minding her young granddaughter. **Feb. 26.**

Alla Czerkasij was born in Ukraine but lived for eight years in Germany and nine in Sweden before moving to the United States in 1960. She and her husband have three adult children and are retired near Collegedale, Tennessee. She enjoys reading, gardening, and singing in the church choir. **Sept. 19.**

Becky Dada, a first-time contributor, writes from Ibadan, Nigeria, where she is the principal of a secondary school. Becky is the mother of four children and a pastor's wife. A published writer, she teaches adult literacy classes in her community, is involved in her local church, and is the part-time director of women's ministries for western Nigeria. Her hobbies include reading, writing, evangelism, and training lay evangelists. **Jan. 28, Mar. 23, May 28, Sept. 21.**

Djane Meiri Pereira Dantas, a Brazilian, was an educator for 12 years before serving as a school administrator in São Paulo, Brazil. She enjoys teaching children, reading, writing, playing the piano, and traveling. Her biggest dream is to write children's books. **Jan. 14.**

Jayne Doswell Darby, retired after 37 years of teaching and secretarial work, has returned to work as an administrative secretary at an academy in Pennsylvania. A local church elder, she enjoys reading, crocheting, knitting, and playing the piano. Her articles have apperared in the *Adventist Review, Guide, Message,* and her local newspaper. **Jan. 17.**

Joella Brown Davis and her husband, Bob, have one grown son and two teenagers whom she is home-schooling. She enjoys reading, writing, painting, baking bread, and quiet life out in the country. **Aug. 31.**

Lynn Marie Davis is a sign language interpreter in the Georgia school system. Facilitating empowerment workshops is one of her favorite pastimes. "Steps to Making Your Dreams Come True" is her favorite workshop. Other hobbies include walking, hospitality, cooking, meeting new people, studying languages, writing, photography, and reading. **July 13.**

Ruth F. Davis lives in Huntsville, Alabama, with her husband. They have three grown children and three granddaughters. She chairs the Family and Consumer Sciences Department at Oakwood College and is an ordained elder of the college church. Ruth is active in other church and professional organizations. She also served as a missionary teacher in Ghana and Liberia, West Africa. **June 5.**

Wanda Grimes Davis is a staff chaplain at a hospital in Portland, Oregon. Preaching, teaching, and facilitating small groups are among her favorite things. She presents seminars and preaches throughout the country. She serves in her local church as an elder and Bible class teacher. Wanda and her husband have three children who provide inspiration for many of her sermons. **Apr. 28, June 23.**

Marjorie Davison is a retired nurse living in the United Kingdom. She is a widow and has two children, four grandchildren, and one great-grandchild. **May 29.**

Hilda Cyrelli de Souza writes from Brazil. She and her minister-husband are the parents of three young adults. Hulda, a teacher for 27 years, has authored several textbooks and articles in Brazil. She is a seminar presenter for women's ministries, family ministries, and education. Her leisure activities include walking, nature hikes, reading, embroidery, and music. **Feb. 12, Mar. 6.**

Candance Graves DeVore, the mother of two teenagers, is a dorm mom at Laurelbrooke Academy in Tennessee, where her husband has served as boys' dean for five years. She has written several articles. **Dec. 9.**

Brenda Forbes Dickerson is a wife and mother of two young children. She enjoys writing, gardening, sewing, and helping with women's and children's ministries in her local church. **Apr. 14, July 31.**

Laurie Dixon-McClanahan, a retired Bible instructor, is a prolific letter writer. She enjoys the culinary arts, quilting, hiking, and people. She volunteers at a hospital in North Carolina, and as a chaplain in Florida. **Feb. 3, Oct. 8, Nov. 25.**

Jodi Eulene Dodson (Eulene Borton), the mother of three children, has composed and published music ("My God Is a Real God"), and with her sister recorded gospel albums. She was the director and composer of Scripture music for The Sowers. She turned from God for 15 years, but He revealed His love to her through the power of the gospel. She has returned to write, publish, and share her story, *I Just Can't Do It, God!* **Mar. 4, Apr. 18, May 9, Aug. 15, Nov. 10, Dec. 18.**

Leonie Donald is a first-time contributor. She writes from Brisbane, Australia, where she and her husband have lived for 10 years. She loves the climate there after having moved there from New Zealand. **Sept. 28, Dec. 10.**

Nelly Piagentine do Prado Souza and her minister-husband and two children live in Brazil. She is a teacher and is involved in women's ministries in Brazil. **July 8.**

Ruti Rodrigues de Carvalho Garcia dos Santos is a public employee in Brazil. She and her husband have one son. Ruti is the women's ministries coordinator for her local church and has had several ariticles and poems published in magazines. **May 22.**

Goldie Down is a freelance writer living in Australia with her minister-husband, both former missionaries to India for 20 years. They have six children and 12 grandchildren. She has had 21 books published, including a creative writing textbook to be used in government schools. She assists her husband writing and editing a 20-page monthly archaeological journal and a 40 page bimonthly archaeological magazine. She also enjoys teaching and preaching. **July 26.**

April Dunnett is returning to lecturing in literature, fine arts, and communications after three years as a gardener. She graduated with a national diploma in horticulture in 1996 and still loves gardening, arts, crafts, handbells, books, nature, and the countryside. **Feb. 28, May 12.**

Joy Dustow lives in a retirement village near Brisbane, Australia, with her husband. She has had a varied educational career in Australia, Fiji, New Guinea, and Thailand. She takes an active part in the church and social activities of the village. **Sept. 23.**

Mary C. Edmister, a widow after 18 years as a military wife, now lives in Riverside, California. She is a retired real estate agent who is now a freelance writer. **Sept. 6.**

Suzanne Elliott has been married for 46 years. She and her husband have six children and 11 grandchildren. Although retired, they have started a new church in Maryland that keeps them busy. Suzanne enjoys writing poetry and painting, and helps people by listening. **Apr. 16.**

Jocelyn Fay is a copy editor at the Review and Herald Publishing Association in Hagerstown, Maryland. She enjoys genealogical research and collects Cat's Meow Village special collection pieces and antique blue-and-white china. Her newest pastime is learning more about the mid-Atlantic states. **Apr. 19.**

Cristina Fernandez, a secretary, teacher, and counselor, was born in Chile. She has dedicated her life to helping young people, adults, and families through her counseling ministry. **Aug. 25.**

Mercy M. Ferrer and her husband have recently been transferred from Cyprus to Moscow, Russia. They are the parents of two young adults. Mercy enjoys traveling with her husband, reading, cooking, and photography. **Feb. 17, Apr. 2, Sept. 9.**

Valeria Fidelia is the health and temperance, children's ministries, and women's ministries director for the Middle East Union of Seventh-day Adventists in Cyprus. A performing musician, she enjoys being part of the music scene in Cyprus whenever work commitments permit. Her greatest joy comes in singing for her Lord. **May 25.**

Edith Fitch taught in elementary schools for 41 years. She compiled four volumes of supplementary helps for grades 1-4 Bible classes for church schools in Canada and has been involved in research for church and school histories. Her hobbies include traveling, writing, cooking, hardanger, and calligraphy. **Mar. 9, Apr. 27.**

Myrna Forbes is a first-time contributor from Nebraska. She enjoys her children and grandchildren, her home, and her church. **Apr. 5.**

Heide Ford is the assistant editor of *Women of Spirit,* a Christian women's magazine. She is a minister's wife living in Maryland and holds a master's degree in counseling. Her interests include reading, learning about different cultures, kayaking, and the outdoors. **June 13, Sept. 26.**

Jennifer Gill Fordham is an elementary school teacher in Berrien Springs, Michigan, where her husband is attending the seminary at Andrews University. She is a recent graduate of Oakwood College and enjoys reading, singing, writing, and reciting poetry. **Nov. 17.**

Sari Karina Fordham is a first-time contibutor to the women's devotional book project. She is a native of Finland who served the Lord as a missionary in East Africa for nine years with her husband and two daughters. She loves to walk and to sing in the shower. Now retired from teaching, she writes from Austell, Georgia. **Dec. 25.**

Edna Maye Gallington lives in Riverside, California, and works in communications. She is a graduate of La Sierra University and has taken public relations studies at the University of California at Riverside. She enjoys playing the piano, creative writing, hiking, and working in her church. **Feb. 13, May 24, July 9.**

Vicki Gallon-Clark is one of four principals of a Christian human resources consultant firm, AGAPE, based in Hartford, Connecticut. She is also a wife and the mother of two children, ages 19 and 6. Vicki loves to read and write. She is also involved in many church and civic activities. **Apr. 10, Oct. 14.**

Evelyn Glass is a wife, mother, grandmother, and farmer. She heads the Women's Ministries Department for the Mid-America Union of Seventh-day Adventists and serves as an elder and clerk at her church. Her interests include folk painting, refinishing furniture, public speaking, and writing for local and state newspapers, as well as Christian publications. **Nov. 28.**

Carmen O. Gonzalez writes from the central New York area. She enjoys people and is the singles ministries coordinator for the New York Conference of Seventh-day Adventists and is actively involved in other ministries. Carmen has one grown son. **Oct. 4, Nov. 24.**

Kathryn Gordon is a medical social worker in a dialysis unit in Saint Joseph, Missouri. She enjoys gardening, windsurfing, skiing, floor hockey, and ballet. **July 6.**

Ellie Green is president of E. Green & Associates, a consulting firm. A prolific writer and full-time lecturer, she enjoys speaking at Christian women's retreats, doing oil, watercolor, and chalk painting, as well as crocheting and knitting. Her son is an attorney, her daughter is a nurse, and her husband is a retired NASA rocket scientist. **May 16.**

Christine Greene lives with her family in Regina, Saskatchewan, Canada. At the time of writing she was a 12-year-old seventh grader. She enjoys writing, skiing, and swimming and is active in her church youth programs. **Nov. 16.**

Glenda-mae Greene is the assistant vice president for student services at Andrews University in Michigan. This third-generation educator has taught at all levels. She enjoys many phases of church work—speaking, teaching, helping. In her spare time she revels in the beauty of nature on her daily walks. Glenda-mae is constantly amazed by the power of the word, especially God's word in the Gospels. **Mar. 26, Apr. 26, June 14, Oct. 10.**

Norma Greenidge works in the Cataloging and Reference departments of the James White Library at Andrews University in Michigan. She is the mother of two children and is a grandmother. Norma is an elder in her church and is involved in women's ministries. At the time of this writing she was completing her Ph.D. in educational psychology. **Mar. 28.**

Donna J. Habenicht teaches child psychology at Andrews University in Michigan. She coordinates the younger Bible school divisions for the campus church and frequently conducts workshops and seminars for parents and teachers. She loves to read, play the piano and organ, travel, and play with her grandchildren. A writer for religious magazines, Donna is also the author of *How to Help Your Child Really Love Jesus.* **Oct. 29.**

Elaine Hagele's life is a journey that has included teaching high school living skills and currently, as a C.P.A., working as an auditor. On her journey she has lived in three Canadian provinces, three American states, Guam, India, and Japan. Young people are her passion. Flower arranging is her hobby. **Aug. 5.**

Dessa Weisz Hardin is a wife and mother of three adult children and two sons-in-law, one French and one British. She likes to travel, read, study languages, and work with children. She works in both public and church school reading programs and chairs her local church school board. **July 30.**

Judith Warren Hawkins writes from Tallahassee, Florida, where she is a county judge. Her husband is a college administrator, and they have one college-age son. She has served or assisted in almost every local church office. **June 20.**

Ursula M. Hedges is a secondary school teacher/administrator, interior designer, and church elder. Born of missionary parents in India, she and her Australian principal-husband have given 10 years in mission service in the Pacific, as well as many in Australia and New Zealand. Ursula has published books, stories, and articles. Other hobbies include reading, producing dramas, writing, sewing, and cooking. Family brings her great pleasure. **July 24, Oct. 28, Nov. 27.**

Eleanor L. Hewes and her husband spent 15 years as missionaries in Zimbabwe and Kenya. She is a retired church school teacher and executive secretary. She has two married daughters and five grandchildren. Her hobbies are soul winning, entertaining, spending time with her grandchildren, and church activities. **Mar. 22.**

Synnova Hill is a senior majoring in social work at Southern Adventist University in Tennessee and plans on going on for her master's degree. In her free time Synnova enjoys hiking, white-water rafting, and reading. **Sept. 12.**

Jo Ann Hilton and her husband have two teenagers. She graduated from the Florida Hospital School of Practical Nursing in 1978. Her hobbies are crafts, writing, nature (especially beachcombing), and bluegrass gospel music. **Mar. 8, Sept. 17, Oct. 16, Nov. 6.**

Roxy Hoehn writes from Topeka, Kansas. She may not know many people on her family tree, but she delights in being a member of the family of God. She is the director of women's ministries for the Kansas-Nebraska Conference of Seventh-day Adventists. **Feb. 20, July 18.**

Carol June Hutchins Hooker is a community health nurse in Maryland. She is married to a math teacher and is the mother of two teen-agers. She enjoys sewing, singing in the church choir, and seeing how God leads people. **Dec. 29.**

Tamyra Horst is the women's ministries director for the Pennsylvania Conference of Seventh-day Adventists. She and her husband have two sons. She has authored a book, *How to Hug a Heart,* a women's ministries manual, and articles. Tamyra enjoys speaking, writing, walking, camping, hiking, biking as a family (though she watches from shore while they kayak) and spending time with her friends. **Feb. 21, July 2, Sept. 4, Oct. 3.**

Lorraine Hudgins has worked with her minister-husband at Faith for Today, the Voice of Prophecy, and the General Conference of Seventh-day Adventists. She is a published writer, author of two books, mother of five grown children, and an elder in her local church. Her poems and articles have appeared in various religious publications. **Apr. 15, May 5, June 4, July 17, Aug. 28, Oct. 31.**

Barbara Huff is the wife of a church administrator, the mother of two adult children, and a grandmother. She is a freelance writer and works as an administrative assistant at the Euro-Asia Division of Seventh-day Adventists in Moscow, Russia. In her job she helps with communication between the mission field and the homeland. **May 23, July 10.**

Carolyn Hurst, single mother of two teenagers, lives in Berrien Springs, Michigan, where she is secretary to the Graduate Dean at Andrews University. Her hobbies include music, reading, and needlework. **Sept. 5.**

Anita L. Jacobs and her husband both work at the Review and Herald Publishing Association in Maryland, where Anita serves as assistant editor of *Listen* and *Winner* magazines. She has three grown children and has been involved in children's ministries for many years. Anita's hobbies include quilting and cross-stitching. **Apr. 8.**

Verena Jaggi-Rechsteiner writes from Blantyre, Malawi, where she and her physician-husband are serving as missionaries. They previously served as missionaries in India. They have two young-adult sons. Verena is originally from Switzerland and speaks German, French, English, and Italian fluently. She is a German language teacher and medical technical assistant. Her hobbies are teaching, reading, writing, and playing the violin and organ. **Sept. 2, Oct. 9.**

Judy Haupt Jagitsch writes from central Illinois, where she and her husband live in retirement. They have five children and four grandchildren. Judy has worked in all the levels of the children's ministries in her local church and is presently the church clerk. Her top priority hobby is the grandchildren. **Sept. 27.**

Wilma C. Jardine, originally from Panama, is retired and living in North Carolina. Mother of six children and grandmother of seven, she is a literature evangelist for the Carolina Conference of Seventh-day Adventists. She is also a jail ministry volunteer at the county jail and teaches a Bible class at her church. She loves to read, sing about the Lord, and travel. **Dec. 11.**

Marianette Johnston is a homemaker at heart. She has served with her husband for 46 years in pastoring, college teaching, evangelism, and church administration. They have three children and four grandsons. She hopes to find time for quilting and cross-stitching. **July 16.**

Margaret Kamara is married with two daughters. She is the loan administration officer at a bank in Sierra Leone. Margaret loves children and is a children's Bible school teacher and Dorcas leader at her church in Freetown. **Feb. 19.**

Faith Keeney, a wife and retired accountant, secretary, and pilot, has flown many missions over the past 26 years into Mexico to bring physicians, dentists, and other health-care workers to isolated villages that have no other care. She loves reading, poetry, painting, and hiking. **Mar. 17.**

Wilma Burton King is a teacher who is currently staying home to be with her two children. She and her pastor-husband live in Wichita, Kansas, among her Noah's ark collection and with her son's animals, which make it seem like a real Noah's ark. **Aug. 7.**

Beverly Sawyer Kinsey currently resides in Greensboro, North Carolina, where she was born. She was raised by her father from the age of 7, because of the untimely death of her mother. Beverly is a wife, mother of one, and an employee of the county government. Her interests include singing, reading, motivating, and being a "new" grandmother. **Nov. 3.**

Helena Klingman is a retired nurse living in Rydöbruk, Sweden. Although she grew up in a Christian home, she didn't care about religion until she fell in love with Jesus 10 years ago. She has always been interested in nature. She likes to read, write, and knit sweaters for an orphanage in Romania. **Dec. 8.**

Eileen Tejada Knight is a clerk for a volunteer organization at a hospital in Delaware. She and her husband of 25 years have three grown children. Church duties include communication/women's ministries director and personal ministries secretary. Karen has written three plays for church programs. **Mar. 19.**

Patty Knittel is a part-time assistant office manager in Oregon, where she lives with her husband and two children. She chairs the Oregon Conference women's retreat committee and is the women's ministries coordinator for her local church. She has led a weekly Bible study for the past three years and assists another woman in jointly publishing a monthly newsletter for her church. Patty enjoys tennis, golf, reading, and writing. **Oct. 2, Nov. 29.**

Hepzibah G. Kore is a minister's wife in Bangalore, India. She is the coordinator for women's ministries and Shepherdess International, as well as the director for the Children's Ministries and Family Life departments for the South India Union of Seventh-day Adventists. She has a son and a daughter. Hepzibah enjoys reading and working with women. **Nov. 8.**

RosaLynda Kosini, known by her friends as "Gina," writes from culturally colorful San Antonio, Texas. She dabbles in lyrics, poetry, humor, and inspirational pieces. **Aug. 22.**

Betty Kossick and her husband live in Cadillac, Michigan. As a newspaper journalist, she writes a popular column, Faces in the Crowd. Betty cofounded the Dayton, Ohio, Christian Scribes in 1979, serving as the group's first president, and continues to be a long-distance member. She is active in her church and in Toastmasters International. **Jan. 3, Feb. 10, May 11, Sept. 3.**

Winnie Kurian has been a teacher for the past 25 years and loves working with children. She is now a homemaker living in Bangalore, India. Winnie and her husband have three grown children. She enjoys nature, reading, and baking. **Jan. 6, Aug. 26.**

Kay Kuzma is a wife, mother of three, and the president of Family Matters in Tennessee, a media ministry providing services to families. A teacher for 25 years, she now has a syndicated daily radio feature, a weekly television broadcast, and a free quarterly newspaper, *Family Times.* Kay has written more than a dozen books. **Jan. 5, June 16.**

Eileen E. Lantry writes from northern Idaho. She is a librarian, teacher, homemaker, minister's wife, Bible instructor, and grandmother. She and her husband spent 16 years as missionaries in Southeast Asia. Eileen has authored 16 books and many articles, and loves nature, gardening, hiking, and cross-country skiing. **Jan. 25, Feb. 8, Mar. 20, June 17, Sept. 18.**

Gina Lee is a freelance writer with more than 450 stories, articles, and poems in print. She teaches a writing workshop for the city of Burbank, California, and works part-time in the local library. **Apr. 20, May 8, Aug. 16, Oct. 11.**

Irene Wakeham Lee is a retired teacher and missionary to the Philippines. **Jan. 22.**

Gerita Liebelt writes from Pueblo, Colorado. She is a registered nurse, pastor's wife, and homemaker. She has written a book, and is a youth and Vacation Bible School leader in her local church. Her devotional first appeared in *The Heart of the Home,* a newsletter for stay-at-home moms. **Mar. 31.**

June E. Loor, a retired registered nurse and minister's wife, writes from her home on top of their favorite western North Carolina mountain ridge. The Loors have two children and five grandchildren. She enjoys people, her grandchildren, mountains, camping at the ocean, traveling, and home decorating. **May 18.**

Pat Madsen lives in California, but does quite a bit of traveling. She likes gardening, water color painting, health, music, and arts and crafts. She has had submissions in previous women's devotionals books and is a former editor-in-chief of her high school paper. Pat is a Sabbath school superintendent and teaches a class after church. **Dec. 20.**

Ann Maloney-Halim and her husband live in Lincoln, Nebraska, where she home-schools her two children and is a full-time stay-at-home mom. Ann is the editor/producer of a newsletter, *The Heart of the Home*, for stay-at-home moms. She serves her local church as an elder, and enjoys biking, camping, reading, and sewing. She is doing an independent study course on nature-opathy. **Feb. 5, May 21.**

Philippa Marshall writes from England, where she is a retired nurse. She is also trained in relaxation and massage therapy. She is the mother of three, grandmother of six. She is the women's ministries coordinator and clerk for her local church. Her interests include walking her dog, writing for Christian magazines, visiting family, art, and music. **Jan. 30, Mar. 7, June 2.**

Sharon Marshall-Randall, nurse/counselor, wife, mother of two grown children, and grandmother, is also the hospitality director and codirector of her church's Sunday soup kitchen. She is also active in women's ministries, family life ministries, and counseling young women. She writes from New Jersey. **May 20, Nov. 30.**

Peggy Mason lives in Wales with her husband and one of her two adult sons. She is an English teacher and writer whose hobbies include growing, drying, and arranging flowers, cooking, sewing, and reading. She is a pianist/composer and enjoys working for her church and community. **Jan. 13, May 7.**

Mary Maxson has been in pastoral ministry with her husband for 25 years and has her own "Kleenex ministry." They have two young adult children. She enjoys traveling and understanding other cultures. Mary enjoys volunteering as a hospital chaplain, reading, walking, and music, and her favorite pastimes are arranging silk flowers and working in her flower garden. She loves popcorn. **Apr. 17.**

Wilma McClarty, widowed in 1997, chairs the English Department at Southern Adventist University in Tennessee. She is the mother of two. She is a public speaker and writer who has received many honors and awards, including the Sears-Roebuck Teaching Excellence and Campus Leadership Award for 1991. **Jan. 2, Aug. 27.**

Marge Lyberg McNeilus is the bookkeeper for her husband's business, McNeilus Auto and Truck Parts. She is also a homemaker, mother of four children, and has four grandchildren whom she enjoys immensely. Her hobbies include photography, crafts, writing, music, and traveling. **Dec. 22.**

Retta Michaelis writes from Loma Linda, California, where she lives with her health educator-husband and two teenage daughters. She works part-time as a medical technologist at the Loma Linda University Medical Center Blood Bank, and is active in her church and community. Her interests include reading, writing, Bible study, and spending time with her family. **July 29, Aug. 18, Oct. 15, Nov. 26, Dec. 26.**

Lonna Tachenko Milburn teaches at the University of North Dakota and serves as a consultant for the U.S. Government in Russia and the Ukraine. The mother of two 7-year-old girls, she has worked on numerous church-related projects in Russia and the Ukraine since 1992. **Sept. 24.**

Marcia Mollenkopf is a retired schoolteacher. She has served on her church school board, given Bible studies, and been a teacher and superintendent in her local church. Bird-watching, crafts, and bread sculpturing are among her special interests. **Apr. 11.**

Virlys Moller, an English teacher in Washington State, has taught in four academies since she began her career in 1970. She also enjoys gardening. Her specialty is growing roses. Virlys wrote this piece while attending a writing workshop in July, 1995. **Aug. 9.**

Nilma Pimentel Monteiro and her pastor-husband and three children live in Fortaleza, Brazil. Nilma is active in women's ministries and child evangelism and is employed as a secretary. She enjoys gardening, flowers, music, and cooking. **Jan. 7.**

Barbara Smith Morris is executive director of a nonprofit retirement center and served for seven years as a Tennessee delegate representing housing and services needs of the low-income elderly. Active in both her church and community, she is a presentor of seminars on elder life issues. Barbara has four children and six grandsons. She writes a daily devotional for the retirement center and loves to be surrounded by people of all ages. **Feb. 11.**

Lillian Musgrave and her family have made northern California their home for more than 35 years. She has been involved with the HIV Spiritual Support ministry for more than five years and leads a parents' support group. As time allows, she enjoys writing (including poetry), music, church responsibilities, and family activities that involve her four grandchildren. **Jan. 4.**

Leila Ribeiro Nadaline and her minister-husband live in Curitiba, Brazil, with their two children. She is a secretary who enjoys helping her husband conduct marriage seminars. She uses her free time to read and to cultivate friendships. **Apr. 23.**

Joan Minchin Neall was born in Australia, lived in England, and now makes her home in Tennessee. She is a registered nurse, and she and her pastor-husband have four children and eight grandchildren. She is the district women's ministries coordinator for her area. She enjoys nature, sewing, journaling, and her grandchildren. **Mar. 25, Apr. 9, Dec. 27.**

Joyce Neergaard is a nurse who, with her husband, has lived several years in the Middle East. She has a special interest in improving the health of mothers and children. She is studying for her master's degree in public health at Loma Linda University in California. Besides learning new things, she likes to hike, cycle, read nontextbooks, write nonresearch materials, travel, and sing. **Nov. 13.**

Ann Elaine Nelson, a retired elementary teacher, has written a book,

Puzzled Parents. She now helps her husband in his business. They live in Michigan and have four children who have blessed them with 11 grandchildren. Active in church work as assistant superintendent for Sabbath school and teacher of the teen class, her favorite activities are music, sewing, traveling, photography, and creating memories with her grandchildren. **Dec. 23.**

Elaine Norman writes from Nashville, Tennessee, where she and her husband and two teenage children live. She is a secretary and enjoys reading, cooking, baking bread, traveling, walking and exercising, music, and computers. She enjoys teaching Bible-based weight-loss programs and has done several for church groups. **Aug. 24, Oct. 30.**

Mabel Rollins Norman resided in Avon Park, Florida, until she passed away February 6, 1998. She has been published in a number of magazines, several newspapers, and two women's devotional books. She and her husband taught a biweekly in-prison Bible class. She was known for her encouraging cards and letters. **Apr. 12, June 24, Aug. 12, Sept. 13, Nov. 19.**

Martha Montgomery Odom, a published author, is a retired teacher and secretary living in Collegedale, Tennessee. She and her missionary husband served 17 years in Spain, Panama, and the Philippines. She has served in her local church as head deaconess, elder, superintendent, and teacher. **July 19.**

Edna May Olsen has lived in England almost seven years since her husband's retirement from the United States Army. Her three daughters and granddaughters live in California. She is actively involved in her small church and is a published writer. Her hobbies include reading, writing, and hiking with the local Ramblers. **Mar. 13.**

Cathy O'Malley has 20 years of experience working with people as teacher, sales consultant, trainer, and workshop director. Her hobbies are reading, painting, and writing poetry. She enjoys living in the Washington, D.C., metropolitan area with her husband and two children on a four-year posting from Ottawa, Ontario, Canada. **Oct. 20.**

Rose Otis, formerly the director of women's ministries for the General Conference of Seventh-day Adventists, is now the director of women's ministries and vice president for ministries for the North American Division of Seventh-day Adventists in Silver Spring, Maryland. She began the women's devotional book project and edited the first five. She enjoys water sports with her family, writing, and being home. **Mar. 21, Oct. 27.**

Jemima Dollosa Orillosa and her husband and two teenage daughters live in Silver Spring, Maryland, where she works as a secretary in the secretariat department of the General Conference of Seventh-day Adventists. She enjoys making friends and telling them about God's love and loves to write articles based on her experiences. She enjoys walking, playing tennis, visiting friends, and is a lover of nature. **June 28.**

Hannele Ottschofski is a pastor's wife and mother of four daughters. Born in Finland, she grew up in Sweden and England and she married a German minister. They have been involved in ministry in Germany and central Africa. She enjoys music, reading, sewing, and writing. **Feb. 9.**

Ofelia A. Pangan, who helps her pastor-husband, worked in Laos and Thailand for 21 years and in Ontario, Canada, for almost 10 years. She taught school for 28 of those years. She is the mother of three children and has six grandchildren. Ofelia loves visiting her grandchildren, gardening, reading, traveling, and playing Scrabble. **Jan. 8, Mar. 18, Sept. 22, Oct. 13.**

Revel Papaioannou and her retired minister-husband live in Veroia, Greece, the biblical town of Berea. They have four sons and four grandchildren. She is involved in teaching Bible seminars, teaching English, and working with the youth at her church and wherever else she is needed. Her hobbies include fell walking, aerobics, stamp and coin collecting, and gardening. **July 11.**

K. Elaine Pascual is a registered nurse who writes from California. She recently earned a master's degree in public health, specializing in maternal and child health. She likes cats, children, and writing (including poetry). **May 4.**

Eunice Peverini writes from Thousand Oaks, California. She and her husband, the speaker/director of La Voz de la Esperanza radio ministry, have three children and six grandchildren. Eunice enjoys community work, interior decorating, flower arrangement, crafts, gardening, sewing, reading, and accompanying her husband in his ministry. **Feb. 23.**

Kathleen Stearman Pflugrad and her husband have pitched their tent in spots as diverse as Guam's beaches and Alaska's mountains. They currently live in Grayling, Michigan. She enjoys reading, listening, volunteer projects, and information collecting. **Aug. 29.**

Alice Heath Prive is the mother of three children. She recently moved to Los Angeles to work on a Ph.D. in ethics and reeligion at the University of Southern California. Good times include being with friends—old and new— and sneaking some time to read "just for fun." **June 25.**

Jeanne d'Harimala Rasoanindrainy writes from Mauritius in the Indian Ocean, where she is the registrar, librarian, and secretary at a seminary. She has had three books published and is working on a fourth one, an educational book for young parents. She is the family life director at her local church and conducts prayer meetings for the children on Wednesdays. Her hobbies include reading, writing stories for her grandsons, and gardening. **Mar. 12, Oct. 25.**

Ruth Rawson and her husband live in the country town of Albury on the Murray River in New South Wales. She is the mother of two children and teaches part-time at a Christian college. Ruth is actively involved in community work and enjoys crafts, writing, reading, camping, bush-walking, cross-country skiing and being with people. **Apr. 3.**

Judith Redman is a wife and the mother of two girls, ages 6 and 9. She works as a child-care giver in her home and is family life leader for her local church. Her interests include crafts, caravaning, and playing squash. **Dec. 15.**

Marian M. Reiber is the trust director for the Adventist Media Center in Simi Valley, California. She is the mother of three and grandmother of seven. Her hobbies include all kinds of stitchery and putting puzzles together. A recent challenge was an 8,000-piece puzzle of the Sistine Chapel. **July 15.**

Julie Reynolds, a registered nurse, is a full-time homemaker and mother living in North Carolina. She is the women's ministries coordinator for her area. Her favorite activities include gardening, hiking in the mountains, walking on the seashore, and playing with her children. **May 13.**

Kay D. Rizzo is a freelance writer living in central California. She is the author of many books, with manuscipts 31 and 32 to be released shortly. She also writes a monthly column for *Signs of the Times* and *Listen* magazines, and hosts *The Family Hour* on KARM-FM radio. She serves as an elder and youth leader, as well as minister of music, in her local church. Kay and her husband have two married daughters who are professional musicians. **July 5.**

Barbara Roberts is a homemaker who does some freelance writing. She enjoys her grandchildren, writing, reading, sewing, and growing orchids. She serves her local church in Washington State as an elder and superintendent. **Jan. 16, Nov. 21.**

Janice Rose, a registered nurse, is pursuing a B.A. degree in psychology. She is married and has two children. Janice has served her local church as an elder, treasurer, and departmental leader. Her hobbies are reading and handcrafts. **Jan. 31.**

Jean Reiffenstein Rothgeb and her husband live in Utah. They have two daughters, four grandchildren, and two great-grandchildren. She is semiretired but works in the clinic of an orthopedic surgeon. She loves the outdoors, especially bird-watching with their daughter and her family in the mountains and deserts of Utah. She enjoys needlework when not occupied with church responsibilities or remodeling her home. **July 23, Oct. 18.**

Cathy L. Sanchez is a full-time homemaker. She and her husband and daughter live in Nebraska, where she is the women's ministries and cooking school coordinator for her church. Her special interests are music, writing, gardening, small group studies, and her family. **June 3.**

Deborah Sanders shares from her personal journal, *Dimensions of Love,* and goes by the pen name Sonny's Mommy. She lives in Canada with her husband of almost 30 years. They have three children. She is an active witness within her church, community, and support-group for parents with autistic children. She enjoys trying to make others feel special, as Jesus makes her feel. **Nov. 14.**

Susan Scoggins moved to Russia at the end of 1995 with her husband, who is the publishing director for the Euro-Asia Division of Seventh-day

Adventists. She likes to do lots of artsy and musical things, but finds that travel is higher on the agenda these days, since the country spans such a big portion of the world. **Aug. 21, Oct. 19, Dec. 12.**

Karon Scott is an executive secretary. She and her attorney-husband have one son, two step-daughters, and two grandsons. She is an animal lover and a cat fanatic. **July 27.**

Esther Arney Larson Shadday, a retired secretary and medical assistant, the mother of four and grandmother of 10, fulfilled a 50-year-old dream in 1996 when she received a degree in religion. She has been very active in her church, working in all the departments at one time or another. She plays the piano, slide trombone, guitar, accordion, and harmonica. Her hobbies include piano, continuing education, reading, writing, studying Greek, oil painting, crochet, and other crafts. **Dec. 24.**

Donna Lee Sharp, formerly a retirement facility administrator, music teacher, assistant editor, secretary, and elementary school teacher, is now retired. Her first love was raising five children, who have given her seven grandchildren. Today she is involved in music at two churches, weekly sing-alongs at the local senior center, travel, and bird-watching. **Aug. 8, Sept. 8.**

Carrol Johnson Shewmake, a retired academy librarian, is a retired minister's wife, a freelance writer, and a seminar and workshop speaker. She is the mother of four and grandmother of eight. She is writing books about developing an intimate relationship with God. **Jan. 12, Mar. 2, June 11.**

Bonita Shields is an associate pastor. She and her husband live in Takoma Park, Maryland. Bonita enjoys writing for Christian magazines, public speaking, reading, walking, crafts, and collecting baskets. **Sept. 16.**

Rose Neff Sikora is a registered nurse who enjoys writing, camping, helping others, and spending time with her three grandchildren. She and her husband live in Hendersonville, North Carolina. **Mar. 29, Dec. 21.**

Sandra Simanton has a master's degree in social work and has worked as a missionary in Guatemala, Colombia, and Mexico. She currently lives in Grand Forks, North Dakota, with her husband and two preschool children and is a full-time homemaker. Sandy is involved with Community Services, women's ministries, and children's programs at her church. She enjoys sewing and reading. **Jan. 27, Mar. 14.**

Carol J. Smith and her husband live in Washington with their two sons. They both work in long-term health-care ministry. They have learned to be flexible with many relocations and serve in church/school ministries as needed. Carol keeps busy giving Bible studies and women's prayer fellowships. Her hobbies include reading, freelance writing, and the family activities of camping, canoeing, hiking, skiing, and swimming. **Nov. 20.**

Ginger Snarr graduated from Walla Walla College School of Nursing in 1960. Currently, she is a homemaker and lives in Vancouver, Washington, with her husband, Dudley. They have made several trips to the former Soviet Union, where they have been involved in humanitarian work. **June 26.**

Bethany Sorenson is a wife and mother of four. She is a health and temperance leader in her church and is an administrative assistant for a company that does fund raising for various law-enforcement agencies nationwide. In her spare time she enjoys running, reading, bowling, and gardening. **Mar. 27.**

Elva E. Springer is a retired medical assistant and X-ray technician whose hobbies are camping, boating, flying, writing, and church activities. She has three children, eight grandchildren, and six great-grandchildren. She and her husband of 53 years still take their annual 5,000-mile motorcycle trip. **Apr. 30.**

Sharon Staddon, a C.P.A., is the deputy finance director for ADRA/Sudan, a development and relief agency. For 23 years prior to her work in Sudan, she and her husband ministered in Minnesota, Nebraska, Alaska, Kansas, and Washington State. She is the mother of two young adult sons and enjoys music, having taught piano for 19 years. **Aug. 17.**

Ardis Dick Stenbakken is the director of women's ministries for the General Conference of Seventh-day Adventists. An Army chaplain's wife for almost 24 years, she moved with her husband to Maryland to work at the Seventh-day Adventist Church headquarters. They have two adult children. Ardis enjoys church work, cross-stitch, quilting, reading, travel, and public speaking. **Jan. 9, Feb. 16, Apr. 4, June 9, Aug. 6, Nov. 12, Dec. 28, Dec. 31.**

Cyndi Stephens is a housewife and home-schooling mom of an 11-year-old boy. She serves on the women's ministries committee and directs the cradle roll/kindergarten class at her church. **June 15.**

Rita Kay Stevens, an administrative assistant, is a church administrator's wife in Texas. She enjoys traveling and has had the opportunity of living in many different places in the United States and overseas. Her pleasures include meeting and entertaining people, walking, reading, encouraging others, and crafting. The mother of two adult sons, Rita is active in women's ministries. **Feb. 18.**

Marilisa Foffa Stina is a women's ministries leader in São Paulo, Brazil. She is a pastor-administrator's wife and the mother of three children. She enjoys playing the piano, swimming, reading, collecting tourism magazines, and nature. **Feb. 6.**

Iris L. Stovall is a wife and the mother of an adult son, a teenage son, and a teenage daughter. Her hobbies are creative writing, singing, and videography. She is an audiovisual technician and an elder at her church and works in women's ministries at the General Conference of Seventh-day Adventists in Maryland. Several of her articles have appeared in religious publications. **Jan. 19, Feb. 15, Mar. 24, May 2, June 22, July 12, Sept. 7.**

Rubye Sue is a first-time contributor who writes from Florida. **Nov. 23.**

Judith A. Sullivan, originally from Jamaica, has lived in the United States for the past 10 years. She teaches English in a middle school in southern Florida and serves her local church as teacher of a collegiate Bible class and communication secretary. Her hobbies are reading and writing short stories and poetry. **Jan. 11.**

Arlene Taylor is risk manager at St. Helena Hospital in northern California as well as founder and president of her own nonprofit corporation, pledged to promoting brain-function research and providing related educational resources. An internationally known speaker, she enjoys traveling around the world, presenting seminars about the brain and personal/spiritual growth. **Feb. 2, Mar. 30, Aug. 14, Nov. 9, Dec. 13.**

Stella Thomas is an administrative secretary in the Office of Global Mission at the General Conference of Seventh-day Adventists in Maryland. She is the mother of two children and enjoys cooking and traveling. Stella teaches the primary-age children's Bible class at her church, and has a burden to see young people dedicate their lives to God. **Nov. 5.**

Kathleen Tonn-Oliver makes her home in California. She is a creative and commercial writer and a seminar presenter who has written 11 books and numerous articles. A recovering victim of child abuse, Katie is working on four major writing projects on the subject of abuse. **Mar. 5.**

Darlyn Townsend lives at Camp Au Sable in northern Michigan with her husband and two sons. She is the craft director and enjoys making baskets, swimming, music, flower gardening, nautical decor, watching the deer, and riding on her quiet golf cart through the woods. **June 10.**

Nicea Ferreira Trindade is a wife, mother of three, and grandmother of three. She is currently working with adolescent youth in Rio de Janeiro, Brazil. Her hobby is writing. **Sept. 20, Oct. 5.**

Lilly Tryon, from Pennsylvania, is a registered nurse, pastor's wife, and home-schooling mother of two boys. Her interests include doing things with her family, flower gardening, rubber stamping, scrapbooks, reading, writing, playing the piano, and singing. **Aug. 2, Sept. 25.**

Olga Valdivia is a wife and mother of three. She writes from Idaho, where she and her family moved 10 years ago. She works as a secretary in the Advertising Department of the Pacific Press Publishing Association. Olga enjoys jogging, interior decorating, reading, and crafts, and is a published writer. **May 10.**

Janis Clark Vance is a registered nurse and licensed counselor with a master's degree in educational psychology. She and her husband are the parents of three grown children. She is the founder of Take Heart Retreats, a spiritual ministry devoted to helping victims of childhood sexual abuse. **May 15.**

Nancy Van Pelt, a certified family life educator and family and consumer science professional, is an author and internationally known speaker. She has written 20 books and has another one under way. Her hobbies are getting organized, entertaining, quilting, and having fun. Nancy and her husband live in California and are the parents of three grown children. **Aug. 20, Sept. 29, Dec. 16**.

Nancy Cachero Vasquez is the volunteer coordinator for the North American Division office at the General Conference of Seventh-day Adventists in Maryland. She is the wife of one of the division's vice presidents and mother of three young adults. Nancy's special interests are reading, writing, crafts, shopping, and baking. **Apr. 6, June 27.**

Julia C. S. Vernon lives on a farm in Grantsville, Utah, with her husband, Peter, and their three children, ages 13 to 17. She is a hospice chaplain in her pastoral care associates ministry and serves four hospices in the Salt Lake City area. She is also a local elder in the Central Church of Salt Lake City and has had several articles published in the *Adventist Review, Liberty,* and *Ministry* magazines. Her hobby is designing crochet patterns, some of which have won blue ribbons at local fairs. **Jan. 21.**

Brianna Renee Walker lives on a farm in eastern Oregon with her parents, two sisters, and a brother, where they raise watermelons and sheep. Her hobbies include waterskiing, playing the piano, reading, drawing, arm wrestling her dad, and getting together with her youth group. A graduate of the class of 1998, her aspiration is a career in writing. **Nov. 4.**

Mae E. Wallenkampf has a master's degree in music and is now a retired music teacher living in California near her two daughters and their families. She enjoys reading, baking bread, and traveling. Mae has three children and five grandchildren. **June 18.**

Anna May Radke Waters and her husband have five children and seven grandchildren. She is a retired administrative secretary. Anna May is involved in her local church as an elder. Her hobbies are knitting, crocheting, counted cross-stitch, writing, entertaining, and traveling. **Nov. 7.**

Elizabeth Darby Watson is an associate professor of social work and the director of GENESIS, a program designed for single parents to earn a college degree at Andrews University in Michigan. She is a local church elder and women's ministries coordinator, and presents workshops and seminars. The mother of three, she enjoys creative writing, cross-stitch and letter writing. **Jan. 24, Aug. 4.**

Ruth Watson, now retired, was previously an office manager, diet consultant, elementary school teacher, bookkeeper, and writer. She and her physician-husband spent 13 years as missionaries in Thailand, where she published a magazine and songbook for children. She has been writing for publication since 1960. This mother of three and grandmother of two is involved in women's ministries and small group Bible studies. She enjoys traveling, relief mission work overseas, writing, flower gardening, exercising, and being a grandmother. **Apr. 21, May 6, Sept. 14.**

Dorothy Eaton Watts was the director of women's ministries for the General Conference of Seventh-day Adventists in Silver Spring, Maryland, at the time of this writing. She is currently an associate secretary of the Southern Asia Division of Seventh-day Adventists. Dorothy, a freelance writer, editor, and speaker, was a missionary in India for 16 years. She has founded an orphanage, taught elementary school, and written more than 20 books. Her hobbies include gardening, hiking, and birding (with more than 1,000 in her world total). **Jan. 1, Feb. 1, Mar. 1, Apr. 1, Apr. 7, May 1, June 1, July 1, Aug. 1, Sept. 1, Oct. 1, Nov. 1, Dec. 1.**

Lois May Watts and her retired minister-husband have two children and two grandchildren. They spent 18 years as missionaries in Japan as well as many years in the midwestern United States. They currently live in West Virginia. Lois is a schoolteacher by profession. **June 7.**

Penny Estes Wheeler spent early mornings last summer sitting on her porch in Maryland watching bumblebees buzz among her morning glories and black-eyed Susans. The editor of *Women of Spirit*, Penny enjoys travel and speaking. Her family is especially dear to her heart. **Jan. 26.**

Dava Benton White works part-time as a nurse and full-time as a mother of three young children. She has served on the executive committee for the local Christian Business and Professional Women's Club for the past five years. Her hobbies include reading, sewing, letter writing, canoeing, and biking. **June 19.**

Bonnie Wilde is the women's ministries coordinator for her church in Canada and writes a column for a newsletter. She is a nurse and homemaker. **Mar. 3.**

Carlene Will teaches seminars on home organization and personal devotions. She is the women's ministries leader for her local church and facilitates a weekly Bible study for women in her neighborhood. The mother of four boys, she enjoys quilting and country life in Battle Ground, Washington. **Aug. 10, Oct. 24.**

Mildred C. Williams and her husband live in southern California. They have two daughters. Mildred works part-time as a physical therapist and enjoys sewing, writing, public speaking, gardening and baby-sitting her granddaughter. She has written a book and has been published in several religious magazines. **June 6.**

Kathy Jo Duterrow Yergen has recently moved from Beltsville, Maryland, to Red Deer County, Alberta, Canada, where her husband is now the secretary of the Alberta Conference of Seventh-day Adventists. She has many interests, including watercolor, and is working on a book telling of God's many miracles in her life. **July 22, Sept. 15.**

Scripture Index

12:1 . . . . Nov. 3
13:2 . . . . July 7

JAMES

1:2, 3 . . . . Sept. 8
1:17 . . . . Aug. 14
1:17 . . . . Dec. 13
4:7 . . . . Jan. 17
4:8 . . . . Apr. 10
5:16 . . . . Feb. 4

1 PETER

3:12 . . . . Feb. 10
4:9 . . . . Feb. 25

4:10 . . . . July 8
5:7 . . . . July 26
5:8 . . . . Dec. 9

2 PETER

3:9 . . . . Sept. 18

1 JOHN

1:9 . . . . May 15
3:1 . . . . Sept. 5
3:1 . . . . Oct. 14
3:16 . . . . Jan. 19
4:7 . . . . Aug. 31

REVELATION

1:7 . . . . Dec. 20
2:4, 5 . . . . . . June 29
2:10 . . . . Nov. 14
3:8 . . . . Oct. 11
3:20 . . . . Apr. 6
4:11 . . . . June 2
7:17 . . . . Dec. 3
12:9 . . . . Oct. 22
19:8 . . . . June 21
20:15 . . . . . . Apr. 12
21:10 . . . . . Aug. 9
22:17 . . . . . . Dec. 18
22:20 . . . . . . Apr. 18